STUDY AND LISTENING GUIDE

FOR

A HISTORY OF WESTERN MUSIC
SIXTH EDITION

AND

NORTON ANTHOLOGY OF WESTERN MUSIC
FOURTH EDITION

STUDY AND LISTENING GUIDE

FOR

A HISTORY OF WESTERN MUSIC
SIXTH EDITION
BY DONALD JAY GROUT AND CLAUDE V. PALISCA

AND

NORTON ANTHOLOGY OF WESTERN MUSIC
FOURTH EDITION
BY CLAUDE V. PALISCA

J. PETER BURKHOLDER

W. W. NORTON & COMPANY
NEW YORK   LONDON

ISBN 0-393-97694-7 (pbk.)

W. W. Norton & Company, Inc.
500 Fifth Avenue, New York, N.Y. 10110
www.wwnorton.com

W. W. Norton & Company Ltd.
Castle House, 75/76 Wells Street, London W1T 3QT

1 2 3 4 5 6 7 8 9 0

CONTENTS

READ THIS SECTION FIRST

The purpose of this *Study and Listening Guide* is to help you learn the material in *A History of Western Music,* Sixth Edition (HWM), by Donald Jay Grout and Claude V. Palisca, and acquaint yourself with the music in the *Norton Anthology of Western Music,* Fourth Edition (NAWM), by Claude V. Palisca. Each chapter of the *Study and Listening Guide* is coordinated with a chapter of HWM and several pieces in NAWM.

There is much to know about the history of Western music and much to discover in the music itself. The best way to learn it is to follow some simple rules of successful learning.

1. Know your goals. It is easier to learn and to chart your progress if you know what you are trying to accomplish.
2. Proceed from what you know to what is new or less familiar. We learn best when what we are learning relates to what we already know. Thus it is usually easiest to start with the big picture and proceed from the general to the specific, from the main points to the details; this helps us see quickly how each element relates to the others, and what is most important. But it is also helpful to get to know a single example and discover broader principles by looking at it closely; indeed, broad statements may not be meaningful or clear until we have a concrete example.
3. Do not try to do everything at once. Trying to do too much, too fast makes learning difficult and frustrating. Divide the task into units small enough to grasp at one sitting. Do not cram for tests; study every day.
4. Write down what you learn. You will retain information and concepts much more readily if you write them down for yourself rather than merely read them or hear them or highlight them in a book. The mental act of putting ideas into your own words and the physical act of writing out names, terms, dates, and other information create multiple pathways in your brain for recalling what you have learned.
5. Apply what you know. You learn and retain the skills and knowledge that you use.
6. Review what you know. We learn through repetition.
7. Have fun. You learn better and remember more when you are having fun. This means allowing yourself to enjoy the process of learning, mastering, and applying concepts and skills, whether riding a bike or discovering music history.

This *Study and Listening Guide* is designed to help you do all of these, through the following features.

Chapter Objectives

Each chapter begins with an outline of what you should learn from reading the texts and studying the music. These are the central issues addressed in the chapter. When you read the objectives before studying the material, they will pinpoint what you are trying to achieve. When you reread them after you have read the chapter, studied the music, and worked through the study questions, they can help you to evaluate your achievement. They direct you to the big picture, so you do not miss the forest for the trees.

Chapter Outline

The chapter outline shows how the corresponding chapter in HWM is divided into sections, summarizes the main points in each section, introduces important terms and names (highlighted in *italics*), and indicates which selections in NAWM relate to each topic. By reading the outline *first,* you begin with an overview of the subject. Then, as you read the chapter, the details presented there will flesh out the general concepts presented in the outline. Since you have already read the main ideas in the outline, as you read the text you are beginning to review and reinforce what you have learned, while increasing the depth of your knowledge. When you have finished a section or chapter, reread the outline to make sure you grasp the main points. The outline will also be useful as you review.

Study Questions

The readings are full of information, and it may sometimes be difficult to figure out what is more and less significant. The study questions are designed to help you focus on the most important issues and concepts addressed in each section of each chapter and apply those concepts to the music in NAWM. Material related to any of the questions may be found in a single place in HWM or scattered throughout the section. Relevant material may also be found in the analytical discussions of individual pieces in NAWM.

Questions are grouped by topic, and each question focuses on a single issue. This divides each chapter into units of manageable size and allows you to proceed step by step. The questions vary in kind, from fill-in-the-blank questions to short essays that ask you to synthesize material and apply it to the music, and even exercises that ask you to sing or play through the music. Tackling the material in small units and doing a variety of things in each section can help to make your work more fun.

Write down your answers. Space is provided to answer the study questions in this book. Writing down what you learn, rather than merely reading or highlighting the text, will help you retain it better. This is particularly helpful for recalling terms, names, and titles in foreign languages, since spelling them out for yourself will make them more familiar. If you have trouble remembering how to spell a foreign or unfamiliar word or name, writing it several times will help you recall it.

The study questions are not review questions, to be filled in after you have finished reading and have closed the book. They are guides to the reading and to the music. After you have read a section of the text, or even while you are reading it, work through the relevant study questions, rereading the text for answers as needed. Always respond to the questions in your own words, rather than copying directly from the text; this will help you to master each concept, making it your own by phrasing it in your own way. If there is anything you do not understand, return to the reading (in HWM, NAWM, or this *Study and Listening Guide*) to find the missing information, or ask for help from your instructor.

Some study questions ask you to define or to use terms that are introduced in the text. There is rote learning in every subject, and in music much of it is of terminology. Each musical repertory has its own specialized vocabulary, often borrowed from Italian, Latin, French, or German. You cannot communicate with others about this music without mastering these terms.

Many questions ask you to apply to the pieces in NAWM concepts and terms that are presented in the text. In this way you will to get to know the music better and will reinforce your grasp of the concepts and terms by applying what you know to the music itself. These study questions on the music are set off in boxes headlined *Music to Study*. Each of these subsections begins with a list of the pieces in NAWM under consideration, indicating the CD number and tracks for each piece on the recordings that accompany NAWM.

You should listen to each piece in NAWM several times, including at least once before reading about it and at least once afterward. The heart of music history is the music itself, and a major part of your study should be listening to and becoming familiar with the music.

Terms and Names to Know

Near the end of each chapter is a list of important terms and names that appear in the texts and are highlighted in italics in the chapter outline. Most of these are covered in the study questions. They are listed separately here to help you review and to test your retention of what you have learned. In addition to these names, you should know the composers and titles of the pieces you studied. Use the lists in reviewing at the end of each chapter and in reviewing for examinations.

Review Questions

Each chapter ends with review questions that ask you to reflect more generally on the material you have learned. Most of them are like essay questions that you might encounter on a test. These may be used as springboards for discussion in class or with your study group, or as essay questions to use for practice as you study for examinations. Others are exercises that ask you to pull together information from several places in the chapter.

How to Proceed

The following procedure is recommended, but any procedure that helps you learn the most effectively and efficiently is the right one for you. You might vary your approach until you find the one that works best.

1. As you start each chapter, **read the chapter objectives** first to see what is expected of you.
2. **Read through the chapter outline.** Notice the topics that are covered, the main points that are made, and the terms that are introduced. Important new terms and names are given in italics.
3. Now work through the chapter section by section, as marked by roman numerals in the chapter outline and centered headings in HWM.
4. Start each section by **listening to the pieces in NAWM** that are listed in this section of the outline. Read through the text and translation before listening to vocal pieces, and listen to every piece with the score. (If you have time, you might first listen to each piece without the score, and you might also sing or play through the piece yourself, which will help you learn it better.) This lets you encounter the music first, just as music. Later, you will come back to it and apply the principles you learn in reading the text.
5. Next, **read the section in HWM,** using the chapter outline as a guide. As the text refers you to pieces in NAWM, look again at the music and read the analytical discussion of each piece.
6. **Work through the study questions** for this section. Refer again to the music when the questions direct you to do so, and study the music or review HWM and the analytical discussions in NAWM to find the information you need to answer the questions. (Instead of reading first and then working through the study questions, you may find it more convenient to answer the study questions as you read through the text.)
7. When you have answered the study questions, **review the chapter outline** for this section and look over your answers to the questions. If there is anything you do not understand, refer back to the text, or make a note of it in the margin and ask your instructor for help.
8. **Listen to the music again,** and check your answers to the relevant study questions. Then congratulate yourself for finishing this section of the chapter. You may move on to the next section, or save it for another day.
9. At the end of the chapter, review by checking your knowledge of the **terms and names to know,** rereading the chapter outline, and reviewing your answers to the study questions. Read the objectives again to make sure you have accomplished them. **Read the review questions** and write brief answers in outline form, or use them as practice essay questions before examinations.

NOTE TO THE INSTRUCTOR

This *Study and Listening Guide* is designed to walk the student through the material in HWM and NAWM step by step. Not every instructor will want to include all the content covered in the texts, and each is likely to emphasize different aspects of the music and its history. Each instructor is encouraged to tailor this study guide to the needs of the individual course.

The study questions are designed to be used as guides for the student, as the basis for work in discussion sessions, or as problem sets to be handed in. There are many questions, so that each significant topic can be covered. The instructor is encouraged to select which of the questions students should do on their own, which they may omit, and which should be handed in, if any. The review questions can also be used in several ways: as guides for individual review, as model test questions, or as short writing assignments in or out of class. For courses in which this *Study and Listening Guide* is a required text, permission is granted to use any of the questions on examinations.

ACKNOWLEDGMENTS

Any book is a collaborative effort, and teaching materials are especially so. The first edition of this *Study and Listening Guide* (1996) originated in a group of study questions for the first twelve chapters of *A History of Western Music,* Fourth Edition, which I developed in collaboration with my associate instructors for Music History and Literature I at Indiana University School of Music in fall 1993: Brian Bourkland, Nicholas Butler, the late Kirk Ditzler, Gesa Kordes, and Mario Ortiz-Acuña. I am grateful for their assistance, their suggestions, and the questions of theirs that remain here in some form. I am grateful also to my associate instructors in fall 1995, John Anderies, Nicholas Butler, Pablo Corá, David Lieberman, Felicia Miyakawa, and Patrick Warfield, who used the first draft of the first edition of this study guide and offered very helpful feedback. My students that semester and my colleagues Austin B. Caswell and Thomas Noblitt provided encouragement and useful comments. Thanks also to Claude V. Palisca for helpful advice and for permitting me to consult materials he had developed, and to Kristine Forney for suggestions.

In undertaking this revision, thanks are due to the many instructors and students who have used the first edition and have shown me how it is helpful and what can be improved. Thanks to Michael Ochs for his careful editing, to Jan Hoeper and Claire McCabe for providing up-to-date drafts, galleys, and proofs of the new editions of *A History of Western Music* and the *Norton Anthology of Western Music,* and to Roy Tedoff for advice on format. Thanks finally and as always to Doug McKinney for his encouragement and support.

STUDY AND LISTENING GUIDE

FOR

A HISTORY OF WESTERN MUSIC
SIXTH EDITION

AND

NORTON ANTHOLOGY OF WESTERN MUSIC
FOURTH EDITION

MUSICAL LIFE AND THOUGHT IN ANCIENT GREECE AND ROME

1

CHAPTER OBJECTIVES

After you complete the reading, study of the music, and study questions for this chapter, you should be able to

1. identify several elements of Western music and music theory that derive from the music of ancient Greece or Israel;
2. describe in general terms ancient Greek music and ideas about music and the musical life of ancient Greece and Rome;
3. explain why the ancient Greeks linked music to numbers, astronomy, and poetry, and how they thought it affected a person's character and behavior;
4. identify some basic terms of Greek music theory and some ancient writers on music;
5. name some aspects of the liturgy and music of the Western Christian Church that parallel or derive from Jewish and Byzantine practices;
6. explain how Gregorian chant came to be the standard repertory of liturgical song for the Western Church; and
7. summarize early Christian attitudes toward music, including the role of music in the church, the place of music among the liberal arts, and the relation of audible music to the mathematical proportions that govern nature and humans, and explain how these views relate to ancient Greek views of music.

CHAPTER OUTLINE

I. The Greek and Roman Heritage (HWM 1–2)

Western culture has roots in ancient Greece and Rome. Although little ancient music survived, ancient writings about music, particularly music theory, had a strong influence on later centuries.

II. Music in Ancient Greek Life and Thought (HWM 2–7)

A. Greek Musical Life
In ancient Greece, music was linked to the gods, miraculous powers, and religious ceremonies. There were three main instruments, played alone or to accompany singing or recitation:

1. The *lyre,* a plucked string instrument associated with Apollo;
2. The *aulos,* a reed instrument linked with Dionysus and Greek drama;
3. The *kithara,* a larger relative of the lyre.

Music festivals and contests were an important part of Greek musical life after the fifth century B.C.E. They fostered the rise of professionals and of increasing virtuosity and complexity in music. About forty-five pieces or fragments of music survive, most from relatively late periods. Greek music was *monophonic,* but was often performed in *heterophony.*

B. Greek Musical Thought

Greek theory associated music with numbers (through the simple ratios that produced the consonant intervals) and therefore with astronomy, as in the notion of the "music of the spheres." Music was closely tied to poetry, which was usually sung.

C. The Doctrine of *Ethos*

The Greeks held that music could directly affect character (*ethos,* related to the English word "ethics") and behavior. According to *Aristotle,* it did so by imitating the *passions* or states of the soul and thus arousing the same passions in the listener. Because of this power, both *Plato* and Aristotle gave music an important role in education but argued that only certain kinds of music were desirable: while the right kind of music disciplines the mind and fosters virtue, music that stimulates undesirable attitudes should be avoided.

III. The Greek Musical System (HWM 8–15, NAWM 1–2)

The Greek musical system shares several elements with later Western systems, such as notes, intervals (including tones, semitones, and thirds), and scales. Greek scales were constructed from *tetrachords,* groups of four notes spanning a perfect fourth. *Pythagoras* (ca. 500 B.C.E.) is credited with having discovered that the consonant intervals are produced by simple number ratios of 2:1 for the octave, 3:2 for the fifth, and 4:3 for the fourth.

Sidebar: **Greek Music Theory in Depth**

There were three *genera* (plural of *genus,* meaning type or class) of tetrachords: *diatonic, chromatic,* and *enharmonic.* The *Greater Perfect System* was an arrangement of four tetrachords covering two octaves. The scale-types used by the Greeks were called *tonoi* (plural of *tonos*); theorists differ in describing them. *Cleonides* and *Ptolemy* recognized seven scale-types, each with a unique series of tones and semitones, like the scales that can be played on the white keys of the modern piano starting on the seven different notes. Surviving examples of Greek music conform very closely to the precepts of the theorists, including the tonoi and the three genera.   **Music: NAWM 1–2**

IV. Music in Ancient Rome (HWM 15–17)

The Romans adopted many aspects of Greek musical culture, including religious and ceremonial music, music in private entertainment, and public festivals and competitions. Roman music shared most characteristics of Greek music.

V. The Early Christian Church (HWM 17–29)

A. Rome's Decline

As the Roman empire declined and the Western Empire collapsed in the fifth century C.E., the Christian Church became the main cultural force in Europe. The Church adapted music to its own needs and rejected pagan uses of and attitudes toward music.

B. The Judaic Heritage

Christian worship services were not modeled directly on Jewish ceremonies, but there are strong parallels, including a symbolic sacrifice, a ceremonial meal, the reading of Scripture, the singing of *psalms,* and the practice of assigning certain readings and psalms to specific days of the calendar.

C. The Spread of Christianity

As the Church spread, it absorbed musical practices from many areas. Among the most important were psalm singing and *hymns* as used in the monasteries in Syria and later cultivated in Byzantium and Milan.

D. Byzantium

Each region of the church in the East developed its own *liturgy* (set of texts and ritual actions). *Byzantium,* later called Constantinople after the Roman Emperor *Constantine,* was the capital of the Eastern Roman Empire from 395 to 1453, and its musical practices influenced the West.

Sidebar: **Byzantine Music in Depth**

Particularly important were the Byzantine hymns, of which there were several types. The *kanones* were poetic elaborations on the biblical *canticles.* Their melodies were created from melodic formulas in a process called *centonization.* Byzantine music used eight modes (called *echoi,* singular *echos*) that resemble the *modes* later adopted in Western music theory.

E. Western Liturgies

Between the fifth and eighth centuries, each region of the Western church developed its own liturgy in Latin and its own repertory of liturgical melodies, called *chants.* The Frankish king *Charlemagne,* crowned Holy Roman Emperor in 800, sought to impose the Roman liturgy and repertory of chant throughout his entire domain (modern France, Switzerland, western Germany, and northern Italy). This led to the rise throughout this region of *Gregorian chant* (named for Pope Gregory I or II), which combined ancient, Roman, and Frankish elements and became the standard repertory of chants for the Western Church from the ninth century on. Modern editions of Gregorian chant, including the *Liber usualis,* were prepared in the late nineteenth and early twentieth centuries by monks at the Benedictine *Abbey of Solesmes* in France. The next most important chant repertory in the West is that of Milan, named *Ambrosian chant* after St. Ambrose. He introduced into the Western church the practice of *responsorial psalmody,* in which a soloist sings the first half of a psalm verse and the congregation responds by singing the rest.

F. The Dominance of Rome

Beginning in the fourth century, the bishop of Rome, also known as the pope, became the leader of the Western church, and Latin its official language. Several popes sought to standardize the chants and improve singing through a papal choir and the Schola cantorum, a group of teachers who trained church singers.

G. The Church Fathers

Christian writers and scholars known as the church fathers regarded music as the servant of religion. They valued music for its power to inspire piety and to influence the character of listeners, but they opposed listening to music for pleasure and excluded instrumental music from church services. Early Christian writers passed on the philosophy and music theory of the ancient world. Martianus Capella (early fifth century) helped to codify the *seven liberal arts*: the three verbal arts called the *trivium* (grammar, dialectic, and rhetoric) and the four mathematical disciplines called the *quadrivium* (geometry, arithmetic, astronomy, and harmonics, or music).

H. Boethius

The heritage of Greek music theory was transmitted to the Middle Ages through *De institutione musica* (The Fundamentals of Music) by *Boethius* (ca. 480–524/26). He described three kinds of music: *musica mundana* (cosmic music), the orderly numerical relations that control the natural world; *musica humana* (human music), which controls the human body and soul; and *musica instrumentalis,* audible music produced by voices or instruments.

STUDY QUESTIONS

The Greek and Roman Heritage (HWM 1–2)

1. Artists and writers of the Middle Ages and later periods imitated the art and literature of ancient Greece and Rome. Why did musicians find it difficult to imitate ancient music? What aspects of ancient music did they draw on?

Music in Ancient Greek Life and Thought (HWM 2–7)

2. What were the three main instruments used by the ancient Greeks? How was each played, and on what occasions was it used? Which instrument was associated with Apollo, and which with Dionysus?

    a. _____

    b. _____

    c. _____

3. In the Greek conception, what were the links between music, numbers, and astronomy?

4. In Greek musical life, how was music related to or dependent upon poetry?

5. According to Plato and Aristotle, how could music affect a person's character and behavior? Why should certain kinds of music be promoted and other kinds suppressed? What is the relevance of this debate for our own time?

The Greek Musical System (HWM 8–15, NAWM 1–2)

6. Who was Pythagoras, and when did he live? According to legend, what did he discover?

7. What is a *tetrachord*?

8. What are the three *genera* of tetrachord? What intervals appear in each, in order from top to bottom?

    1. _____   _____

    2. _____   _____

    3. _____   _____

9. How are tetrachords combined in the *Greater Perfect System*?

Music to Study
    NAWM 1: *Epitaph of Seikilos,* song (ca. first century C.E.)
        CD 1.1 (Concise 1.1)
    NAWM 2: Euripides (?), *Orestes,* tragedy, excerpt: *Stasimon* chorus (either
        408 B.C.E., the date of Euripides' play, or by third century B.C.E.,
        the date of the papyrus on which the music is preserved)
        CD 1.2

10. How do the *Epitaph of Seikilos* (NAWM 1) and the *stasimon* chorus from
    Euripides' *Orestes* (NAWM 2) exemplify the characteristics typical of Greek
    music as described in HWM, pp. 2–7 and the summary on pp. 16–17?

11. Of the three genera you identified in question 8 above, which are used in the
    Epitaph of Seikilos? How can you tell?

    Which are used in the chorus from *Orestes*? How can you tell?

Music in Ancient Rome (HWM 15–17)

12. In what ways did musical life in Rome resemble that of ancient Greece?

The Early Christian Church (HWM 17–29)

13. How did the Christian Church become the main cultural force in Europe? What did it replace in this role?

14. What aspects of ancient Greek and Roman music did the early Church reject, and why?

15. What similarities do you notice between Jewish religious practices and the liturgy and music of early Christian worship? In particular, how are psalms used?

16. What are *hymns*? How far back do they go in Christian worship?

17. What are *canticles*?

18. What is *centonization*?

19. What role did Charlemagne play in relation to liturgy and chant? What is Gregorian chant? What were the sources for Gregorian chant, and what did it replace?

20. What attitudes toward music were held by the leaders of the early Christian Church? How do these views compare to the views of Plato and Aristotle?

21. How does music fit into the seven liberal arts? Why is music (or harmonics) grouped with the mathematical arts, rather than with the verbal arts?

22. Who was Boethius? Why was he important for music in the Middle Ages?

23. In Boethius's view, what was *musica instrumentalis,* and how did it relate to *musica mundana* and *musica humana*? How does this view compare to ancient Greek ideas about music?

TERMS TO KNOW

Terms Related to Ancient Greek Music

aulos
lyre
kithara
monophony, heterophony
doctrine of ethos

tetrachord
genus (pl. genera): diatonic,
   chromatic, enharmonic
Greater Perfect System
tonos (pl. tonoi)

Terms Related to Judeo-Christian Music

psalm
hymn
liturgy
canticle
kanones
centonization
echos (p. echoi)

chant
Gregorian chant
Ambrosian chant
responsorial psalmody
liberal arts, trivium, quadrivium
musica mundana, musica humana,
   musica instrumentalis

NAMES TO KNOW

Pythagoras
Plato
Aristotle
Cleonides
Ptolemy
Byzantium

Constantine
Charlemagne
Liber usualis
Abbey of Solesmes
Boethius
De institutione musica

REVIEW QUESTIONS

1. What are some basic characteristics of ancient Greek music? Which of these are shared with other ancient musical traditions?

2. What are some similarities between Greek music and ours? What are some similarities between Greek music theory and common-practice music theory?

3. The modern piano has white and black keys, and we use scales that span an octave and include a perfect fourth and fifth degree. How do these phenomena relate to ancient Greek music theory?

4. What are some Greek ideas about the power of music and its role in society that are still relevant today?

5. What are some of the sources of Gregorian chant, the repertory of melodies used in the Western church? What were the contributions of the Judaic tradition, Syria, Byzantium, and Europe? How did Gregorian chant come to be standardized?

6. How did early Christian writers, including St. Augustine and Boethius, view music? How do their attitudes compare to those of the ancient Greeks, including Plato and Aristotle?

CHANT AND SECULAR SONG IN THE MIDDLE AGES

2

CHAPTER OBJECTIVES

After you complete the reading, study of the music, and study questions for this chapter, you should be able to

1. describe in general terms the liturgical context for chant in the Roman Church, including the main outline of the Mass and names of the Offices;
2. read a melody in plainchant notation;
3. describe several types of Gregorian chant and explain how the shape and manner of performance of each chant relate to its liturgical function;
4. characterize the eight church modes by their final, tenor, and range and identify the mode of a given chant or song;
5. describe medieval solmisation;
6. name several kinds of secular musicians active during the Middle Ages and the regions and social classes from which they came;
7. describe some examples of medieval secular song by troubadours, trouvères, *Minnesinger,* and *Meistersinger*;
8. describe the *estampie,* the oldest surviving form of instrumental music;
9. name and briefly describe some of the instruments played during the Middle Ages; and
10. name and briefly identify a few of the people who contributed to the repertory of medieval monophonic music.

CHAPTER OUTLINE

I. Roman Chant and Liturgy (HWM 31–38)

A. Chant

The *plainchant* repertory of the Roman Church includes some of the oldest and most beautiful songs in existence. (Plainchant is unmetered monophonic sacred song in which each note is about the same duration.) Tunes vary from simple recitation to elaborate melodies, depending on their role in the religious services for which they were created. Both the liturgy, the texts and actions that make up the service, and the chant melodies developed over time. At first the melodies were learned by heart or improvised according to formulas. By the ninth century, manuscripts had signs over the words to indicate the rise and fall of pitch as an aid to memory, and more precise notation developed by the eleventh century. In the nineteenth and twentieth centuries, new editions were prepared that reflected recent interpretation rather than medieval practice. Chant remains the official music of the Roman Church. Yet since the Second Vatican Council of 1962–65, the traditional chants to Latin texts have largely been replaced by simpler tunes with vernacular texts.

B. The Roman Liturgy
There are two main types of service.
1. The *Office* or *Canonical Hours* evolved from group prayer and psalm-singing. Eight Offices are celebrated at specified times each day, of which Matins, Lauds, and especially *Vespers* are musically the most important. Offices feature the singing of psalms and canticles (poems of praise from the Bible, such as the *Magnificat* at Vespers), each with an associated chant called an *antiphon*. They also include the singing of hymns and the chanting of lessons (passages from Scripture) with musical responses called *responsories*.
2. The *Mass* is the most important service. It opens with introductory prayers and chants, continues with Bible readings, responses, and the creed, and culminates in the Eucharist, a symbolic reenactment of the Last Supper of Jesus and his disciples. Elements were added over time until the liturgy was standardized. The texts for certain portions of the Mass, called the *Proper,* change from day to day. The texts of other parts, called the *Ordinary,* are the same each time, although the melodies may vary. (For this reason, the Proper chants are called by their function, while the Ordinary chants are named by their first words.) The most musically significant parts of the Proper are the *Introit, Gradual, Alleluia* or *Tract, Offertory,* and *Communion.* The main musical portions of the Ordinary are the *Kyrie, Gloria, Credo, Sanctus, Agnus Dei,* and *Ite, missa est* or *Benedicamus Domino.*

C. Modern Plainchant Notation
Chant notation uses a staff of four lines, two movable clefs, and a variety of note-shapes called *neumes,* which may indicate one or more notes. Chant may have been sung rhythmically in the early Middle Ages, but now it is sung in even durations. Before notation, chant melodies were passed down orally. Notation helped to standardize the chant melodies and promote uniformity. (It also reduced the need for memorization and made chant easier to learn than it had been when it was passed down orally.)

II. Classes, Forms, and Types of Chant (HWM 38–46, NAWM 3–4)

A. Classifications of Chant
Chants can be classified in several ways:
1. by the type of text (biblical or nonbiblical, prose or poetical);
2. by the manner of performance (*antiphonal, responsorial,* or *direct*);

3. by the number of notes per syllable (*syllabic,* mainly one note per syllable; *neumatic,* one to five notes per syllable; or *melismatic,* in which many syllables have more than five notes).

Chant melodies often reflect the inflection and rhythm of the words. Each melody divides into phrases and periods, following divisions in the text. Phrases tend to be archlike—rising, sustaining, then falling.

B. Recitation Formulas

The simplest chants are *recitation formulas* for reciting prayers and Bible readings. *Psalm tones* are formulas for singing the psalms in the Office. There is one psalm tone for each of the eight church modes, plus one "wandering tone." Most of the formula consists of recitation on the *tenor* or *reciting note* of the mode, with an initial figure at the beginning of the first verse and cadential figures to mark the middle and end of each psalm verse. The *Lesser Doxology,* praising the Trinity, is sung at the end of each psalm, using the same psalm tone. The Magnificat is sung to a similar, slightly more decorated formula. In performing psalms in the Office, the half-verses alternate between two halves of the choir, a practice called *antiphonal psalmody.* **Music: NAWM 4a, 4c, 4e, 4g, 4i, and 4n**

C. Antiphons

Each psalm tone and canticle in the Office is paired with an antiphon, sung before and after the psalm or canticle. (They are called antiphons because the psalms and canticles are usually sung antiphonally.) Most Office antiphons are relatively simple, although those for the canticles are more ornate. There are also independent antiphons used on other occasions. **Music: NAWM 4b, 4d, 4f, 4h, and 4m**

D. Responsory or Respond

In *responsorial psalmody,* a soloist alternates with the choir or congregation. In a responsory, a soloist sings a *respond,* repeated by the choir, then a Scripture verse and a Doxology, each followed by the respond in the choir. (Responsories were originally sung responsorially, although this is not always true today.) **Music: NAWM 4j**

E. Antiphonal Psalmody

In the Mass, the *Introit* and *Communion* were once full psalms with antiphons (more elaborate than Office antiphons) sung antiphonally by the choir. The Introit now has only one verse (plus Doxology) and the Communion has none. (The antiphonal psalms in the Mass are usually neumatic in style.) **Music: NAWM 3a and 3j**

F. Proper Chants of the Mass

The most ornate chants of the Mass are the Graduals, Alleluias, Tracts, and Offertories. Like the Introit and Communion, they are part of the Proper.

1. *Tracts* are long, melismatic, and formulaic and evolved from *direct* singing of a psalm by a soloist. (Note the link between solo performance and melismatic style.) They are sung only in Advent and Lent.

2. *Graduals* are shortened responsories in terms of their texts, with a respond followed by a single psalm verse, but are long chants because they are melismatic. They are sung responsorially between a

soloist (or solo group) and the choir. (Note again the link between solo performance and melismatic style.)   **Music: NAWM 3d**

3. *Alleluias* include a respond on the word "alleluia," usually closing with a long *melisma* called a *jubilus*; a psalm verse that usually ends with part or all of the refrain melody; and a repetition of the respond. Alleluias are sung responsorially and are melismatic. The Tract substitutes for the Alleluia during Advent and Lent.   **Music: NAWM 3e**

4. The *Offertory* was originally an antiphon with psalm, but became very elaborate, often melismatic. It lost its verses when the ceremony it accompanied was shortened.   **Music: NAWM 3g**

G. Chants of the Ordinary
The chants of the Ordinary began as simple syllabic melodies sung by the congregation. Now they are sung by the choir. The *Gloria* and *Credo,* with their long texts, remain mostly syllabic, while the others are more elaborate. Because of their texts, the *Kyrie, Sanctus,* and *Agnus Dei* tend to have three-part sectional forms.   **Music: NAWM 3b–c, 3f, 3h–i, and 3k**

III. Later Developments of the Chant (HWM 46–50, NAWM 5–7)

A. Historical Conditions
Because of the rise of new cultural centers in western and central Europe and the decline of Christian influence in the south, almost all important developments in music from the ninth century to near the end of the Middle Ages took place north of the Alps.

B. Tropes
Tropes are newly composed additions to existing chants. There were three types: adding both text and music; adding music only; or adding text to existing melismas. Tropes flourished in the tenth and eleventh centuries, then fell out of fashion. Most were banned by the Council of Trent (1545–63).   **Music: NAWM 7**

C. Sequences
Sequences were newly composed chants, usually sung after the Alleluia in the Mass. The first sequences (ca. ninth century) were melismas added to Alleluias, to which prose texts were sometimes added. Later sequences were composed independently. The genre was at its peak in the tenth through thirteenth centuries. The form usually consists of a series of musical phrases, of which all but the first and last are repeated immediately to new lines of text. *Hildegard of Bingen* (1098–1179), a famous abbess and mystic, composed both words and music for several sequences. Like tropes, all but a few sequences were eliminated from the liturgy by the Council of Trent. **Music: NAWM 5**

D. Liturgical Drama
Liturgical dramas were short dialogues set to chant and performed just before Mass. The Easter and Christmas dramas were performed throughout Europe. There were also some nonliturgical sacred music dramas, such as Hildegard of Bingen's *Ordo Virtutum* (The Virtues, ca. 1151).   **Music: NAWM 6–7**

IV. Medieval Music Theory and Practice (HWM 50–57)

A. Treatises

Treatises from the ninth century through the late Middle Ages tend to focus on practical issues such as performance, notation, and the modes. Among the most significant is the *Micrologus* (ca. 1025–28) by *Guido of Arezzo* (ca. 991–after 1033).

B. The Church Modes

Medieval theorists recognized *eight church modes*, defined by their *finalis* or *final*, their *tenor* or *reciting note*, and their *range*. *Authentic modes* have the final near the bottom of their range; *plagal modes* have the final near the middle. There is one plagal and one authentic mode on each of four finals: D, E, F, and G. These modes served as the foundation for music theory for centuries. The note B was sometimes flatted, making the modes on D and F resemble modern minor and major. Medieval theorists applied Greek names to the church modes, which were more commonly identified by number.

C. Solmization

Guido of Arezzo devised a set of *solmization* syllables to help singers locate whole tones and semitones. With some modifications, these same syllables are still in use. The medieval system evolved to include three *hexachords* (*natural* on C, *hard* on G, and *soft* on F, with a B flat) and the idea of changing between hexachords, called *mutation*, to cover a wider range and account for both B flat and B natural. The *Guidonian hand* assigned a pitch to each joint of the left hand as a tool to teach notes and intervals.

D. Notation

Chant notation evolved from *neumes* above the words to indicate rising or falling pitches (ninth century), to *heighted* or *diastematic neumes* which showed the pitches more clearly (tenth century), to the inclusion of one or two lines to indicate certain relative pitches, to the invention of the four-line staff in the eleventh century, which allowed precise notation of relative pitch. This made it possible to learn a melody directly from the written page. Durations were not indicated precisely, and we do not know what the rhythm of chant was like.

V. Nonliturgical and Secular Monody (HWM 57–64, NAWM 8–11)

A. Early Secular Genres

Early forms of secular music (from the eleventh and twelfth centuries) include three types of monophonic song:

1. *Goliard songs* had secular Latin texts celebrating the vagabond life of students and wandering clerics called Goliards.
2. *Conductus* is a term used for any serious, nonliturgical Latin song, sacred or secular, with a metrical text and a newly composed melody.
3. The *chanson de geste* (song of deeds) was an epic narrative poem in the vernacular, sung to melodic formulas. An example is the *Song of Roland,* the French national epic.

B. Jongleurs

Jongleurs or *ménestrals* (minstrels) made a living as traveling musicians and performers, on the margins of society.

C. Troubadours and Trouvères

Troubadours (feminine: *trobairitz*) were poet-composers active in southern France in the eleventh and twelfth centuries. They wrote in the language of the region, called *Provençal* (or *langue d'oc* or *Occitan*), and were from or associated with the aristocracy. Their counterparts in northern France, called *trouvères,* wrote in the *langue d'oïl,* the ancestor of modern French, and remained active through the thirteenth century. The songs of both groups are varied in structure and topic. Many of the troubadour and trouvère songs were about love. Some included dialogue or enacted little dramas, leading to musical plays such as *Jeu de Robin et de Marion* (ca. 1284) by the trouvère Adam de la Halle (ca. 1237–ca. 1287). Others depicted a kind of love—called *courtly love*—in which a discreet, unattainable woman was adored from a distance.   **Music: NAWM 8–10**

D. Troubadour and Trouvère Melodies

Troubadour and trouvère poems are strophic. The melodies are mostly syllabic with a range of an octave or less. The rhythm of troubadour melodies is uncertain in the notation, but later trouvère melodies have clear rhythms. Various patterns of repetition are used, along with free composition. Some trouvère songs feature a *refrain,* a segment of text that returns in each stanza, usually with the same melody.

E. Minnesinger

The *Minnesinger* were knightly poet-composers active in German lands from the twelfth through the fourteenth centuries. They sang of an idealized love (*Minne*), and their melodies are formed of phrases that repeat in orderly patterns.

F. Meistersinger

The *Meistersinger* were German poet-composers of the fourteenth through sixteenth centuries, drawn from the urban middle class of tradesmen and artisans rather than from the aristocracy. Their songs were governed by rigid rules. A common form is *bar form*: a a b, with the melody for the b section (*Abgesang*) often repeating some or all of the a section (*Stollen*). **Music: NAWM 11**

G. Songs of Other Countries

Other types of monophonic song include religious songs not intended for use in church, such as the Spanish *cantiga,* song of praise to the Virgin, and the Italian *lauda.*

VI. Medieval Instrumental Music and Instruments (HWM 64–66, NAWM 12)

A. Estampie

Dances were accompanied both by songs and by instrumental music. The oldest surviving form of instrumental music is the *estampie,* several of which date from the thirteenth and fourteenth centuries. Each section was played twice, first with an *"open"* or incomplete cadence, then with a *"closed"* or full cadence.   **Music: NAWM 12**

B. Musical Instruments

There was a rich variety of instruments in the Middle Ages, including plucked string instruments such as the harp, *psaltery,* and lute; bowed strings such as the *vielle* or *Fiedel;* an ancestor of the hurdy-gurdy called the *organistrum;* wind instruments such as recorders, transverse flutes, *shawms,* and bagpipes; brass instruments such as the trumpet; drums; and church organs, *portative organs,* and *positive organs.*

STUDY QUESTIONS

Roman Chant and Liturgy (HWM 31–38)

1. What are the *Offices* or *Canonical Hours*? From what earlier practice do they derive?

2. Fill in the names of the Offices celebrated at the following times of day. Circle the ones that are most important for music.

before sunrise	_____	about noon	_____
sunrise	_____	about 3 PM	_____
about 6 AM	_____	sunset	_____
about 9 AM	_____	just after the sunset Office	_____

3. What does the *Mass* commemorate?

4. What is the *Ordinary* of the Mass? What is the *Proper*? Which set of chants, the Proper or the Ordinary, are called by the first word or words of the text?

5. Which of the following chants are from the Mass Ordinary, and which are from the Proper?

Introit	_____	Credo	_____
Kyrie	_____	Offertory	_____
Gloria	_____	Sanctus	_____
Gradual	_____	Agnus Dei	_____
Alleluia	_____	Communion	_____
Tract	_____	Ite, missa est	_____

6. When did chant melodies begin to be written down? _____

7. How were chant melodies transmitted before notation was developed? Why was notation useful?

8. Example 2.1 in HWM (p. 39) is a transcription in modern notation of the chant on the facing page. The plainchant notation uses a four-line staff. As in the modern five-line staff, each line stands for a pitch a third lower than the line above it, and the spaces stand for the pitches in between. The first symbol in each line is a clef; here it is a C clef on the top line, indicating that the top line stands for middle C. What pitch does each of the following lines and spaces stand for?

    the second line from the top   _____   the bottom line   _____

    the space below it   _____   the space below it   _____

In plainchant notation, what does a dot after a note signify? (Note: This is a sign added by modern editors and does not appear in medieval manuscripts.)

Musical exercise in reading chant notation (HWM 38–39)

You do not have to know the names of the different note-shapes, or *neumes*. But with a little practice you should be able to read the chant notation. Practice in the following way:

Reading the modern notation in Example 2.1, sing or play on an instrument the first phrase of the chant (the top line of the example). You may omit the words if it is easier for you to do so.

Then sing (or play) the same phrase, using the plainchant notation. Go back and forth between the two ways to notate the phrase until you understand how the plainchant notation indicates the same pitches and rhythms as the modern notation. If you have trouble reading any of the note-shapes, check the explanation on p. 36 of HWM or on p. 7 of NAWM.

Go through the same process for each phrase in turn: sing (or play) it first from the modern notation, then from the plainchant notation.

When you have finished, sing (or play) through the whole chant from the plainchant notation. If you get stuck, refer to the modern transcription.

Classes, Forms, and Types of Chant (HWM 38–46, NAWM 3–4)

9. What manner of performance does each of the following terms describe?

    antiphonal   _____

    responsorial   _____

    direct   _____

Music to Study
   NAWM 3: Mass for Christmas Day, in Gregorian chant
3a: Introit: *Puer natus est nobis*	CD 1.3
3b: Kyrie	CD 1.4 (Concise 1.2)
3c: Gloria	CD 1.5
3d: Gradual: *Viderunt omnes*	CD 1.6–7
3e: Alleluia *Dies sanctificatus*	CD 1.8
3f: Credo	CD 1.9
3g: Offertory: *Tui sunt caeli*	CD 1.10
3h: Sanctus	CD 1.11
3i: Agnus Dei	CD 1.12 (Concise 1.3)
3j: Communion: *Viderunt omnes*	CD 1.13
3k: Ite, missa est	(Not on recording)

   NAWM 4: Office of Second Vespers, Nativity of Our Lord (evening service on Christmas Day), in Gregorian chant
4a: *Deus in adjutorium*	(Not on recording)
4b: Antiphon for first psalm	CD 1.14 (Concise 1.4)
4c: First psalm	CD 1.15 (Concise 1.5)
Reprise of antiphon	(Not on recording)
4d–e: Second antiphon and psalm	(Not on recording)
4f–g: Third antiphon and psalm	(Not on recording)
4h–i: Fourth antiphon and psalm	(Not on recording)
4j: Short Responsory: *Verbum caro*	CD 1.16
4k: Hymn: *Christe Redemptor omnium*	(Not on recording)
4l: Verse: *Notum fecit*	(Not on recording)
4m–n: Antiphon and Magnificat	(Not on recording)

10. Look at the chants of the Mass and Office in NAWM 3 and 4. Find and list two examples of primarily *syllabic* chants, two *melismatic* chants, and two that are *neumatic,* frequently using more than two notes per syllable but rarely using long melismas.

syllabic	neumatic	melismatic
_____	_____	_____
_____	_____	_____

---

11. What are some ways that the music of chant reflects the accentuation and phrasing of the text? For each way you mention, find an example among the chants of the Mass and Office in NAWM 3 and 4.

12. What are *psalm tones*? Where are they used?

13. How are psalm tones shaped, and how do they adjust to suit the many different texts they are used with? Give an example from NAWM 4.

14. What is the *Lesser Doxology*? What does the abbreviation "E u o u a e" indicate (as in NAWM 3a and 4d)?

15. What is an *antiphon*? Diagram the way an antiphon and psalm would be performed in the Vespers in NAWM 4, using A for Antiphon, V for each psalm verse, and D for the Lesser Doxology.

16. The Introit, Offertory, and Communion were all once antiphons with psalms. What is the structure of each now? (Use the same symbols as in #15 above.)

    Introit _____   Communion _____

    Offertory _____

17. What is a *responsory*? Diagram the Short Responsory in the Vespers in NAWM 4j, using R for Respond, V for the verse, and D for the Doxology.

    Which portions would originally have been sung by a soloist?

18. The Gradual and Alleluia are also responsorial chants. What is the structure of each now? (Use the same symbols as in #17 above.)

    Gradual   _____   Alleluia   _____

19. Of the chants in the Ordinary of the Mass in NAWM 3, which ones are generally syllabic, which tend to be neumatic, and which are melismatic? For any of them that use musical repetition, show the pattern of repetition.

	text-setting	form
Kyrie	_____	_____
Gloria	_____	_____
Credo	_____	_____
Sanctus	_____	_____
Agnus Dei	_____	_____
Ite, missa est	_____	_____

Later Developments of the Chant (HWM 46–50, NAWM 5–7)

20. What is a *trope*? What are the three types of trope? When were most tropes created? Why are they not part of the modern liturgy?

21. What is a *sequence*? Where does it occur in the liturgy? When were most sequences composed? Why are there so few sequences in the modern liturgy?

22. Who was Notker Balbulus? Where and when did he work? And what, according to him, was his role in the invention of the sequence?

Music to Study
   NAWM 5: Wipo, *Victimae paschali laudes,* sequence for Mass on Easter Day (first half of the eleventh century)
     CD 1.17 (Concise 1.6)
   NAWM 6: Hildegard of Bingen, *Ordo virtutum* (The Virtues), sacred music drama (ca. 1151), excerpt: closing chorus, *In principio omnes*
     CD 1.18–19 (Concise 1.7–8)
   NAWM 7: *Quem quaeritis in praesepe,* trope (liturgical drama) at Mass on Christmas Day (tenth century)
     CD 1.20

23. Diagram the form of the sequence *Victimae paschali laudes* (NAWM 5). Use a new letter for each new melodic segment (a for the first line of text, b for the second, and so on), and repeat that letter when a segment of melody repeats with a new text.

24. How is melodic repetition used in Hildegard of Bingen's *In principio omnes* (NAWM 6)? How does this song differ from liturgical chant in function and in style?

---

25. In what sense is *Quem quaeritis in praesepe* (NAWM 7) a trope? Where does it fit in the Mass to which it is attached?

26. What makes *Quem quaeritis in praesepe* a *liturgical drama*? (In what sense is it liturgical? In what sense is it a drama?) Why is *Ordo virtutum* not a liturgical drama?

27. How is the music of *Quem quaeritis in praesepe* unified through melodic repetition?

Medieval Music Theory and Practice (HWM 50–57)

28. The eight church modes are labeled by number and name. Each is defined by (1) its *finalis* or *final,* (2) its *tenor* or *reciting note,* and (3) its *range.* Give the name, final, tenor, and range for each of the church modes.

Number	Name	Final	Tenor	Range
1	_____	____	____	_____
2	_____	____	____	_____
3	_____	____	____	_____
4	_____	____	____	_____
5	_____	____	____	_____
6	_____	____	____	_____
7	_____	____	____	_____
8	_____	____	____	_____

29. Which modes are *authentic* (indicate by number)? _____

   Which are *plagal*? _____

   What does a plagal mode share with its corresponding authentic mode?

   How does it differ?

30. Using the criteria of final and range, identify (by number) the mode of each
   of the following chants:

   Quem quaeritis in praesepe (NAWM 7)   _____

   Alleluia Pascha nostrum (NAWM 15a)   _____

   Conditor alme siderum (NAWM 28, verse 1)   _____

31. What is *solmization*? Why was it useful? When was it invented, and by whom?
   How is modern solmization similar to medieval practice? How does it differ?

32. What are the *natural, hard,* and *soft hexachords*? Why was it necessary to
   have all three? What is *mutation,* and how is it useful in singing?

33. What is the *Guidonian hand,* what was it used for, and how was it used?

34. How did chant notation evolve? What stages did it go through? What is one of its limitations?

Nonliturgical and Secular Monody (HWM 57–64, NAWM 8–11)

35. Who were the *Goliards*? Who were the *jongleurs* or *minstrels*? What kinds of music did each perform, and when and where did they perform it?

36. What is a *conductus*? How does it differ from a liturgical chant?

37. What is a *troubadour*? a *trobairitz*? a *trouvère*? When were they active, and what languages did they use? From what social classes did they come?

38. What is *courtly love*?

39. Who were the *Minnesinger*? When and where were they active? How are their songs like troubadour and trouvère songs, and how do they differ?

40. Who were the *Meistersinger*? When and where were they active?

41. What is a *cantiga*? Where is it from? What is a *lauda,* and where is it from?

Music to Study
    NAWM 8: Adam de la Halle, *Robins m'aime,* rondeau or trouvère song, from *Jeu de Robin et de Marion* (ca. 1284)
      CD 1.21
    NAWM 9: Bernart de Ventadorn, *Can vei la lauzeta mover,* troubadour song (ca. 1170–80)
      CD 1.22 (Concise 1.9)
    NAWM 10: Beatriz de Dia, *A chantar,* canso or troubadour song (second half of twelfth century)
      CD 1.23
    NAWM 11: Hans Sachs, *Nachdem David war redlich,* Meisterlied (ca. 1520–76)
      CD 1.24

42. Describe the melodic characteristics of troubadour songs, using Bernart de Ventadorn's *Can vei* (NAWM 9) and Comtessa Beatritz de Dia's *A chantar* (NAWM 10) as examples.

    How many notes are set to each syllable? _____

    How large a range does the melody typically cover? _____

    Does the notation indicate the rhythm? _____

    How else would you characterize the melodic style?

43. How is the trouvère song *Robins m'aime* (NAWM 8) by Adam de la Halle different in style from the troubadour songs (NAWM 9–10)? How is it similar?

44. How do *Can vei, A chantar,* and *Robins m'aime* use melodic repetition? Chart the form of each. (For the first two, chart the form of a single strophe; for the third, use capital letters for repetitions of music *and* text, and lower-case letters for repetitions of music with new words.)

   Can vei   _____

   A chantar   _____

   Robins m'aime _____

45. What is the mode of each of these songs? (Use the mode number.)

   Can vei   _____

   A chantar   _____

   Robins m'aime _____

46. What is *Bar form*? How is it used Hans Sachs's *Nachdem David war redlich* (NAWM 11)? Does the *Abgesang* repeat material from the *Stollen*?

47. Of the secular monophonic songs in NAWM 8–10, which have a form similar to bar form as used in *Nachdem David war redlich*?

Medieval Instrumental Music and Instruments (HWM 64–66, NAWM 12)

Music to Study
>   **NAWM 12:** *Istampita Palamento,* istampita or estampie (fourteenth cen-
>   tury)
>   CD 1.25–29

48. What is an *estampie*? Which of its sections were repeated? How do the
    "open" and "closed" cadences work in the *Istampita Palamento* (NAWM
    12)? (Note: This may be easier to follow while listening to the music.)

---

49. For each of the following medieval instruments, briefly describe it, explain
    how each was played, and name one or more modern instruments of which it
    is an ancestor.

    vielle or Fiedel

    organistrum

    psaltery

    shawm

    portative organ

    positive organ

50. What other instruments were used in the Middle Ages?

TERMS TO KNOW

Terms Related to Liturgy

Office or Canonical Hours
Vespers
Magnificat
Mass
Proper of the Mass: Introit,
  Gradual, Alleluia or Tract,
  Offertory, Communion

Ordinary of the Mass: Kyrie,
  Gloria, Credo, Sanctus,
  Agnus Dei, Ite, missa est or
  Benedicamus Domino
Lesser Doxology (Gloria Patri)

Terms Related to Chant

plainchant
antiphon
responsory
neume
antiphonal, responsorial, or
  direct performance
syllabic, neumatic, melismatic
recitation formula
psalm tone
tenor or reciting note (tone)
antiphonal psalmody
responsorial psalmody
respond

melisma
jubilus
trope
sequence
liturgical drama
mode: the eight church modes
final (finalis)
authentic mode, plagal mode
solmization
hard, soft, natural hexachords
mutation (of hexachords)
Guidonian hand
heighted or diastematic neumes

Terms Related to Other Monophonic Music

Goliard song
conductus
chanson de geste
jongleur or ménestral (minstrel)
troubadour, trobairitz
Provençal or langue d'oc
  (Occitan)
trouvère
langue d'oïl
courtly love
refrain
Minnesinger

Meistersinger
bar form: Stollen, Abgesang
cantiga
lauda
estampie or istampita
open and closed cadences
psaltery
vielle or Fiedel
organistrum
shawm
portative organ, positive organ

NAMES TO KNOW

Notker Balbulus
Wipo
Hildegard of Bingen
Ordo Virtutum

Guido of Arezzo
Micrologus
Song of Roland

REVIEW QUESTIONS

1. Make a time-line from 800 to 1600 and locate on it the pieces in NAWM 5–12, their composers, and these other people and events: Charlemagne, Notker Balbulus, Guido of Arezzo, and the Council of Trent. (The chants in NAWM 3–4 come from many centuries and most cannot be dated accurately, so they cannot be fixed on your time-line.)

2. Why was notation devised, and how was it useful? How would your life as a musician be different if there was no notation?

3. How has the music of chant been shaped by its role in the ceremonies and liturgy of the Roman Church, by the texts, and by the manner in which it has been performed? Use as examples at least two individual chants of varying types, and show in what ways the musical characteristics of each are appropriate for its liturgical role, its text, and its manner of performance.

4. Write a chant melody to the text of the Kyrie, Sanctus, or Agnus Dei from the Mass in NAWM 3. Use the original chant as a model for the form, including repetition of words and of music. Use any of the eight church modes *except* the mode of the original chant or its corresponding plagal or authentic mode. (For instance, since the Kyrie is in mode 1, do not use mode 1 or mode 2 to write your Kyrie.) Try to follow the style of chant as you have come to know it, including melodic contour, phrasing, and accentuation. You may use either modern or chant notation.

5. What practical contributions to the theory and performance of monophonic music were made between the seventh and the twelfth centuries?

6. Trace the history of monophonic secular song from the Goliards to the Meistersinger. For each group of poet-composers, note their region, language, place in society, and time of activity, and briefly describe their music.

7. In what ways are instrumental music and the use of instruments in accompanying singing similar in the Middle Ages and the present time, and in what ways do they most differ?

The Beginnings of Polyphony and the Music of the Thirteenth Century

3

CHAPTER OBJECTIVES

After you complete the reading, study of the music, and study questions for this chapter, you should be able to

1. name the new trends in eleventh-century music that became distinguishing characteristics of Western music;
2. describe the varieties of polyphony practiced between the ninth and thirteenth centuries and trace their historical development;
3. define important terms and identify the people, works, and schools of composition that played a major role in the development of medieval polyphony; and
4. describe the origins and early evolution of the motet.

CHAPTER OUTLINE

I. Historical Background of Early Polyphony (HWM 70–71)

The eleventh century brought prosperity and a cultural revival to much of western Europe, including the beginning of modern cities and the rise of Romanesque architecture. This was also a time of change for music.

1. *Polyphony,* music of two or more independent voices, became prominent in the church, starting a development unique in music history.
2. Precise notation allowed composers for the first time to fix a work in definitive form and transmit it accurately to others, so it could be performed by someone who had not already learned it by ear.
3. Music was increasingly structured by precepts such as the eight church modes and rules governing rhythm and consonance.

II. Early Organum (HWM 71–73, NAWM 13)

A. Parallel Organum and Organum with Oblique Motion

Polyphony was probably improvised before it was written down. It was first described in the ninth-century treatise *Musica enchiriadis* and dialogue

Scolica enchiriadis. In this early *organum,* an added voice (*organal voice* or *vox organalis*) appears below a chant melody (*principal voice* or *vox principalis*), moving either in parallel motion at the interval of a fourth or fifth (*parallel organum*) or in a mixture of parallel and oblique motion (*organum with oblique motion*).

B. Eleventh-Century Organum

In *eleventh-century organum* (also called *note-against-note organum*), the added voice usually sings above the chant (although the voices may cross), moving most often in contrary motion to the chant and forming consonant intervals with it (unison, fourth, fifth, and octave). Only the portions of chant that were sung by soloists were set polyphonically, so that in performance sections of polyphony alternate with sections of chant. The oldest collection of pieces in this style is the *Winchester Troper* (eleventh century) and instructions on how to compose or improvise organum of this type are preserved in the treatise *Ad organum faciendum* (To Make Organum, ca. 1100).   **Music: NAWM 13**

III. Florid Organum (HWM 73–76, NAWM 14)

New types of polyphony, called *Aquitanian polyphony,* appeared early in the twelfth century in southwestern France and Spain. In *florid organum,* the chant is sustained in long notes in the lower voice (called the *tenor*), while the upper voice sings from one to many notes above each tenor note. This style was called *organum, organum duplum* (double organum), or *organum purum* (pure organum); *organum* could also refer to a piece that used this style. A contrasting style in which voices move mainly note against note was called *discant.* Texts for these works include tropes on Benedicamus Domino, sequences, and newly composed Latin poems called *versus*; polyphonic settings of the last are the earliest polyphony not based on chant. Manuscripts for these types of polyphony use *score notation* (one part above the other, with notes that sound together aligned vertically), but do not indicate rhythm or duration.   **Music: NAWM 14**

IV. Notre Dame Organum (HWM 76–83, NAWM 15a–c, 15e, 16)

A. The Rhythmic Modes

A notation to indicate patterns of long and short notes was developed during the twelfth and early thirteenth centuries. By about 1250, these patterns were codified as the six *rhythmic modes.* The modes were based on divisions of a threefold unit called a *perfection.* Each mode was indicated by a different succession of note groupings or *ligatures.*

B. Polyphonic Composition

From the twelfth through the mid-fourteenth century, polyphonic music developed mainly in northern France and disseminated from there across western Europe. The first composers of polyphony known to us by name are *Léonin* (ca. 1135–ca. 1201) and *Pérotin* (ca. 1170–ca. 1238). They worked in Paris at the *Notre Dame cathedral,* the center for a style called

Notre Dame polyphony. (We know their names because a treatise known as *Anonymous IV* describes their music and names some of their works.)

C. Léonin

Léonin wrote or compiled the *Magnus liber organi* (The Great Book of Organum), a cycle of organa for the solo portions of the Graduals, Alleluias, and Responsories for major feasts for the entire church year. (As in earlier styles of organum, the portions sung by the choir remain in Gregorian chant.) Léonin's organa are in two voices and alternate sections of organum style with sections in discant style, called *clausulae* (singular *clausula*). The discant sections use the rhythmic modes and tend to appear where there are melismas in the original chant. The upper voice of the sections in organum style may be in free rhythm, although some editors and performers treat it in *modal rhythm* (i.e., using the rhythmic modes). **Music: NAWM 15b–c**

D. Pérotin Organum

Pérotin and his contemporaries revised Léonin's work, writing discant clausulae to replace sections of organum and *substitute clausulae* in place of older sections of discant. The tenors often repeat rhythmic patterns and segments of melody. Pérotin also wrote new organa in three and four voices, called *organum triplum* and *organum quadruplum,* respectively, in which the upper parts are in the rhythmic modes and often use *voice exchange.* The second voice (reading up from the bottom) was called the *duplum,* the third the *triplum,* and the fourth the *quadruplum.* **Music: NAWM 15e, 16**

V. Polyphonic Conductus (HWM 84, NAWM 17)

The *polyphonic conductus* is a setting of a metrical Latin poem, either sacred or secular (like the earlier monophonic conductus). The tenor is newly written, not based on chant. The two, three, or four voices move in similar rhythm and declaim the text together, in a predominantly syllabic and homorhythmic texture known as *conductus style,* Works in other genres were sometimes written in this style. Some conductus feature long melismas called *caudae* (tails), especially at the beginning or end. As in the organa and discant clausulae of Léonin and Pérotin, vertical consonances of the fifth and octave are prominent throughout and required at cadences, and the music is written in score notation. Both organum and conductus fell out of favor after 1250. **Music: NAWM 17**

VI. The Motet (HWM 84–91, NAWM 15d, 15f–g, 18)

A. Origins and General Features

Starting in the early thirteenth century, words were often added to the upper voice or voices of a discant clausula. This produced a new genre, the *motet* (from the French word *mot,* for "word"). The duplum of a motet is called the *motetus.* Composers created motets by freely reworking existing clausulae and motets, adding or substituting texts and in some cases new upper lines. Motets were also newly composed, instead of being adapted from existing clausulae, but still used segments of chant in their tenors. Later in the thirteenth century, some tenors were taken from secular tunes. Tenors were often laid out in repeating rhythmic patterns and were probably played rather than sung. Once removed from the liturgy, motets came to be sung on secular occasions. Their texts could be sacred or secular and need not relate to the text of the tenor. In three-voice motets, the most common type, there were often two texts: both in Latin, both in French, or (more rarely) one in each language. Although the texts differ between voices, they are usually on related subjects. A motet is identified by a compound title with the first word(s) of each text, including the tenor. Frequently, the upper voices would cadence at different places to maintain forward momentum.   **Music: NAWM 15d, 15f, and 15g**

B. Motet Texts

Motet texts were often written to existing music and had to follow its shape and rhythm. Frequently the same vowels or syllables appear in different texts, binding them together through sound as well as sense. Later motet texts are predominantly secular, and most are love songs.

C. The Franconian Motet

In many motets from the second half of the thirteenth century, the upper voice moves more quickly and has a longer text than the middle voice, while the tenor remains the slowest. This type is called the *Franconian motet,* after composer and theorist *Franco of Cologue* (fl. ca. 1250–80). Rhythm continued to be based on the rhythmic modes, but in the upper parts notes were often broken into shorter notes, using *fractio modi* (breaking up of the mode). *Petrus de Cruce* or Pierre de la Croix (fl. ca. 1270–1300) used even more notes and shorter note values in the top voice in a style named *Petronian,* after him. Harmonically, these later motets were similar to the earlier ones, with perfect consonances on the main beats and free dissonance in between. Toward the end of the century, cadences began to be standardized, with the lowest voice moving down by step and the upper voices up by step to form a fifth and octave above the lowest voice. In this type of cadence, the outer voices expand from a harmonic sixth to an octave, and the bottom and middle voice move from a harmonic third to a fifth.   **Music: NAWM 18**

D. Hocket

Hocket (from the French word for "hiccup") is a technique in which a melody is interrupted by rests, while the missing notes are supplied by another voice. It was used in motets and conductus in the late thirteenth and early fourteenth centuries. Works that use it extensively, whether vocal or instrumental, are called *hockets.*

E. Notation in the Thirteenth Century

Notation for the rhythmic modes used patterns of ligatures, but the syllabic text-setting of motets made ligatures impossible. This required a notation that indicated the duration of each note. *Franconian notation,* codified by Franco of Cologne in *Ars cantus mensurabilis* (The Art of Measurable Music, ca. 1280), solved this problem by using different note shapes for different relative values. (This same principle underlies modern notation.) With this more exact notation, polyphonic works no longer needed to be written in score and were notated instead in *choirbook format,* in which the voices all appear on the same or facing pages but are not aligned.

Sidebar: **Thirteenth-Century Notation in Depth**

Franconian notation used four note shapes: the *double long,* the *long,* the *breve,* and the *semibreve.* The basic time unit was the *tempus* (pl. *tempora*), the length of one unaltered breve, and there were three tempora in a *perfection,* equivalent to a modern measure of three beats. A long was either perfect (three tempora) or imperfect (two), a breve could be altered to be two tempora, and divisions of the breve were notated by semibreves. Although this notation still emphasized three-fold divisions, it gave new freedom from the rhythmic modes.

VII. Summary (HWM 92–93)

Polyphony developed from the eleventh through the thirteenth centuries as a process of elaborating on existing pieces. New voices were added to existing chants in note-against-note organum, florid organum, and discant. New discant clausulae substituted for older sections of organum or discant. Adding words to the upper parts of clausulae—a kind of troping—produced motets. Additional voices and texts could be added in turn, and motets were also newly composed using segments of chant and other melodies. At each step, composers elaborated on existing material. New technical developments focused on rhythm and notation, from the rhythmic modes to Franconian notation. Whereas until the early thirteenth century almost all polyphony was sacred, by the end of the century secular texts were also being set polyphonically.

STUDY QUESTIONS

Historical Background of Early Polyphony (HWM 70–71)

1. What important new developments in European music were under way in the eleventh century? Which of the trends that were new then are still typical of Western music?

Early Organum (HWM 71–73, NAWM 13)

2. In what treatise was polyphony first described? _____

    Name the textbook that accompanied this treatise. _____

    About when were they written? _____

    What two kinds of organum do they describe?

3. State the rules that govern the composition of Example 3.1 in HWM, p. 72 (parallel organum in two voices, with a modified cadence).

4. Following the model in Example 3.1, write parallel organum at the fourth below for the first verse of the sequence *Victimae paschali laudes.*

Vic - ti - mae   pa - scha - li   lau - des   im - mo - lent   Chri - sti - a - ni.

5. In Example 3.3 in HWM, p. 72, why can the chant (the upper line, marked *vox principalis*) *not* be accompanied by a voice a parallel fourth lower? What adjustments have been made to solve this problem?

6. Describe the style of organum common in the eleventh century.

What is this style called? _____

Name a manuscript that contains examples of this style. _____

Name a treatise in which this style is described. _____

7. What are the main harmonic intervals of early polyphony? Why were these intervals considered consonant, while others were considered dissonant?

Music to Study
   NAWM 13: *Alleluia Justus ut palma,* organum from *Ad organum faciendum*
      (ca. 1100)
   CD 1.30 (Concise 1.10)

8. In the eleventh-century organum *Alleluia Justus ut palma* (NAWM 13),
   some sections are not set in polyphony. Why not?

   In the sections in two-voice polyphony, which part is the original chant, and
   which is the added voice? Which of the two is more disjunct (fewer steps,
   more skips)? Why?

9. Using *Alleluia Justus ut palma* as a model, add an organal voice in eleventh-
   century style (note-against-note organum) to the first two verses of *Victimae
   paschali laudes,* given below. Here the organal voice will be above the
   chant, rather than below it (although it may cross below on occasion). Start
   the first phrase on a unison *D* with the chant, and end each verse on an
   octave *D–D*. Each vertical sonority should be a unison, a perfect fourth, a
   perfect fifth, an octave, or (rarely) a perfect eleventh, with a third or sixth
   permissible just before a unison or octave cadence. Use contrary motion
   most often and parallel and oblique motion for variety, but avoid parallel
   octaves and unisons. Make the organal voice as smooth as possible, and
   avoid leaps larger than a fifth. Do not go higher than the *A* above the staff.
   Do not use any accidental other than *B* flat, and avoid using both *B* natural
   and *B* flat in close proximity. Have fun with this, and try to write something
   you like while following all these rules.

Vic - ti - mae pa - scha - li   lau - des   im - mo - lent   Chri - sti - a - ni.

A - gnus red - e - mit o - ves: Chri - stus in - no - cens Pa - tri   re - con - ci - li - a - vit pec - ca - to - res.

Florid Organum (HWM 73–76, NAWM 14)

10. In florid organum, which voice has the chant? _____

    What is this voice called? _____

    Why did it receive this name?

    Describe the relationship between the parts in florid organum. What is each voice like?

11. What is a *versus*? How does it differ from organum in respect to the derivation of its text and its music?

Music to Study
> **NAWM 14:** *Jubilemus, exultemus,* florid organum (twelfth century)
> CD 1.31

12. How does *Jubilemus, exultemus* (NAWM 14) differ from the eleventh-century organum *Alleluia Justus ut palma* (NAWM 13)? How are the two similar?

Notre Dame Organum (HWM 76–83, NAWM 15a–c, 15e, 16)

13. Show the rhythmic pattern for each of the six rhythmic modes:

    Mode I   _____

    Mode II   _____

    Mode III   _____

    Mode IV   _____

    Mode V   _____

    Mode VI   _____

14. For which chants of the Mass and Office did Léonin write organa?

    Of these chants, which portions did he set in polyphony?

    What was his collection of organa called? _____

15. According to the treatise called Anonymous IV, what was Léonin best at?

    What was Pérotin noted for?

16. What is a *clausula*?

    What is a *substitute clausula*? What does it substitute for?

Music to Study
   NAWM 15a–c and e: *Alleluia Pascha nostrum,* plainchant and Léonin's
      setting (late twelfth century), with later anonymous substitutions
   15a: Plainchant   (Not on recording)
   15b: Léonin, organum duplum (pp. 53–54, 56, 58–59)
                                 CD 1.32–34, 1.36, 1.38–40
   15c: Anonymous discant clausula on "nostrum" (pp. 54–55)
                                      (Not on recording)
   15e: Anonymous substitute clausula on "-la-" (pp. 56–57)
                                      (Not on recording)

There are several stages of elaboration represented in NAWM 15:

   15a: The original chant is in three sections: the respond ("Alleluia"),
      the verse, and the repetition of the respond. Each section begins with
      the soloist and ends with the choir.
   15b: Léonin substituted polyphony for the portions of chant originally
      sung by the soloist, alternating organum and discant. The original
      chant appears in the lowest voice, the tenor, notated a fifth lower to
      make room for the upper part.
   15c & 15e: Later composers substituted new sections of discant, called
      substitute clausulae, for ones by Léonin. Léonin's original settings
      for these sections (on "nostrum" and "-latus") do not appear in the
      manuscript from which this example is taken and are omitted here.
   15d, 15f, & 15g: Finally, some of the sections of discant were given texts
      for the upper voices, making them into *motets.* The earliest motets
      have one added text, as in NAWM 15d and 15f, heard on the record-
      ing in place of 15c and 15e, on which they are based.

Text	Perf.	15a: Chant	15b: Léonin (Page/Track)	15c and 15e: Substitute clausulae	15d and 15f: Motets
Respond					
Alleluia.	Solo	intonation	organum (54/1.32)		
Alleluia	Choir	response	chant (55/1.33)		
(-a.)	Choir	jubilus	chant (55/1.33+)		
Verse					
Pascha	Solo	syllabic	organum (55/1.34)		
nostrum	Solo	melismatic	[discant]	discant (55–56)	(55–56/1.35)
immola-	Solo	syllabic	organum (57/1.36)		
(-la)tus	Solo	melismatic	[discant]	discant (57–59)	(57–59/1.37)
(-tus) est	Solo	syllabic	organum (59/1.38)		
Christus.	Choir	melismatic	chant (59/1.38+)		
Respond					
Alle-	Solo	syllabic	organum (60/1.39)		
lu-	Solo	melismatic	discant (60/1.40)		
(-lu)ia	Solo	syllabic	organum (60/1.40+)		
(-a).	Choir	melismatic	chant (60/1.40+)		

17. The setting of *Alleluia Pascha nostrum* in NAWM 15b, c, and e includes sections in both organum duplum and discant style. What are the main features of each style?

    organum duplum

    discant style

18. Which sections of *Alleluia Pascha nostrum* use organum style?

    Which sections use discant style? Why is discant used in these passages?

19. Which sections of NAWM 15b use no polyphony? Why are these sections not sung polyphonically?

20. In the discant clausula on the word "nostrum" (NAWM 15c), which rhythmic mode predominates in the upper voice? in the lower voice?

    upper voice _____   lower voice _____

    Besides the rhythmic mode itself, what repeated rhythmic pattern is used in the lower voice?

21. How does the lower part of NAWM 15c compare to the chant melody on "nostrum" in NAWM 15a? What happens in the lower voice at m. 19, where the editor has added a double bar and a Roman numeral II?

22. In NAWM 15c, where do cadences occur? What vertical sonorities appear on the cadential note?

What sonorities tend to precede cadences? Do the voices tend to move in parallel or in contrary motion at cadences?

How many times does each of these vertical sonorities appear on a downbeat?

octave ____   perfect fifth ____   third ____   unison ____   other ____

23. Using questions 20–21 above as guides, describe the use of rhythmic modes and rhythmic and melodic repetition in the discant clausula on "-lu-" in NAWM 15b (p. 60, CD 1.40).

24. What are the names for the various voices in an organum?

    bottom voice   _____

    second voice from the bottom   _____

    third voice from the bottom (if any)   _____

    fourth voice from the bottom (if any)   _____

    Which voice carries the chant?   _____

Music to Study
   NAWM 16: Pérotin, *Sederunt,* organum quadruplum (late twelfth or early
          thirteenth century), respond only
       CD 1.42–44 (Concise 1.11–13)

25. Compare the organum of Léonin in NAWM 15b with that of Pérotin in
    NAWM 16, an organum quadruplum on *Sederunt.* How is Pérotin's style
    like Léonin's, and how is it different?

26. Which rhythmic mode predominates in each of the following passages of
    Sederunt?

    the top three voices, mm. 2–10   _____

    the top voice, mm. 13–23   _____

    the top voice, mm. 35–40   _____

27. What vertical sonority is used most often at the cadences in *Sederunt*?

28. Compare the passages of Pérotin's *Sederunt* in mm. 13–23 and 24–34. How are they related?

    What is this technique called? _____

    Where else in the piece does this technique occur?

Polyphonic Conductus (HWM 84, NAWM 17)

29. How is a polyphonic conductus like a monophonic conductus?

Music to Study
> **NAWM 17:** *Ave virgo virginum,* conductus (thirteenth century)
>   CD 1.45

30. In what ways is *Ave virgo virginum* (NAWM 17) typical of the polyphonic conductus, as described in HWM?

    How is it different from organum and from discant?

The Motet (HWM 84–91, NAWM 15d, 15f–g, 18)

31. How did the motet originate, and how did it acquire its name?

32. What does the title of a motet indicate?

Music to Study

    NAWM 15d: *Gaudeat devotio fidelium,* motet (thirteenth century)
        CD 1.35
    NAWM 15f: *Ave Maria, Fons letitie,* motet (thirteenth century)
        CD 1.37
    NAWM 15g: *Salve, salus hominum / O radians stella / Nostrum,* bitextual
        motet (thirteenth century)
        CD 1.41
    NAWM 18: *Amours mi font / En mai / Flos filius eius,* motet in Franconian
        style (late thirteenth century)
        CD 1.46 (Concise 1.14)

33. How are the motets in NAWM 15d, 15f, and 15g related to the discant clausulae on *nostrum* and *-latus* in NAWM 15c and 15e? What has been added, deleted, or changed in creating these new works? What has stayed the same?

---

34. In the motet *Gaudeat devotio fidelium* (NAWM 15d), the tenor is on the word "nostrum." Where in the text of the motet do the sounds "no-" and "-um" appear? Where else do the vowels "o" and "u" appear?

   How do these similarities of sound help to bind together the tenor and the motetus?

35. How does the meaning of the motet text relate to the meaning of the original chant text, "Alleluia, Christ, our paschal lamb, is sacrificed"? How does the motet text relate to the occasion (Easter Mass) on which this chant was originally sung?

36. What makes *Amours mi fonr / En mai / Flos filius eius* (NAWM 18) a *Franconian motet,* and how does it differ from earlier motets?

37. When were Franconian motets written? _____

   After whom were they named? _____

   About when was this person active? _____

38. What makes *Aucun vont / Amor qui cor / Kyrie,* shown in Example 3.13 of HWM, p. 88, a *Petronian motet,* and how does it differ from earlier motets and from Franconian motets?

39. When were Petronian motets written? _____

    After whom were they named? _____

    About when was this person active? _____

40. What new notational system was devised to indicate rhythm in motets? How was it different from the notation for the rhythmic modes? Why was this change necessary, and what results did it have?

41. In what treatise was this notational system codified? Who wrote it, and when?

Summary (HWM 92–93)

42. Summarize the most significant developments in music during the period between about 1160 and 1300.

TERMS TO KNOW

Terms Related to Early Polphony

polyphony
organum
principal voice (vox principalis),
    organal voice (vox organalis)
parallel organum
organum with oblique motion
eleventh-century organum (or
    note-against-note organum)

Aquitanian polyphony
florid organum
tenor (in florid organum, discant,
    and motet)
organum duplum, organum purum
discant
versus
score notation

Terms Related to Notre Dame Polyphony

rhythmic modes
perfection (Latin *perfectio*)
ligatures
Notre Dame polyphony
clausula (pl. clausulae)
discant clausula
modal rhythm
substitute clausula

organum triplum, organum
    quadruplum
voice exchange
duplum, triplum, quadruplum
polyphonic conductus
conductus style
cauda (pl. caudae)

Terms Related to the Thirteenth-Century Motet

motet
motetus
Franconian motet
fractio modi
Petronian motet
hocket, hockets

Franconian notation
choirbook format
double long, long, breve, semibreve
tempus
perfection

NAMES TO KNOW

Musica enchiriadis
Scolica enchiriadis
Winchester Troper
Ad organum faciendum
Notre Dame, Cathedral of Paris
Léonin

Pérotin
Anonymous IV
Magnus liber organi
Franco of Cologne
Petrus de Cruce (Pierre de la Croix)
Ars cantus mensurabilis

REVIEW QUESTIONS

1. Take the time-line you made in chapter 2 and add the pieces in NAWM
   13–14, 15b–15g, and 16–18, their composers (when known), France of
   Cologne and Petrus de Cruce, and the treatises *Musica enchiriadis, Scolica
   enchiriadis, Ad organum faciendum,* and *Ars cantus mensurabilis.*

2. What different forms of polyphony can be found between the ninth century and the first half of the twelfth century? Describe an example of each type.

3. Describe the music of Notre Dame polyphony. Include in your discussion the major composers, the genres they cultivated, the rhythmic and harmonic style of their music, and the way new pieces used, embellished, or substituted for existing music.

4. Write a passage in Notre Dame organum, following the model of Léonin's setting of the opening "Alleluia" from *Alleluia Pascha nostrum* (NAWM 15b). For a tenor, use the opening "Alleluia" (just the first ten notes, up to the asterisk) from the *Alleluia Dies sanctificatus* (NAWM 3e) from the Mass for Christmas Day.

5. Write a passage in discant style, following the model of the two-voice discant clausulae in NAWM 15b, 15c, and 15e. For a tenor, use the seventeen notes to the word "Dies" in the *Alleluia Dies sanctificatus* (NAWM 3e) from the Mass for Christmas Day, laid out in a repeating rhythmic pattern like those in the tenors of the discant clausulae in NAWM 15b, 15c, and 15e. In the duplum, use rhythmic patterns derived from at least two of the rhythmic modes (but do not mix modes 1 and 2 in the same discant clausula, and do not mix modes 1, 3, or 4 in the same phrase).

6. Trace the development of the motet from its origins through the end of the thirteenth century, using NAWM 15d, 15g, and 18 as examples of three stages in that development.

7. How did changing musical styles and changing notational practices for polyphonic music interrelate during the period 900–1300?

8. In your view, looking back over chapters 2 and 3, what developments during the period 900–1300 were most significant for the later evolution of music? What styles, practices, techniques, attitudes, or approaches that were new in this time have continued to affect Western music in the last 700 years? In your opinion, which of these have most set music in the western European tradition apart from music of other cultures?

FRENCH AND ITALIAN MUSIC IN THE FOURTEENTH CENTURY

4

CHAPTER OBJECTIVES

After you complete the reading, study of the music, and study questions for this chapter, you should be able to

1. explain the increased prominence of secular literature and music in the fourteenth century;
2. describe some of the rhythmic and other stylistic features that characterize the music of the *ars nova, trecento,* and late-fourteenth-century *ars subtilior*;
3. describe isorhythm and its use in fourteenth-century motets and Mass movements;
4. name and describe the forms of secular song practiced in France and Italy during the fourteenth century;
5. identify some of the major figures, works, and terms associated with music in the fourteenth century.

CHAPTER OUTLINE

I. General Background (HWM 96–98)

A. The Church's Declining Authority

The fourteenth century was an unstable and increasingly secular age. Church authority was undermined by the move of the pope to Avignon (1305–78) and a schism between rival popes (1378–1417). Human reason became an authority in its own sphere, independent of church control.

B. Social Conditions

The growth of cities, the Black Death (1348–50), the Hundred Years War (1338–1453), and political changes challenged the old order. Great works of literature by Dante, Boccaccio, Petrarch, and Chaucer appeared in vernacular languages, and interest in Greek and Latin writings revived.

C. Musical Background

The new musical style in France was the *Ars nova* ("new art"), named after a treatise attributed to *Philippe de Vitry* (1291–1361). The principal innovations of the *ars nova* are the use of duple divisions of the note (in addition to triple) and the use of notes shorter than the semibreve. These changes gave fourteenth-century music a rhythm distinct from that of earlier periods.

II. The *Ars Nova* in France (HWM 98–105, NAWM 19–21)

A. The *Roman de Fauvel* and Vitry
The *Roman de Fauvel* (1310–14) is a satirical poem with interpolated music, including 34 motets. By this time, motet texts were usually secular and often referred to contemporary events. Five three-part motets in this work are by Vitry, considered the outstanding French poet and composer of the early fourteenth century. The motets of Vitry and other fourteenth-century composers use *isorhythm* ("same rhythm").

B. The Isorhythmic Motet
The tenor in an *isorhythmic motet* is composed of a repeating series of pitches, called the *color,* and a repeating rhythmic pattern, called the *talea.* These can be combined in various ways: one may be longer than the other, their endings may coincide or overlap, and when the color repeats, the talea may appear in diminished durations. Upper voices may also be isorhythmic in whole or in part, if they feature repeating rhythmic patterns coordinated with repetitions in the tenor. Isorhythm gave unity and form to motets.   **Music: NAWM 19**

C. Guillaume de Machaut
Guillaume de Machaut (ca. 1300–1377) was the leading poet and composer of fourteenth-century France. His isorhythmic motets are longer and more complex than Vitry's. Machaut wrote many secular songs: 19 monophonic and polyphonic *lais,* 25 monophonic and 7 polyphonic *virelais,* 22 polyphonic *rondeaux,* and 41 polyphonic *ballades.* The virelai, rondeau, and ballade are called *formes fixes* (fixed forms); each features a set pattern of rhymes and repeating lines of poetry called *refrains,* and the rhymes and refrains are coordinated with repeating segments of music.
   1. The virelai has the form A b b a . . . A, in which A is the refrain and a uses the same music as A. There are usually three stanzas, for a form of A b b a A b b a A b b a A. The b section often has open and closed endings.
   2. The ballade has the form a a b C and usually has three or four stanzas, each ending with the same line of text (C). Musically, the endings of the a section and the C section may be similar or identical. Ballades with two texted voices are called *double ballades.*
   3. The rondeau has the form A B a A a b A B, with a refrain in two sections (A and B), the first repeating in the middle of the stanza. The stanza uses the same two sections of music as the refrain, a and b, but with different words.   **Music: NAWM 20**
The polyphonic songs are for one or two singers and instruments. Unlike the motet, in which the tenor provides structure and was written first, in these songs the *cantus* (the top part, sung by the voice) is the principal line and was written first. This treble-dominated style of voice and instrumental

accompaniment is known as *ballade style* or *cantilena style.* The vocal melodies often feature long melismas near the beginning or in the middle of lines of poetry.

Machaut's *Messe de Notre Dame* (Mass of Our Lady, ca. 1364) is a four-part setting of the Mass Ordinary. The Gloria and Credo are syllabic, with all four voices declaiming the text together, and end with isorhythmic Amens. The other movements are isorhythmic, often including isorhythm in all or most voices, and their tenors are drawn from plainchant melodies for the same texts from the Ordinary of the Mass.   **Music: NAWM 21**

The predominance of secular works in Machaut's output was typical of his day, reflecting a secularization of the arts and concern in the Church that complex, virtuosic music distracted from worship.

III. Italian *Trecento* Music (HWM 106–11, NAWM 22–23)

A. The Trecento
In Italy, the fourteenth century is known as the *Trecento* (tray-CHEN-toe), from "mille trecento," Italian for 1300. Most Italian music of the time was monophonic and unwritten, and most church polyphony was improvised. Secular polyphony was cultivated among the elite in certain cities in northern Italy, especially Florence, where the *Squarcialupi Codex,* the most important manuscript of Trecento music, was copied.

B. The Madrigal
The fourteenth-century *madrigal* (not to be confused with the sixteenth-century form) is for two voices without instruments. It has two or more three-line stanzas, all set to the same music, with a closing couplet called the *ritornello,* set to new music in a different meter.   **Music: NAWM 22**

C. The Caccia
The *caccia,* a mid-fourteenth-century form, features two voices in canon at the unison over a free instrumental part. The texts are often about hunting or other action scenes, with the appropriate sounds imitated in the music.

D. The Ballata
The *ballata* (from "ballare," to dance) evolved from monophonic dance songs with choral refrains. The polyphonic ballata of the late fourteenth century was a lyrical piece whose form resembles the French virelai.

E. Landini
Francesco Landini (ca. 1325–1397) was the leading Italian composer of the fourteenth century. He is best known for his ballate and wrote no sacred music. In a ballata, a three-line *ripresa* or refrain (A) precedes and follows a seven-line stanza. The stanza's first two pairs of lines, called *piedi,* present a new phrase (b), and the last three lines, the *volta,* use the music of the refrain (a), for an overall form of A b b a A. Most lines of the poem are set with melismas on the first and next-to-last syllables. Landini has lent his name to the *"Landini" cadence,* in which the usual cadence formula of a sixth expanding to an octave between cantus and tenor is decorated by the upper voice descending a step before resolving to the octave. In the late fourteenth century, Italian composers began to absorb

aspects of the French style, and northern composers and musicians began to settle in Italy.   **Music: NAWM 23**

F. Performance

The *superius* (top part) of a secular song is vocally conceived, while the tenor and often the *contratenor* (third part, filling out the harmony) appear to have been intended for instrumental performance. However, any part could be sung or played or shared between voice and instrument. Vocal pieces were sometimes played by instruments, with embellishments added to the vocal line, and some instrumental versions were written down.

IV. French Music of the Late Fourteenth Century (HWM 111–13, NAWM 24)

A. Late-Fourteenth-Century French Secular Music

In the late fourteenth century, many French and Italian composers were active at Avignon and other courts in southern France. They wrote mainly French secular songs, using the formes fixes, in a style that was both refined and complex.

B. Rhythm

Rhythm in this style was especially complex, with subdivisions, syncopations, hocket, and different meters in different voices. Because of its intricate rhythms and notation, this style has been called the *ars subtilior* ("the subtler manner"). This sophisticated style, intended for the most cultivated listeners and the most practiced performers, began to wane by the end of the fourteenth century. *Partial signatures,* in which the voices have different signatures (most often, the lower voice or voices have a signature of one flat while the others do not), were often used in the fourteenth and fifteenth centuries.   **Music: NAWM 24**

V. Musica Ficta (HWM 113–18)

Performers often altered notes chromatically, a practice known as *musica ficta.* In cadences in which a minor sixth expanded to an octave, the top note was often raised to make a major sixth, so that the top line resolved upward by half step, like a leading tone. A three-voice cadence in which both octave and fifth are approached from a half step below is called a *double leading-tone cadence.* Other chromatic alterations were made to avoid tritones or to create smooth lines. Chromatic notes outside Guido's hexachord system were called *ficta* ("feigned"), and composers and scribes tended not to notate them, leaving it to performers to judge where they were needed. Modern editors often suggest where changes should be made by indicating accidentals above or below the affected notes.

Sidebar: **Fourteenth-Century Notation in Depth (HWM 116–17)**

Both Italian and French musicians developed notations for the new styles of the fourteenth century. In the Italian system, dots were used to mark groupings of two, three, or four semibreves. In the French system, which became standard, the long, breve, and semibreve could each be divided into either two or three of the next smaller note value. These divisions were called *mode, time,* and *prolation,* respectively; triple divisions were *perfect* and duple *imperfect* (*major* and *minor,* respectively, for prolation). Combining time and prolation produced four possible meters (corresponding to 9/8, 6/8, 3/4, and 2/4). The *minim* and *semiminim* were introduced for notes smaller than a semibreve. About 1425, noteheads began to be left open ("white notation") instead of being filled in. The resulting note-shapes evolved into modern notation (whole note, half note, and so on).

VI. Instruments (HWM 118–20)

Music manuscripts of the fourteenth century do not specify which parts are vocal and which are instrumental, for each piece could be performed in a variety of ways. Polyphonic music was probably most often performed with one voice or instrument on a part, usually featuring various types of instruments rather than instruments from a single family. Instruments were classified as loud (*haut* or "high") or soft (*bas* or "low"). Loud instruments such as shawms, *cornetts* (wooden instruments with cup mouthpiece and fingerholes), slide trumpets, and *sackbuts* (predecessors of the trombone) were often used outdoors; soft instruments such as the harp, vielle, lute, psaltery, portative organ, transverse flute, and recorder were used indoors, and percussion was used in both environments. Larger organs were used in churches.

VII. Summary (HWM 120)

The fourteenth century is characterized by an emphasis on secular music; greater diversity and complexity in rhythm; a growing sense of harmonic organization; more use of imperfect consonances; musica ficta; cantilena style; the continuation of the motet as a secular genre; and new genres of secular polyphony.

STUDY QUESTIONS

General Background (HWM 96–98)

1. What currents in religion, philosophy, politics, and literature helped to make the fourteenth century a secular age?

2. What does the Latin phrase "ars nova" mean? _____

   How do we use the term now?

The *Ars Nova* in France (HWM 98–105, NAWM 19–21)

3. What is the *Roman de Fauvel*? When was it written? What music does it contain?

4. How is the tenor of an isorhythmic motet constructed? What are the names of the elements that repeat?

Music to Study
    NAWM 19: Philippe de Vitry, *In arboris / Tuba sacre fidei / Virgo sum,* motet (ca. 1320)
      CD 1.47–48

5. What is Vitry's motet *In arboris / Tuba sacre fidei / Virgo sum* (NAWM 19) about? What does each text say, and how do the texts relate to each other?

6. Write out the color of this motet as a series of note names (*C G A* etc.).

    How many notes does the color contain? _____

    How many times is the color stated in the motet? _____

7. Write out the talea of this motet as a series of durations. Include the rests. To make it easier to follow the rhythm, reduce the value of each note or rest to a third of its value, so that a dotted whole note becomes a half note, a dotted half note becomes a quarter note, and so on. In this notation, the first note would be a whole note, the second a half note, and so on.

    How many notes does the talea contain? _____

    How many times is the talea stated in the motet? _____

    How is the talea altered after the midpoint of the motet?

    In this motet, how are the talea and color coordinated? How does this give form to the motet?

8. How does the tenor of this piece compare in its structure with those of the motets in NAWM 15d, 15f, and 18? In what ways is it structured according to similar ideas, and in what ways is it more complex?

9. Are there any places in the upper voices of this motet where the rhythm is the same as in a previous parallel passage? If so, where? Locate and describe these passages where the rhythm repeats exactly in all three parts. (This kind of repetition of rhythm is also called isorhythm, even when a repeating series of pitches is not involved.)

10. What is *hocket*? Where and how is it used in this motet?

11. Where in this Vitry motet (that is, in which measures) can you find parallel octaves between the voices?

Where can you find parallel fifths between the voices?

Where can you find a double leading-tone cadence (defined and illustrated on pp. 113–15 of HWM)?

12. Briefly describe Guillaume de Machaut's career. Where did he live, whom did he serve, and what did he do?

13. Diagram the form of the three *formes fixes,* using letters to indicate musical repetitions and capital letters to show the refrains.

    virelai _____   ballade _____   rondeau _____

14. How does the fourteenth-century rondeau resemble *Robins m'aime* (NAWM 8) by the thirteenth-century trouvère Adam de la Halle?

Music to Study
   NAWM 20: Guillaume de Machaut, *Rose, liz, printemps, verdure,* rondeau
       (mid-fourteenth century)
     CD 2.1–3 (Concise 1.15–17)
   NAWM 21: Guillaume de Machaut, *Messe de Notre Dame* (Mass of Our
       Lady, ca. 1364), excerpt: Agnus Dei
     CD 2.4–6 (Concise 1.18–20)

15. Note the rondeau form in your answer to question 13. Which measures in the music of *Rose, liz, printemps, verdure* (NAWM 20) correspond to each letter of your diagram?

    How do the rhymes in the poetry coordinate with this form?

    How do cadences help to delineate the form?

---

16. In this rondeau, what relation does the music in mm. 32–37 have to music heard previously? How does this help to delineate the form?

17. Describe the melodic and rhythmic style of the two upper parts of this rondeau—the triplum and the cantus. How do these compare to the upper parts of the motets in NAWM 18–19 and to the thirteenth-century monophonic rondeau in NAWM 8? Describe what is distinctive about Machaut's style, as compared with melodies of the late thirteenth and early fourteenth centuries.

18. What is the *Messe de Notre Dame*? What is special about it?

Which movements are isorhythmic?

What other style is used, and in what movements? Why is it appropriate for these movements?

19. The tenor in Machaut's Agnus Dei is the second line from the bottom. It is adapted from a Gregorian chant Agnus Dei. To confirm this, sing the tenor part to the "Agnus Dei" text as underlaid below it, but instead of using Machaut's rhythms, sing the pitches in the unmeasured rhythm of chant, with each note receiving an equal time value (and double value on the last note of each phrase of text).

   Where are there repetitions of music in this chant melody?

   How does the form of Machaut's Agnus Dei follow the form of the chant melody?

20. In the Agnus Dei, the isorhythm begins at the words "qui tollis" after each "Agnus Dei." Each time, the color is stated only once, the talea more than once. The last note of each section follows the last statement of the talea.

   (Note that in certain cases, some repetitions of an isorhythmic pattern will subdivide a few notes. For example, compare mm. 15–17 in all four voices with mm. 8–10. For each voice, the rhythm is virtually the same in both passages, but in the top three voices there is a half note in one passage that is divided into smaller note values in the other. This kind of small difference embellishes but does not negate the basic isorhythmic structure.)

   Write out the talea for the first "qui tollis." _____

   How many measures long (in this modern transcription) is this talea? _____

   How many times is it stated? _____

   To what extent are the other three voices isorhythmic?

   Write out the talea for the second "qui tollis." _____

   How many measures long (in this modern transcription) is this talea? _____

   How many times is it stated? _____

   To what extent are the other three voices isorhythmic?

21. How does Machaut's Agnus Dei compare to his rondeau *Rose, liz, printemps, verdure*? How do the upper two voices of each piece compare in melodic and rhythmic style? How do the two lower voices of each compare?

22. What factors led to a decline in the composition of sacred music in fourteenth-century France and Italy?

Italian *Trecento* Music (HWM 106–11, NAWM 22–23)

23. What is the *Squarcialupi Codex,* and why is it important?

Music to Study
NAWM 22: Jacopo da Bologna, *Fenice fù,* madrigal (mid-1300s)
    CD 2.7

24. What is a fourteenth-century madrigal? Describe the type of poetry used, the poetic form, the form of the piece, and the melodic style, and show how Jacopo da Bologna's *Fenice fù* exemplifies these traits.

25. How does the melodic style of *Fenice fù* differ from that of Machaut's rondeau (NAWM 20)?

26. Define and describe the fourteenth-century *caccia*.

Music to Study
> **NAWM 23:** Francesco Landini, *Non avrà ma' pietà,* ballata (second half of fourteenth century)
> CD 2.8–10 (Concise 1.21–23)

27. In a ballata, what is the *ripresa*? What measures of Landini's *Non avrà ma' pietà* (NAWM 23) correspond to this part of the form?

What are the *piedi* and *volta*? Where do these appear in Landini's ballata?

How is the form of a ballata similar to that of a virelai? How is it different?

28. What is a "Landini cadence"? Where do Landini cadences appear in Landini's ballata?

29. Compare the melodic, rhythmic, and harmonic style of Landini's ballata to that of Machaut's rondeau (NAWM 20). Where do melismas occur in each piece, and how is the composers' practice similar or different in this respect? What other similarities and differences do you observe?

30. What combinations of voices and instruments were possible in performing secular polyphonic songs in the fourteenth century?

French Music of the Late Fourteenth Century (HWM 111–13, NAWM 24)

31. What are the special traits of the late-fourteenth-century *ars subtilior,* particularly in the realm of rhythm?

32. What are *partial signatures*? Which pieces studied in this chapter use them?

Music to Study
   NAWM 24: Baude Cordier, *Belle, bonne, sage,* rondeau (early 1400s)
      CD 2.11

33. How does Baude Cordier's *Belle, bonne, sage* (NAWM 24) resemble Machaut's rondeau (NAWM 20), and how is it different in style? What aspects of the Cordier link it to the *ars subtilior*?

34. In what shape is Cordier's rondeau presented in the manuscript, and why?

Musica Ficta (HWM 113–18)

35. What is *musica ficta*? Under what circumstances is it used, and why? Why were accidentals not written down?

36. The editor has suggested where musica ficta should be applied in Jacopo da Bologna's *Fenice fù* (NAWM 22) by placing accidentals above certain notes. Using the rules given by Prosdocimo de' Beldomandi (in HWM, p. 115) and summarized in HWM (pp. 113–18), explain why the editor has suggested each of these alterations.

   m. 15, third beat   _____

   m. 15, fourth beat   _____

   m. 17   _____

Fourteenth-Century Notation in Depth (HWM 116–17)

37. Briefly describe fourteenth-century French notation. What are the divisions of the long, breve, and semibreve called? What are the four prolations, and how do they correspond to modern meters?

Instruments (HWM 118–20)

38. What types of instruments were in use in the 1300s? What are *haut* ("high") and *bas* ("low") instruments? How were instruments used in vocal music?

Summary (HWM 120)

39. What characteristics distinguish fourteenth-century music from music of earlier periods?

TERMS TO KNOW

Terms Related to Ars Nova Music

ars nova
isorhythm
isorhythmic motet
color (pl. colores)
talea (pl. taleae)
lai
virelai

rondeau
ballade
formes fixes
refrain
double ballade
cantus
cantilena style

Terms Related to Trecento and Late-Fourteenth-Century French Music

Trecento
madrigal (fourteenth-century)
ritornello (in fourteenth-century
   madrigal)

caccia
ballata
ripresa, piedi, volta
ars subtilior

Terms Related to Music Theory and Instruments

Landini cadence
superius
contratenor
partial signature
musica ficta
double leading-tone cadence
mode, time, prolation

perfect and imperfect time
major and minor prolation
minim, semiminim
haut and bas instruments
cornett
sackbut

NAMES TO KNOW

Ars nova
Philippe de Vitry
Roman de Fauvel
Guillaume de Machaut

La Messe de Notre Dame
Squarcialupi Codex
Jacopo da Bologna
Francesco Landini

REVIEW QUESTIONS

1. Make a time-line for the pieces, composers, and treatises discussed in this chapter.

2. What is new about the *ars nova*? How does it compare to thirteenth-century music? How does late-fourteenth-century French music (the *ars subtilior*) extend the ideas of the ars nova?

3. Describe isorhythm as practiced in Vitry's motets and Machaut's Mass.

4. Write a short textless isorhythmic piece in three voices, in 6/8, modeled on the style and procedures of Vitry's *In arboris / Tuba sacre fidei / Virgo sum* (NAWM 19) and the Agnus Dei from Machaut's Mass (NAWM 21). Follow these steps:

    a. For the color in the tenor, use the fourteen notes on "hodie" in the *Alleluia Dies sanctificatus* (NAWM 3e) from the Mass for Christmas Day. Devise a talea of seven notes and one to four rests, using only notes and rests that are one or two longs (dotted half notes) in length; the 6/8 measures should be laid out in groups of two. Using this color and talea, write out the tenor.

    b. Write a duplum above the tenor, using only quarter, eighth, dotted quarter, and dotted half notes (and rests). Write it as a series of phrases separated by rests, making sure that all sonorities on downbeats are consonant and that the beginnings and ends of phrases form perfect consonances with the tenor. Do not cross below the tenor. Avoid resting during rests in the tenor.

    c. Add a triplum in the same style as the duplum or slightly more florid. It can cross below the duplum but not below the tenor. Avoid resting during rests in the other voices. Make sure that all sonorities on downbeats are consonant and that phrases end on perfect consonances.

5. Name and describe the forms of secular song practiced in France and Italy during the fourteenth century. How are French and Italian music similar? How do they differ?

6. Describe the melodic, rhythmic, and harmonic style of Machaut. How do the works of Vitry, Jacopo da Bologna, Landini, and Cordier resemble or differ from those of Machaut in melodic, rhythmic, and harmonic style? What features do they all share?

ENGLAND AND THE BURGUNDIAN LANDS IN THE FIFTEENTH CENTURY

5

CHAPTER OBJECTIVES

After you complete the reading, study of the music, and study questions for this chapter, you should be able to

1. describe the characteristics of medieval English music that distinguished it from French and Italian styles;
2. describe genres practiced in England during the thirteenth through fifteenth centuries;
3. explain how English music influenced music on the Continent during the fifteenth century;
4. describe fauxbourdon, chant paraphrase, and cantus-firmus techniques;
5. explain how an international musical style developed in the mid-fifteenth century and the historical and cultural circumstances that placed Burgundian composers at the center of these developments;
6. describe the music of Burgundian composers, particularly Du Fay, and explain the differences between their musical practices and those of the fourteenth century; and
7. name and describe the various types of polyphonic Mass cycle composed in the fifteenth century, particularly the cantus firmus Mass.

CHAPTER OUTLINE

I. English Music (HWM 123–29, NAWM 25–26, 28)

English, French, and Italian composers contributed to the development of an international style in the fifteenth century. The cantilena style began to be used in some motets and Mass settings as well as in secular music.

A. General Features
Medieval English music favored the major mode, homophony, fullness of sound, and much use of parallel thirds and sixths.

B. Fourteenth Century
The main surviving sources of fourteenth-century English music are the *Worcester fragments,* a group of manuscripts from Worcester Cathedral,

containing works for the Mass, motets, and conductus. The English cultivated forms that resemble rounds, such as the *rondellus,* in which voices in the same range exchange phrases to create an effect like a round. A frequent occurrence in English music is parallel motion in thirds and sixths, often in combination (that is, parallel sixths between the outer voices and parallel thirds between the bottom and middle voices, resolving to an octave and fifth, respectively, at cadences).

C. Fauxbourdon
The streams of parallel sixths and thirds typical of English music may have inspired the Continental practice of *fauxbourdon,* prominent ca. 1420–50. A fauxbourdon is a piece in which two notated voices, usually a paraphrased chant and the tenor below it, move mostly in parallel sixths, resolving to an octave at cadences, and a third unwritten part is sung a fourth below the superius, producing parallel thirds with the tenor. The same texture was often used in fully notated music. This led to a new style in which the principal melody was in the upper voice, the others moved in a similar rhythm and became almost equally important, and the music was suffused with imperfect consonances.   **Music: NAWM 28**

D. The Old Hall Manuscript
The main source for early-fifteenth-century English music is the *Old Hall manuscript.* It includes motets, hymns, sequences, and Mass movements in styles ranging from isorhythm and cantilena style to *cantus firmus* settings on a plainchant melody. (A cantus firmus is a plainchant or other melody used as the basis for a polyphonic composition, often moving in longer notes than the other voices.) The influence of English style on Continental composers was celebrated in a poem of about 1440 that praised the *"contenance angloise"* (English guise) of "lively consonance."

E. Dunstable
John Dunstable (ca. 1390–1453) was the leading English composer of the first half of the fifteenth century. He served for a time in the English possessions in France, which helped bring his music to the Continent. He wrote in all the prevailing genres and styles of polyphony.

F. Dunstable's Three-Part Sacred Works
Dunstable is best known for his three-voice sacred works. They use a variety of techniques, including a cantus firmus in the tenor, an ornamented chant melody in the top voice, and free counterpoint not based on chant.
Music: NAWM 25

G. The Fifteenth-Century Motet
In the fifteenth century, the isorhythmic motet waned in popularity. The term *motet* came to be applied to a polyphonic setting of a Latin text other than part of the Mass Ordinary.

H. The Carol
The fifteenth-century *carol* is a setting of a religious poem in English or Latin (or a mixture of both), often on the birth of Jesus, with a recurring *burden* or refrain and a series of stanzas. It evolved from an earlier form of carol, a monophonic dance song with a refrain.   **Music: NAWM 26**

II. Music in the Burgundian Lands (HWM 129–41, NAWM 27–30)

A. Duchy of Burgundy

The late fourteenth and the fifteenth centuries saw a great expansion in the size and power of the duchy of *Burgundy,* until the death of the last duke in 1477. The dukes maintained a *chapel* that included about two dozen musicians, and they also employed a number of instrumentalists for secular music. Their lavish patronage for music helped nurture musicians, so that most of the leading composers of the late fifteenth century came from their lands, mainly from modern-day Belgium and northeastern France. Church musicians were trained as choir boys, learning music theory and academic subjects as well as singing; women were excluded from church choirs and thus from musical careers, but some novices and nuns received musical training and wrote music. Musicians traveled with their patrons or moved to new posts in other regions, and their interactions with musicians from all over Europe aided the development of a common international style that blended elements of French, Italian, and English styles.

B. Du Fay

Guillaume Du Fay (c. 1397–1474) was educated at Cambrai in the duchy of Burgundy, served several patrons in Italy and Savoy in the 1420s and 1430s, returned to Cambrai, went back to Savoy in the 1450s, and finished his career at Cambrai, making him a truly international composer.

The main genres of the period were Masses, Magnificats, motets, and secular *chansons* (songs) to French texts. The chansons continued the formes fixes and three-voice treble-dominated texture of the fourteenth century, but the melodic style was smoother and the harmony more consonant. Triple meter and compound meters were far more common than duple meter. The traditional sixth-to-octave cadence between tenor and superius was sometimes harmonized with a contratenor that leapt up an octave from a fifth below the tenor to a fifth above the tenor's note of resolution, creating a sound similar to a modern dominant-tonic cadence.

C. The Burgundian Chanson

In the fifteenth century, *chanson* (song) was the term for any polyphonic setting of a French secular poem. Most chansons were in the form of a rondeau. Ballades were typically reserved for ceremonial occasions and given a more florid vocal part than in a rondeau.   **Music: NAWM 27**

D. Binchois

Gilles Binchois (c. 1400–1460) served the Burgundian court chapel for most of his career. He was best known for his chansons, especially his rondeaux.   **Music: NAWM 30**

E. Burgundian Motets

Motets in this period were often written in the style of the chanson, with the main melody (often paraphrased from chant) in the treble, supported by the tenor, with a contratenor to fill out the harmony. Isorhythmic motets were still sometimes composed for special occasions.   **Music: NAWM 28**

F. Masses

After about 1420, composers regularly set the Mass Ordinary as a unified cycle, creating the genre of the *polyphonic Mass cycle.*

1. Some Masses were unified simply by musical style.

2. A *plainsong Mass* based each movement on a plainchant for that text.

3. Musical unification was achieved by using the same material in each movement. One early form was the *motto Mass,* in which each movement begins with the same music, called a *head motive* or *motto.*

4. The most important form was the *cantus-firmus Mass* or *tenor Mass,* which used the same cantus firmus in each movement (some also had a head motive). This type was developed by English composers and became predominant throughout Europe by 1450.

In the cantus-firmus Mass, the cantus firmus was usually placed in the tenor in long notes and treated in isorhythmic fashion. Below it was a *contratenor bassus* (low contratenor) or *bassus* (bass) to provide a harmonic foundation; above it was the *contratenor altus* (high contratenor) or *altus* (alto); the top part was called *cantus* (melody), *discantus* (discant), or *superius* (highest part). This four-voice texture became standard by 1450.

The cantus firmus could be taken from a chant, a secular song, or the tenor of a chanson, and the Mass was named after the borrowed tune. One of the most frequently borrowed secular tunes was *L'homme armé* ("the armed man"). Although cantus-firmus Masses used learned devices such as isorhythm, they conformed to the style that prevailed after 1430, with careful control of dissonance, emphasis on consonance, smooth melody, nearly equal importance of voices, four-voice texture, and some use of imitation.   **Music: NAWM 29**

STUDY QUESTIONS

English Music (HWM 123–29, NAWM 25–26, 28)

1. What characteristics of English music in the thirteenth through early fifteenth centuries set it apart from music on the European continent?

2. What is a *rondellus,* and how does it work? Describe how the voices exchange phrases in *Fulget coelestis curia / O Petre flos / Roma gaudet,* discussed in HWM, pp. 124–25.

3. What is *fauxbourdon*? How does it work? How does it relate to English music and what was its importance for future developments?

4. What is the Old Hall manuscript? What types of composition does it contain, and what compositional procedures does it feature?

5. What was the "*contenance angloise*"? What was its importance to music outside England? What historical circumstances may have led to the spread on the Continent of English music and musical style?

6. What genres of music did Dunstable compose? What compositional techniques appear in his music?

7. Describe the relationship between the Dunstable melody and the plainchant melody it paraphrases in Example 5.3 on p. 127 of HWM. How does Dunstable embellish the chant?

Music to Study

NAWM 25: John Dunstable, *Quam pulchra es,* motet (first half, fifteenth century)
  CD 2.12 (Concise 1.24)
NAWM 26: *Salve, sancta parens,* carol (fifteenth century)
  CD 2.13

8. In what sense is *Quam pulchra es* (NAWM 25) a motet? Which part, if any, has the chant? How are the parts related to each other? How had the definition of "motet" changed by the early fifteenth century to include a piece such as this?

9. How does Dunstable shape the music of *Quam pulchra es* to reflect the divisions of the text and the rhythms of the words?

10. Where are there passages in *Quam pulchra es* that feature parallel thirds, sixths, or tenths? (Note that the middle voice is performed an octave lower than written, so that all three parts begin on middle C.)

    About how often during the work are imperfect consonances sounding?

11. How often in *Quam pulchra es* do harmonic dissonances appear? How often do parallel unisons, fifths, or octaves occur? How does this compare with the thirteenth-century conductus *Ave virgo virginum* (NAWM 17) and with Machaut's fourteenth-century Agnus Dei (NAWM 21)?

12. Compare the melodic style of the top voice in Dunstable's motet to that of the vocal lines in Machaut's *Rose, liz, printemps, verdure* (NAWM 20) and Landini's *Non avrà ma' pietà* (NAWM 23). What are the main differences between the English style of the first half of the fifteenth century and these fourteenth-century styles?

13. Now do the same for the melodic style of the tenors, and for the relationship between the vocal line and the tenor.

14. What is a *carol*? How does *Salve, sancta parens* (NAWM 26) conform to the description of a fifteenth-century carol in HWM?

15. Where are there parallel sixths, thirds, or tenths between the outer voices in the carol *Salve, sancta parens* (NAWM 26)? In the three-voice Burden II, where is there a texture in which the outer voices move in parallel sixths and the bottom two voices in parallel thirds? (Note: Sometimes the rhythm of the parts is slightly different, while the voices still essentially move in parallel.)

16. Where are there cadences in this carol? Which ones are Landini cadences? What harmonic interval is used at the cadences in the two-voice sections? What harmonic sonorities appear at the cadences in the three-voice sections?

17. If you had to assign the top voice of this carol to one of the church modes (not a rhythmic mode), which mode would you choose? Why? (The mode of a polyphonic work is generally the mode of its superius and its tenor.)

    What is the final of this mode? _____ Where do cadences occur on this note?

    What is the the tenor or reciting tone of the mode? _____ Where do cadences occur on this note?

    In what ways does this pattern of cadences show a concern for clarity of mode and for tonal planning?

Music in the Burgundian Lands (HWM 129–41, NAWM 27–30)

18. What political conditions aided the rise of Burgundian musicians to prominence in the fifteenth century? What kinds of musicians were employed by the Dukes of Burgundy? How did the music at the Burgundian court influence music across Europe?

19. What circumstances limited musical training and careers for women in the fifteenth century?

20. Briefly summarize Du Fay's career. How was it typical of musicians of his era? How did such a career facilitate the creation of an international style?

21. How does the fifteenth-century cadence described in HWM, pp. 134–35, resemble fourteenth-century cadences, and how is it like cadences in common-practice tonal music?

Music to Study
>   **NAWM 27:** Guillaume Du Fay, *Resvellies vous et faites chiere lye,* ballade
>   (1423)
>   CD 2.14–16
>   **NAWM 30:** Gilles Binchois, *De plus en plus,* rondeau (ca. 1425)
>   CD 2.26–27 (Concise 1.32–33)
>   **NAWM 28:** Guillaume Du Fay, *Conditor alme siderum,* motet (hymn para-
>   phrase) in alternation with chant (middle third of fifteenth century)
>   CD 2.17–18

22. In Du Fay's *Resvellies vous et faites chiere lye* (NAWM 27), which segments
    of the upper line seem to suggest instrumental performance? Why?

23. Where are there double leading tone cadences in *Revellies vous,* either writ-
    ten or created through musica ficta?

24. Du Fay composed *Resvellies vous* in 1423 when he was in Italy, and it shows
    strong influences from fourteenth-century French and Italian music. Which
    elements in this piece resemble Machaut's *Rose, liz* (NAWM 20)? Which
    suggest the late-fourteenth-century *ars subtilior* style? How does the me-
    lodic line in the texted portions suggest Italian rather than French influence?

25. How does the musical and poetic form of Binchois's *De plus en plus*
    (NAWM 30) compare to that of Machaut's *Rose, liz* (NAWM 20)?

26. Compare the melodic style of the top voice in Binchois's *De plus en plus* to those of the vocal line of Machaut's *Rose, liz* and of the top voice of Dunstable's *Quam pulchra es* (NAWM 25). (See question 12 above for your comparison of the latter two.) What traits does Binchois share with his English contemporary that differ from Machaut's style?

27. How do the Machaut, Dunstable, and Binchois pieces compare in harmonic style? For each piece, what cadence formulas are characteristic? What vertical sonorities are common? Where do parallel fifths and octaves occur, if at all? Where do successions of parallel sixths and thirds appear? Again, what traits does Binchois share with Dunstable that differ from Machaut?

28. In Du Fay's polyphonic setting of the even-numbered verses of the chant hymn *Conditor alme siderum* (NAWM 28), how is the chant melody embellished? Where in the phrase do embellishments occur? (Note that the chant melody itself is notated here in longs and breves, producing a pattern like the first rhythmic mode.)

29. How does Du Fay's setting of *Conditor alme siderum* fit the description of *fauxbourdon* in HWM, pp. 125–26?

30. In what church mode is the chant hymn *Conditor alme siderum*? _____

How does the polyphonic setting reinforce the mode?

31. Why did composers begin to write polyphonic settings of the Ordinary of the Mass? What different ways were used to create unity among the movements, and what different types of Mass resulted?

32. What are the four voices of a fifteenth-century Mass called? What is the general character of each part?

top part

second part down

third part down

bottom part

33. What kinds of borrowed melodies were used in cantus-firmus Masses?

    In which voice does the cantus firmus usually occur? _____

Music to Study
   NAWM 29a: Guillaume Du Fay, *Se la face ay pale,* ballade (1430s)
      CD 2.19 (Concise 1.25)
   NAWM 29b: Guillaume Du Fay, *Missa Se la face ay pale,* Mass (ca.
      1450s), excerpt: Gloria
      CD 2.20–25 (Concise 1.26–31)

34. How does Du Fay use the tenor of his chanson *Se la face ay pale* (NAWM
    29a) in the tenor of the Gloria from his *Missa Se la face ay pale* (NAWM
    29b)? How is this like isorhythm? How does it provide a form for the Gloria
    movement? How does it affect how easy it is to hear and recognize the
    source melody?

35. Where in the Gloria does Du Fay borrow material from the other two voices
    of his chanson? What purpose might this borrowing serve?

36. How do the four voices of the Gloria differ from each other in function and
    style?

---

37. Examine the upper voices in the Gloria. How often do two successive measures have the same rhythm? How often do the top two voices move in the
same rhythm at the same time? What does this suggest about Du Fay's use
of rhythm?

38. In the isorhythmic works of Vitry (NAWM 19) and Machaut (NAWM 21),
we can find parallel fifths and octaves and double leading-tone cadences.
Can any of these be found in Du Fay's Gloria? How would you describe the
harmony?

39. Summarize the differences in musical style between the mid-fourteenth and
mid-fifteenth centuries, using Machaut's rondeau and Mass movement
(NAWM 20 and 21) and Dufay's ballade and Mass movement (NAWM 29a
and 29b) as the basis for your comparison.

TERMS TO KNOW

rondellus
fauxbourdon
cantus firmus
"contenance angloise"
motet (fifteenth-century and
   later)
carol
burden
chapel

chanson
polyphonic Mass cycle
plainsong Mass
motto Mass
head motive or motto
cantus-firmus Mass or tenor Mass
bassus (contratenor bassus)
altus (contratenor altus)
cantus, discantus, superius

NAMES TO KNOW

the Worcester fragments
the Old Hall manuscript
John Dunstable
Burgundy

Guillaume Du Fay
Gilles Binchois
L'homme armé

REVIEW QUESTIONS

1. Make a time-line for the pieces and composers discussed in this chapter. Include dates for the poem that mentions the "contenance angloise"; dates for the end of the duchy of Burgundy and the reigns of Philip the Good and Charles the Bold; the dates and places of Du Fay's birth, death, and employment; and dates for any historical events listed on p. 138 of HWM with which you are familiar, to help orient you to the fifteenth century.

2. What characteristics and procedures of English music set it apart from music on the Continent in the thirteenth, fourteenth, and early fifteenth centuries? How did the Continental style change as it absorbed the influence of English music in the first half of the fifteenth century?

3. What new ways of using and reworking Gregorian chant developed during the fifteenth century?

4. What special role did the duchy of Burgundy and Burgundian composers play in the development of music during the fifteenth century?

5. Using Du Fay's *Conditor alme siderum* (NAWM 28) as a model, set the first verse of *Victimae paschali laudes* (NAWM 5) in fauxbourdon style, with the chant paraphrased in the top voice, a second voice in parallel fourths below, and a tenor moving mostly in parallel sixths with the top line, cadencing on octaves. Use triple meter as in the Du Fay, alternating long and short notes.

6. Describe the music of Du Fay and explain how he synthesized elements from France, Italy, and England in a cosmopolitan style.

7. Describe the varieties of polyphonic Mass cycle composed in the fifteenth century, and compare Du Fay's *Missa Se la face ay pale* (a cantus-firmus Mass) to Machaut's *Messe de Notre Dame* (a plainsong Mass).

THE AGE OF THE RENAISSANCE: MUSIC OF THE LOW COUNTRIES

6

CHAPTER OBJECTIVES

After you complete the reading, study of the music, and study questions for this chapter, you should be able to

1. describe some aspects of the influence of humanism on the culture and music of the fifteenth and sixteenth centuries;
2. name some of the most significant theorists and treatises of the time and explain their importance;
3. describe the beginnings and early development of music printing and its effects on musical life;
4. describe and explain the change from the composition of each successive line of a polyphonic work one after another to the composition of all parts simultaneously; and
5. describe the music and briefly describe the careers of some of the major composers active at the end of the fifteenth century and the beginning of the sixteenth century.

CHAPTER OUTLINE

I. General Characteristics (HWM 144–54)

A. Humanism

The *Renaissance* was not a musical style, but a period of history marked by the rediscovery and renewed influence of ancient Greek and Roman culture, led by the movement called *humanism*. Although no ancient music was known, during the fifteenth century many ancient writings on music were rediscovered and the major Greek writings were translated into Latin. Ancient writers' descriptions of the emotional effects of music caused some in the sixteenth century to criticize the lack of such effects in the music of their own time. Several theorists made important contributions:

1. *Liber de arte contrapuncti* (Book on the Art of Counterpoint, 1477) by *Johannes Tinctoris* laid out strict rules for controlling dissonances, limiting them to unstressed beats and to *suspensions* at cadences.

2. *Franchino Gaffurio* incorporated Greek theory into his treatises, the most influential of the late fifteenth and early sixteenth centuries.
3. *Dodekachordon* (The Twelve-String Lyre, 1547) by *Heinrich Glareanus* added four new modes (authentic and plagal modes on A and C, akin to later minor and major modes) to the eight earlier modes.
4. *Le Istitutioni harmoniche* (The Harmonic Foundations, 1558) by *Gioseffo Zarlino* codified the rules for dissonance treatment, counterpoint, and emotional expressivity.

B. Tuning Systems

Although thirds and sixths were treated as consonances in music, the traditional *Pythagorean tuning* system rendered them out of tune so that perfect fourths and fifths would be pure. In the fifteenth and sixteenth centuries, new tuning systems were introduced that allowed imperfect intervals to sound well, such as *just intonation.* (This was in accord with the humanist insistence on pleasing the ear, rather than making it subservient to an abstract ideal such as the creation of consonance through simple ratios.) Composers began to use accidentals further up and down the circle of fifths.

C. Words and Music

Humanism encouraged composers to pay increasing attention to the meaning, sound, form, and rhythm of the texts they set. Whereas text underlay had often been left to the singers, sixteenth-century composers sought to fix it precisely, for good accentuation. There was not a single musical style in the Renaissance, but a general search for means to please the human senses and express human emotions.

D. Italy

Humanism and the arts thrived particularly in Italy, where rulers of small city-states and principalities sought to outdo each other in their patronage of literature and the arts. Many of the composers they employed were from France, Flanders, and the Netherlands, particularly from the formerly Burgundian lands. These composers were influenced by the simple popular music of Italy, and the combination of northern and Italian elements helped to produce the international style of the sixteenth century.

E. Music Printing

Printing allowed wider distribution of music at a lower cost with greater accuracy and less time spent recopying by hand, creating the first true market for music as a commodity. Johann Gutenberg developed the art of printing words from movable type in 1450, and by 1473 books of chant were being printed the same way. *Ottaviano de' Petrucci* (1466–1539) of Venice was the first to print polyphonic music from movable type in 1501, using three impressions (for the staff lines, for the notes, and for the text) to create beautiful, clear collections of chansons, motets, or Masses. Others used a more complex type that allowed printing in a single impression. Most works were published as *partbooks,* one book for each voice or instrumental part (superius, altus, tenor, and bassus).

F. Compositional method

In a style that featured full harmony, careful treatment of dissonance, and imitative counterpoint, it became difficult to keep to the old method of writing a complete superius or tenor, then adding the second part, then the bassus, and finally the altus. Instead, by the early sixteenth century composers began to work out all the voices simultaneously, sometimes using a score to see all the parts at once. (This practice is sometimes called "simultaneous composition," in contrast to the "successive composition" of voices one after another in music of the fifteenth century and before.)

II. Northern Composers and Their Music (HWM 154–63, NAWM 31)

Most prominent composers in the period 1450–1550 came from France, Flanders, or the Netherlands. Many served some of their career in Italy.

A. Johannes Ockeghem

Johannes Ockeghem (ca. 1420–97) was born in the north and spent most of his career in the service of the kings of France. He was famous as a composer and as a teacher of many leading composers of the next generation. He wrote 13 Masses (some cantus-firmus Masses and some of other types), 10 motets, and about 20 chansons. He extended the range of the bassus down to low F, giving a fuller and darker sound, and all four voices tend to be equally active. The harmony is consonant and often includes full triads. He creates contrasts of light and dark by varying the texture, setting some passages for only two or three voices and sometimes alternating between high and low pairs of voices.   **Music: NAWM 31**

B. Canon

Ockeghem seldom uses *imitation* (echoing a motive or phrase in another voice, often at a different pitch level) but does use *canon,* which at this time meant a procedure for deriving more than one voice from a notated voice. His *Missa prolationum* uses *mensuration canons,* in which one notated line generates two voices through a different mensuration sign. Ockeghem's *Missa cuiusvis toni* (Mass in any mode) can be read in any of four clef combinations, each resulting in music in a different authentic mode. These arcane procedures demonstrated the composer's skill, but often went unheard and did not disturb the appealing surface of the music.

C. The Generation after Ockeghem

Many composers of the next generation were taught or influenced by Ockeghem. They worked in Italy as well as the north and blended northern polyphony, intricacy, and subtly flowing rhythms with the Italian preferences for homophony, simplicity, distinct rhythms, and clearly articulated phrases.

D. Jacob Obrecht

Jacob Obrecht (1457 or 1458–1505) was trained in the Low Countries and worked there and in Italy. His works include 29 Masses, 28 motets, and numerous songs and instrumental works. His treatment of the cantus firmus in his Masses is quite varied and shows considerable originality. Like others of his generation, Obrecht often uses imitative counterpoint.

E. The *Odhecaton*

The first volume of polyphonic music printed from movable type was the *Harmonice musices odhecaton A,* published by Petrucci in Venice in 1501. This was an anthology of chansons from ca. 1470–1500 in both older and newer styles. The newer style favored a four-voice texture instead of three voices; more imitation between the voices; greater equality of the voices; and a clearer harmonic structure. By the early sixteenth century, composers abandoned the formes fixes for more varied poetic and musical forms. Many chansons were settings of popular tunes, treating the borrowed tune like a cantus firmus or in paraphrase.

III. Josquin des Prez (HWM 164–69, NAWM 32–33)

A. Career

Josquin des Prez (ca. 1450s–1521) was considered the best composer of his time and is one of the greatest of all time. He was born in northern France and served patrons in Italy and France. His works, which include about 18 Masses, 100 motets, and 70 secular vocal works, were published and recopied more widely than those of any other composer of his day.

B. The Chanson

Composers of Ockeghem's generation introduced more imitation into the chanson, but continued to use the old formes fixes. *Antoine Busnois* (d. 1492) was one of the best-known chanson composers of the late fifteenth century. Some chansons were very popular, being recopied and published repeatedly. Chansons were freely altered, arranged, and transcribed for instruments, and either the superius or the tenor of a chanson could be used as a cantus firmus for a Mass.

C. Masses

Most of Josquin's Masses use a secular tune as a cantus firmus. One Mass honors his patron, the duke of Ferrara, by using a theme derived from his name as rendered in solmization syllables. An *imitation Mass* (also called *parody Mass*) borrows, not a single line, but the entire multivoice texture of a polyphonic work, and reworks it to create something new in each movement of the Mass. Josquin's *Missa Pange lingua* is based on a chant hymn. Instead of placing the chant in a single voice, he paraphrased it in all voices (a procedure called a *paraphrase Mass*).   **Music: NAWM 32**

D. Text Setting

The influence of humanism and of Italian popular songs (which were mostly syllabic) led Josquin and others to match the music more carefully to the accents and rhythms of the words.

E. Musica Reservata

Some sixteenth-century writers use the term *musica reservata* for music that reflects the meaning and emotions of the words. Josquin may have originated this practice.

F. Motets

The large number of motets by Josquin reflects the interest composers had in setting a variety of texts and exploring word-music relationships. Josquin's music may be the first (or among the first) to be expressive of the emotions suggested by its text. In a Josquin motet, each phrase of text receives its own musical figure, which is usually treated in a point of imitation, with the full four-voice texture reserved until the drive to the cadence at the end of a musical sentence.   **Music: NAWM 33**

IV. Some Contemporaries of Obrecht and Josquin (HWM 170–72, NAWM 34)

A. Heinrich Isaac

Heinrich Isaac (ca. 1450–1517) was born in Flanders and served patrons in Italy, Austria, and elsewhere. He wrote many songs, about 30 Masses, and the three-volume *Choralis Constantinus,* a cycle of motets based on the texts and melodies for the Proper of the Mass for most of the church year. His later music was influenced by the style of Italian popular music. **Music: NAWM 34**

B. Other Contemporaries

Other significant composers of this generation were Pierre de la Rue (ca. 1460–1518) and *Jean Mouton* (1459–1522), who served the kings of France.

V. Summary (HWM 172)

The international style of the early sixteenth century featured a four-voice texture with independent, singable lines of nearly equal importance, composed simultaneously rather than line by line around a cantus firmus. The Mass, motet, and chanson were the preferred genres, and all used phrases in imitation interspersed with homophonic textures.

STUDY QUESTIONS

General Characteristics (HWM 144–54)

1. What is *humanism*? What was its role in Renaissance intellectual life? What aspects of music did it influence, and how was its influence manifested?

2. Compare and contrast the comments of Cirillo and Zarlino in the vignettes on pp. 145 and 147 of HWM. Which side does each take in the argument about polyphony? How do they relate their understanding of music to humanistic concepts and to ancient Greek writings on music?

3. Who were the most important theorists of the late fifteenth and sixteenth centuries, and what were their contributions?

4. Why was the traditional Pythagorean tuning no longer ideal for Renaissance music?

5. How did humanism influence the relation between music and text in vocal pieces? How did the new understanding of text setting relate to ancient Greek ideas?

6. Why did Italy provide an ideal ground for Renaissance humanism as a movement and for the development of the international musical styles of the late fifteenth and sixteenth centuries?

7. When did printing of polyphonic music from movable type begin? _____

    Who was the first printer to use this technique, and where was he active?

    _____   _____

    What was the name of his first publication? _____

    What kind of music did it contain? _____

    Describe the usual format for printing polyphonic music in the sixteenth century.

    What impact did printing have on the dissemination of musical works?

8. Why did Pietro Aron consider it important to compose all the parts at once (see vignette, p. 153 of HWM)? How does this practice differ from that of composers in the fourteenth or mid-fifteenth centuries, such as Machaut or Du Fay?

Northern Composers and Their Music (HWM 154–63, NAWM 31)

9. Summarize Ockeghem's career and reputation.

Music to Study
    NAWM 31: Johannes Ockeghem, *Missa De plus en plus,* Mass (second half of the fifteenth century), excerpts: Kyrie and Agnus Dei
    31a: Kyrie   CD 2.28–30
    31b: Agnus Dei   CD 2.31–32

10. In his *Missa De plus en plus* (NAWM 31), what does Ockeghem borrow from Binchois's *De plus en plus* (NAWM 30)? How does he use the borrowed material? How does he alter it?

---

11. How does Ockeghem's treatment of borrowed material here compare to that of Du Fay in the Gloria from *Missa Se la face ay pale* (NAWM 29b)?

12. How do the ranges of the four voice parts in the Ockeghem Mass compare to the ranges in Du Fay's Mass?

13. How does Ockeghem use changes of texture, especially in the number of simultaneous parts? How does this compare to the Du Fay Mass?

14. Describe Ockeghem's harmonic practice and treatment of dissonance.

15. Locate (by measure number, voices involved, and notes used) two examples of each of the following kinds of dissonance allowed by Johannes Tinctoris in his *Liber de arte contrapuncti*.

dissonance on an unstressed beat   suspension at a cadence

_____   _____

_____   _____

16. If you had to assign the tenor of this Mass to one of the church modes, which one would you choose? Why?

    What is the final of this mode? _____ Where do cadences occur on this note (or on a consonant sonority with this as the lowest note)?

    What is the the tenor or reciting tone of the mode? _____ Where do cadences occur on this note?

    Where do cadences occur on notes other than the final and reciting tone, and on what notes?

    Summarize how this polyphonic work projects its mode. (The mode of a polyphonic work is generally the mode of its tenor and superius.)

17. What is a *mensuration canon,* and how does it work in Ockeghem's *Missa prolationum*?

    What is special about Ockeghem's *Missa cuiusvis toni*?

    What was the attitude of Ockeghem and his contemporaries toward such ingenious compositional techniques?

18. Where and when did Jacob Obrecht live and work?

19. What is *Harmonice musices odhecaton A*? Who published it, and where? Why is it important?

Josquin des Prez (HWM 164–69, NAWM 32–33)

20. Where and when did Josquin live and work? How was he regarded by his contemporaries and by later sixteenth-century commentators?

21. In what genres did Josquin compose? Why did he choose to write so many motets?

22. How were chansons reworked and reused by composers and performers?

Music to Study
> **NAWM 32:** Josquin des Prez, *Missa Pange lingua,* Mass (ca. 1515–20), excerpts: Kyrie and portion of Credo
>   32a: Kyrie   CD 2.33–35 (Concise 1.34–36)
>   32b: Credo, excerpt: *Et incarnatus est*   CD 2.36–38
> **NAWM 33:** Josquin des Prez, *De profundis clamavi ad te,* motet (first or second decade of the sixteenth century)
>   CD 2.39–42 (Concise 1.37–40)

23. How are the opening two phrases of the chant hymn *Pange lingua gloriosi* used and varied in the first Kyrie of Josquin's *Missa Pange lingua* (NAWM 32)? Describe how each of the four voices treats the chant. How does this compare to the way borrowed material is used in Du Fay's *Missa Se la face ay pale* (NAWM 29b) and Ockeghem's *Missa De plus en plus* (NAWM 31)?

24. How does Josquin use the chant melody in the Christe and second Kyrie? In the *Et incarnatus est* from the Credo?

25. How does Josquin vary the texture, especially in the number of simultaneous parts? How does this compare to the Ockeghem and Du Fay Masses?

26. How does Josquin use imitation between the voices in the Kyrie? What different arrangements of voices does he use for his points of imitation? How does his use of imitation compare to the Ockeghem and Du Fay Masses?

27. How does Josquin's music convey the images and feelings of the text in the *Et incarnatus est*?

28. How does Josquin's music reflect the meaning of the opening words of his motet *De profundis clamavi ad te* (NAWM 33)?

    How does the music reflect the natural accentuation of the words elsewhere in the motet?

29. Where do cadences occur in Josquin's motet *De profundis clamavi ad te*? How does the location of cadences relate to the structure of the text?

30. In what mode is Josquin's motet? How can you tell? How is the mode projected in the music?

31. In a motet of Josquin's generation, each segment of the text is given its own musical phrase, which is either treated in a point of imitation or presented homophonically. Most phrases close with cadences, although some points of imitation overlap. One of Josquin's trademarks is his alternation of voices in pairs with each other and with the full four-voice texture. These changes of texture, along with the frequent cadences, help to make the structure clear.

   In Josquin's motet, where do phrases begin with a point of imitation? List each instance, including the measure number it begins, the first words of the phrase, and the number of voices that participate in the point of imitation.

Some Contemporaries of Obrecht and Josquin (HWM 170–72, NAWM 34)

32. Where did Isaac live and work? How is his music different from that of others in his generation?

Music to Study
> **NAWM 34:** Heinrich Isaac, *Innsbruck, ich muss dich lassen,* lied (early sixteenth century)
> CD 2.43

33. How does Isaac's setting of *Innsbruck, ich muss dich lassen* (NAWM 34) show the influence of Italian popular music?

Summary (HWM 172)

34. Describe the musical style current in Europe around 1500–1520. How does it differ from the style of Du Fay?

TERMS TO KNOW

Renaissance
humanism
suspension
Pythagorean tuning
just intonation
partbooks

canon
mensuration canon
imitation Mass (or parody Mass)
paraphrase Mass
musica reservata

NAMES TO KNOW

Liber de arte contrapuncti, by
   Johannes Tinctoris
Franchino Gaffurio
Dodekachordon, by Heinrich
   Glareanus
Le istitutioni harmoniche, by
   Gioseffo Zarlino
Ottaviano de' Petrucci

Johannes Ockeghem
Missa prolationum
Missa cuiusvis toni
Jacob Obrecht
Harmonice musices odhecaton A
Josquin des Prez
Antoine Busnois
Heinrich Isaac

REVIEW QUESTIONS

1. Make a time-line for the pieces, composers, treatises, and theorists discussed in this chapter.

2. Define humanism as a movement in the Renaissance, and explain how it was reflected in the culture, arts, and music of the time.

3. Trace the development of the motet from the fourteenth through the early sixteenth centuries, using the motets in NAWM by Vitry, Dunstable, Du Fay, and Josquin as examples.

4. Write a point of imitation for two voices, about eight to fifteen measures of cut time, in the style of Josquin. Use as models the opening points of imitation in both halves of his motet *De profundis clamavi ad te* (NAWM 33). Either the upper or the lower voice may enter first, but the upper must enter a fifth higher than the lower. The first few measures should be in exact imitation; the rest may be in freer counterpoint, ending with a cadence on an octave or unison. Follow the same rules of counterpoint and dissonance treatment that Josquin followed, and try to make your vocal lines as varied in rhythm as his, with no two successive measures having the same rhythm. (Your goal in this exercise is to learn about Josquin's style by imitating it.)

5. Compare the Masses of Machaut, Du Fay, Ockeghem, and Josquin that are excerpted in NAWM. What type of Mass is each one? What existing musical material does each borrow? How is this material used and varied in each? How do these Masses compare to each other in the role of each voice, the setting of the text, melodic style, harmonic practice, use of imitation, and other general aspects of style?

6. Trace the early history of music printing, describing the variety of printing methods, the important publishers, and the effects music printing had on musical life.

7. Compare the careers and music of any two of the following composers: Machaut, Du Fay, Ockeghem, Josquin.

NEW CURRENTS IN THE SIXTEENTH CENTURY

7

CHAPTER OBJECTIVES

After you complete the reading, study of the music, and study questions for this chapter, you should be able to

1. describe the principal styles and genres of sixteenth-century secular vocal music and instrumental music;
2. describe the relation of music and words in sixteenth-century vocal music and contrast it with earlier practices of setting texts;
3. identify some of the major composers of the sixteenth century; and
4. identify the characteristics of national schools of composition in the sixteenth century.

CHAPTER OUTLINE

I. The Franco-Flemish Generation (1520–1550) (HWM 177–81)

A. General
The years 1520–1550 saw a growing diversity of styles, genres, and forms in vocal music and the growing importance of instrumental music. The imitation Mass gradually replaced the cantus-firmus Mass. Composers increasingly wrote for five or six voices rather than four, the standard of the previous generation.

B. Nicolas Gombert
The motets of *Nicolas Gombert* (ca. 1495–ca. 1556) move in a continuous texture of overlapping phrases, most set as points of imitation.

C. Jacobus Clemens
Jacobus Clemens ("Clemens non Papa," ca. 1510–ca. 1556) wrote numerous imitation Masses, over 200 motets, and four collections of psalm settings in Dutch.

D. Adrian Willaert
Adrian Willaert (ca. 1490–1562) was one of the most important composers of his generation. Director of music at St. Mark's Church in Venice for the second half of his life, he exercised a great influence through his

teaching, his compositions, and his ideas for the treatment of text. He specified which syllable was to be sung to each note and sought to ensure that the text was correctly accented and punctuated, marking major breaks in the text with full cadences and lesser breaks with weaker or evaded cadences. His melodic lines and cadences convey the mode by emphasizing the final and other important notes in the mode.

II. The Rise of National Styles (HWM 181–83, NAWM 35)

A. Italy
The sixteenth century saw the rise to prominence of national styles. Italian music became particularly important. By the end of the sixteenth century, Italy had displaced France and the Lowlands as the center of European musical life, and it continued to dominate for the next two centuries.

B. The Frottola
The *frottola,* an Italian genre common in the late fifteenth and early sixteenth centuries, was a strophic secular song with an amorous or satirical text set in a simple, syllabic, and homophonic style. The melody in the upper voice was accompanied by diatonic harmonies in the lower parts, which were often played on instruments.   **Music: NAWM 35**

C. The Lauda
The polyphonic *lauda* was a nonliturgical religious song similar in style to the frottola.

III. The Italian Madrigal (HWM 183–94, NAWM 36–40)

A. General
The *madrigal* was the leading secular genre in sixteenth-century Italy. Unlike the fourteenth-century madrigal or the frottola, the sixteenth-century madrigal did not use a refrain or a set form, but was a through-composed work that sought to capture the ideas and feelings in the words through a series of changing musical textures and images. The poems used were elevated in tone, often by major poets and on sentimental or erotic subjects. Madrigals were sung in courtly gatherings and academies, usually by amateurs for their own enjoyment. They were also sung in plays and theatrical productions, and after about 1570 some patrons employed professional singers to perform them. Madrigals were perhaps the first commercial popular music in the modern sense; more than 2000 madrigal collections were published and sold between 1530 and 1600, and they remained popular into the next century. Madrigals of 1520–1550 are usually for four voices and later ones for five or more, with one singer to a part, sometimes doubled or replaced by an instrument.

B. Early Madrigal Composers
The leading early madrigal composers were active in Florence and Rome. Their madrigals are mostly homophonic, like the frottola. Franco-Flemish composers such as *Jacob Arcadelt* (ca. 1505–ca. 1568) brought into the madrigal the imitative counterpoint, overlapping cadences, changing textures, and novel harmonic effects of the motet.   **Music: NAWM 36**

C. The Petrarchan Movement
The rise of the madrigal was closely connected to renewed interest in the poetry and ideals of fourteenth-century Italian poet *Francesco Petrarca* or *Petrarch* (1304–1374). Early madrigalists often set his poetry, especially his sonnets, and later composers set sixteenth-century poets influenced by him. *Pietro Bembo* (1470–1547) edited Petrarch's poems and showed that Petrarch sought to reflect the mood or imagery of the words in the sound of the language itself. Bembo identified two qualities that were often contrasted in Petrarch's poetry, *"pleasingness" (piacevolezza)* and *"severity"* (*gravità*). The madrigals of Adrian Willaert often exemplify this contrast, and Willaert's student Gioseffo Zarlino described the musical means for representing it in *Le Istitutioni harmoniche*. **Music: NAWM 37**

D. Cipriano de Rore
Cipriano de Rore (1516–1565), a student of Willaert's, was the leading madrigalist of his generation. His music was famed for its vivid expression of the feelings in the text. **Music: NAWM 38**

E. Chromaticism
Composers in the middle and late sixteenth century began to use chromatic progressions, which had previously been forbidden. They were inspired in part by interest in reviving the ancient Greek chromatic and enharmonic genera, as in the music and writings of *Nicola Vicentino* (1511–ca. 1576). Some composers used black-note notation to suggest images of the dark, a sign that madrigals were written mostly for the singers' enjoyment.

F. Later Madrigalists
Among the important madrigal composers of the late sixteenth century were both northern composers and native Italians, notably *Luca Marenzio* (1553–1599). Some patrons employed professional vocal ensembles, such as the *concerto delle donne* (women's ensemble) established at Ferrara in 1580, and several composers wrote virtuosic madrigals for these groups. **Music: NAWM 39**

G. Gesualdo
Carlo Gesualdo (ca. 1561–1613) is known for using chromaticism. His vertical sonorities are mostly consonant, but the motion through successive sonorities can be quite unpredictable. The contrast between chromatic and diatonic sections to convey the changing moods of the text is also a hallmark of his style. **Music: NAWM 40**

H. Claudio Monteverdi
Claudio Monteverdi (1567–1643) was the most important Italian composer of the late sixteenth and early seventeenth centuries. He was born in Cremona, worked in Mantua, and was choirmaster at St. Mark's in Venice for the last 30 years of his life. His madrigals show a variety of techniques, including increased use of unprepared dissonance, declamatory passages, and other methods of conveying the feeling of the text.

I. Other Italian Secular Vocal Genres
In addition to madrigals, Italian composers also wrote lighter genres of secular vocal music, such as the *villanella, canzonetta,* and *balletto*.

IV. Secular Song outside Italy (HWM 194–205, NAWM 41–44)

A. France
Composers centered in Paris around 1520–1550 cultivated the *Parisian chanson.* These were strophic songs in a light, fast style, mostly syllabic and homophonic, with the melody in the upper voice, occasional brief points of imitation, and short repeated sections. The principal publisher of Parisian chansons was *Pierre Attaingnant* (ca. 1494–ca. 1551). Prominent composers included *Claudin de Sermisy* (ca. 1490–1562) and *Clément Janequin* (ca. 1485–ca. 1560), who was renowned for his descriptive chansons. **Music: NAWM 41**

B. The Later Franco-Flemish Chanson
Outside of Paris, northern composers continued the older Franco-Flemish chanson, absorbing elements of the Parisian chanson and Italian madrigal.

C. Musique Mesurée
The poet Jean-Antoine de Baïf wrote French verse that imitated the long and short syllables of ancient Greek and Latin poetry, a style called *vers mesurés à l'antique* (measured verse in antique style). *Claude Le Jeune* (1528–1600) and others set these to music, giving each long syllable a long note and each short syllable a note half as long. This style was called *musique mesurée* (measured music). **Music: NAWM 42**

D. Germany
Secular polyphony came late to Germany, where the monophonic songs of the Meistersinger were important through the sixteenth century.

E. The Lied
The polyphonic *lied* (song) developed in Germany around the mid-fifteenth century. It usually wove Franco-Flemish counterpoint around a familiar German tune. After 1550, lieder adopted features of the Italian madrigal and villanella.

F. Major Composers
Orlando di Lasso (1532–1594) served the duke of Bavaria in Munich for almost forty years and was the most important composer active in Germany. He wrote Italian madrigals, French chansons, and German lieder in madrigal style. *Hans Leo Hassler* (1564–1612) united German and Italian characteristics in his music.

G. Spain
The principal Spanish secular form in the late fifteenth and early sixteenth centuries was the *villancico,* a short strophic song with refrain. *Juan del Encina* (1469–1529) was the principal composer of villancicos.

H. Eastern Europe
Several Polish and Bohemian composers were familiar with musical trends in Western Europe and participated in the same developments.

I. The English Madrigal
Nicholas Yonge's 1588 publication *Musica transalpina,* a collection of Italian madrigals in English translation, launched a fashion for madrigal

singing and composition in England. Among the leading composers were *Thomas Morley* (1557–1602) and *Thomas Weelkes* (ca. 1575–1623). Morley was particularly skilled in lighter forms such as the *ballett* and *canzonet* (from the Italian balletto and canzonetta). Madrigals were often sung by amateurs for their own pleasure. **Music: NAWM 43**

J. English Lute Songs
Solo songs with lute accompaniment, known as *lute songs,* became popular in England after about 1600, especially the songs or *airs* of *John Dowland* (1562–1626). These feature less text-painting than the madrigal but carefully follow the natural declamation of the text. In addition to the lute song and madrigal, which were indebted to foreign models, there was a native tradition of *consort songs,* songs for voice accompanied by a *consort of viols.* **Music: NAWM 44**

K. Summary
The generation after Josquin continued and extended his style. Influenced by humanism, Willaert and others sought to match the rhythm and meaning of the text in both sacred and secular music. Later madrigal composers used varied textures, chromaticism, and dissonance to express more vividly the feelings in the text. Popular styles emerged in England, France, and Germany as well as Italy, and French composers tried to revive ancient Greek meters in musique mesurée.

V. Instrumental Music of the Sixteenth Century (HWM 205–19, NAWM 45–46)

A. The Rise of Instrumental Music
The period 1450–1550 saw a rise of independent styles and forms of writing for instruments. Earlier, instruments accompanied or substituted for voices in vocal works, played transcriptions of vocal works, and performed dances, fanfares, and other works from memory. But now instrumental music was written down more often, reflecting an increase in status (and perhaps in musical literacy) for instrumentalists.

B. Books on Instruments
A sign of growing regard for instruments is the appearance of books that describe them and tell how to tune them, play them, and embellish a musical line. *Sebastian Virdung*'s *Musica getutscht und ausgezogen* (A Summary of the Science of Music in German, 1511) was the first book to describe instruments and how to play them, and *Michael Praetorius*'s *Syntagma musicum* (A Systematic Treatise of Music, 1618) is one of the most important. Instruments were built in *families,* with different sizes and registers from bass to soprano, giving a homogeneous sound throughout the entire range. A complete set of a single type of instrument, often made by a single maker, was called a *chest* or *consort.*

    1. Wind instruments included recorders, shawms, capped-reed instruments, transverse flutes, cornetts, trumpets, and sackbuts.

    2. The main bowed string instrument was the *viol,* which had frets, six strings, and a delicate tone. The usual type was the *viola da gamba*

(leg viol), held on or between the legs; the *viola da braccio* (arm viol) was played on the arm.

3. Keyboard instruments included the organ, *clavichord,* and *harpsichord.*

C. The Lute

The lute was the most popular polyphonic household instrument in the Renaissance. The *vihuela* was a related instrument from Spain. Both lute and vihuela music was notated in *tablature,* which showed not the pitches to play but which string to pluck and where to stop the string to produce the correct pitch. (For examples of tablature, see HWM, pp. 217 and 317, and NAWM 44.)

D. Relation of Instrumental to Vocal Music

Many different types of instrumental music emerged over the sixteenth century, ranging from music derived from vocal music to new independent genres: (1) arrangements of vocal pieces; (2) elaborations of existing melodies; (3) types modeled on vocal genres; (4) introductory pieces; (5) dance music; and (6) variations.

E. Instrumental Arrangements

Many instrumental works were transcriptions of madrigals, chansons, or motets, embellished in a style that was idiomatic for the instruments.

F. Polyphonic Elaborations of Chant or Secular Melodies

Some instrumental works were based on a cantus firmus, such as the *In nomines* in England. Chant melodies were sometimes set in *versets* played on the organ, often alternating with the original chant in the choir.

G. Compositions Modeled on Vocal Genres: The Canzona

The Italian instrumental *canzona* originated as a work in the same style as a Parisian chanson, with a typical opening figure of a note followed by two notes of half its value (e.g., a half note and two quarter notes). The early canzonas were for organ; canzonas for instrumental ensemble were written after 1580 and evolved into the seventeenth-century sonata da chiesa. Canzonas were often based on a series of different figures, most treated in imitation. The result was a piece in a series of sections.

H. Sonata

Sonata (Italian for "sounded") is a term with many different meanings throughout music history. It was first used for a piece of purely instrumental music. The Venetian sonata at the end of the sixteenth century was more serious and motet-like than the canzona. Among the most important Venetian composers of sonatas and canzonas was *Giovanni Gabrieli* (ca. 1557–1612). His *Sonata pian' e forte* (ca. 1597), for two instrumental choirs, was among the first instrumental ensemble pieces to designate specific instruments and dynamic markings.

I. Preludes and Other Introductory Pieces

Keyboard and lute players improvised polyphonic pieces, and works in the same general style were written down under names such as *prelude, fantasia,* or *ricercare.* Preludes and fantasias often served to establish the mode for a following vocal piece. The chief keyboard genre in improvisatory style in the second half of the sixteenth century was the *toccata* (Italian for "touched"). The ricercare or ricercar evolved from an early improvisatory form into a work for ensemble or solo instrument based on a series of subjects treated in imitation, like an instrumental relative of the motet.

J. Dance Music

Social dancing was important to Renaissance society, and thus much of its instrumental music was written for dancing or based on dance forms. Here the top melody usually dominates, and there is little contrapuntal interplay. In stylized dance pieces, an instrumental style independent of vocal models could develop. An important theatrical dance form was the *ballet*. Dances were often grouped in pairs or in threes, usually a slow dance in duple meter followed by a fast one in triple meter, such as a *pavane* and *galliard* or *passamezzo* and *saltarello*. The *allemande* and *courante* appeared about mid-century and a century later become part of the dance suite. Renaissance musicians improvised both in embellishing a given line and in adding contrapuntal lines to a given melody. The fifteenth-century *basse danse* was improvised over a borrowed tenor, but later basses danses were written out with the melody on top.   **Music: NAWM 45**

K. Variations

Written sets of *variations* first appear in the early sixteenth century. There are both variations on tunes presented in the treble and variations over *ostinatos* in the bass. In the late sixteenth and early seventeenth centuries, English *virginalists*—composers for virginal, or harpsichord—wrote many variations and other keyboard works. The most important manuscript collection is the *Fitzwilliam Virginal Book*. The themes chosen were simple and songlike, often familiar tunes. Variations preserved the phrasing and harmony while changing the figuration.   **Music: NAWM 46**

L. English Composers on the Continent

Several English composers were active in Denmark, the Netherlands, and Germany during the early seventeenth century and influenced composers in the region.

M. Summary

In the sixteenth century, instrumental music rose to a new prominence in publications of dance music and in genres independent of dance or song.

STUDY QUESTIONS

The Franco-Flemish Generation (1520–1550) (HWM 177–81)

1. Where did Willaert live and work? Who were some of his students?

2. What principles did Willaert follow in setting words to music? How does this approach differ from earlier approaches in setting text?

The Rise of National Styles (HWM 181–83, NAWM 35)

3. During the sixteenth century, what idioms coexisted with the Franco-Flemish style? Which nation or region eventually displaced France and the Lowlands as the center of musical life in Western Europe?

Music to Study
NAWM 35: Marco Cara, *Io non compro più speranza,* frottola (ca. 1500)
CD 2.44–50

4. What is a *frottola*? Where and when was it popular? What traits of the genre are exemplified in Cara's *Io non compro più speranza* (NAWM 35)?

The Italian Madrigal (HWM 183–94, NAWM 36–40)

5. Describe the sixteenth-century Italian *madrigal*. How does it differ from the fourteenth-century madrigal? How does it differ from the frottola?

6. In what circumstances were madrigals performed, and by whom?

Music to Study
   NAWM 36: Jacob Arcadelt, *Il bianco e dolce cigno,* madrigal (ca. 1538)
      CD 2.51–52 (Concise 1.41–42)

7. In what ways does Arcadelt's madrigal *Il bianco e dolce cigno* (NAWM 36) resemble a frottola, such as Cara's *Io non compro più speranza* (NAWM 35)?

   In what ways is it different from a frottola?

8. In the sixteenth century, sexual climax was known as "the little death," and poets often used this image in erotic poetry. How does your interpretation of this poem change, once you know this fact? What is the speaker saying?

---

9. In what ways does Arcadelt reflect in his music the feelings or the imagery of the text?

10. Who was Francesco Petrarch? When did he live? What was his importance for the sixteenth-century madrigal?

11. Who was Pietro Bembo? When did he live? What was his importance for the madrigal?

Music to Study
NAWM 37: Adrian Willaert, *Aspro core e selvaggio,* madrigal (ca. 1540s)
    CD 2.53–57
NAWM 38: Cipriano de Rore, *Da le belle contrade d'oriente,* madrigal (1566)
    CD 2.58–60 (Concise 1.43–45)
NAWM 39: Luca Marenzio, *Solo e pensoso,* madrigal (late sixteenth century)
    CD 3.1–5

12. In what ways is Willaert's *Aspro core* (NAWM 37) like a sixteenth-century motet, such as Josquin's *De profundis clamavi ad te* (NAWM 33)?

13. According to Pietro Bembo, how did Petrarch convey "pleasingness" (*piacevolezza*) and "severity" (*gravità*) in his poetry?

How is this contrast reflected in mm. 1–21 of Willaert's *Aspro core*?

What suggestions for setting a text does Zarlino (who was Willaert's student) make in the passage on p. 198 of HWM? How does this reflect Willaert's practice in the opening passage of *Aspro core*?

14. In what other ways does Willaert's music illustrate the images in the text?

15. Willaert's text is a sonnet by Petrarch. A sonnet has fourteen lines divided into an octave (the first eight lines) and a sestet (the remaining six lines). In a Petrarchan sonnet, the usual rhyme scheme is abba abba cde cde, and the sestet introduces a new thought or feeling as well as new rhymes. How does Willaert set off the sestet from the octave? In what other ways does his setting reflect the structure of the text?

16. In Rore's *Da le belle contrade d'oriente* (NAWM 38), how does the music reflect the presence of two speakers in the poem?

How does the music reflect the meaning and mood of the words?

How does the music reflect the accentuation and rhythm of the words?

17. Where in Rore's madrigal is there direct chromatic motion from a note to a chromatically altered form (for example, from *B* to *B♭* or *F* to *F♯* or the reverse), within a single melodic line?

Where does direct chromatic motion occur in the madrigal by Nicola Vicentino excerpted in HWM, p. 200?

In which earlier piece(s) in NAWM does direct chromatic motion occur?

What connections do you see between the musical culture that produced these madrigals by Rore and Vicentino and the musical culture(s) that produced the earlier piece or pieces?

18. Both Rore's *Da le belle contrade d'oriente* and Marenzio's *Solo e pensoso* (NAWM 39) set sonnets. How does each composer set off the sestet from the octave? In what other ways does each setting reflect the structure of the text?

19. How does Marenzio's music suggest the poetic imagery of *Solo e pensoso*?

20. What was the *concerto delle donne* (women's ensemble) at Ferrara? Who established it, when, and who took part? How did the formation of such ensembles affect the vocal techniques composers used in their madrigals?

Music to Study
   NAWM 40: Carlo Gesualdo, *"Io parto" e non più dissi,* madrigal (1590s?)
      CD 3.6–8

21. In *"Io parto" e non più dissi* (NAWM 40), how does Gesualdo suggest the two speakers?

22. How does Gesualdo use chromaticism, contrasting diatonic sections, melodic motion, and rhythm to reflect the emotional sense and imagery of the text?

23. How does the music project a single mode, despite all the chromaticism?

24. Briefly outline Monteverdi's career, including his date and place of birth, his early training, and his employment, including place, position, and dates of service.

Secular Song outside Italy (HWM 194–205, NAWM 41–44)

25. Who was the major publisher of the Parisian chanson in the early sixteenth century?

Who were the principal composers of these chansons?

What evidence is there for the popularity of this type of chanson?

Music to Study
> **NAWM 41:** Claudin de Sermisy, *Tant que vivray,* chanson (second quarter of the sixteenth century)
>> CD 3.9–10 (Concise 1.46–47)
> **NAWM 42:** Claude Le Jeune, *Revecy venir du printans,* chanson (late sixteenth century)
>> CD 3.11–19

26. How does the Parisian chanson, exemplified by Sermisy's *Tant que vivray* (NAWM 41), compare to the Italian frottola, such as Cara's *Io non compro più speranza* (NAWM 35), and the early madrigal, such as Arcadelt's *Il bianco e dolce cigno* (NAWM 36)?

27. What are the characteristics of *musique mesurée*? How are these qualities exemplified in Le Jeune's *Revecy venir du printans* (NAWM 42)?

28. In this strophic song with refrain, how does Le Jeune vary the verses? How does this give shape to the whole work?

29. What are the characteristics of German secular polyphony in the fifteenth and sixteenth centuries?

30. How are Lasso's lieder similar to or different from the earlier German lieder and contemporary Italian madrigals? Compare Example 7.9 on p. 199 of HWM with Isaac's setting of *Innsbruck, ich muss dich lassen* (NAWM 34) and Willaert's *Aspro core* (NAWM 37) or Rore's *Da le belle contrade d'oriente* (NAWM 38).

31. What is a *villancico*? Where and when were villancicos popular?

32. What was *Musica transalpina,* and when did it appear? What effect did it have on the development of the English madrigal?

Music to Study
   NAWM 43: Thomas Weelkes, *O Care, thou wilt despatch me,* madrigal (ca. 1600)
      CD 3.20–23 (Concise 1.48–51)
   NAWM 44: John Dowland, *Flow, my tears,* air or lute song (ca. 1600)
      CD 3.24–26 (Concise 1.52–54)

33. In Weelkes's madrigal *O Care, thou wilt despatch me* (NAWM 43), how are the images and feelings in the text conveyed in the music?

34. Locate where the following unusual vertical sonorities occur in Weelkes's madrigal. (Some occur more than once.)

    a diminished seventh   _____

    an augmented triad   _____

    a diminished octave   _____

    What purposes do these dissonances serve? How can you explain their presence?

35. Thomas Morley, in the passage reprinted on p. 216 of HWM, says to would-be composers of madrigals that "the more variety you show the better shall you please." What kinds of variety does he mean (that is, variety in what aspects of the music), and how does Weelkes provide that variety?

36. Comparing Weelkes's madrigal to the madrigals in NAWM 36–40, what similarities and what differences do you notice between English and Italian madrigals?

37. What are the characteristics of an English lute song ca. 1600, as exemplified by Dowland's *Flow, my tears* (NAWM 44)? How is it like a madrigal, and how is it different?

38. In tonal music of the common-practice period (ca. 1670–ca. 1900), there is a strong sense of direction toward the tonic (or local tonic). In familiar tonal progressions such as I-IV-vii-iii-vi-ii-V-I or I-vi-IV-ii-V-I, there is a strong tendency for root motion to progress up by fourths (the same as down by fifths) or down by thirds, rather than in the opposite direction. Modal music does not have this strong directional quality, so that motion up by thirds or down by fourths is just as likely as the reverse.

    Given this difference, is Dowland's *Flow, my tears* more likely to be tonal (in A minor, as NAWM suggests on p. 220) or modal (in the Hypoaeolian mode, the plagal mode on A)? Can you find a passage whose harmonies progress by thirds or by fourths or fifths? Does this passage follow the expectations of tonal music, or of modal music?

Instrumental Music of the Sixteenth Century (HWM 205–19, NAWM 45–46)

39. Why do we have so little instrumental music from before 1450? How and why did this change after about 1450? What evidence is there for a rising interest in instrumental music during the Renaissance?

40. What are *Musica getutscht und ausgezogen* and *Syntagma musicum*? Who wrote them, and when? Why are they important?

41. What is an *instrument family*? Why is it significant that instruments were built in families?

42. Which were the principal instrument families in the sixteenth century? How do they relate to their medieval ancestors, and how do they relate to their modern relatives?

43. What is *tablature*? What does it convey to the performer?

44. What are the main kinds of instrumental music in the sixteenth century? Which of them were derived from vocal music, and how were they related?

45. What is a *canzona*? What vocal form was it related to, and what did it develop into? Describe the characteristics of a sixteenth-century canzona.

46. What was a *sonata* in the sixteenth century?

47. What is special about Giovanni Gabrieli's *Sonata pian' e forte*?

48. What role did improvisation play in sixteenth-century musical performance and education? What forms and genres relate to improvisation?

49. What is a *toccata*? On which instruments was it performed? What are its main musical characteristics, and how are they exemplified in the toccata by Claudio Merulo excerpted in Example 7.13 on pp. 212–13 of HWM?

50. What is a *ricercare* (or *ricercar*) in the sixteenth century? What are its main characteristics? What vocal genre does the late-sixteenth-century ricercare resemble?

51. What are some of the main characteristics of Renaissance dance music?

52. How were Renaissance dances grouped? What combination were popular?

Music to Study
    NAWM 45: Pierre Attaingnant (editor, compiler, and printer), *Danseries a 4 parties, Second Livre* (Dances in Four Parts, Second Book, published 1547), excerpts

45a: Basse danse	CD 3.27 (Concise 1.55)
45b: Branle gay	CD 3.28 (Concise 1.56)

53. How do the Basse danse and Branle gay from Pierre Attaingnant's *Danseries a 4 Parties,* second book (NAWM 45) exemplify the characteristics of Renaissance dance music?

54. What types of variations were written in the sixteenth century? In the music of the English virginalists, what kinds of tunes were used as themes for variations, and how were they treated in the variations?

55. What is the *Fitzwilliam Virginal Book,* when was it compiled, and what does it contain?

Music to Study
NAWM 46: William Byrd, *Pavana Lachrymae,* keyboard variations on NAWM 44, Dowland's *Flow, my tears* (early seventeenth century) CD 3.29–31 (Concise 2.1–3)

56. How is Dowland's *Flow my tears* (NAWM 44) treated in Byrd's *Pavana Lachrymae* (NAWM 46)? How does Byrd use figuration to vary the music?

TERMS TO KNOW

Terms Related to Sixteenth-Century Vocal Music

frottola
lauda (polyphonic)
madrigal (sixteenth-century)
"pleasingness" (piacevolezza)
    and "severity" (gravità)
the *concerto delle donne*
villanella, canzonetta, balletto
Parisian chanson

vers mesurés à l'antique
musique mesurée
lied
villancico
ballett and canzonet
lute song
air
consort song

Terms Related to Sixteenth-Century Instrumental Music

instrument family
chest or consort
viol (viola da gamba, viola
    da braccio)
clavichord
harpsichord
lute
vihuela
tablature
In nomine
verset
canzona

sonata (sixteenth-century)
prelude
fantasia
toccata
ricercare
pavane and galliard
passamezzo and saltarello
allemande and courante
basse danse
variations
ostinato
the English virginalists

NAMES TO KNOW

Names Related to Sixteenth-Century Vocal Music

Nicolas Gombert
Jacobus Clemens
Adrian Willaert
Jacob Arcadelt
Petrarch (Francesco Petrarca)
Pietro Bembo
Cipriano de Rore
Nicola Vicentino
Luca Marenzio
Carlo Gesualdo
Claudio Monteverdi

Pierre Attaingnant
Claudin de Sermisy
Clément Janequin
Claude Le Jeune
Orlando di Lasso
Hans Leo Hassler
Juan del Encina
Musica transalpina
Thomas Morley
Thomas Weelkes
John Dowland

Names Related to Sixteenth-Century Instrumental Music

*Musica getutscht und ausge-
    zogen,* by Sebastian Virdung
Syntagma musicum, by
    Michael Praetorius

Giovanni Gabrieli
Sonata pian' e forte
The Fitzwilliam Virginal Book

REVIEW QUESTIONS

1. Make a time-line for the sixteenth century and place on it the pieces, composers, and treatises discussed in this chapter. (You will add to this time-line in the next chapter.)

2. Trace the development of secular vocal music in Italy from the frottola to the madrigals of Marenzio and Gesualdo.

3. Describe the varieties of secular vocal music practiced in France, England, and Germany during the sixteenth century. Which of these forms were influenced by the Italian madrigal, and in what ways?

4. In what ways can you compare the madrigal in England (or Italy, or both) to popular music of the present or recent past? Try to come up with as many examples as you can of parallels between the madrigal, the popular music of the sixteenth century, and top-40 pop music, rock, rap, country, or any other type of popular music current today. What are some important differences?

5. Trace the influence of humanism and the revival of ideals associated with ancient Greek music on vocal music in Italy and France during the sixteenth century, focusing on the genres most affected by these influences.

6. Describe the relation of music and words in the various forms of sixteenth-century vocal music and contrast it with earlier practices of setting texts.

7. Name and describe the various types of notated instrumental music in the sixteenth century. Which ones were related to vocal models, to dancing, or to improvisation, and how?

CHURCH MUSIC OF THE LATE RENAISSANCE AND REFORMATION

8

CHAPTER OBJECTIVES

After you complete the reading, study of the music, and study questions for this chapter, you should be able to

1. describe attitudes toward and uses of music in Protestant churches in the sixteenth century and the genres they used;
2. recount the effect of the Counter-Reformation on sixteenth-century Catholic music;
3. identify some of the most important composers and terms associated with these trends; and
4. describe the styles of Palestrina, Victoria, Lasso, and Byrd.

CHAPTER OUTLINE

I. The Music of the Reformation in Germany (HWM 224–28)

A. Music in the Reformation
Martin Luther (1483–1546), leader of the *Reformation* in Germany, loved music and gave it a central position in the Lutheran Church. Lutheran services used parts of the Roman liturgy in Latin, parts in translation, or Luther's German version of the Mass liturgy, the *Deudsche Messe* (1526). The music used was also a mixture of plainsong, Latin polyphony, and German hymns. Luther believed that the congregation should take part in the music of the service, so he made congregational hymn singing part of the liturgy.

B. The Lutheran Chorale
The *chorale* was a strophic hymn sung by the congregation in unison. Chorales later became the basis for polyphonic compositions. Luther wrote many chorale texts and some of the tunes. There were four sources for chorale tunes: newly written melodies; translations or arrangements from Gregorian chant; existing German devotional songs; and secular tunes.

C. Contrafacta
Many chorales were adapted from secular songs by revising the text to give it a spiritual meaning or by replacing it with a new sacred text. The new works that resulted are called *contrafacta* (singular *contrafactum*).

D. Polyphonic Chorale Settings
Composers soon began to arrange the monophonic chorales in polyphonic settings for choirs to perform, using a variety of styles including cantus-firmus and imitative motet styles. Settings in *cantional style*—simple chordal settings with the chorale in the top voice—became common in the late sixteenth century, and after 1600 it was customary for the organ to play all the parts while the congregation sang the tune.

E. The Chorale Motet
By the end of the sixteenth century, Protestant composers began to write *chorale motets,* free polyphonic elaborations of a chorale.

II. Reformation Church Music outside Germany (HWM 228–33, NAWM 50)

A. The Psalter
Reformation movements in France, the Low Countries, and Switzerland, led by *Jean Calvin* (1509–1564) and others, rejected the Catholic liturgy, artistic trappings, and nonbiblical texts in favor of rhymed translations of the Psalms. These were published in *Psalters* and set to melodies that were newly composed or adapted from plainchant or secular songs and sung in unison. The main French Psalter used tunes composed or adapted by *Loys Bourgeois* (ca. 1510–ca. 1561). Psalm tunes were sometimes set in simple chordal style, less often in polyphony. The psalm texts were translated and the melodies often borrowed by churches in other countries, including the New England colonies. Early reformers in Bohemia virtually banished polyphony from church. The later Moravian Brethren cultivated music in Bohemia and in America, where they emigrated in the eighteenth century.

B. Pre-Reformation Music in England
For reasons of war and politics, England was relatively isolated in the latter fifteenth and first half of the sixteenth centuries, and the newer style of imitative counterpoint was rare before 1540. The leading English composer of this period was *John Taverner* (ca. 1490–1545), renowned for his Masses and Magnificats. The most important mid-century English composer was *Thomas Tallis* (ca. 1505–1585), known for his music for both the Catholic and Anglican liturgies.

C. Anglican Church Music
The Church of England separated from the Roman Catholic Church in 1534, largely for political reasons (Henry VIII wanted an annulment of his first marriage, and the pope refused to grant it). A new liturgy in English was printed in *The Book of Common Prayer* (1549), and composers wrote church music in English. Among the most important composers of Anglican music were *William Byrd* (1542–1623), a Catholic who also wrote Latin motets and Masses, and *Orlando Gibbons* (1583–1625). The two main genres were the *service* and the *anthem:*

1. A *service* consisted of music for Morning and Evening Prayer and for Holy Communion, and could be either a *Great Service* (contrapuntal and melismatic) or a *Short Service* (chordal and syllabic).
2. The *anthem* was equivalent to a motet. There were two varieties: the *full anthem,* sung by the full choir throughout, and the *verse anthem,* for solo voice or voices with organ or viol accompaniment, with brief passages for chorus.   **Music: NAWM 50**

III. The Counter-Reformation (HWM 234–47, NAWM 47–49)

In response to the Protestant Reformation, the Catholic Church undertook its own internal program of reform, the *Counter-Reformation.*

A. The Council of Trent
The *Council of Trent* met periodically between 1545 and 1563 to reform the Catholic Church. Music was only one factor that was considered. The Council urged very general reforms designed to ensure that the words of the liturgy were clear and the music religious in tone. There is a legend that Palestrina convinced the Council not to abolish polyphony by writing the *Pope Marcellus Mass* (NAWM 47).

B. Palestrina
Giovanni Pierluigi da Palestrina (1525 or 1526–1594) spent his entire career in Rome as a church musician. Most of his music was sacred, including 104 Masses and about 250 motets. He supervised the revision of Gregorian chant to conform to the edicts of the Council of Trent.

C. The Palestrina Style
Palestrina's style became a model for later composers of polyphonic church music. His Masses use a range of techniques, from cantus firmus to imitation Masses and from paraphrase to canon. His vocal lines move mostly by step in a smooth, flexible arch. He avoids chromaticism and uses a limited harmonic vocabulary, but employs different spacings to create variety in sonority. His counterpoint is smooth and mostly consonant, with dissonance restricted to suspensions, passing notes, and *cambiatas.* The voices move in flexible rhythms, mostly independent of each other, within a regular harmonic rhythm. Each phrase has its own motive, and phrases overlap. Unity is created by repeating motives and cadencing on important notes in the mode. The text is declaimed very clearly, and changes of texture lend variety and illustrate the words.   **Music: NAWM 47**

D. Palestrina's Contemporaries
Laude continued to be written and sung in Rome.

E. Spain
Spanish sacred polyphony was based on the Franco-Flemish style but was marked by heightened expression and adventurous harmonies.

F. Victoria
Tomás Luis de Victoria (1548–1611) was a Spanish composer active in Rome and in Spain whose music is more intense than Palestrina's in text expression and use of accidentals.   **Music: NAWM 48a and 48b**

G. Lasso

Orlando di Lasso (mentioned in chapter 7) is as important for his motets as Palestrina is for Masses. His motets often use pictorial, rhetorical, and dramatic devices and are written in a variety of styles.   **Music: NAWM 49**

H. Byrd

William Byrd (mentioned above) wrote three Masses and numerous motets, in addition to secular music and music for the Anglican church.

IV. Summary (HWM 248)

The year 1600 is only an approximate date for the end of the Renaissance. Some Renaissance traits continued into the seventeenth century, and several aspects of Baroque music are already evident before 1600. The texture of similar voices in counterpoint was characteristic of the Renaissance but was increasingly replaced by homophony during the sixteenth century. Rhythm became comparatively steady and predictable by 1600. Sacred polyphony was marked by smooth vocal parts, full triadic harmonies, and a strong projection of the mode.

STUDY QUESTIONS

The Music of the Reformation in Germany (HWM 224–28)

1. In what ways was the early Lutheran service similar to the Catholic liturgy, and how was it different? What languages were used? What further changes were made in the *Deudsche Messe*?

2. What is a *chorale*? How was a chorale they sung, and by whom?

3. What are the chief sources of tunes for chorales? What are *contrafacta*?

4. In what ways did chorales receive polyphonic treatment in the sixteenth and early seventeenth centuries? How were these polyphonic settings performed? Include in your answer descriptions of *cantional style* and the *chorale motet.*

Reformation Church Music outside Germany (HWM 228–33, NAWM 50)

5. How was music used in the Calvinist churches outside Germany? How does this differ from usage in the Lutheran Church?

6. What is a *Psalter,* and what does it contain?

7. How is English polyphonic music of the late fifteenth and early sixteenth centuries different from Franco-Flemish polyphony of the same time? What types of English pieces survive from this period?

8. What are the principal forms of Anglican church music? How does a *Great Service* differ from a *Short Service*?

Music to Study
   NAWM 50: William Byrd, *Sing joyfully unto God,* full anthem (late sixteenth century)
   CD 3.47–50 (Concise 2.9–12)

9. Why is *Sing joyfully unto God* (NAWM 50) a full anthem and not a verse anthem?

10. How does Byrd illustrate the text in *Sing joyfully unto God*? How does he highlight the accentuation and phrasing of the text?

11. What compositional traits mark this as a work by Byrd? (One not mentioned
    in NAWM is the English fondness for cross-relations in different voices,
    here between *A* and *Ab*.)

The Counter-Reformation (HWM 234–47, NAWM 47–49)

12. What was the Council of Trent? When was it held, and what was its purpose?
    What matters relating to music were discussed, and what actions relating to
    music did the Council take?

13. Briefly summarize Palestrina's career. Why was his music important for later
    composers?

14. How many Masses did Palestrina write? _____

    What compositional techniques did he use in his Masses?

Music to Study
> **NAWM 47:** Giovanni da Palestrina, *Pope Marcellus Mass* (published 1567),
>   excerpts
> 47a: Credo   CD 3.32–36
> 47b: Agnus Dei I   CD 3.37 (Concise 2.4)

15. Describe Palestrina's style in terms of melody, harmony, counterpoint and
    dissonance treatment, sonority, and rhythm, using examples from the Credo
    and first Agnus Dei of the *Pope Marcellus Mass* (NAWM 47a and 47b).

    melody:

    harmony:

    counterpoint and dissonance treatment:

    sonority:

    rhythm:

Music to Study
   NAWM 48a: Tomás Luis de Victoria, *O magnum mysterium,* motet (published 1572)
      CD 3.38–40
   NAWM 48b: Tomás Luis de Victoria, *Missa O magnum mysterium,* Mass (published 1592), excerpt: Kyrie
      CD 3.41–42

16. How is each phrase of text treated in Victoria's motet *O magnum mysterium* (NAWM 48a)? How does the placement of cadences help to give shape to the piece and make clear the divisions of the text?

17. Compare the Kyrie of Victoria's *Missa O magnum mysterium* (NAWM 48b) to the motet on which it is based (NAWM 48a). What has Victoria borrowed from his earlier motet, and how has he varied it?

18. What is an *imitation Mass* or *parody Mass* (see the definition in HWM, p. 166)? How does Victoria's *Missa O magnum mysterium* exemplify this kind of Mass? How does this differ from or resemble a cantus-firmus Mass (such as Du Fay's *Missa Se la face ay pale,* NAWM 29b) and a paraphrase Mass (such as Josquin's *Missa Pange lingua,* NAWM 32)?

19. How do Orlando di Lasso's career, music, and musical output contrast with those of Palestrina? (Note: There is additional information on Lasso in chapter 7 of HWM.)

Music to Study
   NAWM 49: Orlando di Lasso, *Tristis est anima mea,* motet (pub. 1565)
      CD 3.43–46 (Concise 2.5–8)

20. How does Lasso use pictorial, rhetorical, or dramatic devices to convey the meaning of the words in his motet *Tristis est anima mea* (NAWM 49)?

21. Briefly recount William Byrd's career. What kinds of music did he write? How did the situation of religion in England affect his career and compositional output? (You may wish to refer back to parts of chapter 7 of HWM in answering this question.)

Summary (HWM 248)

22. According to the summary on pp. 248 of HWM, what were the general characteristics of music in the sixteenth century in respect to the treatment of texture, rhythm, melody, and harmony?

TERMS TO KNOW

Reformation
chorale
contrafacta
cantional style
chorale motet

Psalter
service: Great Service, Short Service
anthem: full anthem, verse anthem
Counter-Reformation
cambiata

NAMES TO KNOW

Martin Luther
Deudsche Messe
Jean Calvin
Loys Bourgeois
John Taverner
Thomas Tallis
The Book of Common Prayer

William Byrd
Orlando Gibbons
the Council of Trent
Giovanni Pierluigi da Palestrina
Pope Marcellus Mass
Tomás Luis de Victoria

REVIEW QUESTIONS

1. Add to the time-line you made for the sixteenth century in chapter 7 the pieces, composers, and events discussed in this chapter.

2. How was music regarded, how was it used, and what musical genres were cultivated in the Lutheran church, in Calvinist churches, and in the Church of England during the sixteenth century?

3. Many chorales were adapted from Gregorian chant. Create a chorale tune based on the Gregorian hymn *Christe Redemptor omnium* (NAWM 4k). Use for your text the first four lines of the English translation ("Jesus! Redeemer of the world!"), which is rhymed and metrical. Since chorales are almost entirely syllabic, you will need to eliminate some of the extra notes in the Gregorian melody. (One strategy might be to match the eight syllables of each line of the English verse to the eight notes or neumes in the corresponding line of music, and then, for syllables with more than one note, choose the one you like best. Or you can follow the melody more flexibly.) Use any rhythm that fits the accentuation of the poetry and features only half, quarter, and eighth notes. You might create several different chorale tunes, all based on this chant.

4. How did the Counter-Reformation affect music for the Catholic church?

5. Describe Palestrina's style in his Masses.

6. How did composers of church music in the later sixteenth century treat the words they set? What are some of the approaches to setting or expressing a text, as exemplified by the pieces treated in this chapter?

MUSIC OF THE EARLY BAROQUE PERIOD

9

CHAPTER OBJECTIVES

After you complete the reading, study of the music, and study questions for this chapter, you should be able to

1. describe the characteristics that distinguish Baroque music from music of earlier periods;
2. relate music of the Baroque period to the culture and art of the time;
3. describe the various styles of music that flourished and competed in the first half of the seventeenth century;
4. trace the evolution of opera in Italy from its forerunners through the middle of the seventeenth century;
5. describe the genres and styles of secular and sacred vocal music practiced in the early seventeenth century;
6. explain what is distinctive about Venice and Venetian music in the late sixteenth and early seventeenth centuries; and
7. name and briefly describe the most important genres and styles of instrumental music in the early Baroque period.

CHAPTER OUTLINE

I. General Characteristics (HWM 251–60, NAWM 53)

A. Baroque as Term and Period

The word "baroque" was used in the mid-eighteenth century to describe music or art regarded as bizarre or exaggerated. Later it was used by art historians in a positive way to describe the flamboyant decorative and expressive tendencies of seventeenth- and early-eighteenth-century art and architecture. Music historians now use it for the period of about 1600 to 1750. The *Baroque period* embraced a variety of musical styles that share some general conventions and ideals, including the belief that music should move the emotions of the listener.

B. Geographical and Cultural Background

Italy remained the most influential region, with important centers at Florence, Rome, Venice, Naples, and Bologna. French music absorbed Italian influences before an Italian, Jean-Baptiste Lully, established a French style after mid-century. German music also had Italian roots, and a native English tradition was eventually largely displaced by the Italian style. Many rulers supported music, as did the church, many cities, and independent academies. Literature and art flourished throughout Europe in the Baroque period, from the poetry of Milton to the paintings of Rembrandt. New developments in philosophy and science were particularly spectacular, as Bacon, Descartes, Leibniz, Galileo, Kepler, Newton, and others helped lay the foundations of modern thought.

C. New Musical Idiom
Musicians around 1600 sought to give expression to a wider range of emotions and ideas than before. Their search for new methods involved considerable experimentation and led to the codification of a new musical language by the middle of the century.

D. The Two Practices
When his madrigals were attacked by theorist *Giovanni Maria Artusi* for incorrect treatment of dissonance, Claudio Monteverdi defended them by distinguishing between the *prima pratica* (first practice), in which a composer follows the rules of dissonance treatment codified by Zarlino, and the *seconda pratica* (second practice), in which those rules could be violated in order to express better the feelings in the text. The former came to be called *stile antico* (old style), as opposed to the *stile moderno* (modern style). By the mid-seventeenth century, commentators divided music into church, chamber, and theatrical styles.   **Music: NAWM 53**

E. Idiomatic Writing
Renaissance polyphony might be sung or played by various combinations of voices and instruments, but the growing importance of soloists led seventeenth-century composers to write with a specific medium in mind. As a result, distinctive idiomatic styles developed for the voice, violin family, viol family, wind instruments, keyboard, and other instruments.

F. The Affections
Baroque composers sought to write music that was expressive of *the affections,* or states of the soul. These are not the composer's own emotions, but generalized states of feeling.

G. Rhythm
Music before the seventeenth century was conceived primarily in terms of durations, but Baroque and later composers thought in terms of strong and weak beats grouped in *measures.* On the other hand, free and irregular rhythms were used in vocal recitative and instrumental preludes and toccatas. Some standard forms paired a relatively free section with a strictly metered section, such as a recitative and aria or a toccata and fugue.

H. The Basso Continuo
Renaissance polyphony used a texture of equal voices, but in Baroque music the melody and bass were the two essential lines. In the notational system called *thoroughbass* or *basso continuo,* the accompaniment was not fully written out; instead, *continuo instruments* such as harpsichord,

organ, or lute would play the notated bass line and fill in the appropriate chords above it, while often a sustaining instrument like a bass viola da gamba, violoncello, or bassoon would reinforce the bass. Accidentals, nonharmonic tones, and chords other than root-position triads could be indicated by numbers and other figures; a part notated in this way is called a *figured bass*. A basso continuo part can be *realized* by the performer(s) in various ways from simple chords to elaborate improvisations.

I. The New Counterpoint

A new kind of counterpoint evolved in which the lines had to fit the chords of the basso continuo, so that the counterpoint was governed by harmony.

J. Dissonance

The new importance of harmony led by the middle of the seventeenth century to a conception of dissonance as a note outside a chord, rather than an interval between two voices, and to an increased role for dissonance in defining the tonal direction of a piece.

K. Chromaticism

Chromaticism was used in the early seventeenth century for expression of extreme emotions or to give harmonic interest to improvisations. Later in the century, it also gained a role in defining tonal direction.

L. Major-Minor Tonalities

These and other developments led by the last third of the seventeenth century to *tonality,* the system of major and minor keys organized around a tonic triad, which replaced the older system of modes.

II. Early Opera (HWM 260–78, NAWM 51–52 and 54–56)

A. Forerunners

An *opera* is a staged drama set to continuous (or nearly continuous) music. The first operas were written around 1600, but many earlier forms of theater used music, including Greek tragedies, liturgical dramas, religious plays, and Renaissance theater.

B. Intermedi

Intermedi or *intermezzi* were theatrical interludes performed between acts of a sixteenth-century play. The more elaborate intermedi often included madrigals, solo songs, and other music.

C. Madrigal Cycles

Madrigal cycles were groups of madrigals that presented a plot or series of scenes.

D. The Pastoral

A *pastoral* was a poem, sometimes staged as a drama, about rustic youths and maidens in an idealized setting.

E. Greek Tragedy as a Model

The ancient Greek tragedies were a model for the dramatically effective theater Renaissance dramatists sought to achieve. Some felt that only the choruses of Greek tragedy were sung, but *Girolamo Mei (1519–1594)* argued that the tragedies were sung throughout. This set the stage for the invention of opera.

F. The Florentine Camerata

Mei's theory that the Greeks achieved powerful emotional effects through melody that followed the inflections and rhythms of the human voice was a strong influence on the *Florentine Camerata,* an informal group that met at the house of *Giovanni Bardi* (1534–1612) in Florence during the 1570s and 1580s. Following Mei, *Vincenzo Galilei* (d. 1591) attacked counterpoint and argued that only a single melodic line could express the feelings of poetry, by following the natural inflections of a good orator.

G. The Earliest Operas

The poet *Ottaviano Rinuccini* (1562–1621) and singer-composer *Jacopo Peri* (1561–1633) produced *Dafne,* the first pastoral sung throughout, in Florence in 1598. The first opera was *L'Euridice* (1600) by the same pair. In that same year, *Giulio Caccini* (1551–1618) also set Rinuccini's *L'Euridice,* and *Emilio de' Cavalieri* (ca. 1550–1602) produced in Rome *Rappresentatione di anima e di corpo* (The Representation of the Soul and the Body), a religious musical play. All three wrote *monody,* music for solo voice and accompaniment, and sought a style between speech and song that conveyed the text clearly, expressively, and naturally. Peri developed a new style for dialogue, known as *stile recitativo* or *recitative style.* Other kinds of monody at the time included the *air* (or *aria),* which was strophic, and the *solo madrigal,* which was through-composed. Both types are included in Caccini's collection *Le nuove musiche* (The New Music, 1602). Singers were expected to add embellishments to written music, but Caccini wrote them out to show the correct approach. **Music: NAWM 51**

H. The Recitative Style

In recitative style, Peri sought to imitate speech by allowing the natural rhythms of speech to determine the rhythm of the melodic line; harmonizing the syllables that were naturally stressed or intoned in speech; letting the bass follow these main syllables, rather than making the voice "dance to the movement of the bass"; and setting the syllables in between to notes that might be either consonant or dissonant with the bass, to resemble the continuous motions of speech. The various styles of monody—recitative, air, and solo madrigal—were used in many kinds of music in the early seventeenth century, and they made a dramatic musical theater possible by allowing composers to represent a great variety of situations and emotions. **Music: NAWM 52**

I. Claudio Monteverdi

Monteverdi's opera *L'Orfeo* (Mantua, 1607), to a libretto by Alessandro Striggio, is on the same subject as Peri's *Euridice* and also uses contrasting styles. The recitative is more continuous and tonally organized; there are more airs and madrigals; repeating ritornellos and choruses create large-scale form; and the orchestra is large and varied. Most of Monteverdi's next opera, *Arianna* (1608), is lost, but the widely admired lament of Arianna survives. **Music: NAWM 54**

J. Francesca Caccini

Only a few more operas were staged in Florence through the 1620s. The court preferred ballets and intermedi, such as *La liberazione di Ruggiero* (1625), an opera-like blend of ballet and intermedio by *Francesca Caccini* (1587–ca. 1640). The daughter of Giulio Caccini, she was known as both a singer and a composer and was the highest-paid musician at court.

K. Rome

Opera became established in Rome in the 1620s. Writers wrote texts for operas, called *librettos,* on the lives of saints, mythology, or epics, and the comic opera became established as a separate genre. Solo singing separated into two distinct types, *recitative* and *aria.* By mid-century, operas often included comic episodes, scenic spectacle, extraneous characters, and other elements that were entertaining as theater but no longer conformed to the Florentine ideal of a unified drama akin to that of ancient Greece.

L. Venetian Opera

Opera was introduced to Venice in 1637 in a public theater; this marked the first time opera was staged for a paying public. Venice was ideal for opera, with many visitors in Carnival season (from the day after Christmas to the day before Lent), wealthy backers, and a steady audience. Plots were drawn from mythology, epics, and Roman history and featured dramatic conflicts and striking stage effects. Monteverdi's last two operas, *Il ritorno d'Ulisse* (The Return of Ulysses, 1641) and *L'incoronazione di Poppea* (The Coronation of Poppea, 1642), were written for Venice. They alternate passages of recitative, aria, and *arioso* (a style between recitative and aria) as appropriate to convey the drama. *Pier Francesco Cavalli* (1602–1676) and *Antonio Cesti* (1623–1669) were important composers of opera in Venice. Their arias are full separate pieces and use a new vocal idiom later known as *bel canto* (beautiful singing), with smooth diatonic lines and easy rhythms. By the mid-seventeenth century, Italian opera was characterized by traits it would retain for the next two centuries: a focus on solo singing, with little ensemble or instrumental music; a separation of recitative and aria; the use of distinctive types of aria; and the primacy of music over poetry.   **Music: NAWM 55–56**

III. Vocal Chamber Music (HWM 278–85, NAWM 57)

A. Strophic Forms and Bass Patterns

Most secular vocal music was chamber music. Like opera, chamber works used monody and basso continuo. *Strophic arias* used the same music for each strophe or stanza; *strophic variations* used the same harmonic and melodic plan for each stanza, but varied the melodic details. Composers often based works on the *romanesca* and other standard patterns for singing poetry in *ottave rime* (stanzas of eight eleven-syllable lines) or on a repeating bass figure called a *ground bass* or *basso ostinato.* The *chaconne* and *passacaglia* both feature a repeating bass figure in a slow triple meter.

B. The Concertato Medium

The seventeenth-century *concerto* brought together contrasting sounds into a harmonious whole, in what is called the *concertato medium.* A *concertato madrigal* uses instruments as well as voices; a *sacred concerto* likewise combines a vocal setting of a sacred text with parts for instruments; and an *instrumental concerto* pits groups of instruments against each other, usually soloists against a larger group. Monteverdi's later books of madrigals include a number of concertato madrigals. His Book 8, *Madrigali guerrieri et amorosi* (Madrigals of War and Love, 1638), includes a variety of concerted pieces, along with two staged ballets and *Il Combattimento di Tancredi e Clorinda* (The Combat of Tancred and Clorinda), a theatrical piece of 1624. The latter uses pictorial music to suggest the action and introduces a new style, *stile concitato* (excited style), to suggest warlike feelings and actions. Monteverdi and his contemporaries mixed diverse elements in order to represent a variety of emotions, situations, and characters. In arias by younger composers such as Cavalli and Cesti, the creation of a graceful melody became more important than portraying every image or feeling in the text.

C. Genres of Vocal Solo Music

Monodies were very popular in early-seventeenth-century Italy and were published in large number. The *cantata* (Italian for "sung") was a work for solo voice and continuo. Early cantatas often used strophic variations, and later ones, such as those by *Barbara Strozzi* (1619–after 1664) alternated recitatives and arias, like an operatic scene. Composers outside Italy absorbed Italian influences but also worked in native forms like the French *air de cour.*   **Music: NAWM 57**

D. Influences on Church Music

Elements of the stile moderno (modern style), such as monody, the basso continuo, and the concertato medium, were used in church music as well as in secular music. But Renaissance polyphony was not abandoned; the counterpoint of Palestrina became the model for elevated church style. New pieces in Palestrina's style were said to be in stile antico (old style), codified in the treatise *Gradus ad Parnassum* (Steps to Parnassas, 1725) by *Johann Joseph Fux.*

IV. Venice (HWM 285–87, NAWM 58)

A. Social Conditions in Venice

Venice was an independent city-state, a major trading center with the East, and the second most important city in Italy (after Rome). *Saint Mark's Church,* the state church, was a center of music and pageantry, and many great composers served as choirmaster (including Willaert, Rore, Zarlino, and Monteverdi) or organist (including Giovanni Gabrieli). Venetian music was often homophonic, richly textured, and varied in sonority.

B. Venetian Polychoral Motets

Many Venetian motets used two or more choirs, each accompanied by instruments or organ and placed apart from the others. In these motets for *cori spezzati* (divided choirs), called *polychoral motets,* the choirs sing alone, answer each other in antiphony, and join together for large climaxes.   **Music: NAWM 58**

C. Venetian Influence
The Venetian style influenced many composers throughout Europe.

V. Genres of Catholic Church Music (HWM 287–90, NAWM 59–61)

A. The Grand Concerto
A *grand concerto* was a large work for singers and instruments, often arranged in two or more separate choirs.

B. The Concerto for Few Voices
More common were concertos for one to three voices with organ continuo. *Lodovico Viadana* (1560–1627) was among the first to use this medium, in his 1602 collection *Cento concerti ecclesiastici* (One Hundred Sacred Concertos). *Alessandro Grandi* (ca. 1575/80–1630) was noted for his sacred works in the new style.   **Music: NAWM 59–60**

C. Oratorio
An *oratorio* is a sacred drama like an opera, sung throughout with recitatives, arias, ensembles, and instrumental preludes and ritornellos, but performed without staging or costumes. Most were performed in a church hall called an "oratorio," from which the musical genre took its name around the middle of the seventeenth century. Oratorios often featured a narrator, and the chorus was more prominent than in opera. *Giacomo Carissimi* (1605–1674) was the leading Italian composer of oratorios in the mid-seventeenth century.   **Music: NAWM 61**

D. Private Music of the Convent
Nuns and novices in *convents* made and studied music despite obstacles to their training raised by church regulations, and some such as *Lucrezia Vizzani* became composers.

VI. Lutheran Church Music (HWM 290–94, NAWM 62)

A. The New Styles
Lutheran composers in Germany in the seventeenth century also wrote grand concertos and concertos for few voices, along with chorale motets. An important collection of small sacred concertos was *Opella nova* (1618 and 1626) by *Johann Hermann Schein* (1586–1630).

B. Heinrich Schütz
Heinrich Schütz (1585–1672) was the leading German composer of his time. He studied in Venice and was chapelmaster for the elector of Saxony at Dresden for over half a century. He is renowned for his church music; he apparently wrote no independent instrumental music, and most of his secular vocal music is lost. His sacred music includes simple German psalm settings, Latin motets, polychoral works, sacred concertos for few voices, concertato motets (three books of *Symphoniae sacrae*), and oratorios, such as *The Seven Last Words* (ca. 1645).   **Music: NAWM 62**

VII. Instrumental Music (HWM 294–304, NAWM 63–65)

A. Types of Instrumental Music

Basso continuo and vocal styles influenced instrumental music in the seventeenth century, particularly in the sonata for solo instrument with accompaniment. Over the first half of the century, instrumental music gradually became the equal of vocal music in quantity and content. The following major types can be distinguished, several of which carry over from the sixteenth century:

1. Fugal works in continuous imitative counterpoint, such as the ricercare, fantasia, *fuga,* and related genres.
2. Canzonas that feature sections in imitative counterpoint and in other styles. By mid-century, the canzona was succeeded by the related form of the *sonata da chiesa* (church sonata).
3. Pieces that vary a given melody or bass, such as the *partita,* passacaglia, chaconne, *chorale partita,* and *chorale prelude.*
4. Dances and pieces in dance rhythms, as separate pieces and as part of dance *suites.*
5. Pieces in improvisatory style for solo keyboard or lute, called toccata, fantasia, or prelude.

In practice, these categories intertwine and overlap.

B. Ricercare

Most seventeenth-century *ricercares* are short, serious pieces for keyboard that treat a single subject in imitation throughout. *Girolamo Frescobaldi* (1583–1643), organist at St. Peter's in Rome, composed organ ricercares for use in church services.

C. Fantasia, Fancy

A longer imitative work on a single subject was usually called a *fantasia.* English composers wrote imitative fantasias and *fancies* for viol consort.

D. Canzona

Canzonas featured a series of sections, most in imitative counterpoint. A *variation canzona* uses variants of the same subject in each section.

E. Sonata

In the seventeenth century, *sonata* came to refer to works for one or two instruments with basso continuo. The solo writing was often idiomatic and expressive, as in solo vocal works. Sonatas tend to be sectional, with contrasting mood and figuration in each section. In violin sonatas, the idiomatic violin style includes runs, trills, double stops, and improvised embellishments called *affetti.* A common scoring for a sonata was two treble instruments and continuo, called a *trio sonata.*

F. Variations

Variations were common in the seventeenth century, sometimes under titles such as *partite* (divisions). There were several types:

1. In *cantus-firmus variations,* the melody was largely unchanged and was surrounded by other contrapuntal lines.

2. In another type, the melody was in the top voice and was embellished differently in each variation.

3. Other types of variations are based on a bass or harmonic plan rather than on a melody.

German composers wrote variations for organ on chorale melodies.

G. Dance Music

In addition to music for dancing and stylized dance movements, other types of pieces also used dance rhythms.

H. Suites

German composers cultivated the dance *suite,* a series of dances of varied character that often were melodically related.

I. French Lute and Keyboard Music

French composers arranged dances for lute, playing chords one note at a time (this is the *style brisé,* or broken style) and using ornaments called *agréments* to highlight or prolong a note. These features were adapted to the harpsichord and became characteristic of French keyboard music and of French style in general. *Denis Gaultier (1603–1672)* was the most important French lute composer of the early seventeenth century. *Johann Jakob Froberger (1616–1667)* took the French style to Germany and standardized the sequence of dances in the suite as *allemande, courante, sarabande,* and *gigue.* **Music: NAWM 63a, 63b, and 64**

J. Improvisatory Compositions

Frescobaldi's toccatas feature a series of diverse sections, and Froberger's alternate free improvisation with imitative sections. **Music: NAWM 65**

STUDY QUESTIONS

General Characteristics (HWM 251–60, NAWM 53)

1. What did the term "baroque" mean in the eighteenth century?

   How was it later used in writing on art history?

   How is it used now in music history? Why is it more helpful to refer to "the Baroque period" than to "Baroque style"?

2. What nation or region exercised the most influence on music during the Baroque period? How was its influence felt elsewhere in Europe?

3. How was music supported financially in the seventeenth and eighteenth centuries, and by whom?

4. Which famous artists, writers, philosophers, and scientists were active in the seventeenth century? How does music show a similar intellectual ferment?

Music to Study
    NAWM 53: Claudio Monteverdi, *Cruda Amarilli,* madrigal (ca. 1600)
        CD 3.59–63 (Concise 2.13–17)

5. How does Monteverdi use dissonances, and particularly unprepared dissonances, to convey the meaning of the text in *Cruda Amarilli* (NAWM 53)?

6. To what did Giovanni Maria Artusi object in *Cruda Amarilli*? How might the
   notion of written-out embellishments answer Artusi's objections?

7. Monteverdi defended himself, not with an appeal to written-out embellishments, but with the claim that he was following a "second practice" (*seconda pratica*). What was the basis for this second practice? With what other
   practice does Monteverdi contrast it, and how do the two practices differ?

---

8. How did the Renaissance ideal of writing music that could be performed by
   any combination of voices and instruments change in the seventeenth century? What was the effect on composition?

9. What are *the affections*? How does the representation of affections in music differ from the later idea of expressing an individual artist's feelings?

10. What is new about rhythm in seventeenth-century music, in contrast to earlier music?

11. How does the typical musical texture in the Baroque period differ from that of the Renaissance?

12. Define the following terms, and explain the significance of each concept.

basso continuo or thorough bass

figured bass

continuo instruments

13. How did the emphasis on the bass and the use of basso continuo change how counterpoint was conceived and written and how dissonance was defined?

14. What is *tonality*? How does it differ from the older system of church modes? How did it evolve? Why was figured bass important in its development?

Early Opera (HWM 260–78, NAWM 51–52 and 54–56)

15. What forms of theater before 1600 used music? In what ways did they resemble opera?

16. What was the function of an *intermedio* (pl. *intermedi*)? How was it like and unlike an opera?

17. What is a *pastoral*? What is the importance of pastoral subjects and poetry in the development of opera? In what sense is *L'Euridice* (excerpted in NAWM 52) a pastoral?

18. In what sense was ancient Greek tragedy a model for opera? Who were Girolamo Mei, Giovanni Bardi, and Vincenzo Galilei, and what did each one do to promote the revival of Greek ideals that ultimately led to opera?

19. What was the *Florentine Camerata,* and what is its significance?

20. What were the roles of Ottavio Rinuccini, Jacopo Peri, and Giulio Caccini in the creation of the first musical dramas (what we now call operas)? What was their relationship to the Camerata?

21. What does the term *monody* mean? What different types of monody did Peri and Caccini use in their vocal music? How did monody make musical theater possible?

Music to Study
    NAWM 51: Giulio Caccini, *Vedrò 'l mio sol,* continuo madrigal (ca. 1590)
        CD 3.51–53

22. Compare the opening of Giulio Caccini's *Vedrò 'l mio sol* as it appears in
    NAWM 51 with the original publication, shown in HWM, p. 259. (In the
    latter, note that the vocal line is notated in soprano clef.) What notes are pre-
    sent in the NAWM edition that are not present in the original publication?

    How are these notes differentiated from the others on the page?

    Why are they present in the NAWM edition? Why are they absent in the
    original publication?

23. How does *Vedrò 'l mio sol* differ from other madrigals we have seen?

    What traits does it share with other sixteenth-century Italian madrigals? Why
    is it a madrigal, and not an air?

24. What kinds of ornaments does Caccini use in the vocal line of *Vedrò 'l mio
    sol,* and where do they appear? What other ornaments might have been per-
    formed by the singer?

Music to Study

> **NAWM 52:** Jacopo Peri, *Le musiche sopra l'Euridice* (The Music for *The Euridice*), opera (1600), excerpts
>
> > 52a: Prologue, *Io, che d'alti sospir,* strophic air with ritornello
> >
> > CD 3.54
> >
> > 52b: *Nel pur ardor,* canzonet (dance-song) with ritornello
> >
> > CD 3.55
> >
> > 52c: *Per quel vago boschetto,* recitative   CD 3.56–58

25. What is the *stile recitativo* or *recitative style*? How does Peri describe it in the preface to *Euridice* (excerpted in HWM, p. 267)? How does the dialogue from his setting of *L'Euridice* (NAWM 52c) reflect his conception?

26. How does Peri use harmony, dissonance, and rhythm in Orfeo's response to the death of Euridice (mm. 63–87) to convey the meaning of the words and the feelings they reflect?

27. What style of monody does Peri use in the other excerpts from *Euridice* (NAWM 52a and 52b)? How does this style differ from recitative style?

28. Compare and contrast Monteverdi's *Orfeo* with Peri's *Euridice,* including the excerpts in NAWM 54 and 52 respectively and the description of each in HWM. In what ways is the Monteverdi similar and different?

29. Monteverdi's prologue (NAWM 54a) is a *strophic variation,* in which the harmony and general melodic contour are the same for each strophe of the text, but details in the music are changed to fit the new text. How are the first two strophes different? Note the changes Monteverdi has made.

How does the last strophe differ from the others in the way it ends, and how does that illustrate the text? (Hint: Look at the melody, the harmony, and the last few words of the text.)

30. In what ways does Orfeo's canzonet (NAWM 54b) resemble a frottola?

31. How does Monteverdi use dissonance, rhythm, melodic contour, and other elements to convey the meaning of the text and the feelings it reflects in Orfeo's recitative *Tu se' morta* (NAWM 54c, mm. 43–64)?

32. How do the music and the text of the choral madrigal that concludes NAWM 54c relate to what has preceded it?

33. In *Orfeo,* Monteverdi uses particular musical forms and styles to convey the changing dramatic situation and the feelings of the characters. What characteristics make each of the following forms and styles appropriate for the scene in which it is used?

    54a: La Musica, strophic variation with ritornello

    54b: Orfeo, strophic canzonet with ritornello

    54c: Messenger, recitative

       Orfeo, expressive recitative

       Chorus, choral madrigal

34. Who was Francesca Caccini, when and where did she live and work, and for what was she renowned?

35. How was opera supported and financed in Rome in the period 1620–50?

    How was Roman opera of this period different from earlier opera in Florence and Mantua?

36. When and where was opera first made available to the paying public?

    What made this city ideal for opera?

37. Compare the performance context of Venetian opera to that of *L'Euridice* and *L'Orfeo*. What effects did the shift in audience and performing context have on the development of opera?

38. Who were Francesco Cavalli and Marc' Antonio Cesti? When and where did each live and work, and what were their contributions?

Music to Study

    NAWM 55: Claudio Monteverdi, *L'incoronazione di Poppea,* opera (1642), Act I, Scene 3

        CD 4.16–20

    NAWM 56: Antonio Cesti, *Orontea,* opera (1649), Act II, Scene 17, *Intorno all'idol mio*

        CD 4.21–22

39. Compare and contrast the scene from Monteverdi's *L'incoronazione di Poppea* in NAWM 55 with the scene from *Orfeo* in NAWM 54c. What devices does Monteverdi use in each case to depict the text and portray the dramatic situation?

40. In this scene from *L'incoronazione di Poppea,* the music shifts back and forth often between recitative and aria styles. Why does Monteverdi set Poppea's "Deh non dir di partir" (mm. 280–87) as recitative, and her words "Vanne, vanne ben mio" (mm. 303–9) as a brief aria? (Hint: Do not be fooled by the notation of the latter; it is in a fast triple time.)

41. Contrast the aria from Cesti's *Orontea* (ca. 1649) in NAWM 56 with the airs from Peri's *Euridice* (1600) in NAWM 52a and 52b. How did the style of operatic song change from the beginning to the middle of the seventeenth century?

42. How does the aria from *Orontea* exemplify the *bel canto* style?

43. What important characteristics of opera took shape in Italy by the middle of the seventeenth century? How did opera in Rome and Venice at mid-century differ from Florentine operas of about 1600?

Vocal Chamber Music (HWM 278–85, NAWM 57)

44. Define the following terms:

strophic aria

strophic variation

ground bass or basso ostinato

concertato medium

concertato madrigal

sacred concerto

instrumental concerto (in the seventeenth century)

45. What is the title of Monteverdi's eighth book of madrigals (in either Italian or English), and what is special about the collection?

46. What is the *stile concitato*? Who first used it? When, and in what piece? What does it represent, and how does it achieve its effects?

47. What is a *cantata* in the seventeenth century? How does it resemble opera, and how is it different?

Music to Study
   NAWM 57: Barbara Strozzi, *Lagrime mie,* cantata (published 1659)
      CD 4.23–27

48. In her cantata *Lagrime mie* (NAWM 57), Strozzi uses sections of recitative, aria, and arioso (a style between recitative and aria, usually more metric than recitative). Where is each kind of monody used? (Indicate by measure numbers.)

   recitative   _____

   aria   _____

   arioso   _____

In what ways are the sections of text set as aria particularly appropriate for that style of music?

---

49. What musical devices does Strozzi use to represent the following words and the feelings or actions behind them?

"lagrime" (tears)

"respiro" (breath)

"tormenti" (torments)

50. What are the *stile moderno* and *stile antico* in seventeenth-century church music?

51. What is *Gradus ad Parnassum*? Who wrote it, and when? What was its significance?

Venice (HWM 285–87, NAWM 58)

52. What was distinctive about Venice and its music in the sixteenth and early seventeenth centuries?

Music to Study
> **NAWM 58:** Giovanni Gabrieli, *In ecclesiis,* motet or grand concerto (published 1615)
>> CD 4.28–33

53. What are *cori spezzati*? What is a *polychoral motet*? How does Gabrieli's motet *In ecclesiis* (NAWM 58) exemplify the characteristics of the genre?

Genres of Catholic Church Music (HWM 287–90, NAWM 59–61)

54. What varieties of sacred concerto were written in the seventeenth century? For what circumstances and occasions was each type suited?

55. What is an *oratorio*? From what does its name derive? How is an oratorio like an opera, and how does it differ?

Music to Study

NAWM 59: Lodovico Viadana, *O Domine Jesu Christe,* sacred concerto (ca.1602)

    CD 4.34

NAWM 60: Alessandro Grandi, *O quam tu pulchra es,* motet (1625)

    CD 4.35–37

NAWM 61: Giacomo Carissimi, *Historia di Jephte,* oratorio (ca. 1650), excerpt

    61a: *Plorate colles,* expressive recitative   CD 4.38

    61b: *Plorate filii Israel,* chorus   CD 4.39

56. How is Viadana's *O Domine Jesu Christe* (NAWM 59) like a sixteenth-century motet, such as Victoria's *O magnum mysterium* (NAWM 48a), and how is it different?

57. How is Viadana's sacred concerto like secular monody of around the same time, such as Caccini's *Vedrò 'l mio sol* (NAWM 51), and how is it different?

58. How is Grandi's *O quam tu pulchra es* (NAWM 60) like a sixteenth-century motet, and how is it different?

59. How does Grandi's motet compare to the alternation of recitative and aria styles in the scene from Monteverdi's *L'incoronazione di Poppea* in NAWM 55? How does each work respond to its text?

60. Compare the excerpt from Carissimi's *Historia di Jephte* in NAWM 61 with the scene from Monteverdi's *Orfeo* in NAWM 54c. What elements does each use?

How do Monteverdi and Carissimi use harmony to convey emotions?

How does each use the chorus?

61. What obstacles lay in the way of women in convents who sought musical training? Name a composer who was a nun, and describe her career and music.

Lutheran Church Music (HWM 290–94, NAWM 62)

62. Describe Johann Hermann Schein's *Opella nova* and its significance.

63. Summarize Heinrich Schütz's career. What Italian influences did he absorb, and how are they reflected in his music? How were his career and music affected by the Thirty Years' War?

Music to Study
   NAWM 62: Heinrich Schütz, *Saul, was verfolgst du mich* (SWV 415), grand
           concerto (ca. 1650)
   CD 4.40–41 (Concise 2.27–28)

64. How does Schütz use changes of texture and other musical effects to depict the events and text of *Saul, was verfolgst du mich* (NAWM 62)? What types of style and texture does he use?

Instrumental Music (HWM 294–304, NAWM 63–65)

65. What main types of instrumental music were practiced in the first half of the seventeenth century? How do these types compare to the forms used in the sixteenth century?

66. In the first half of the seventeenth century, what is the difference between a ricercare and a fantasia?

    What is the difference between a canzona and a sonata?

67. What kinds of variations were written in the seventeenth century? In each type, what stayed the same in each variation, and what changed?

68. What is a dance *suite*? What dances typically appear in a suite by Froberger?

69. What is *style brisé* (broken style)?

What are *agréments*?

On what instrument did *style brisé* and *agréments* originate? _____

Why were they necessary or useful on that instrument?

To what instrument were they later adapted? _____

Music to Study
> **NAWM 63a:** Ennemond Gaultier, *La Poste,* gigue for lute (early to mid-seventeenth century)
> > CD 4.42
> **NAWM 63b:** Jean-Henri D'Anglebert, arrangement for harpsichord of Ennemond Gaultier's *La Poste* (seventeenth century)
> > CD 4.43
> **NAWM 64:** Johann Jakob Froberger, *Lamentation on the Death of Emperor Ferdinand III* (1657)
> > CD 4.44
> **NAWM 65:** Girolamo Frescobaldi, Toccata No. 3 (1615, rev. 1637)
> > CD 4.45 (Concise 2.29)

70. Compare Gaultier's gigue for lute (NAWM 63a) with its arrangement for harpsichord (NAWM 63b). How does the keyboard version imitate the style of the lute?

71. What features of Froberger's *Lamentation on the Death of Emperor Ferdinand III* (NAWM 64) mark it as a piece in French style?

What features are particularly appropriate to its subject?

72. How is Frescobaldi's Toccata No. 3 (NAWM 65) divided into sections? Where does the style or figuration change?

73. Frescobaldi's toccata is in the Dorian mode on G (i.e., transposed up a fourth). Where are the main cadences, and on what scale degrees do they occur? How is the modal final of G established?

What clues are there that this piece is in G Dorian rather than in G Minor? (Hint: Think of the notes and chords that are more likely to occur in G Dorian than in G Minor—and the reverse—and look for them. For example, a C minor triad may occur in either, but a C major or A minor triad is unlikely in G Minor, which has an *E♭* in the key signature.)

TERMS TO KNOW

Terms Related to the Baroque Period

Baroque period
prima pratica, seconda pratica
stile antico, stile moderno
the affections
measures
thoroughbass

basso continuo
continuo instruments
figured bass
realization of a figured bass
tonality

Terms Related to Early Opera

opera
intermedio (pl., intermedi) or
   intermezzo (pl., intermezzi)
madrigal cycle
pastoral
monody
recitative style (stile recitativo)

air or aria
solo madrigal
libretto
recitative
aria
arioso
bel canto

Terms Related to Vocal Music

strophic aria
strophic variation
romanesca
ottave rime
ground bass or basso ostinato
chaconne
passacaglia
concerto (seventeenth-century)
concertato medium
concertato madrigal
sacred concerto

instrumental concerto
   (seventeenth century)
stile concitato
cantata (seventeenth century)
air de cour
cori spezzati
polychoral motet
grand concerto
oratorio
convent

Terms Related to Instrumental Music

fuga
sonata da chiesa
partita (or partite)
chorale partita
choral prelude
suite
ricercare (seventeenth-century)
fantasia (seventeenth-century)
fancy
canzona (seventeenth-century)

variation canzona
sonata (seventeenth-century)
affetti
trio sonata
cantus firmus variations
style brisé
agréments
allemande, courante, sarabande,
   gigue

NAMES TO KNOW

Names Related to Early Opera

Girolamo Mei
Florentine Camerata
Giovanni Bardi
Vincenzo Galilei
Ottaviano Rinuccini
Jacopo Peri
Dafne
L'Euridice
Giulio Caccini
Emilio de' Cavalieri
*Rappresentatione di anima e
 di corpo*

Le nuove musiche
L'Orfeo
Arianna
Francesca Caccini
La liberazione di Ruggiero
Il ritorno d'Ulisse
L'incoronazione di Poppea
Pier Francesco Cavalli
Antonio Cesti

Names Related to Vocal Music

Madrigali guerrieri et amorosi
*Il Combattimento di Tancredi e
 Clorinda*
Barbara Strozzi
Gradus ad Parnassum, by
 Johann Joseph Fux
Saint Mark's Church
Lodovico Viadana
Cento concerti ecclesiastici

Alessandro Grandi
Giacomo Carissimi
Lucrezia Vizzani
Opella nova
Johann Hermann Schein
Heinrich Schütz
Symphoniae sacrae
The Seven Last Words

Names Related to Instrumental Music

Girolamo Frescobaldi
Denis Gaultier

Johann Jakob Froberger

REVIEW QUESTIONS

1. Make a time-line for the pieces, composers, treatises, and theorists discussed in this chapter.

2. What are the principal characteristics that distinguish music of the Baroque period from music of the Renaissance?

3. What new concepts or procedures were developed in the period 1600–1650 as composers sought to find ways to capture human emotions in music?

4. Trace the development of opera in Italy from its origins to 1650. Include in your answer changes of aesthetic aims and ideas as well as changes of style and procedure.

5. What connections do you see between Monteverdi's madrigals and his operas? What effects did his experience as a madrigal composer have on his operas?

6. Write an expressive recitative in the style Monteverdi used in *L'Orfeo*. Use for your text the first two lines of his madrigal *Cruda Amarilli* (NAWM 53) in either the original Italian or in the English translation. Write it for male voice and continuo, as in Orfeo's recitative *Tu se' morta* from *L'Orfeo* (in NAWM 54c), and use the latter as a model for how to write a recitative, how to fit the music to the accentuation of the poetry, and how to use gestures and dissonances for expressivity. You may write only the voice and bass line or may fill in the harmony, and you may stop after a few measures or write an entire recitative using all eight lines of the poem, as you wish; the goal is to see how recitative in this style works, from the inside.

   (If you use the Italian, please note that in Italian, adjacent vowels elide into a single syllable. Thus the first line has eleven syllables, with the "-da" of "Cruda" elided into a single syllable with the "A-" of "Amarilli" and the "-me" of "nome" elided with the "an-" of "ancora.")

7. What new forms and styles of secular vocal music were introduced in the first half of the seventeenth century?

8. How was sacred music affected by the new developments in secular music in the first half of the seventeenth century? What new forms or styles of sacred music emerged during this time?

9. What was the concertato medium, and where was it used?

10. What types of instrumental music were practiced during the early seventeenth century? Which of these genres and styles were new, and which continued trends from the sixteenth century? Of the latter, how were the older genres or styles changed in the seventeenth century?

11. What are some elements that distinguish French from Italian instrumental style in the early Baroque?

OPERA AND VOCAL MUSIC IN THE LATE SEVENTEENTH CENTURY
10

CHAPTER OBJECTIVES

After you complete the reading, study of the music, and study questions for this chapter, you should be able to

1. describe developments in Italian opera in the second half of the seventeenth century and the beginning of the eighteenth century;
2. trace the origins and development of musical theater in France, England, and Germany during the seventeenth and early eighteenth centuries and explain what makes each national tradition distinctive;
3. describe the cantata and other secular vocal genres in the late seventeenth century;
4. describe the varieties of sacred music composed in the late seventeenth and early eighteenth centuries; and
5. define and use the most important terms and identify some of the composers and works associated with opera and vocal music in the late seventeenth and early eighteenth centuries.

CHAPTER OUTLINE

I. Opera (HWM 309–24, NAWM 66–70)

A. Venice

In the second half of the seventeenth century, opera spread throughout Italy and Europe. The main Italian center was Venice. Musical interest in operas lay primarily in the arias, which became more numerous. Singers were the stars, and popular singers commanded much higher fees than composers (just as today film and popular music stars earn more than the screenwriters and songwriters whose works they perform). There were many types of aria, including strophic songs; two-part and three-part forms; arias over ostinato basses or a *running bass* (also called a *walking bass*), in which the bass moves in steady eighth notes; and arias that used march or dance rhythms. *Continuo arias* were accompanied only by continuo, with or without an orchestral ritornello.

B. Venetian Opera Exported

Many Italian composers made careers writing Italian operas in Germany. A common type of aria was a *motto aria,* in which the singer states the opening motive (the motto), the instruments interrupt, and then the singer begins again. Arias often included coloratura passages and mood or text painting.

C. Naples

A new operatic style that emphasized elegant melodies over dramatic force developed in Naples and became dominant in the early eighteenth century. There were two types of recitative, later called *recitativo semplice* or *secco* (simple or dry recitative, with basso continuo), for dialogue or monologue, and *recitativo obbligato* or *accompagnato* (accompanied recitative, with orchestra), for dramatic situations. Composers also used *arioso,* a type of singing between aria and recitative. The principal type of aria was the *da capo aria,* in which the first section (with or without the opening ritornello) is repeated after a middle section that contrasts in key, figuration, and often mood. *Alessandro Scarlatti* (1660–1725) was a leading composer of this kind of opera.   **Music: NAWM 66**

D. France

A distinctive style of opera developed in France in the 1670s under the patronage of King *Louis XIV* (1638–1715, reigned 1643–1715). *Jean-Baptiste Lully* (1632–1687) drew on two strong French traditions, *court ballet* and classical French tragedy, to create the *tragédie lyrique* (tragedy in music). The court ballet included solo songs, choruses, *entrées* (entrances), and dances for costumed and masked dancers, and a closing *grand ballet* that included the king and nobility.

E. Louis XIV

Louis XIV was a talented dancer who performed frequently in the court ballets and established the Royal Academy of Dance in 1661. He valued public entertainments for making the court and people more loyal and impressing foreigners with the power of the state.

F. Jean-Baptiste Lully

Lully was born in Italy, came to Paris at age fourteen, became a violinist with Louis XIV's twenty-four-piece string orchestra (the *vingt-quatre violons du roy*), and composed music for court ballets and *comédie-ballets* (plays with dances and songs). In 1672 he was put in charge of sung drama in France (where Louis controlled his realm in part through centralized control of the arts). He collaborated with *Jean-Philippe Quinault,* whose librettos featured mythological plots often interrupted by *divertissements,* long interludes of choral singing and dancing. Lully's recitative is in a new style, more dramatic and compelling than Italian recitativo secco and perfectly matched to the rhythms and inflections of French, especially as declaimed on the dramatic stage. There are two types: *récitatif simple,* in which the meter shifts freely between duple and triple, and *récitatif mesuré,* in a more songlike, measured style. Lully's airs are simpler and much less florid than Italian arias.   **Music: NAWM 67 and 68b**

G. The *Ouverture*

Lully codified the *ouverture* or *French overture* as an introduction to a ballet, opera, suite, or other large work. A French overture usually has two parts: the first slow, stately, homophonic, and marked by dotted rhythms, and the second fast and imitative, often closing with a return to the slower first tempo. Lully's orchestra influenced others across Europe. *Georg Muffat* (1653–1740) introduced Lully's style into Germany, where it found many imitators. French composers also mixed elements of opera and ballet in the *opera-ballet*. **Music: NAWM 68a**

H. England

Musical theater in seventeenth-century England included the *masque,* akin to the French court ballet; plays with extensive incidental music, called *semi-operas*; and only two musical dramas that were sung throughout.

I. John Blow

John Blow (1649–1708) was organist and composer at Westminster Abbey and in the Chapel Royal. His masque *Venus and Adonis* (1684 or 1685) is sung throughout, like an opera. It combines French overture and dance styles, Italian recitative and bel canto, and English song and choral styles.

J. Henry Purcell

Henry Purcell (1659–1695) is considered the greatest English composer of the Baroque era. He wrote a large amount of music for chorus, voice, chamber ensembles, and keyboard, and incidental music for forty-nine plays, including five semi-operas such as *The Fairy Queen* (1692). His opera *Dido and Aeneas* (1689) combined French overture, dance, and choral styles with Italian and English vocal styles, including Italian ground bass arias and a distinctively English style of recitative. **Music: NAWM 69–70**

K. Germany

Some German cities, notably Hamburg, supported opera in German, called *Singspiel* (play with music). These usually used spoken dialogue instead of recitative and featured a variety of air and aria types drawing on German song, French airs, and Italian styles.

L. Reinhard Keiser

Reinhard Keiser (1674–1739) was the leading composer of German opera in the early eighteenth century, unifying German and Italian traits.

II. Vocal Chamber Music (HWM 324–27)

A. The Cantata in Italy

In the second half of the seventeenth century, the Italian *cantata* was a dramatic narrative or soliloquy for voice and continuo laid out as a series of two or three recitative-aria pairs. It was like a scene from an opera, but performed in a chamber setting without staging. Many opera composers wrote cantatas.

B. Alessandro Scarlatti
Scarlatti wrote over 600 cantatas. His music is fully tonal and uses diminished seventh chords, distant modulations, and unusual harmonies for expressive effect.

C. Other Vocal Chamber Music
Other types of Italian vocal chamber music included the vocal duet and the *serenata,* a semidramatic work for several singers and small orchestra.

D. Song in Other Countries
French and German composers also wrote cantatas, following Italian models. Solo songs continued to be written in the national styles of France, Germany, and England. English composers also wrote *catches,* canons on usually humorous texts, and *odes,* large works for soloists, chorus, and orchestra celebrating state occasions and holidays.

III. Church Music (HWM 327–41)

A. General
Catholic church music was written in old, modern, and mixed styles.

B. Italy
The basilica of San Petronio in Bologna was a center of church music in both old and modern concerted styles. The church music of Scarlatti and others exemplifies the plaintive chromaticism and sentimentality of much Italian religious music of the early eighteenth century. German writers called this style Empfindsamkeit (sentimentality).

C. South Germany
South German composers of church music blended old and new styles and Italian and German traits. Masses often featured chorus and soloists with full orchestral preludes and accompaniment.

D. Vienna
The Masses of *Antonio Caldara* (ca. 1670–1736) include concerted arias and duets, choral movements, and movements that mix chorus and soloists.

E. Oratorio
Oratorios were performed in sacred concerts. Most were in Italian rather than Latin and were in two parts with a sermon or intermission in between. Oratorios were written in the same style as operas and substituted for opera during Lent and other seasons when theaters were closed.

F. French Church Music
Marc-Antoine Charpentier (1634–1704) brought the Latin oratorio to France, combining Italian and French traits. At Louis XIV's chapel, the leading genres were the motet for solo voice and continuo and the *grand motet* (large motet) for soloists, choruses, and orchestra.

G. Anglican Church Music
Services and anthems continued to be the leading genres of Anglican church music. Purcell and others wrote anthems and odes for special occasions and nonliturgical songs and ensembles for private devotional use.

H. Lutheran Church Music

Lutheran music reached its height in the period 1650–1750. Orthodoxy was challenged by *Pietism,* which emphasized individual freedom and simple expression of feelings in music.

I. Chorales

Johann Crüger (1598–1662) wrote many new chorale tunes and edited the most influential Lutheran songbook of the second half of the seventeenth century. Many of these songs were intended for use in the home, but began to be used in church in the eighteenth century. Four-part settings of the chorales in cantional style were popular.

J. Concerted Church Music

Orthodox composers wrote sacred concertos that included concertato arias and choruses, concerted chorale settings, or a mixture of both. *Dietrich Buxtehude* (ca. 1637–1707) wrote *chorale variations,* in which each verse elaborates a chorale in a different way, as well as freer concerted pieces. Much of his church music was composed for the Abendmusiken, concerts after the afternoon church services. A standard format for concerted church music was an opening chorus, solo movements, and a choral setting of one verse of a chorale.

K. The Lutheran Church Cantata

The *Lutheran church cantata* was devised around 1700 by *Erdmann Neumeister* (1671–1756) as a series of recitatives and arias meditating on a biblical text and closing with a chorale. Neumeister blended orthodoxy with Pietism, and composers setting his cantata texts to music blended elements of chorale settings, solo song, the sacred concerto, and opera. Today J. S. Bach is considered the greatest exponent of the church cantata, but in his time *Georg Philipp Telemann* (1681–1767) was more highly regarded. Telemann wrote more than a thousand cantatas and published four complete cycles for the entire church year.

L. The Passion

The *historia* was a German genre setting a Bible story to music. The most important type was the *Passion,* telling the story of the suffering and death of Jesus. Plainchant Passions survive from the Middle Ages. Passions in the sixteenth and early seventeenth centuries were written in motet style throughout (the *motet Passion*) or alternating plainsong and motet style (the *dramatic* or *scenic Passion*). In the late seventeenth century a new type appeared that resembled an oratorio and is known as the *oratorio Passion.* Beyond relating the Bible story, Passions came to include chorales sung by the choir or congregation and poetic texts set as solo arias.

STUDY QUESTIONS

Opera (HWM 309–24, NAWM 66–70)

1. What were the most important elements of Italian opera in the late seventeenth and early eighteenth centuries? How did drama and music relate in Italian opera of this period, and how did this compare with the ideals of the Florentine Camerata?

2. Describe each of the following types of aria.

   continuo aria

   motto aria

   da capo aria

   Why is it possible for the same aria to be all three types?

3. Describe each of the following. In what circumstances was each used?

   recitativo semplice or secco

   recitativo obbligato or accompagnato

Music to Study
NAWM 66: Alessandro Scarlatti, *Griselda,* opera (1721), Act II, Scene 1, *Mi rivedi*
CD 4.46–48

4. What type of aria is Scarlatti's *Mi rivedi* (NAWM 66)? Chart the form of this aria as it would be performed.

5. Look at the words of this aria in translation. What emotions is Griselda experiencing?

How does Scarlatti's music convey Griselda's feelings? How does the musical form help to capture the conflicting emotions Griselda feels?

6. On what two French traditions did French opera draw?

Of these two, in which did Louis XIV participate himself? Of what did his participation consist? What did this genre include? Why did Louis XIV value it and other public entertainments?

7. Name the composer and librettist who founded the French opera tradition.

_____   _____

How do their *tragédies lyriques* compare to Italian operas of the time?

Music to Study

NAWM 67: Jean-Baptiste Lully, *Le bourgeois gentilhomme: Ballet des nations* (1670), excerpts

67a: L'Entrée des Scaramouches, Trivelins et Arlequins
CD 4.49

67b: Chaconne des Scaramouches, Trivelins et Arlequins
CD 4.50

NAWM 68: Jean-Baptiste Lully, *Armide,* opera (1686), excerpts

68a: Ouverture   CD 5.1–3

68b: Act II, Scene 5: *Enfin il est en ma puissance*
CD 5.4–6

---

8. In Lully's *Ballet des nations,* how does the *entrée* of the Scaramouches, Trivelins, and Harlequins (NAWM 67a) suggest an entrance? How does it suggest the comic character of the figures it accompanies?

9. In the following chaconne (NAWM 67b), where does the chaconne bass (*G–F♯–E–D* or a variant) or harmonic progression (I–V–IV–V, each lasting a measure) occur? List each occurrence by measure number. What happens when it does not appear?

10. What characteristics of the overture to Lully's *Armide* (NAWM 68a) mark it as a French overture?

11. How does the musical setting of Armide's recitative *Enfin il est en ma puissance* (NAWM 68b) reflect the form and accentuation of the text?

12. How does the musical setting reflect the dramatic situation and the emotional conflict Armide is feeling?

13. The scene ends with a minuet played by instruments and then sung by Armide. The minuet was associated at the time with surrender to love. In what ways is this appropriate to the dramatic situation? How does the use of a dance reflect the origins of French opera?

14. How does this scene from *Armide* differ from the recitative and aria of Italian opera?

15. What are the characteristics of the following genres of musical theater? What nation is each from, and how does it differ from Italian opera?

masque

semi-opera

Singspiel

Music to Study
   NAWM 69: Henry Purcell, *Dido and Aeneas,* opera (1689), Act III, Scene 2
   Recitative: *Thy hand, Belinda*   CD 5.7 (Concise 2.30)
   Aria: *When I am laid in earth*   CD 5.8–9 (Concise 2.31–32)
   Chorus: *With drooping winds*   CD 5.10
   NAWM 70: Henry Purcell, *The Fairy Queen,* semi-opera (1692), *Hark! the ech'ing air a triumph sings*
      CD 5.11

16. Compare Purcell's recitative *Thy hand, Belinda* (in NAWM 69) to Lully's recitative from *Armide* (in NAWM 68b) and Peri's recitative in *L'Euridice* (in NAWM 52c). How does Purcell's music follow the accentuation of the English text? How does the music convey Dido's emotions?

17. Laments in Italian operas were often written over a descending ground bass, and Purcell's aria *When I am laid in earth* (in NAWM 69) follows this tradition. Part of the expressivity comes from dissonances or conflicts in phrasing between the ostinato bass and the vocal line. Where do these dissonances or conflicts in phrasing occur?

    Besides these conventions, what other devices does Purcell use to give this music the feeling of a lament?

18. In the closing chorus of *Dido and Aeneas* (in NAWM 69), how does the music reinforce the mood of lamentation?

19. How does the air from Purcell's *The Fairy Queen* (NAWM 70) compare to the aria from Scarlatti's *Griselda* (NAWM 66) and the air from Lully's *Armide* (in NAWM 68b)? Would you say this Purcell air is more Italian or more French in style?

Vocal Chamber Music (HWM 324–27)

20. Describe the form and style of the secular Italian cantata in the late seventeenth and early eighteenth centuries. How does it compare to opera?

21. In addition to opera and cantata, what other vocal forms (other than church music) were popular in Italy, France, Germany, and England in the second half of the seventeenth century?

Church Music (HWM 327–41)

22. Describe the varieties of sacred music practiced in the late seventeenth and early eighteenth centuries in Catholic Europe, including Italy, southern Germany, and France.

23. Where and when were oratorios performed, and what were they like? What does André Maugars praise in oratorios in the passage on p. 329 of HWM?

24. What is *Pietism,* and what is its significance for music?

25. How did Lutheran composers in the second half of the seventeenth century use the concertato medium? Include in your discussion brief descriptions of at least three pieces excerpted or described in HWM, pp. 334–39.

26. How did Lutheran composers in the second half of the seventeenth century use chorales in their music? Include in your discussion brief descriptions of the works by Tunder and Buxtehude excerpted or described in HWM, 335–38.

27. Describe the Lutheran church cantata. Who devised it, and when? What was the text like? From what sources might parts of the text be borrowed, and what portions were newly written? What was the music like, and from what traditions did it draw?

28. What is a *historia*? What is a *Passion*? What kinds of Passion are there, and when was each important?

TERMS TO KNOW

Terms Related to Opera and Ballet

running bass (walking bass)
continuo aria
motto aria
recitativo semplice or secco
recitativo obbligato or
  accompagnato
da capo aria
court ballet
tragédie lyrique
entrée

grand ballet
comédie-ballet
divertissement
récitatif simple
récitatif mesuré
French overture (ouverture)
opéra-ballet
masque
semi-opera
Singspiel

Terms Related to Other Vocal Music

cantata (in late-seventeenth-
  century Italy)
serenata
catch
ode
grand motet
Pietism

chorale variations
Lutheran church cantata
historia
Passion
motet Passion
dramatic or scenic Passion
oratorio Passion

NAMES TO KNOW

Alessandro Scarlatti
Louis XIV
Jean-Baptiste Lully
vingt-quatre violons du roy
Jean-Phillippe Quinault
Georg Muffat
John Blow
Venus and Adonis
Henry Purcell

The Fairy Queen
Dido and Aeneas
Reinhard Keiser
Antonio Caldara
Marc-Antoine Charpentier
Johann Crüger
Dieterich Buxtehude
Erdmann Neumeister
Georg Philipp Telemann

REVIEW QUESTIONS

1. Make a time-line for the pieces, composers, and librettists discussed in this chapter.

2. How did Italian opera develop and change during the seventeenth and early eighteenth centuries, from Monteverdi through Scarlatti?

3. Trace the origins and development of musical theater in France during the seventeenth century. Explain what distinguishes it from Italian opera, and describe the importance of dance in French musical theater.

4. What factors influenced the development of English musical theater in the seventeenth century? What genres did the English use? What did the English borrow from the French and Italian traditions?

5. Write a new setting in the style of Lully's French recitative for Dido's four lines of recitative in NAWM 69 (from "Thy hand, Belinda" through "Death is now a welcome guest"). Use as a model the opening of Armide's recitative in NAWM 68b, which is also a setting of a rhymed quatrain (from "Enfin" to "son invincible coeur"). You may write only the voice and bass line or may fill in the harmony. Why is Purcell's recitative so different from Lully's, and what is he trying to achieve that Lully's style does not accomplish?

6. Trace the history of opera in Germany through the early eighteenth century.

7. Describe the secular Italian cantata of the late seventeenth century, using Scarlatti's *Lascia, deh lascia* as an example (see HWM, pp. 325–26).

8. Describe the varieties of sacred music being composed in the late seventeenth and early eighteenth centuries, including works in the Catholic, Anglican, and Lutheran traditions.

INSTRUMENTAL MUSIC IN THE LATE BAROQUE PERIOD

11

CHAPTER OBJECTIVES

After you complete the reading, study of the music, and study questions for this chapter, you should be able to

1. name and describe the genres of instrumental music composed in the second half of the seventeenth century and the early eighteenth century;
2. trace the development of keyboard music in this period and describe the styles of various regions and individual composers; and
3. trace the development of ensemble music and orchestral music in this period and describe the style of Corelli.

CHAPTER OUTLINE

I. Introduction (HWM 345)

In the later Baroque, composers suited their music to specific instruments. The principal genres of keyboard music are these:
1. Toccata, prelude, or fantasia and fugue;
2. Settings of chorales or chants, such as a chorale prelude;
3. Variations;
4. Passacaglia and chaconne;
5. Suite; and
6. Sonata (after 1700).

The principal genres of ensemble music are these:
1. Sonata (sonata da chiesa), sinfonia, and related forms;
2. Suite (sonata da camera) and related forms; and
3. Concerto.

II. Organ Music (HWM 345–51, NAWM 71–72)

A. The Baroque Organ

Baroque organs could achieve a variety of timbres, with several keyboards and many different ranks of pipes available for each keyboard. The organist selected the *registration* by pulling out a knob (called a stop) for each desired set of pipes. Much organ music was written for Protestant services, where it served as a prelude to part of the service.

B. The Toccata
The seventeenth-century German toccata or prelude includes both sections in toccata style and one or more sections in imitative counterpoint. The toccata sections have an improvisatory feel, with unpredictable harmony, surprising contrasts of texture, and virtuoso passagework. The imitative sections are like fugues embedded between toccata sections. From this contrast evolved the eighteenth-century form of toccata and fugue or prelude and fugue.   **Music: NAWM 71**

C. The Fugue
The ricercare was gradually replaced by the *fugue,* composed as an independent piece or as part of a prelude. A fugue opens with an *exposition,* in which the *subject* in the tonic is imitated by the *answer* in the dominant and the other voices alternate subject and answer. Later appearances of the subject, also called expositions, alternate with *episodes* where the subject is absent and modulation may occur. Preludes and fugues were used both in church services and as teaching pieces for performance and composition.

D. Temperament
Keyboard players in the Baroque era often used *meantone temperament,* which gave better thirds and triads than Pythagorean tuning. Lute players could play in all twenty-four major and minor keys because their frets were equally spaced and thus every semitone was the same size, giving *equal temperament,* and keyboard players gradually adopted this system.

E. Chorale Compositions
Lutheran chorales were used in several types of organ composition. Chorales could be accompanied with harmonizations or counterpoint; varied in *chorale variations* (also called *chorale partita*); fragmented and developed in a *chorale fantasia*; or presented in embellished form.   **Music: NAWM 72**

F. The Chorale Prelude
A *chorale prelude* presents a chorale once, varied or elaborated in a contrapuntal setting. Most chorale preludes use one of the following procedures: (1) each phrase of the melody is treated in imitation; (2) each phrase is presented cantus-firmus style and is preceded by an imitative foreshadowing of the phrase in smaller note values; (3) the melody is ornamented over a contrapuntal accompaniment that may draw motives from the chorale; (4) the melody is presented unadorned over an accompaniment marked by a repeating rhythmic figure not drawn from the chorale.

G. Organ Music in the Catholic Countries
Organ composers in Italy, south Germany, and Spain continued to use early-seventeenth-century forms, writing ricercares, variation canzonas, settings of liturgical cantus firmi, and nonimitative toccatas. French composers wrote airs, antiphonal "dialogues" between parts of the organ, and versets and interludes for the Mass.

III. Harpsichord and Clavichord Music (HWM 351–56, NAWM 73)

The main genres for stringed keyboard instruments were the *theme and variations* and the *suite*.

A. Theme and Variations
Variation sets continued to be popular. Composers often wrote variations on an original melody rather than an existing tune.

B. Suite
There were two main types of suite, German and French. In Germany, the suite (also called *partita*) by 1700 always featured four dances of varying meter, tempo, and national origin in a set order:
   1. *allemande,* a German dance in a moderately fast duple meter that moves in continuous eighth or sixteenth notes, with a short upbeat;
   2. *courante,* a French dance in moderate 6/4 or 3/2 time (often motivically related to the allemande);
   3. *sarabande,* a Mexican-Spanish dance in slow triple meter with a stress on the second beat, generally the most homophonic; and
   4. *gigue,* an Anglo-Irish dance (the jig) usually in a fast 12/8 or 6/8 with a skipping melody and often in imitative counterpoint.
A suite might also contain an introductory prelude or one or more dances added after one of the last three standard dances.
   The French *clavecinists* (harpsichordists) wrote suites using a wider variety of dance movements in no set order. *Elisabeth-Claude Jacquet de la Guerre* (1665–1729) was hailed as a child prodigy and became renowned for her harpsichord, ensemble, and vocal music. The *ordres* (suites) of *François Couperin* (1668–1733) contain any number of short movements, most in dance rhythms and most with evocative titles. The passacaglia and chaconne often appeared in suites or as independent works. Couperin's treatise *L'Art de toucher le clavecin* (The Art of Playing the Clavecin, 1716) detailed how to play the harpsichord, including fingering and performing the agréments (French ornaments).   **Music: NAWM 73**

C. The Keyboard Sonata
The sonata, mainly a genre for ensembles, was transferred to the keyboard by Johann Kuhnau (1660–1722) at the end of the seventeenth century.

IV. Ensemble Music (HWM 356–69, NAWM 74–75)

A. Italy
Italian composers continued to dominate instrumental chamber music during the seventeenth and early eighteenth centuries, as they did in opera and cantata. This was also the the era of the great Cremona violin makers, Niccolò Amati (1596–1684), Antonio Stradivari (1644–1737), and Giuseppe Bartolomeo Guarneri (1698–1744).

B. The Ensemble Sonata
The sonata was a work in several contrasting sections or movements for a small number of instruments with basso continuo. After about 1660, there were two main types, although in practice the two types mixed:

1. *Sonata da chiesa* (church sonata), a series of mostly abstract movements mixed with dance movements;
2. *Sonata da camera* (chamber sonata), a suite of stylized dances, often opening with a prelude.

A *trio sonata* is a sonata (of either type) for two treble instruments (usually violins) and basso continuo. This is the most common instrumentation for a sonata, followed by the *solo sonata* for one treble instrument and continuo. There are also sonatas for larger groups and for unaccompanied string or wind instrument.   **Music: NAWM 74**

C. Italian Chamber Music
The church of San Petronio in Bologna was an important center for chamber music.

D. Arcangelo Corelli
Arcangelo Corelli (1653–1713) was the greatest master of seventeenth-century Italian instrumental music. After studies at Bologna, he lived in Rome. He published two sets each of trio sonatas da chiesa and da camera, a set of solo violin sonatas, and a set of concerti grossi, with twelve works in each set.

His trio sonatas feature lyrical violin lines within a limited range of technique. Suspensions and *sequences* drive the music forward and help create the directed harmonic motion characteristic of common-practice tonality (which was new in Corelli's generation). His church sonatas most often include four movements in the pattern slow–fast–slow–fast, usually consisting of a majestic prelude, a fugue, a slow aria or duet, and a fast binary dance, such as a gigue. His chamber sonatas typically begin with a prelude and include two or three dance movements. Each movement presents and develops a single melodic idea.   **Music: NAWM 75**

Corelli's solo violin sonatas use the same format as his trio sonatas but demand more virtuosity, including double and triple stops, rapid runs and arpeggios, and perpetual-motion passages. His playing and teaching were as influential on later violinists as his music was on later composers.

E. Improvisation in Musical Performance
Performers in the seventeenth and eighteenth centuries were expected to embellish written melodies, whether with small figures such as trills, turns, appoggiaturas, and mordents or with freer, more extended embellishments such as scales, runs, and arpeggios. Ornamentation was not only decorative but added interest and helped to convey the affections. A *cadenza* was an improvised extension of the six-four chord in a cadence near the end of a movement. Performers could also omit movements or sections and add instruments as desired. (In sum, pieces were seen as opportunities for performance, not as hallowed works that were only to be performed as the composer intended.)

F. Ensemble Sonatas outside Italy
Composers in England, Germany, and France wrote trio sonatas, following the Italian model. The most important trio sonatas in France are those by François Couperin, who sought a union of Italian and French styles.

G. The Solo Sonata after Corelli

Composers in Germany, England, and France also wrote solo sonatas on the Italian model. An influential pupil of Corelli's was *Francesco Geminiani* (1687–1762), active in London as violinist and composer and author of the important treatise *The Art of Playing on the Violin* (1751).

H. Works for Larger Ensembles

Sonatas, dance suites, and other types of composition were also written for larger ensembles. In Germany, music was cultivated not only at courts by the nobility but also in the cities by the middle class. Many towns had a *collegium musicum,* a group that played and sang music for their own pleasure, and a town band, the *Stadtpfeifer.*

I. Orchestral Music

In the late seventeenth century, musicians began to distinguish between *chamber music* for one player on a part and *orchestral music* for more than one on a part. It is not clear from most scores which medium the composer preferred. Opera overtures and dances were always conceived as orchestral music. The Paris opera orchestra was the most famous in Europe, renowned for its discipline.

J. The Orchestral Suite

The German *orchestral suite* (also called *ouverture,* after the opening movement) was modeled on Lully's suites from his operas and ballets.

K. The Concerto

The instrumental *concerto* was a new genre that emerged in the 1680s and became the most important Baroque orchestral genre. In the *orchestral concerto,* the first violin dominated and the texture was less contrapuntal than in the sonata and sinfonia. More important were the *concerto grosso,* which contrasted a small ensemble (or *concertino*) with a large ensemble (or *concerto grosso*), and the *solo concerto,* which set a solo instrument with continuo against the orchestra. In both, the full orchestra was called *tutti* (all) or *ripieno* (full). Concerto-like textures were frequent in seventeenth-century vocal and instrumental music before the concerto emerged as a separate form. Like sonatas and sinfonias, concertos were played in church before certain segments of the Mass or as a substitute for the Offertory. Corelli's concerti grossi were like sonatas punctuated by changes of texture, and some later composers followed this model, especially in Germany and England.

L. Torelli

Giuseppe Torelli (1658–1709) helped to codify the concerto as a work in three movements in the pattern fast–slow–fast. The fast movements are in *ritornello form,* in which the large group states a *ritornello* in the tonic at the beginning; the soloist or soloists contribute an episode, which usually modulates; the large group states the ritornello (or a part of it) in the new key; this alternation of episode and ritornello continues for some time; and the movement ends with the reappearance of the ritornello in the tonic.

STUDY QUESTIONS

Introduction (HWM 345)

1. What are the main types of keyboard music in the later Baroque period? How do these compare to the types of keyboard music practiced in the sixteenth century and in the early seventeenth century?

2. What are the main types of ensemble music in the later Baroque period? How do these compare to the main types of instrumental ensemble music practiced in the sixteenth century and in the early seventeenth century?

Organ Music (HWM 345–51, NAWM 71–72)

3. What were the components of a large Dutch or German organ around 1700?

4. What role did toccatas and chorale preludes play in the Protestant church?

Music to Study
    NAWM 71: Dieterich Buxtehude, Praeludium in E Major, BuxWV 141,
        prelude for organ (late seventeenth century)
      CD 5.12–16

5. How does Buxtehude's Praeludium in E (NAWM 71) fit the definition of a
late-seventeenth-century toccata or prelude given in HWM, pp. 346–48?
What types of texture and figuration does it use? How does it fall into sections?

6. The first fugal section of Buxtehude's Praeludium begins in m. 13. Taking
the subject to be eight beats long (from the second beat of m. 13 to the
downbeat of m. 15), list here the measure and staff (right-hand [top], left-
hand [middle], and pedal [bottom]) of each entrance of the subject. (Note:
The last one is somewhat disguised, and then the fugue blends into the following toccata section.)

measure	staff	measure	staff
1. _____	_____	8. _____	_____
2. _____	_____	9. _____	_____
3. _____	_____	10. _____	_____
4. _____	_____	11. _____	_____
5. _____	_____	12. _____	_____
6. _____	_____	13. _____	_____
7. _____	_____		

7. The passages between statements of the fugue subject, when the subject is not sounding, are called *episodes*. (Practically speaking, a passage is usually not considered an episode unless it is at least a measure long, which here is four beats.) Below, list where each episode of at least four beats begins (the beat after the subject concludes) and how many beats long each episode is.

begins in measure	number of beats	begins in measure	number of beats
_____	_____	_____	_____
_____	_____		

What does the longest episode take from the theme, and how does it treat this idea?

8. What are the advantages and disadvantages of Pythagorean tuning, meantone temperament, and equal temperament for keyboard music?

9. What types of organ composition in the late seventeenth and early eighteenth centuries were based on chorales? In each type, how was the chorale treated?

Music to Study
> **NAWM 72:** Dieterich Buxtehude, *Danket dem Herrn,* BuxWV 181, chorale
> variations (late seventeenth century)
> CD 5.17–19

10. How does Buxtehude treat the chorale melody in his variations on *Danket dem Herrn* (NAWM 72)? What other material does he introduce, and how does he treat it?

11. How does organ music in Italy, Spain, and France differ from that in northern Germany during the late seventeenth and early eighteenth centuries?

Harpsichord and Clavichord Music (HWM 351–56, NAWM 73)

12. What four dances are typically part of the German keyboard suite, and in what order? What are the meter, relative speed (fast or slow), nation of origin, and character of each?

dance	meter	speed	nation of origin	other characteristics
_____	____	_____	_____	_____
_____	____	_____	_____	_____
_____	____	_____	_____	_____
_____	____	_____	_____	_____

What other movements might be part of a German suite?

Music to Study
  NAWM 73: François Couperin, *Vingt-cinquième ordre* (Twenty-fifth Order), keyboard suite (1730)
    73a: *La Visionaire* (The Dreamer)   CD 5.20–21
    73b: *La Misterieuse* (The Mysterious One)
                                                CD 5.22
    73c: *La Monflambert*   CD 5.23 (Concise 2.33)
    73d: *La Muse victorieuse* (The Victorious Muse)
                                                CD 5.24 (Concise 2.34)
    73e: *Les Ombres errantes* (The Roving Shadows)
                                                CD 5.25

13. In what sense is *La Visionaire* (NAWM 73a) "a French overture," as it is described in HWM, p. 354?

14. What elements of *La Misterieuse* (NAWM 73b) suggest that it is an allemande? What in *La Monflambert* (NAWM 73c) suggests that it is a gigue?

15. What are the names of the following *agréments* in the upper melody of *La Misterieuse,* and how is each one played? (Hint: See HWM, pp. 354–55.)

    first measure, second note (*E*)

    first measure, notes 6–7 (*A–B*)

    measure 25, fifth note (*A*)

Ensemble Music (HWM 356–69, NAWM 74–75)

16. What two main types of sonata began to be distinguished after about 1660? Describe each type as practiced by Corelli.

17. What was the most common instrumentation for sonatas in the late seventeenth century? What was a sonata in this instrumentation called?

Music to Study
> **NAWM 74:** Giovanni Legrenzi, *La Raspona,* trio sonata (published 1655)
>   CD 5.26–27
> **NAWM 75:** Arcangelo Corelli, Trio Sonata in D Major, Op. 3, No. 2 (published 1689)

1. Grave	CD 5.28
2. Allegro	CD 5.29
3. Adagio	CD 5.30 (Concise 2.35)
4. Allegro	CD 5.31–32 (Concise 2.36–37)

18. In what ways are the violin melodies in Legrenzi's *La Raspona* (NAWM 74) idiomatic for instruments and unlike seventeenth-century vocal style?

19. How many sections are there in Legrenzi's *La Raspona,* where does each begin, and how are they distinguished from each other?

---

20. *La Raspona* is modal, not tonal. The absence of a key signature suggests the Mixolydian mode on G, not G major, and three aspects of the harmony confirm this. (1) The note *F* is quite common, as are the chords D minor and F major; these appear frequently in pieces in the Mixolydian mode but seldom in pieces in G major. (2) The music modulates more often and more prominently to C (IV) than to D (V); the reverse would be true for pieces in G major. (3) Several passages move harmonically up the circle of fifths in sequence; tonal pieces often feature sequences that move *down* the circle of fifths (as in the chord progression vi–ii–V–I), but motion up the circle of fifths contradicts the strong sense of direction characteristic of tonal music.

For each of these three characteristics, find the evidence in the piece to support the statement that *La Raspona* is modal, not tonal. List below the evidence you find, including measure numbers as appropriate.

21. Using the modal *La Raspona* as a point of comparison, what characteristics of the first movement of Corelli's Trio Sonata in D major, Op. 3, No. 2 (NAWM 75) mark it as a tonal rather than as a modal work? "Tonal" here means that the music follows the common practice of major-minor tonality. (Hint: Look again at each characteristic listed in the previous question, and see if the reverse is true in the Corelli.)

22. Corelli's trio sonatas are marked by sequences and by suspensions, especially chains of suspensions in sequence. For each technique, indicate by measure numbers two passages in Corelli's sonata in which it is prominent.

  sequence   _____ _____

  chain of suspensions _____ _____

  How do these techniques lend these passages a sense of forward momentum toward the next cadence?

23. Is Corelli's Op. 3, No. 2 a church sonata or a chamber sonata? What traits mark it as this type of sonata?

24. In what ways are Corelli's solo violin sonatas like his trio sonatas, and in what ways are they different?

25. How did Baroque musicians regard ornamentation of written melodies?

26. Describe the two main ways of ornamenting a melody in the Baroque period.

27. Why did Couperin seek to unite the French and Italian styles of instrumental music? Which composers did he invoke as representatives of each style?

28. What is a *collegium musicum*? What are *Stadtpfeifer*? Where and when was each of these institutions active?

29. What is the difference between *chamber music* and *orchestral music*? In the seventeenth century, what kinds of pieces might have been played by either type of ensemble?

30. Describe the *orchestral suite* of about 1690–1740 and its components.

31. Name and describe the three main types of *concertos* composed around 1700. How were Baroque principles of contrast embodied in each of them?

32. How many movements does a typical concerto by Giuseppe Torelli have, and what is the relative tempo of each movement?

33. Describe *ritornello form* as used by Torelli. How does this form embody the Baroque interest in contrast, and how does it draw contrasting parts into a unified whole?

TERMS TO KNOW

Terms Related to Keyboard Music

registration (on an organ)
fugue
exposition, episode (in fugue)
subject, answer (in fugue)
meantone temperament
equal temperament
chorale variations (or partita)
chorale fantasia

chorale prelude
theme and variations
suite (or partita)
allemande, courante, sarabande,
  gigue
clavecinist
ordre

Terms Related to Ensemble Music

sonata da chiesa
sonata da camera
trio sonata
solo sonata
sequences (in Baroque music)
cadenza
collegium musicum
Stadtpfeifer
chamber music, orchestral
  music

orchestral suite (or ouverture)
orchestral concerto
concerto grosso
solo concerto
concertino, concerto grosso
tutti, ripieno
ritornello form
ritornello

NAMES TO KNOW

Elisabeth-Claude Jacquet de la
  Guerre
François Couperin
L'Art de toucher le clavecin

Arcangelo Corelli
Francesco Geminiani
The Art of Playing on the Violin
Giuseppe Torelli

REVIEW QUESTIONS

1. Make a time-line for the pieces, composers, and treatises discussed in this chapter.

2. Name the varieties of keyboard music being composed in the late seventeenth and early eighteenth centuries. Name and briefly describe an example for as many of these genres as you can.

3. What functions did keyboard music serve in the late seventeenth and early eighteenth centuries? Name the functions for as many genres as you can.

4. As a review of this and previous chapters, trace the evolution of keyboard music from ca. 1500 to ca. 1700.

5. Name the varieties of ensemble music composed in the late seventeenth and early eighteenth centuries. Name and briefly describe an example for as many of these varieties as you can.

6. What functions did ensemble music serve in the late seventeenth and early eighteenth centuries? Name the functions for as many genres as you can.

7. As a review of this and previous chapters, trace the development of music for instrumental chamber ensembles from ca. 1500 to ca. 1700.

8. What characteristics distinguish tonal music from modal music in the seventeenth century? What makes Legrenzi's *La Raspona* (NAWM 74) modal, and what makes Corelli's Trio Sonata, Op. 3, No. 2 (NAWM 75) tonal? Couperin's *La Visionaire* (NAWM 73a) has a tonal center of E flat and a key signature of two flats, suggesting it might be in a transposed Lydian mode; what elements in the music make clear that it is actually in E-flat major and is tonal, not modal?

9. What did Corelli and Torelli contribute to the development of instrumental ensemble music?

MUSIC IN THE EARLY EIGHTEENTH CENTURY

12

CHAPTER OBJECTIVES

After you complete the reading, study of the music, and study questions for this chapter, you should be able to

1. summarize the careers, describe the musical styles, and name and describe some of the most significant works by each of four major composers of the early eighteenth century: Antonio Vivaldi, Jean-Philippe Rameau, Johann Sebastian Bach, and George Frideric Handel;
2. compare the music of each to that of his predecessors and contemporaries; and
3. explain the historical significance of each of these composers.

CHAPTER OUTLINE

I. Background (HWM 373–75)

Between 1720 and 1750, high Baroque styles competed with simpler, more songful music. Musical life in Paris embraced both and included French and Italian music. Venice had several opera companies, and public and private groups sponsored elaborate church and festival music.

II. Antonio Vivaldi (HWM 375–80, NAWM 76–77)

A. Vivaldi's Career

Antonio Vivaldi (1678–1741), nicknamed "il prete rosso" (the red-headed priest), was trained as a musican and priest. He was music director, teacher, conductor, and composer at the *Pio Ospedale della Pietà* in Venice, a home and school for orphaned or abandoned girls. Music was an important part of the curriculum, and the concerts at the Pietà were well attended. At this time, there were no musical "classics," and audiences expected new music each season. Vivaldi composed quickly and always for a specific occasion and group of performers, writing concertos, oratorios, and church music for the Pietà and 49 operas for theaters in Venice and other cities. About 500 of his concertos survive, along with about 90 sonatas and many operas and religious works.

B. The Vocal Works

Vivaldi is best known today as an instrumental composer, but was also successful and prolific as a composer of church music and of opera.

C. The Concertos

Vivaldi's concertos are marked by clear forms, memorable melodies, rhythmic energy, and masterful contrasts of sonority and texture. Two-thirds are for solo with orchestra, usually violin, but also cello, flute, or bassoon. Others feature two soloists or a concertino group of which one or two members are the main soloists. The soloist in the fast movements is a real virtuoso, standing apart from the orchestra as a singer does in an opera. Most Vivaldi concertos are in three movements, with fast outer movements in ritornello form and a slow aria-like middle movement in a closely related key. In Vivaldi's hands ritornello form is infinitely variable, not at all a rigid scheme. Vivaldi's *sinfonias* mark him as a founder of the Classic-era symphony. Some of his works are programmatic, such as the four concertos in *The Four Seasons.*   **Music: NAWM 76–77**

D. Vivaldi's Influence

Vivaldi had a strong influence on other composers, including J. S. Bach, who arranged several of Vivaldi's concertos for keyboard.

III. Jean-Philippe Rameau (HWM 380–86, NAWM 78)

A. Rameau's Career

Jean-Philippe Rameau (1683–1764) was the foremost French composer of the eighteenth century. He had a unique career, becoming known first as a theorist and only later as a composer and writing his major works late in life. His early training and positions were as an organist. His *Traité de l'harmonie* (Treatise on Harmony, 1722) made his reputation as a theorist, but he had difficulty establishing himself as a composer.

B. La Pouplinière

In 1731, Rameau became organist, conductor, and composer for Alexandre-Jean-Joseph Le Riche de la Pouplinière, a rich nobleman and tax collector and an avid patron of music. With the aid of his patron, Rameau wrote numerous operas and opera-ballets that were produced in Paris. His operas secured his reputation as a composer, but they also inspired a debate between his devotées (the Ramists) and those who attacked him as a subverter of the tradition of Lully (the Lullists).

C. Rameau's Theoretical Works

Rameau sought to put music theory on a solid acoustical basis. He was the first to write a theory of tonal music (or functional harmony), as opposed to modal music, and all subsequent tonal theory is derived in some measure from his work. He posited the chord as the basic unit in music; derived it from the overtone series; suggested that a chord maintained its identity and its original root even when inverted; and established the tonic, dominant, and subdominant chords as the pillars of harmony and related all other chords to them.

D. Musical Style

French interest in spectacle is exemplified in Rameau's *Les Indes galantes* (The Gallant Indies, 1735), an opera-ballet in four acts set in exotic locales in Asia and North and South America. Rameau's operas are like Lully's in using dramatic declamation, mixing recitatives with airs, choruses, and instrumental interludes, and including long divertissements. But his style is quite different. Rameau believed that melody was rooted in harmony; his melodies often are triadic, they plainly reveal their underlying harmony, and much of Rameau's expressivity comes from his use of harmonic dissonance and modulation. His overtures expanded on the Lully model, and later he adapted the Italian three-movement sinfonia. His airs, like those of other French composers, are restrained in comparison to Italian arias, while his choruses are effective and his instrumental interludes remarkable in their ability to depict scenes. His clavecin pieces recall those of Couperin. **Music: NAWM 78**

E. Summary

Rameau was typical of French artists of his time in combining clarity and elegance with a talent for depiction. Like his contemporary Voltaire, he was a philosopher as well as a creator.

IV. Johann Sebastian Bach (HWM 386–87)

Johann Sebastian Bach (1685–1750) was not the most famous composer of his time but has become so in the last two centuries. He was born in Eisenach into a family of professional musicians and was trained by his father and elder brother. He blended German, French, and Italian styles, which he learned by copying and arranging music by leading composers of each region. He served as church organist at Arnstadt (1703–7) and Mühlhausen (1707–8), court organist and concertmaster for the duke of *Weimar* (1708–17), music director for a prince in *Cöthen* (1717–23), and cantor of *St. Thomas Church and School* in *Leipzig* (1723–50), writing music for his immediate use in each post.

V. Bach's Instrumental Music (HWM 387–96, NAWM 79–80)

A. The Organ Works

Bach's first positions were as an organist, and his first major works were for organ. His early works were influenced by Buxtehude. At Weimar, he arranged Vivaldi concertos for keyboard, learned the Italian style, and adopted ritornello form and other Vivaldi traits in his own works. From Italian, French, and German elements he forged his own style.

B. The Preludes and Fugues

Some of Bach's organ toccatas intersperse fugue and toccata sections, but more common are works with separate fugues. Some fugues have more than one subject and more than one section. Most of Bach's important organ preludes and fugues date from his Weimar years, and many use elements from the Italian concerto. **Music: NAWM 79**

C. Bach's Trio Sonatas

Bach adapted the Italian trio sonata to the organ in his six trio sonatas for organ solo, composed in Leipzig.

D. The Chorale Preludes

Bach wrote about 170 chorale settings for organ, using all current types of setting. His *Orgelbüchlein* (Little Organ Book), compiled at Weimar and Cöthen, contains short chorale preludes that state the chorale once, usually in the soprano, accompanied with counterpoint or embellished. In some chorale preludes, visual images in the chorale texts are suggested by appropriate figures in the accompaniment. In addition to their practical use for church services, Bach also intended these chorale preludes as teaching pieces for organists. Bach dedicated the *Orgelbüchlein* and many other works to the glory of God and made no distinction between sacred and secular music. He also made three later compilations of chorale settings for organ; these settings are longer and more varied in type than his earlier ones.   **Music: NAWM 80**

E. The Harpsichord and Clavichord Music

Bach wrote in all genres of harpsichord and clavichord music of his era. Most of these works were written at Cöthen or Leipzig, and they show the intermingling of Italian, French, and German elements in his music.

F. The Toccatas

Bach wrote several notable toccatas for harpsichord or clavichord.

G. *The Well-Tempered Keyboard*

Bach's best-known work for harpsichord or clavichord is *The Well-Tempered Keyboard* (Book I, 1722; Book II, ca. 1740), two cycles of twenty-four preludes and fugues in all twelve major and minor keys in rising chromatic order from C to B. Both sets demonstrate the usability of all keys with equal or near-equal temperament. Book I is a teaching manual in offering diverse technical challenges to the player, exemplifying numerous genres and forms in the preludes, and using a variety of approaches in the fugues. Book II includes pieces from many different periods in Bach's life.

H. The Harpsichord Suites

Bach wrote three sets of six suites each: the English Suites (Weimar, ca. 1715), the French Suites (Cöthen, 1722–25), and the six Partitas (1726–31). All contain the standard four dances with additional dances after the sarabande, and the English Suites begin with preludes. He also wrote keyboard works that imitate the French overture and Italian concerto.

I. *Goldberg* Variations

The *Goldberg Variations* (published 1741 or 1742) is a set of thirty variations on a sarabande. Every third variation is a canon; the interval of imitation grows from a unison in variation 3 to a ninth in variation 27. The last variation is a quodlibet incorporating two popular songs of the time, followed by a reprise of the theme. The noncanonic variations are of many types.

J. Works for Solo Violin and Cello

Bach wrote six sonatas and partitas for unaccompanied violin, six suites for cello alone, and a partita for solo flute. These works suggest a polyphonic texture by using multiple stops or jumping back and forth between implied independent lines.

K. Ensemble Sonatas

Bach wrote sets of sonatas for violin and harpsichord, viola da gamba and harpsichord, and flute and harpsichord. Most have four movements in the pattern slow–fast–slow–fast, like a sonata da chiesa, and are like trio sonatas, with the right hand of the harpischord acting as the other solo instrument while the left hand supplies the continuo.

L. Concertos

Bach composed a set of six concertos for the Margrave of Brandenburg in 1721 (the *Brandenburg Concertos*). These follow Italian models but expand the form. He also wrote violin concertos and was perhaps the first to write or arrange concertos for one or more harpsichords and orchestra. He reworked several chamber and orchestral works as cantata movements.

M. The Orchestral Suites

Bach's four orchestral suites (ouvertures) are sprightly and appealing.

N. Other Works

Two works are surveys of musical possibilities. *A Musical Offering* (1747) is based on a theme by King Frederick the Great of Prussia, on which Bach improvised while visiting the king; the finished work shows the possibilities of the theme by setting it in a trio sonata, two ricercares, and ten canons. *The Art of Fugue* (1749–50) sums up the fugue in a series of eighteen canons and fugues of increasing complexity, all based on the same subject.

VI. Bach's Vocal Music (HWM 396–405, NAWM 81–82)

A. Bach at Leipzig

As cantor in Leipzig, Bach was a city employee. He oversaw the music at St. Thomas and St. Nicholas churches and taught Latin and music in the St. Thomas school. Each Sunday, he directed a cantata, alternating between the two churches. The service also included a motet, a Lutheran Mass (Kyrie and Gloria), and chorales, using a choir of at least twelve singers (three for each part). The cantatas were accompanied by an orchestra of eighteen to twenty-four players drawn from the school, town musicians, and the university's collegium musicum.

B. The Church Cantatas

The cantata followed the Gospel reading in the liturgy and often was related in subject. Bach composed four complete cycles of cantatas for the church year (1723–29), plus cantatas for various occasions such as weddings. About 200 cantatas survive, representing a variety of forms and approaches.

C. Neumeister Cantatas

Bach set five cantata texts by Erdmann Neumeister and was influenced by his combination of chorale verses, Bible passages, and new poetry. In his cantatas, Bach frequently combined secular genres such as French overture, recitative, and da capo aria with chorale settings.

D. Chorale Cantatas

Bach's cantatas use chorales in various ways. He often based the opening chorus on a chorale and ended with the same chorale in simple four-part harmony, with independent solos and duets and sometimes a chorale setting in between. For example, *Wachet auf, ruft uns die Stimme* BWV 140 sets the first verse of the chorale in an elaborate chorus, the second for tenor solo, and the third in simple harmonization; in between each chorale verse and the next are a recitative and duet whose words and music are not derived from the chorale.   **Music: NAWM 81**

E. Secular Cantatas

Bach wrote secular cantatas for various occasions. In some he experimented with the new operatic style. He reworked some movements for church cantatas.

F. Motets

A *motet* in Bach's time was a sacred choral work, usually in contrapuntal style, without obligatory instrumental accompaniment. His six surviving motets were written for special occasions, and some use chorale texts or tunes. Bach also wrote a Magnificat and the *Christmas Oratorio,* a set of six cantatas for the Christmas and Epiphany season with the Bible story in recitative, and with arias and chorales that comment on the story.

G. Passions

Bach's *St. John Passion* (1724) and *St. Matthew Passion* (1727) are settings of the Passion story from the Gospels of John and Matthew, respectively, that were performed during Good Friday services. In both, the Bible story is narrated by the tenor soloist in recitative, with characters played by other soloists and the crowd by the chorus, and chorales, recitatives, and arias are interpolated as commentary on the story. All these elements but the chorale derive from opera.

H. Mass in B Minor

Bach's Mass in B Minor was assembled in 1747–49 from existing and some newly composed movements. It includes styles from stile antico and cantus firmus to the modern galant style. Bach may have intended it as a universal statement of religious feeling.   **Music: NAWM 82**

I. Summary

Even before his death, Bach's music was seen as old-fashioned in comparison to the newer, more tuneful style of contemporary Italian opera. His music was known to relatively few in the latter eighteenth century, then gradually revived in the nineteenth. His blending of styles, genres, and forms and the balance in his music between harmony, melody, and counterpoint and between expressivity and technique have helped to make Bach seem in retrospect the greatest musician of his age.

VII. George Frideric Handel (HWM 405–17, NAWM 83–84)

George Frideric Handel (1685–1759) was a truly international composer. He was the first composer to be remembered by all later generations and to have his music performed in a continuous tradition down to the present.

A. Handel's Career

Handel was born in Halle and studied organ and composition. In 1703 he moved to Hamburg, where he wrote his first opera. In 1706, he went to Italy, where he associated with the leading composers and patrons of music, including Corelli, Alessandro Scarlatti, and Domenico Scarlatti. He composed several cantatas, an oratorio, and an opera and solidified his command of the Italian style.

B. Handel in London

In 1710, Handel was named music director for the elector of Hanover, who in 1714 was crowned King George I of England. Handel preceded his patron to London, first going there in 1710, and quickly established himself as a composer of Italian opera. Throughout the 1720s, Handel composed operas for the *Royal Academy of Music*. After that company failed, he formed his own company to produce operas. When rising costs and falling interest made the opera no longer viable in 1739, Handel turned to oratorios in English, which could be performed in a concert hall without expensive Italian singers, sets, or costumes, and which attracted a broader audience. The oratorios gave him a great and enduring popularity in England.

C. Suites and Sonatas

Handel's instrumental music includes three sets of concertos for harpsichord or organ, two collections of harpsichord suites, and numerous solo sonatas and trio sonatas in a style influenced by Corelli.

D. The Concertos

Handel's most significant instrumental works are for orchestra, including the suites *Water Music* (1717) and *Music for the Royal Fireworks* (1749), six concertos for winds and strings, and twelve concerti grossi. Corelli is the main influence on the concertos, which follow the sonata da chiesa format (slow–fast–slow–fast) and only rarely feature extensive or virtuosic solo playing.

E. The Operas

Handel's operas were among the most successful of his time and were produced in Germany and Italy as well as England. The plots are freely adapted from history and literature, and the music consists mainly of recitatives to forward the action and arias that reflect on the characters' feelings, using a variety of aria types. His later operas adopt the light melodic style then current in Italy.   **Music: NAWM 83**

F. The Oratorios

Handel's English oratorios constitute a new genre, a blend of operatic recitative and aria with elements from the English masque and choral anthem, the German historia, and French and ancient Greek drama. The oratorios were in English and often used Old Testament stories, which appealed to a broader audience than the Italian language and historical or mythological plots of opera. They were written for the concert hall, not for church, and some are on mythological or allegorical subjects rather than religious ones. The prominence of the chorus in his oratorios is indebted to choral music in both Germany and England.

G. Choral Style

Handel's choruses often comment on the action, as in a Greek drama or German Passion. At other times, the chorus participates in the action. In his choruses and elsewhere, Handel often borrowed and reworked material from his own music and from other composers. Borrowing, transcribing, and reworking were universally accepted practices. When Handel borrowed, he "repaid with interest," using the borrowed material in new and more ingenious ways. Handel often uses musical figures to depict images in the text or convey a feeling. His choral style was simpler and less contrapuntal than Bach's, but perhaps more dramatic in his use of contrasting textures.   **Music: NAWM 84**

H. Summary

Handel was the first composer whose music endured after his death in an unbroken tradition of performance, particularly in his oratorios. His music's simpler texture, emphasis on melody, grandiose choruses, interest in contrast, and appeal to middle-class audiences suited the taste of the late eighteenth century and laid the foundation for his permanent place in the repertoire.

STUDY QUESTIONS

Background (HWM 373–75)

1. Describe the role of and conditions for music in Paris and Venice in the early eighteenth century.

2. What does Charles Burney's report on Venetian opera (HWM, p. 375) indicate about the stature of opera singers in the early eighteenth century?

Antonio Vivaldi (HWM 375–80, NAWM 76–77)

3. In which city and for what institution did Vivaldi work for most of his career? Describe the institution's purpose, the role of music in it, and Vivaldi's role.

4. What was the eighteenth-century attitude toward new music? How did this attitude affect Vivaldi?

5. In Vivaldi's concertos, which instruments does he favor as soloists?

6. What is the typical pattern of movements in Vivaldi's concertos, including the number of movements and their tempo, forms, and key relationships?

Music to Study
   NAWM 76: Antonio Vivaldi, Concerto Grosso in G minor, Op. 3, No. 2 (published 1712), excerpts
      76a: Adagio e spiccato (first movement)   CD 5.33
      76b: Allegro (second movement)   CD 5.34–40 (Concise 2.38–44)
   NAWM 77: Antonio Vivaldi, Concerto for Violin and Orchestra, Op. 9, No. 2, RV 345 (published 1728), Largo (second movement) CD 5.41

7. How does Vivaldi treat texture and contrasts of texture in his concertos? How is this exemplified in the concerto movements in NAWM 76 and 77?

8. How are dissonances treated in the first movement of Vivaldi's Op. 3, No. 2 (NAWM 76a)? (For example, how are they prepared, how are they resolved, and how do they work together with the harmony?) How does this compare to the treatment of dissonance in a work of the early sixteenth century such as Josquin's *De profundis clamavi ad te* (NAWM 33) and to a work of the early seventeenth century such as Monteverdi's *Cruda Amarilli* (NAWM 53)? How do the dissonances in Vivaldi's concerto reinforce the tonality?

9. Chart the form of the second movement of Vivaldi's Op. 3, No. 2 (NAWM 76b) by completing the table below. Use the abbreviations "Rit" for ritornello, "Epi" for the solo episodes, and letters for the melodic material as it returns. (See the discussion of ritornello form in chapter 11 if needed, and the discussion of this work in HWM and NAWM.)

Before you begin, what is the relationship between b and c in the table below?

Beginning measure	Section	Tutti or soloists	Melodic material	Key
14	Rit	Tutti	a	g minor
17	↓	↓	b	↓
20	↓	↓	c	↓
23	Epi	Soloists	d	↓

10. What characteristics of the mid- to late-eighteenth-century Classic style are already present in Vivaldi's music? Which of these characteristics do you find in the slow movement from Op. 9, No. 2 (NAWM 77)?

Jean-Philippe Rameau (HWM 380–86, NAWM 78)

11. Briefly trace Rameau's career. What were his various occupations? How did he earn a living? What (and who) made it possible for him to write operas and opera-ballets?

12. What were Rameau's contributions to the theory of music?

Music to Study

NAWM 78: Jean-Philippe Rameau, *Hippolyte et Aricie,* opera (1733), Act IV, Scene 1, *Ah! faut-il*
CD 5.42 (Concise 2.45)

13. At the opening of Act IV of Rameau's *Hippolyte et Aricie,* the noble young man Hippolyte is alone in the woods, banished from home, and despairing. How does Rameau use harmony, melody, rhythm, and choice of instrument in the instrumental prelude (NAWM 78, mm. 1–13) to convey his situation and mood? In particular, what suggests that he is in despair? in a rural setting? alone?

14. Diagram the form of this excerpt by completing the table below. Label sections in recitative "recit." and all other melodic material by letter; label modulatory sections "mod." and sections in stable keys by the key. (Note that the vocal line is in alto clef.)

Beginning measure	Singer or orchestra	Melodic material	Key
1	orchestra	A	a minor
4	↓	B	mod. to C
9	↓	C	mod.
11	↓	D	e minor
14	singer	A	a minor

How would you describe this form? How does it reflect Hippolyte's emotions?

15. How does this excerpt compare with the scene from Lully's *Armide* in NAWM 68b? How are Rameau's approach and style similar to Lully's, and how are they different? What is the role of dissonance in each excerpt?

Johann Sebastian Bach (HWM 386–87)

16. How did Bach learn music? How did he absorb the Italian style?

17. Where did Bach work, and when? What were his duties in each position? How did his employment affect the music he composed?

Bach's Instrumental Music (HWM 387–96, NAWM 79–80)

18. What types of organ works did Bach write? For each type, what are its main characteristics, and when during his career did Bach write organ works of this kind?

19. What collections of his organ works did Bach compile, and what was the aim and focus of each collection?

Music to Study
    NAWM 79: Johann Sebastian Bach, Praeludium et Fuga in A minor, BWV
        543, for organ (1710s?)
        CD 5.43–44 (Concise 2.46–47)

20. Diagram the form of the fugue in Bach's Praeludium et Fuga in A minor
    (NAWM 79) by completing the chart below. Indicate each appearance of
    the subject and each episode; show the staff on which each entrance of the
    subject appears by "top," "middle," or "pedal" (bottom); and give the im-
    plied key of each entrance of the subject and its relation to the tonic, a
    minor. The first four entrances of the subject comprise the exposition of the
    fugue, as each of the four fugal voices enters in turn. Several entrances of
    the subject are disguised through embellishment of the opening few notes.
    Note that the piece ends with a free toccata section after the last entrance of
    the subject in the tonic.

Beginning measure	Subject or episode	Staff	Key	Relation of key to tonic a minor
1	subject	top	a minor	i
6	subject	top	e minor	v
11	episode			
15	subject	middle	a minor	i
20	episode			
26	subject	pedal	e minor	v

21. In what ways does the form of Bach's fugue resemble the ritornello form of Vivaldi's concertos?

22. In what ways do the melodies in both the fugue and the prelude show the influence of Italian violin style? Use the solo violin portions of Vivaldi's Op. 3, No. 2, second movement (NAWM 76b) for comparison.

23. How does this Bach fugue compare to the first fugal section of Buxtehude's Praeludium in E Major (NAWM 71) in form and in other respects? (See chapter 11, study questions 6 and 7.)

24. How does Bach's prelude compare to the opening section and other toccata-like passages in Buxtehude's prelude (mm. 1–12, 48–59, etc.)?

25. Based on the comparisons you have made above, write a brief summary of how Bach's prelude and fugue blends North German and Italian influences.

Music to Study
> **NAWM 80:** Johann Sebastian Bach, *Durch Adams Fall,* BWV 637, cho-
> rale prelude from the *Orgelbüchlein* (ca. 1716–23)
> 80a: Chorale melody   not on recordings
> 80b: Bach setting   CD 5.45

26. How does Bach employ musical imagery in his chorale prelude on *Durch Adams Fall* (NAWM 80b) to convey the images in the chorale text?

27. What types of pieces did Bach write for harpsichord or clavichord? What are the characteristics of each type of piece?

28. When was *The Well-Tempered Keyboard* written? What does it contain, and how is it ordered? What are the characteristics of this collection?

29. Describe the *Goldberg* Variations. How is this work structured?

30. What types of chamber music and orchestral music did Bach write? Where were most of his works of this type written?

31. What are *A Musical Offering* and *The Art of Fugue*? When was each written, and what does each contain?

Bach's Vocal Music (HWM 396–405, NAWM 81–82)

32. What were Bach's duties as Cantor of St. Thomas and Music Director of Leipzig?

33. What kinds of musicians (and how many of each) did Bach have available for performing cantatas in Leipzig?

34. Where in the liturgy was the cantata performed? How did its subject matter relate to the rest of the liturgy?

Music to Study
  NAWM 81: Johann Sebastian Bach, *Wachet auf, ruft uns die Stimme,* BWV
       140, cantata (1731)
  1: Chorus, *Wachet auf*   CD 6.1–5 (Concise 2.48–52)
  2: Tenor recitative, *Er kommt*   CD 6.6
  3: Duet for soprano and bass, *Wann kömmst du, mein Heil?*
                                             CD 6.7
  4: Chorale, *Zion hört die Wächter singen* CD 6.8
  5: Bass recitative, *So geh' herein zu mir*   CD 6.9
  6: Duet for soprano and bass, *Mein Freund ist mein!*
                                             CD 6.10–11
  7: Chorale, *Gloria sei dir gesungen*   CD 6.12

35. In Bach's cantata *Wachet auf, ruft uns die Stimme* (NAWM 81), which texts
    are newly written? Which are from existing sources, and from where do they
    derive? How does the structure of this text relate to the cantata texts by
    Erdmann Neumeister, and how is it typical of Bach?

36. For which day of the church calendar did Bach write this cantata? How do
    the words of the preexisting and added texts relate to the Gospel reading for
    the day?

37. How are the words and images of the text reflected in the music, particularly
    in the opening chorus and the two duets?

38. The second recitative is accompanied by strings. What does that symbolize? Why are the third and sixth movements written as duets?

39. How is the chorale tune *Wachet auf, ruft uns die Stimme* used in the first movement?

    In the fourth movement?

    In the final movement?

40. What Italian forms and textures, adapted from opera, concerto, and sonata, are used in this cantata, and in which movements? What other Italian traits do you notice?

41. How do Bach's secular cantatas relate to his church cantatas?

42. What did the word *motet* mean in Bach's time? How was a motet different from a cantata?

43. In the *St. Matthew Passion,* where do the words come from?

What are the functions of the tenor soloist? of the chorus?

In what respects do Bach's passions resemble operas?

Music to Study
NAWM 82: Johann Sebastian Bach, Mass in B Minor, BWV 232 (1747–49), excerpts from the Credo (*Symbolum Nicenum*)
82a: Bass Aria, *Et in Spiritum sanctum Dominum*
                                   CD 6.13–14
82b: Chorus, *Confiteor*   CD 6.15–17
82c: Chorus, *Et expecto resurrectionem*   CD 6.18–19

44. In what ways does the music of *Et in Spiritum sanctum Dominum* from Bach's Mass in B Minor (NAWM 82a) show traces of an up-to-date style?

45. Where and in which voices does the cantus firmus (a Gregorian chant) appear in the chorus *Confiteor* (NAWM 82b)? How is it treated?

46. In addition to cantus-firmus technique, what other Renaissance traits can you find in the *Confiteor*? What Baroque traits make clear that this is a Baroque composition in *stile antico,* not a work from the Renaissance?

47. How does Bach use changes of musical style and texture to convey the sense of the words "and I await the resurrection of the dead"? (Note that these words are set twice, in two different styles, to bring out two different aspects of their meaning.)

48. On what grounds was Bach's music criticized during his lifetime?

49. What are some of the factors that have led later centuries to regard him as the greatest composer of his era?

George Frideric Handel (HWM 405–17, NAWM 83–84)

50. By the age of 25, where had Handel lived, studied, and worked? What genres had he tried? What influences had he absorbed? What made his music international in style?

51. In which genre was Handel first successful in England? Why and when did his success fade? Which new genre supplanted the first and allowed Handel to continue his career?

Music to Study
   NAWM 83: George Frideric Handel, *Giulio Cesare* (Julius Caesar), opera, (1724), Act II, Scene 2, Recitative and Aria, *V'adoro pupille*
   CD 6.20–24 (Concise 2.53–57)

52. Baroque opera plots typically centered on love, drew on history or mythology, created opportunities for spectacle, and often involved secrecy and disguise. How are these elements reflected in the libretto for Handel's *Giulio Cesare,* particularly in this excerpt (NAWM 83)?

---

53. A typical operatic scene involved recitative followed by a da capo aria with an opening ritornello, first section, contrasting middle section, and reprise of the first section. In this excerpt, how does Handel modify this series of events? How do these changes aid the drama? How do they make the final statement of the aria's first section more than a conventional repetition?

54. What elements does Handel draw from instrumental forms, including the concerto and the dance? How does he use these elements expressively?

55. Compare this aria to Scarlatti's *Mi rivedi* (NAWM 66) from *Griselda,* written just three years earlier. How does Handel's aria resemble Scarlatti's, and how does it differ?

56. What national styles and genres did Handel combine in his oratorios?

57. What language is used in Handel's oratorios? How did the language and the subject matter influence the success of his oratorios? Where were they performed, and for whom?

58. How did Handel use the chorus in his oratorios? How does this differ from the practice of Italian composers? What traditions influenced Handel in this regard?

Music to Study
   NAWM 84: George Frideric Handel, *Saul,* oratorio (1739), Act II, Scene 10
      84a: Accompagnato, *The Time at length is come*
                                    CD 6.25
      84b: Recitative, *Where is the Son of Jesse?*
                                    CD 6.26
      84c: Chorus, *O fatal Consequence of Rage*
                                    CD 6.27–29

59. In the recitatives from *Saul* (NAWM 84a and 84b), how does the music portray Saul's rage?

60. In the following chorus (NAWM 84c), how does Handel use musical symbolism to convey the meaning of the text?

61. In this chorus, where does Handel use fugue? What other textures does he employ? Why do you think he used these elements in this way? How do the changes of texture delineate the form and convey the meaning of the text?

62. Where does Handel employ exact or near-exact repetition of entire passages? Chart the form of this chorus, noting these repetitions and the changes of texture you observed in the previous question.

63. How does Handel's choral writing in this work differ from that of Bach in the choral movements from his cantata *Wachet auf* (NAWM 81) and Mass in B Minor (NAWM 82), and how is it similar?

64. What is the role of borrowing in Handel's music? What is borrowed in these excerpts from *Saul,* and how is this material treated? How does this example illustrate the comment in HWM, p. 416, that when Handel borrowed he "repaid with interest"?

65. What characteristics of Handel's music helped to earn it a lasting place in the repertoire of music?

NAMES TO KNOW

Antonio Vivaldi
Pio Ospedale della Pietà
The Four Seasons
Jean-Philippe Rameau
Traité de l'harmonie
Les Indes galantes
Johann Sebastian Bach
Weimar
Cöthen
Leipzig
St. Thomas Church and School
Orgelbüchlein
The Well-Tempered Keyboard

Goldberg Variations
Brandenburg Concertos
A Musical Offering
The Art of Fugue
Wachet auf, ruft uns die Stimme,
  BWV 140
Christmas Oratorio
St. John and *St. Matthew Passions*
Mass in B Minor
George Frideric Handel
Royal Academy of Music
Water Music
Music for the Royal Fireworks

REVIEW QUESTIONS

1. Add to the time-line you made for the previous chapter the *Traité de l'harmonie* and the composers and pieces discussed in this chapter.

2. Describe the career and music of Vivaldi. How did the circumstances of his employment relate to the music he wrote? How are his concertos similar to those of Corelli and Torelli, and how are they different?

3. How do the operas and opera-ballets of Rameau continue the tradition of Lully, and how do they differ?

4. Trace Bach's career and explain how the circumstances of his training and employment influenced the types of music he wrote and the styles he drew upon.

5. What did Bach's instrumental music draw from German sources? What did he draw from Italian models and from French models? Describe a piece by Bach that blends at least two of these national traditions, and explain how Bach combined elements from different nations into a coherent idiom.

6. Adopting the aesthetic position of Johann Adolph Scheibe (as quoted on p. 405 of HWM), describe what is wrong with Bach's Praeludium et Fuga in A minor (NAWM 79) and the opening chorus of his cantata *Wachet auf, ruft uns die Stimme* (NAWM 81).

7. Trace Handel's career and explain how his experiences as a composer influenced the types of music he wrote and the styles he drew upon.

8. Compare and contrast the musical ideals and styles of Bach and Handel, focusing particularly on their vocal music.

9. What was the historical significance of Vivaldi, Rameau, Bach, and Handel? What trends did each absorb, what influence did each have on later music, and in what respects did each achieve a unique musical idiom?

SONATA, SYMPHONY, AND OPERA IN THE EARLY CLASSIC PERIOD

13

CHAPTER OBJECTIVES

After you complete the reading, study of the music, and study questions for this chapter, you should be able to

1. briefly describe the intellectual, cultural, and aesthetic background to music in the Classic period;
2. name and describe the principal musical styles and genres current in the second half of the eighteenth century;
3. diagram and describe some of the principal forms used in this period, particularly aria forms, sonata form, and concerto first-movement form;
4. use and define terms appropriate to this period; and
5. name some of the composers of the period, describe their individual styles, and identify some of their works.

CHAPTER OUTLINE

I. The Enlightenment (HWM 420–32)

A. Enlightenment Thought

The *Enlightenment* was an intellectual movement that valued reason and asserted the equal rights of every person. Enlightenment ideas led to advances in science and were incorporated into the American Declaration of Independence and Constitution.

B. Aspects of Eighteenth-Century Life

Eighteenth-century politics, culture, and the arts were cosmopolitan. Music that combined features of many nations and thus was universally pleasing was considered to be the best music. Musicians from across Western Europe were active in Vienna, enabling a mixing of styles and the synthesis of the "Viennese" Classical style. Humanitarian ideals were strong. A growing middle-class public pursued learning and the arts and helped to support the new institutions of the public concert of music and the journal of musical news and criticism. As more people could afford instruments, had time to play them, and learned to read music, the market grew for published music that amateurs could play and enjoy.

C. Eighteenth-Century Musical Taste
The latter eighteenth century preferred music that was universal in appeal, both noble and entertaining, expressive yet tasteful, natural, simple, and immediately pleasing. Yet old and new styles, and national and cosmopolitan styles, coexisted and competed. (The entire eighteenth century can be viewed as a long argument about taste, as the attacks on Rameau and Bach discussed in chapter 12 might suggest.)

D. Terminology in the Classic Period
Several terms have been used for the styles current in the mid- to late eighteenth century. *Classic* was applied retrospectively to the music of Haydn and Mozart and has been expanded to include the entire period of about 1730–1815. The term *galant* (elegant) was used in the eighteenth century to describe the new style that featured melody in clearly marked phrases over light accompaniment. *Empfindsamkeit* (sentimentality) was a related style that added surprising harmonies, chromaticism, nervous rhythms, and speech-like melody, especially in slow movements.

E. New Concepts of Melody, Harmony, and Form
In contrast to the constant spinning-out of Baroque music, the new styles were *periodic*, divided into short *phrases* that combine into *periods* and larger sections, like the phrases, sentences, and paragraphs of a speech (a characteristic called *periodicity*). Phrases were related through motivic similarities or through *antecedent-consequent* pairing. Harmonic change slowed down. In compensation, the texture was animated through devices such as the *Alberti bass*. Composers no longer sought to express one single *affection* in a movement, as in many Baroque works, and instead explored contrasting styles and feelings within a single movement.

Sidebar: **Musical Rhetoric in Depth**
Several writers on music compared it to rhetoric, the art of giving an oration. The most thorough guide for beginning composers was that by *Heinrich Christoph Koch* (1749–1816), who showed how to assemble short units into phrases, phrases into periods, and periods into larger forms.

II. Opera (HWM 432–40, NAWM 85–86)

Many style elements of the Classic era derive from Italian opera, especially comic opera.

A. Early Italian Comic Opera
An *opera buffa* was a full-length Italian comic opera, sung throughout, with several characters. Plots usually counterpoised comic and serious characters, and librettos often used dialect, especially for the comic characters. Dialogue was set in rapid *recitative* with keyboard accompaniment, and the *arias* used short tuneful phrases and periods over simple harmonies. The same style is typical of the *intermezzo*, a series of short comic scenes performed between acts of a serious opera or play. Plots revolved around a small number of characters drawn from ordinary life. The best-known intermezzo is *La serva padrona* (The Maid as Mistress, 1733) by *Giovanni Battista Pergolesi* (1710–1736).   **Music: NAWM 85**

B. *Opera Seria*

An *opera seria* was a serious opera on a heroic classical theme without comic interludes. The form was codified by the librettist *Pietro Metastasio* (1698–1782), whose librettos were set hundreds of times. His plots show a conflict of passions resolved through heroism or renunciation. His aim was to promote morality and show examples of enlightened rulers. The action proceeds in recitative, and characters comment on the situation in arias.

C. The Aria

The standard aria form was the *da capo aria,* featuring a large A section with two vocal statements surrounded by orchestral ritornellos based on the main melodic material; a shorter contrasting B section with a new text and in a related key, usually without orchestral interludes; and a reprise of the A section. This format was sometimes shortened by omitting the first ritornello on the reprise of A, or by expanding the A section and omitting the rest. Singers were expected to ornament the written line as appropriate, especially on the reprise. Some composers treated the da capo format too rigidly, and some singers added excessive embellishment or forced composers to alter or substitute arias to suit their voices. But the da capo form evolved over time, as composers introduced a greater variety of moods and figuration and borrowed formal ideas from the sonata and concerto.

D. Hasse

Johann Adolph Hasse (1699–1783), music director at the Saxon court in Dresden, was the leading composer of opera seria around the middle of the eighteenth century. He wrote in an Italianate style marked by careful accentuation of the text and melodies grateful to the voice. *Faustina Bordoni* (1700-1781), Hasse's wife, was one of the century's leading sopranos. She performed all over Europe, including for Handel in London, and sang in most of Hasse's operas.   **Music: NAWM 86**

III. Comic Opera (HWM 440–45, NAWM 87)

A. General

Comic opera grew in importance after 1760. Each nation or region had its own type, using the national language and musical styles. Comic opera exercised an important influence on later music, in its style, its preference for naturalness, and its use of national characteristics.

B. Italy

From the middle of the century, Italian operas—sometimes called *dramma giocoso* (cheerful drama) as well as opera buffa—incorporated serious and sentimental plots as well as comic ones. The *ensemble finale* at the end of an act brought the characters on stage one by one until all were singing together.

C. France

French *opéra comique* began as a show with *vaudevilles* (popular songs) or other simple tunes. The 1752 visit to Paris of an Italian troupe performing *La serva padrona* instigated a debate that became known as the *Querelle des bouffons* (Quarrel of the comic actors), about the relative merits of traditional French opera and the new comic Italian opera. This inspired French composers to write comic operas in a style that mixed vaudevilles with original airs called *ariettes,* and by 1770 all the music was newly composed. Although the Italians set dialogue as recitative, the French and other national comic opera traditions used spoken dialogue. Later in the century, opéra comique was also used for serious subjects.

D. England
Ballad opera became popular in England after *John Gay*'s success with *The Beggar's Opera* (1728), a mostly spoken play that sets new words to popular tunes and parodies operatic conventions.   **Music: NAWM 87**

E. Germany
The success of ballad opera inspired a revival of *Singspiel* in Germany. Some Singspiel tunes became so popular that they have virtually become folksongs. In the north, Singspiel merged with native opera in the early nineteenth century; in the south, it was influenced by Italian comic opera.

IV. Beginnings of Opera Reform (HWM 445–47, NAWM 88)

A. Italian Reformers
Niccolò Jommelli (1714–1774) and *Tommaso Traetta* (1727–1779) sought to make opera more natural, expressive, flexible, and varied, in part by uniting French and Italian traits.

B. Gluck
Christoph Willibald Gluck (1714–1787), working with librettist *Raniero de Calzabigi* (1714–1795), reformed opera by making music once again subservient to the poetry and the plot. As exemplified in *Orfeo ed Euridice* (1762) and *Alceste* (1767), Gluck's reform opera blends Italian, German, and French traits; emphasizes the chorus, dance, and orchestra and links them closely with the dramatic action; restrains the freedom of singers to indulge in vocal display; lessens the gulf between aria and recitative; and unifies a variety of elements in extended scenes. Gluck brought his new style to Paris and French opera with *Iphigénie en Aulide* in 1774 and scored a great triumph. Gluck's new style was praised and imitated, establishing a new tradition of serious opera in French.   **Music: NAWM 88**

V. Song and Church Music (HWM 447–50)

A. The Lied
Many collections of *Lieder* (German songs) were published in the eighteenth century, intended primarily for amateur performance at home. Composition of lieder was centered in Berlin. Most lieder were syllabic settings in folksong style with simple accompaniment and were strophic in form.

B. Church Music
Masses, motets, and especially oratorios increasingly adopted operatic style in the late eighteenth century, although some composers continued to use older styles or mixed old and modern elements. English composers often wrote in Baroque styles, partly due to the continuing influence of Handel.

VI. Instrumental Music: Sonata, Symphony, and Concerto (HWM 450–60, NAWM 89–93)

A. Domenico Scarlatti

Domenico Scarlatti (1685–1757), son of Alessandro Scarlatti, worked in Portugal and Spain. His 555 harpsichord *sonatas* are typically in one movement (or two paired movements) in rounded binary form: two sections, both repeated, the first moving from tonic to dominant or relative major, the second modulating back to the tonic and ending with a tonic-key restatement of the material that closed the first section. Rather than themes, Scarlatti often presents a series of strongly etched ideas that plainly project the key through pedal points, arpeggiation, and other figuration. **Music: NAWM 89**

B. The Sonata

Sonatas, symphonies, and chamber works typically have three or four movements in related keys and contrasting moods and tempos. What we now call *sonata form* (or *first-movement form*) was described by Koch as an expanded binary form in two sections, both normally repeated. The first has one large period comprising a series of four or five extended phrases, the first two presenting the movement's main idea in the tonic, the third phrase modulating to the dominant (or relative major in a minor key), and the others in the new key. The second section has two large periods, the first modulating back to the tonic, and the second shaped like the first section but transposing the latter part into the tonic. Theorists writing in the 1830s and later divided the form not into two parts, but into three, corresponding to Koch's three periods: (1) an *exposition* with a first theme in the tonic, a modulatory transition, and second and closing themes in the dominant or relative major; (2) a *development* section that modulates to new keys and may fragment and vary the themes; and (3) a *recapitulation,* restating all three themes in the tonic, sometimes followed by a *coda.* Koch's description emphasizes the tonal plan, whereas the later (and now more familiar) description emphasizes the thematic content.

C. Early Symphonies and Chamber Music

In the early eighteenth century, the Italian opera overture, called *sinfonia,* had three movements in the order fast–slow–fast, ending with a dance. These were also performed independently, and composers such as *Giovanni Battista Sammartini* (1701–1775) began to write *symphonies* for concert performance, works in the same form that were not attached to operas. Sammartini's first movements often follow Koch's description of the form and present a number of ideas.   **Music: NAWM 90**

D. The *Empfindsam* Style

The *empfindsam* style, originated by Italians, is closely identified with *Carl Philipp Emanuel Bach* (1714–88), the most famous of Johann Sebastian Bach's sons and a very influential composer in his own right. He wrote in many genres but is best known for his keyboard music, especially several sets of sonatas, marked by constantly changing rhythms, sudden surprising changes of harmony, texture, or dynamic level, and instrumental evocations of recitative and aria. His *Essay on the True Art of Playing Keyboard Instruments* is an important source for ornamentation and performance practice.   **Music: NAWM 91**

E. German Symphonic Composers

Composers at *Mannheim,* Vienna, and Berlin were the leading German composers of symphonies at mid-century. The Mannheim orchestra, led by *Johann Stamitz* (1717–1757), was renowned for its virtuosity, dynamic range, and controlled crescendo. Viennese taste tended to pleasant lyricism and contrasting themes, while Berlin symphonists preferred less contrast and adopted a more serious tone marked by counterpoint and thematic development.   **Music: NAWM 92**

F. J. C. Bach

Johann Christian Bach (1735–1782), J. S. Bach's youngest son, studied and worked in Italy before going to London. There he had a successful career and met the young Mozart, on whom he had a profound influence. His *concertos* for piano or harpsichord and orchestra follow in their first movements a form that alternates orchestral ritornellos with solo episodes, as in the Baroque concerto, but also features the key structure and contrasting themes of sonata form.   **Music: NAWM 93**

G. Orchestral Music in France

Many publishers and composers were active in Paris. An important genre was the *symphonie concertante* for two or more soloists and orchestra.

H. The Symphony Orchestra

The orchestra of the Classic era was smaller than today's, with about twenty to thirty-five players, including strings, winds in pairs, horns, and harpsichord. The practice of basso continuo was gradually abandoned, and conducting duties passed from the harpsichordist to the leader of the violins. The winds, often used to double the strings and fill in harmonies, gained more independent roles late in the century. The *serenade* was a hybrid Viennese form combining aspects of the symphony and the concerto.

I. Chamber Music

Instrumental roles were unequal in chamber music, with the piano dominating any group it played with and the first violin dominating in string quartets.

VII. Summary (HWM 460)

The early Classic period saw many innovations, especially in comic opera. The desire to reach a wide and varied audience led to music, both vocal and instrumental, that was simple, natural, and easy to grasp. Its intelligibility made possible the increasing independence—and therefore ever greater significance—of instrumental music in the Classic period.

STUDY QUESTIONS

The Enlightenment (HWM 420–32)

1. What was the Enlightenment? How did the wider cultural climate of the eighteenth century affect music?

2. How did musical life change in response to growing public interest in music?

3. According to Johann Joachim Quantz (quoted in HWM, p. 424) and others in the late eighteenth century, what were the characteristics of the best music?

4. What distinguishes the stylistic tendencies known as the *galant* style and *Empfindsamkeit* from Baroque style, and from each other?

5. According to Johann Nikolaus Forkel (as quoted in HWM, p. 429), how is a piece of music like a speech?

6. According to Heinrich Christoph Koch, how is a melodic period put together from smaller units? How does this process resemble that of an orator making an argument?

Opera (HWM 432–40, NAWM 85–86)

7. What are the characteristics of an *opera buffa*? How does the aria by Leonardo Vinci excerpted in HWM, pp. 433–34, exemplify some of these characteristics? How does an *intermezzo* differ from an opera buffa, and how are the two genres similar?

Music to Study
   NAWM 85: Giovanni Battista Pergolesi, *La serva padrona* (The Maid as Mistress), intermezzo (1733), excerpt
   Recitative: *Ah, quanto mi sta male*   CD 7.1–2 (Concise 3.1–2)
   Aria: *Son imbrogliato io*   CD 7.3–6 (Concise 3.3–6)

8. What is funny in Uberto's recitative soliloquy in this scene from Pergolesi's *La serva padrona* (NAWM 85)? How do his vocal line, the changes of harmony, and the interjections of the string orchestra convey yet parody his emotions?

---

9. How are repeated notes and phrases and sudden changes of texture and mood used in Uberto's aria *Son imbrogliato io* to create a comic flavor? What other humorous touches do you notice?

10. What are the characteristics of the *opera seria* libretto as established by Pietro Metastasio? What moral lessons did his operas aim to teach?

11. What are the musical characteristics of opera seria?

12. Describe and chart the typical form of an aria in an opera seria. What alterations in this form were made by some composers? What do the indications "da capo" and "dal segno" indicate to a performer?

Music to Study
> **NAWM 86:** Johann Adolph Hasse, *Cleofide,* opera seria (1731), Act II,
> Scene 9, *Digli ch'io son fedele*
> CD 7.7–11

13. Compare Cleofide's aria *Digli ch'io son fedele* (NAWM 86) to the standard da capo form you charted in question 12. Where does each section begin and end? In what respects does it follow this form? Where does it deviate?

14. Where does material from the opening ritornello (mm. 1–10) return later in the aria, either in the vocal statements or in later ritornellos, and how is it changed?

15. In what ways does the B section contrast with the A section?

16. What characteristics of the new Classic-era styles (as described in the first section of this chapter) appear in the music of both sections of this aria?

17. How does the embellished melody in the upper staff of Example 13.5 in HWM (p. 439) relate to the written melody in the staff below? It was transcribed (by King Frederick the Great of Prussia, no less) from a live performance. What can you deduce from this example about how singers embellished arias in opera seria? (You may also consider the embellishments added by Emma Kirkby in the performance that accompanies NAWM.)

Comic Opera (HWM 440–45, NAWM 87)

18. What was the importance of comic opera for later developments in music of the late eighteenth and nineteenth centuries?

19. How did Italian comic opera change after the mid-eighteenth century?

20. What are the distinctive features of comic opera in France, England, and Germany in the eighteenth century?

Music to Study
  NAWM 87: John Gay (librettist and arranger), *The Beggar's Opera,* ballad
          opera (1728), Scenes 11–13
  CD 7.12–16

21. In what ways does *The Beggar's Opera* (NAWM 87) differ from Italian opera and French comic opera? What is this type of musical theater called? What did John Gay do to "compose" this work?

Beginnings of Opera Reform (HWM 445–47, NAWM 88)

22. How did Jommelli and Traetta seek to reform Italian opera in the 1750s?

Music to Study

> **NAWM 88:** Christoph Willibald Gluck, *Orfeo ed Euridice,* opera (1762), excerpt from Act II, Scene 1
>
> CD 7.17–21

23. What operatic reforms did Gluck introduce in *Orfeo ed Euridice* and *Alceste*? How are those reforms apparent in the scene from *Orfeo ed Euridice* in NAWM 88? How does this differ from the other operas we have seen so far in this chapter, and particularly from Hasse's *Cleofide* as composed and performed?

24. What dramatic musical devices does Gluck use to set the scene and portray the characters (the Furies in the underworld, and Orfeo, who has come down to bring back his beloved Euridice)?

Song and Church Music (HWM 447–50)

25. In what ways is J. F. Reichardt's *Erlkönig* (excerpted in HWM, pp. 448–49) typical of eighteenth-century *Lieder*?

26. How was eighteenth-century church music influenced by opera? Where did older styles continue, and why?

Instrumental Music: Sonata, Symphony, and Concerto (HWM 450–60, NAWM 89–93)

Music to Study
   NAWM 89: Domenico Scarlatti, Sonata in D Major, K. 119 (ca. 1749)
      CD 7.22–23 (Concise 3.7–8)

27. In the first half of his Sonata in D Major, K. 119 (NAWM 89), Scarlatti introduces a string of ideas with contrasting figuration and function. For each of the following passages (indicated by measure numbers), indicate the implied key when it is tonally stable or "mod." if it changes key, and briefly describe the figuration (e.g., arpeggios, scales, octaves, repeated notes or chords, trills, stepwise melody, or a combination of these).

    Some of these ideas return in the second half, and some do not. For those that do, indicate where in the second half they begin and in what key they are presented.

Mm.	Implied key	Figuration	Where in 2nd half?
a. 1–5	_____	_____	_____
b. 6–13	_____	_____	_____
c. 14–17	_____	_____	_____
d. 18–35	_____	_____	_____
e. 36–55	_____	_____	_____
f. 56–64	_____	_____	_____
g. 65–72	_____	_____	_____
d'. 73–95	_____	_____	_____

28. Based on your answers above, write a brief description of the form and the kinds of figuration Scarlatti uses in his sonata.

29. In this sonata, how does Scarlatti imitate the sound or style of Spanish guitar music?

30. Diagram a sonata first movement as described by Koch. Then diagram it as described by theorists of the 1830s and later, and show the correspondences between these two descriptions by indicating which elements of the later description parallel particular elements of the Koch model.

31. What role did opera play in the birth of the independent symphony?

Music to Study
NAWM 90: Giovanni Battista Sammartini, Symphony in F Major, No. 32 (ca. 1744), Presto (first movement)
    CD 7.24–26
NAWM 91: Carl Philipp Emanuel Bach, Sonata in A Major, H. 186, Wq. 55/4 (1765), Poco adagio (second movement)
    CD 7.27–28 (Concise 3.9–10)
NAWM 92: Johann Wenzel Anton Stamitz, Sinfonia a 8 in E-flat Major (published 1758), Allegro assai (first movement)
    CD 7.29–33

32. How does the first movement of Sammartini's Symphony in F Major, No. 32 (NAWM 90) compare in style to the aria from Pergolesi's *La serva padrona* in NAWM 85 or the Scarlatti sonata in NAWM 89? What elements does it have in common with each?

33. Which description of sonata form or first-movement form applies better to this movement, that of Koch or that of theorists of the 1830s and later? Why?

34. In the second movement of C. P. E. Bach's Sonata in A Major (NAWM 91), where does the opening material repeat, and in what key? What else is repeated, and in what key does it appear each time? Diagram the form of the piece. How does it relate to sonata form, and how is it different?

35. What elements of this movement are typical of Bach's expressive style?

36. Compare the melodic writing in this sonata movement to the vocal embellishments added to Hasse's aria from *Cleofide* (NAWM 86), as shown in the upper staff of Example 13.5 in HWM (p. 439; see also question 17, above). Although the melodic range in the sonata is too wide for a singer, how does Bach create the sense in this instrumental work of a vocal melody, like a slow aria?

37. What are some of the techniques that made the Mannheim orchestra famous, and how are they used in the Stamitz symphony movement in NAWM 92?

38. Compare this movement to the Sammartini symphony movement in NAWM 90. How are they similar, and how are they different, in instrumentation, style, and form?

Music to Study
> **NAWM 93:** Johann Christian Bach, Concerto for Harpsichord or Piano and Strings in E-flat Major, Op. 7, No. 5 (ca. 1770), Allegro di molto (first movement)
> CD 7.34–46

39. What traits mark Johann Christian Bach's keyboard concerto movement (NAWM 93) as *galant* in style?

40. How does this differ from the *empfindsam* style of C. P. E. Bach's sonata movement (NAWM 91)?

41. In the J. C. Bach concerto movement, what elements of the opening orchestral ritornello return later, and where does each return?

42. When the keyboard solo enters, what new material does it introduce? Which of these new ideas are later recapitulated, and where?

43. How does the form of this first movement resemble a Baroque concerto movement in ritornello form (in which the orchestra interjects transposed and often abbreviated statements of the ritornello between solo episodes), and how does it differ? How does it resemble a Classic-era movement in sonata form, and how does it differ?

44. How large was the orchestra in the Classic period? In addition to the strings, what other instruments were members, about how many of each were there, and what was their function? Who conducted, and how did this differ from earlier practice?

Summary (HWM 460)

45. How did the new Classic-era styles make possible the rise of instrumental music to a position of unprecedented prominence and prestige?

TERMS TO KNOW

Terms Reviewed from Earlier Chapters

affection
recitative
aria

da capo aria
Singspiel

Terms Related to the Classic Style

the Enlightenment
Classic period, Classic style
galant style
Empfindsamkeit (*empfindsam* style)

phrase, period
periodic, periodicity
antecedent and consequent phrases
Alberti bass

Terms Related to Opera and Vocal Music

opera buffa
intermezzo (eighteenth-century)
opera seria
dramma giocoso
ensemble finale
opéra comique

vaudeville
querelle des bouffons
ariette
ballad opera
lied (eighteenth-century)

Terms Related to Instrumental Music

keyboard sonata (late-eighteenth-century)
sonata form (first-movement form)
exposition, development, recapitulation, coda

sinfonia (eighteenth-century)
symphony
concerto (late-eighteenth-century)
symphonie concertante
serenade

NAMES TO KNOW

Names Related to the Classic Style and to Opera

Heinrich Christoph Koch
La serva padrona
Giovanni Battista Pergolesi
Pietro Metastasio
Johann Adolph Hasse
Faustina Bordoni
John Gay
The Beggar's Opera

Nicolò Jommelli
Tommaso Traetta
Christoph Willibald Gluck
Raniero de Calzabigi
Orfeo ed Euridice
Alceste
Iphigénie en Aulide

Names Related to Instrumental Music

Domenico Scarlatti   Mannheim
Giovanni Battista Sammartini   Johann Stamitz
Carl Philipp Emanuel Bach   Johann Christian Bach
Essay on the True Art of Playing
  Keyboard Instruments

REVIEW QUESTIONS

1. Make a time-line for the pieces, composers, librettists, and theorists discussed in this chapter.

2. How did the Enlightenment ideals of reason and naturalness help to create a climate in which the older Baroque styles were replaced by simpler, immediately pleasing styles with wide appeal?

3. What parallels did eighteenth-century writers observe between music and rhetoric? How do Cleofide's aria (NAWM 86) or C. P. E. Bach's sonata movement (NAWM 91) resemble a speech?

4. Describe the varieties of comic opera in the eighteenth century in Italy, France, England, and Germany.

5. What did comic opera styles contribute to instrumental music in the second half of the eighteenth century?

6. Trace the development of serious opera from the 1730s to the 1770s, including both opera seria and reform opera. How does the reform opera of Gluck and Calzabigi differ from opera seria?

7. If you are familiar with jazz improvisation on a standard tune, what comparisons can you draw between jazz performance and the improvised embellishments in opera seria, as exemplified in Example 13.5 in HWM (p. 439)? What is similar about the two approaches to improvisation, and what differs?

8. What social functions were served by the various instrumental works discussed in this chapter? Which were concert pieces, and which were for amateur or private performance?

9. What elements of form do all or most of the instrumental works in NAWM 89–93 have in common? (For instance, do they all have similar harmonic plans? Do they repeat musical material in similar ways? What elements does each share with the standard model of sonata form?) Can you distill from these five movements a short list of formal strategies that are shared by all or most of these pieces?

THE LATE EIGHTEENTH CENTURY: HAYDN AND MOZART

14

CHAPTER OBJECTIVES

After you complete the reading, study of the music, and study questions for this chapter, you should be able to

1. trace the careers of Haydn and Mozart and the development of their musical idioms;
2. describe the principal genres and forms practiced by Haydn, Mozart, and their contemporaries; and
3. name several important works by each of these composers and describe some works by each in their mature styles.

CHAPTER OUTLINE

I. Introduction (HWM 465)

The greatest composers of the Classic era were *Franz Joseph Haydn* (1732–1809) and *Wolfgang Amadeus Mozart* (1756–1791). They were friends, influenced each other, and composed in many of the same genres and in closely related styles, yet their careers were strikingly different.

II. Franz Joseph Haydn (HWM 465–68)

Haydn learned music through lessons, experience as a choirboy, and studies in counterpoint and composition. He served Prince Paul Anton Esterházy from 1761; then, on the latter's death in 1762, *Prince Nicholas Esterházy* succeeded to the title and became Haydn's patron until the prince died in 1790. From 1766, the prince lived most of the year at his country estate, *Eszterháza*. Haydn's duties were to compose music at the prince's request, lead the 25-person orchestra in weekly concerts and operas, train singers, supervise the musicians, and keep the instruments in repair. He composed numerous chamber pieces with *baryton,* a string instrument the prince played. Writing so much music for immediate performance allowed Haydn to experiment and develop a fresh, effective style that made him the most popular composer in Europe. He also wrote music for publication and on commission. When Prince Nicholas died in

1790, his son Anton disbanded the orchestra and gave Haydn a pension. In 1791–92 and 1794–95, Haydn went to London, where he gave concerts for the impresario *Johann Peter Salomon* and wrote his last twelve symphonies. From 1795 he was again in Vienna as music director for Anton's son Prince Nicholas II with much lighter duties. His major works of this period are six Masses and two oratorios.

III. Haydn's Instrumental Music (HWM 468–85, NAWM 94–98)

A. Symphonic Form

Many early Haydn symphonies use the three-movement plan of the Italian opera sinfonia or have four movements in the order Andante, Allegro, Minuet, and Presto. Soon he adopted a standard pattern of four movements: Allegro, Andante, *Minuet and Trio,* and Allegro or Presto. The first movement is in sonata form, alternating harmonically stable and symmetrically phrased periods (the themes) with unstable transitions and developments. There may be a slow introduction. Haydn often repeats and alters the opening theme to lead into the transition, an orchestral tutti (passage for full orchestra) which modulates to the dominant or relative major. The second thematic section is lightly scored and may introduce a new theme or rework the opening idea, and the exposition closes with a cadential tutti. The development, which grew longer in his later symphonies, varies and recombines material from the exposition, changing keys and often taking sudden digressions. The recapitulation repeats all the themes in the tonic, sometimes altered, and often amplifies the transition and closing section. The slow movement provides a lyrical respite after the speed and strong contrasts of the first. The Minuet and Trio pairs two minuets, graceful triple-meter dances in rounded binary form, the second of which (the Trio) is more lightly scored and is followed by a return of the first, for an overall A B A form. The fourth movement is in sonata form or *rondo form* (in which a recurring theme alternates with episodes—for example, in the pattern A B A C A). It is faster and shorter than the first movement and is usually full of high spirits and surprises. Several of the symphonies have acquired names, few from the composer himself.

B. Early Symphonies

Haydn used themes that were readily broken up and recombined. Symphonies Nos. 6–8, titled *Le Matin, Le Midi,* and *Le Soir* (Morning, Noon, and Evening, 1761) have several unusual features.

C. The Symphonies of 1768–74

The symphonies of 1768–74 are longer and more serious than earlier symphonies and require the listener's close attention. The emotional, agitated, minor-key character of some has been linked to the slightly later literary movement *Sturm und Drang* (storm and stress, from the title of a 1776 play). Haydn introduces more startling dramatic contrasts, richer harmonies, more distant modulations, and more counterpoint. Increasingly, each symphony has unique features that mark it as an individual, as in the *Farewell* Symphony.

D. The Symphonies of 1774–88

After 1774, minor keys and experiments in form and expression give way to major keys, clarity, and wide appeal. The six Paris symphonies (Nos. 82–87) were commissioned for a concert series in Paris. In Symphonies Nos. 88–92, Haydn often begins with a slow introduction; uses contrasting second themes less often; features the winds more; and infuses the finale with counterpoint, increasing its weight without sacrificing popular appeal. **Music: NAWM 94–95**

E. The *London* Symphonies

Haydn wrote music to suit particular occasions, performers, and halls and to please both the expert and the untutored music lover. His *London* symphonies (Nos. 93–104) were aimed at the public, with greater tunefulness (including Slovenian and Croatian peasant tunes), more varied orchestration (including clarinets, trumpets, and timpani), and striking changes of key. First movements tend to focus on the first theme rather than introducing a contrasting second theme; the slow movements use theme and variation or a variant of sonata form; and the Minuet and Trio movements are faster and often humorous. The finales use sonata form, rondo form (usually in the pattern A B A C A or A B A C A B A), or a blend of the two (such as *sonata-rondo,* in which A functions as a sonata-form first theme, B the second theme, and C the development).   **Music: NAWM 96**

F. The Quartets up to 1781

Haydn's Opp. 17 (1771) and 20 (1772) collections established him as the first great master of the *string quartet.* The same movement types are used as in the symphony, although the minuet and trio may precede the slow movement. Three finales in Op. 20 are fugal. The Op. 33 quartets (1781) are lighter, with the minuet transformed into a *scherzo* (joke) through a fast tempo and witty hemiolas, syncopations, and rhythmic surprises. Quartets were intended primarily for amateurs to play for their own pleasure, and Haydn's playfulness must have added to the fun.   **NAWM 97**

G. The Quartets of 1785–90

The quartets of 1785–90 tend toward monothematic first movements and slow movements in theme and variation form.

H. The Last Quartets

Haydn's late quartets (1793–1803) are marked by widely ranging harmonies, stark contrasts of style, and many witty touches.   **Music: NAWM 98**

I. Keyboard Sonatas

Haydn's early keyboard sonatas are suitable for harpsichord, clavichord, or piano, but his later ones are intended for the piano. His piano sonatas generally develop in parallel with his symphonies and quartets.

IV. Haydn's Vocal Works (HWM 485–88)

A. Operas

Haydn wrote many operas, most of them Italian comic operas. They met with success but soon passed from the repertory and are now rarely heard.

B. Masses

Haydn's most important works for church were six late festive Masses (1796–1802) in symphonic style, with full orchestra, soloists, and chorus.

C. Oratorios

While in England, Haydn heard some of Handel's oratorios. His own late oratorios *Die Schöpfung* (The Creation, 1798) and *Die Jahreszeiten* (The Seasons, 1801), both on librettos by *Baron Gottfried van Swieten,* show Handel's influence.

V. Wolfgang Amadeus Mozart (HWM 488–95)

A. Early Life

Mozart was born in Salzburg, where his father Leopold Mozart served the archbishop as performer and composer. Wolfgang and his sister Marianne ("Nannerl") were child prodigies in performance (as was Wolfgang as improviser and composer), and Leopold took them on tour around Europe. Through touring, Mozart learned all styles of music then current in western Europe and imitated them in his own compositions. His mature works synthesize these various styles in music of unprecedented variety. His more than 600 works are identified by their number in the catalogue of his works by Ludwig von Köchel.

B. Early Works

Mozart's first teacher was his father. On tour in London, he met Johann Christian Bach, whose use of thematic contrast and infusion of Italian opera style into instrumental works became hallmarks of Mozart's style. Stays in Italy and Vienna resulted in strong influences from Italian opera and symphony and from Haydn and other Viennese composers.

C. The Salzburg Years

Mozart was in Salzburg for most of 1774–81 but sought a post elsewhere. His reputation as a composer was growing. He was commissioned to compose an opera seria for Munich.

D. Piano and Violin Sonatas

Mozart wrote numerous sonatas and variation sets for piano. The sonatas are varied in form, style, and content. Mozart's themes are usually graceful, singing melodies. In his early violin sonatas, the violin is an optional reinforcement of the melody in the piano, but by the late 1770s was a virtually equal partner.

E. Serenades and Divertimentos

Mozart wrote many serenades and *divertimentos,* pieces for background music or entertainment. They are scored for strings, strings and winds, or winds in pairs (if meant for outdoor performance).

F. Solo Concertos

Also dating from the Salzburg years are several violin concertos and piano concertos and the Symphonie Concertante.

VI. Mozart's Vienna Years (HWM 495–509, NAWM 99–100)

A. Mozart in Vienna

Mozart moved to Vienna in 1781, hoping to earn a living as a freelance pianist and composer. He met with great initial success but failed to find a permanent position, and his popularity and earnings later declined. His music struck a perfect balance between immediate universal appeal and the depth of feeling and technique that earned the respect of the learned. He was strongly influenced by Haydn and by Johann Sebastian Bach, whose music he discovered through Baron Gottfried van Swieten.

B. Piano Works

Among Mozart's most important piano works are the Fantasia and Sonata in C Minor, K. 475 and 457.

C. Chamber Works

In 1785 Mozart published six quartets dedicated to Haydn (known as the *Haydn quartets*). The fruit of long effort and much revision (unusual for Mozart, who normally wrote quickly and easily), they show his ability to absorb Haydn's techniques yet remain original.

D. The Vienna Symphonies

Mozart wrote only six symphonies after 1781, but they were longer and more substantial than their predecessors. Each is highly individual, but together they are characterized by striking openings, more difficult wind parts, more harmonic and contrapuntal complexity, weightier finales, and frequent witty and unexpected touches. These traits are exemplified in Symphony No. 41 in C Major (the *Jupiter,* 1788), whose finale combines its fugal first theme in counterpoint with five other motives.

E. Concertos for Piano and Orchestra

Mozart wrote seventeen piano concertos in Vienna for his own performances as a soloist, primarily during his first five years there. In them, as in all his music, he sought to please both the connoisseur and the less learned listener, although they challenge the best players. The first movements are like those of Johann Christian Bach's concertos in blending ritornello and sonata-form procedures. Before the final tutti, the orchestra pauses on a tonic six-four chord and the soloist plays a *cadenza.* Mozart's second movements are like slow arias, and the finales are rondos or sonata-rondos. **Music: NAWM 99**

F. Operas

In Vienna, Mozart composed a Singspiel, *Die Entführung as dem Serail* (The Abduction from the Harem, 1786); three Italian comic operas on librettos by *Lorenzo da Ponte* (1749–1838)—*Le nozze di Figaro* (The Marriage of Figaro, 1786), *Don Giovanni* (premiered at Prague in 1787), and *Così fan tutte* (Thus Do They All, 1790); an opera seria, less well known than the others (*La clemenza di Tito* or The Mercy of Titus, 1791); and a German opera, *Die Zauberflöte* (The Magic Flute, 1791). Unlike Gluck (and Monteverdi), Mozart thought that in opera the poetry should serve the music rather than the other way around. Mozart's music captured each character, and the ensembles showed them interacting in dramatic ways. *Don Giovanni* was the first work on the Don Juan theme to take the character seriously, resulting in characters and a drama of unprecedented depth. *Die Zauberflöte* mixes comedy with the humanistic imagery and symbolism of the Freemasons, and Mozart's music for it blends elements of opera seria, Singspiel, opera buffa, accompanied recitative, sacred choral style, and Baroque counterpoint.   **Music: NAWM 100**

G. Church Music

Mozart's Masses are written in the modern symphonic-operatic style, alternating chorus and soloists. His Requiem was unfinished at his death and was completed by his student and collaborator Franz Xaver Süssmayr.

VII. Epilogue (HWM 509)

Haydn and Mozart wrote in all major genres and represent the best music the Classic era produced. Yet there are many other composers who made significant contributions.

STUDY QUESTIONS

Introduction (HWM 465)

1. What are some significant differences between the careers of Haydn and Mozart? (See also the accounts of their careers throughout the chapter.)

Franz Joseph Haydn (HWM 465–68)

2. Who was Haydn's principal patron? What was Haydn required to do as part of his employment?

3. What other sources of income did Haydn have during his service with this patron?

4. Trace Haydn's career after 1790, including his sources of income and his major compositions.

Haydn's Instrumental Music (HWM 468–85, NAWM 94–98)

5. What are the standard four movements of a Haydn symphony, and what are the main characteristics of each?

6. What is *Sturm und Drang* style, and what are its typical features?

Music to Study
   NAWM 94: Franz Joseph Haydn, Symphony No. 56 in C Major, Hob. I:56
      (1774), Allegro di molto (first movement)
      CD 7.47–53 (Concise 3.11–17)
   NAWM 95: Franz Joseph Haydn, Symphony No. 92 in G Major (*Oxford*),
      Hob. I:92 (1789), Adagio cantabile (second movement)
      CD 7.54–57
   NAWM 96: Franz Joseph Haydn, Symphony No. 104 in D Major, Hob.
      I:104 (1795), Finale (fourth movement)
      CD 7.58–68

(Note on reading scores: Instruments like the horn and clarinet are written as they are fingered to allow players to move easily between different members of the same family. For instance, clarinets in A, in B♭, and in E♭ will all use the same fingering when they see a *C*, but the instrument will produce an *A*, a *B♭*, or an *E♭* respectively. In the eighteenth and nineteenth centuries, these "transposing instruments" were given in the score as they are notated for the player, which means the conductor or score-reader must transpose in the same way the instrument does to determine the pitch that will sound. In the latter two movements, Haydn uses horns in D, which sound a minor seventh lower than written—*D* when *C* is notated. In Symphony No. 104, he also uses trumpets in D, sounding a whole step higher, and clarinets in A, sounding a minor third lower—*A* when *C* is notated.)

7. In the first movement exposition of Haydn's Symphony No. 56 (NAWM 94), how are the following sections distinguished from each other? Mention these and other features you find significant: harmonic stability or instability; key (when stable); use of chromaticism; phrasing (clearly articulated or continuous and overlapping); dynamics; orchestration; and melodic content.

first theme area (mm. 1–28)

transition (mm. 29–52)

second theme area (mm. 53–67, with a contrasting extension in mm. 68–78)

closing group (mm. 79–99)

Notice how many different ways there are to follow the form. A listener may attend to any of these distinguishing features and will still be able to follow the course of the music clearly. This is one of the ways in which Classic-era music is notable for its intelligibility to a wide range of listeners.

8. In what measure does the recapitulation begin? _____

The recapitulation repeats material from the exposition, but with some changes. What is different in the recapitulation, in comparison to the exposition?

9. What happens in the development in terms of harmony and key?

   How are orchestration and dynamics used in the development?

   What ideas from the exposition are used in the development, where do they appear, and how are they changed from the exposition?

10. Chart the form of the slow movement of Haydn's Symphony No. 92 (NAWM 95), and give the key of each main section.

   How do the opening motives of the first two sections relate?

   What elements of both sections appear in the coda (mm. 94–111)?

11. Compare the melodic writing in this movement to the vocal embellishments added to Hasse's aria from *Cleofide* (NAWM 86 and Example 13.5 in HWM, p. 459) and to the melodic style in the slow movement from C. P. E. Bach's piano sonata (NAWM 91; see also chapter 13, questions 17 and 37). How does Haydn embellish his melodies?

12. How are the wind instruments used in this movement? How does this compare to the earlier Haydn symphony movement in NAWM 94?

13. What elements give the finale of Symphony No. 104 (NAWM 96) its popular character?

14. In what ways does the exposition of this sonata-form movement differ in form from the first movement of Haydn's Symphony No. 56 (NAWM 94)? How are these differences typical of Haydn's later symphonies?

15. What occurs in the development section of the Symphony No. 104 finale, in terms of harmonic plan; orchestration and dynamics; and use of material from the exposition? How does this compare to the development section of Haydn's Symphony No. 56, first movement (compare question 9, above)?

16. In the Symphony No. 104 finale, at the end of the recapitulation there is a long coda (mm. 265–334) instead of the expected closing material. What happens during this coda, in terms of harmonic plan; orchestration and dynamics; phrasing; and use of material from the exposition?

17. What characteristics of these three movements (NAWM 94–96) are typical of Haydn symphonies from the mid-1770s, late 1780s, and London period respectively?

No. 56, first movement (1774):

No. 92, second movement (1789):

No. 104, finale (1795):

18. String quartets were written primarily for amateurs to play for their own enjoyment. What aspects of Haydn's quartets were particularly well suited to give pleasure to the players themselves?

Music to Study

NAWM 97: Franz Joseph Haydn, String Quartet in E-flat Major, Op. 33, No. 2 (*The Joke*), Hob. III:38 (1781), Presto (fourth movement)
CD 8.1–6 (Concise 3.18–23)

NAWM 98: Franz Joseph Haydn, String Quartet in C Major, Op. 76, No. 3, Hob. III:77 (1797), Poco adagio, cantabile (second movement)
CD 8.7–11

19. The theme of a rondo is normally a little binary form with two repeated sections, often a rounded binary form (in which both sections end with the same music) in the pattern ‖: a :‖: b a :‖. This is true of the finale of Haydn's String Quartet in E-flat Major, Op. 33, No. 2 (NAWM 97), where the theme appears in mm. 1–36. In this theme, b (mm. 9–28) is much longer than a. What does Haydn do to extend b and prepare for the return of a?

20. In what measures does the theme reappear in its entirety, including both sections but without the repeat signs?

Where does it appear in varied or abridged form? What is changed?

How do the passages just before the return of the theme prepare for it?

21. This quartet acquired the nickname "The Joke" because of this movement. Describe what is witty or funny in this finale.

22. In the second movement of his String Quartet in C Major, Op. 76, No. 3 (NAWM 98), Haydn presents a series of variations on a tune that later became the Austrian and German national anthems. In each variation, how is the tune varied? How is the accompaniment changed?

variation I:

variation II:

variation III:

variation IV:

23. What elements in Haydn's keyboard music parallel his symphonies and quartets composed around the same time? Which of these elements made the piano more suitable than the harpsichord for playing his music?

Haydn's Vocal Works (HWM 485–88)

24. Briefly describe Haydn's late Masses and oratorios. What music influenced Haydn's music in each genre, and how is this influence evident?

Wolfgang Amadeus Mozart (HWM 488–95)

25. Describe Mozart's career and the influences on his music to 1781. Why was his music so diverse in style?

Mozart's Vienna Years (HWM 495–509, NAWM 99–100)

26. How did Mozart make a living in Vienna?

27. How did Mozart become acquainted with the music of Johann Sebastian Bach? How was he influenced by Bach's music?

28. What are the characteristics of the quartets and symphonies Mozart wrote in Vienna? How do they compare to Haydn's works in the same forms?

Music to Study
NAWM 99: Wolfgang Amadeus Mozart, Piano Concerto in A Major, K.
    488 (1786), Allegro (first movement)
   CD 8.12–27

29. In the first movement of Mozart's Piano Concerto in A Major (NAWM 99), which segments of the opening orchestral ritornello return later in the work, and where does each return? How is each segment varied on its return?

30. How does the form of this first movement resemble a Baroque concerto movement in ritornello form, how does it resemble a sonata-form first movement, and how does it differ from each? How does it compare in this regard with the first movement of J. C. Bach's concerto in NAWM 93 (see chapter 13, question 44)?

31. Describe Mozart's melodic style. How do his melodies compare those in Haydn's symphonies (NAWM 94–96)?

32. In a Classic-period concerto, what is a *cadenza*?

    Where does it fall in the form, and how is it prepared?

    The cadenza in NAWM 99 is Mozart's own. How would you describe it, in terms of melodic figuration, harmony, and treatment of the instrument?

33. What are Mozart's five best-known operas of his Vienna period, and what year was each premiered?

    _____   _____

    _____   _____

    _____   _____

    _____   _____

    _____   _____

34. In Mozart's view, what was the proper relationship between the words and the music in opera? How does this differ from Gluck's view (see HWM, pp. 446–47 and question 23 in chapter 13 above)? Why do you think Mozart felt this way?

Music to Study
> **NAWM 100:** Wolfgang Amadeus Mozart, *Don Giovanni,* K. 527, opera
> (1787), Act I, Scene 5
>> 100a: No. 3, Aria, *Ah chi mi dice mai,* and Recitative, *Chi è là?*
>> CD 8.28–30 (Concise 3.24–26)
>> 100b: No. 4, Aria: *Madamina! Il catalogo è questo*
>> CD 8.31–32 (Concise 3.27–28)

35. How does Mozart's music help to delineate the three characters and portray their feelings in *Ah chi mi dice mai* from *Don Giovanni* (NAWM 100a)?

36. In what ways does the form of this aria resemble sonata form? What element of sonata form does it omit?

37. In Leporello's "catalogue" aria (100b), how are the different characteristics of Don Giovanni's victims depicted in the music? That is, what musical means does Mozart use to depict the images in the text?

TERMS TO KNOW

baryton
Minuet and Trio
rondo form
Sturm und Drang
sonata-rondo

string quartet
scherzo
divertimento
cadenza

NAMES TO KNOW

Franz Joseph Haydn
Wolfgang Amadeus Mozart
Prince Nicholas Esterházy
Eszterháza
Johann Peter Salomon
Le Matin, Le Midi, and *Le Soir*
the *Farewell* Symphony
the *London* Symphonies
Die Schöpfung (The Creation)
Die Jahreszeiten (The Seasons)
Baron Gottfried van Swieten

Mozart's *Haydn* quartets
Jupiter symphony
Die Entführung aus dem Serail (The
    Abduction from the Harem)
Lorenzo da Ponte
Le nozze di Figaro (The Marriage of
    Figaro)
Don Giovanni
Così fan tutte (Thus Do They All)
Die Zauberflöte (The Magic Flute)

REVIEW QUESTIONS

1. Add Haydn, Mozart, and the major events and works discussed in this chapter to the time-line you made for chapter 13.

2. Compare the careers of Haydn and Mozart, including the circumstances of their lives and the genres and styles they cultivated. What are the main similarities between their careers, and what are the major differences?

3. Briefly describe each of the following genres as practiced by Mozart and Haydn in terms of form, style, content, and social function: symphony, string quartet, piano sonata, concerto, and comic opera.

4. Describe the principal characteristics of Haydn's mature style in his instrumental works. Use NAWM 94–98 as examples for your discussion, referring to and describing passages from them as appropriate.

5. Building on the previous question, what aspects of Haydn's style did Mozart absorb into his own? And in what ways does Mozart's mature music differ from that of Haydn? Use NAWM 99–100 and other works described in HWM as examples for your discussion, referring to and describing passages as appropriate.

LUDWIG VAN BEETHOVEN

15

CHAPTER OBJECTIVES

After you complete the reading, study of the music, and study questions for this chapter, you should be able to

1. briefly recount Beethoven's career and the circumstances of his life;
2. list the main characteristics of the music of each of his three periods; and
3. name several important works and describe at least one complete movement for each period.

CHAPTER OUTLINE

I. The Composer and His Music (HWM 513–16)

A. Background
Ludwig van Beethoven (1770–1827) was born in Bonn in northwest Germany and was taught music by his father and a local organist. In 1792, he went to Vienna and studied with Haydn and other composers. Building on the genres, styles, and conventions of the Classic period, he created highly individual works that brought him unprecedented success and became models for later composers, including nine symphonies, five piano concertos, sixteen string quartets, thirty-two piano sonatas, and many other orchestral, chamber, and vocal works. He was neither as prolific nor as speedy a composer as Haydn or Mozart, but took each piece through many drafts and revisions, as we can see in his surviving *sketchbooks*. Starting in his twenties, Beethoven gradually went deaf, writing movingly of his suffering in an 1802 letter called the *Heiligenstadt Testament*. His deafness tended to isolate him from society.

B. Beethoven's "Three Periods"
Beethoven's career is usually divided into *three periods*. In the first, to about 1802, he assimilated the musical language, genres, and styles of his time. In the second, ca. 1803–15, his works were more individual, longer, and grander than before. In the last period, ca. 1816–27, his music became more introspective (and often more difficult to play and understand).

II. First Period (HWM 516–22, NAWM 101–2)

A. Patrons

Beethoven was supported by aristocratic patrons. three of whom gave him an annuity to keep him in Vienna. He also sold his works to publishers, performed as a pianist, and taught piano. Thus he was able to make a living without being employed by a single patron, as Haydn had been.

B. The Piano Sonatas

Beethoven's piano sonatas follow Haydn's example but show individual features. Several traits of his piano style may be indebted to the sonatas of *Muzio Clementi* (1752–1832) and *Jan Ladislav Dussek* (1760–1812): economy of material, symphonic breadth, sudden changes of harmony, dynamics, texture, and mood, and certain kinds of pianistic figuration. **Music: NAWM 101–2**

C. Chamber Music

Beethoven's first six string quartets, Op. 18 (1798–1800), follow Haydn in motivic development and use of counterpoint but show Beethoven's individuality in their themes, surprising modulations and turns of phrase, and formal structure. Other chamber works of the first period include piano trios, violin sonatas, cello sonatas, and a septet for strings and winds.

D. First Symphony

Beethoven's First Symphony in C Major (1800) also follows the example of Haydn, but has a scherzo as the third movement and features long codas in the other movements.

E. The Second Symphony

Beethoven's Second Symphony in D Major (1802) is longer than previous symphonies, with more thematic material and long codas that develop the main ideas.

III. Second Period (HWM 522–33, NAWM 103)

A. Human Relations

By his early 30s, Beethoven was renowned as a pianist and composer, had many aristocratic patrons, and was sought after by publishers.

B. The *Eroica* Symphony

The Third Symphony (titled the *Eroica Symphony,* 1803), was unprecedented in length and complexity, with many unusual features. The first movement has a great number of melodic ideas, including an apparently "new theme" in the development, but almost all derive from the material presented near the beginning. Most novel is that the main theme is treated as a person in a drama, struggling and finally triumphing. The sketches show that many of the unusual features, such as the horn's "too-early" entrance at the recapitulation, were planned from early on. Beethoven first titled the work "Bonaparte," after Napoleon, but changed the title to *Sinfonia Eroica* (Heroic Symphony). The second movement is a funeral march that evokes the style of French Revolutionary marches and hymns. The third movement is a scherzo. The finale mixes variations on a theme from one of Beethoven's ballets with elements of fugue and march style. **Music: NAWM 103**

C. *Fidelio*
Links to the idealism of the French Revolution are also evident in Beethoven's one opera, *Fidelio* (1804–5, rev. 1806 and 1814), Leonore disguises herself as a man in order to free her husband from wrongful imprisonment. Beethoven revised the work repeatedly before it was a success.

D. The *Rasumovsky* Quartets
Beethoven's second set of string quartets was Op. 59 (1806), known as the *Rasumovsky quartets* because Beethoven dedicated them to Count Rasumovsky, Russian ambassador to Vienna. These three quartets are novel in style, and two movements include Russian themes.

E. The Fourth to Eighth Symphonies
Beethoven's Fourth and Fifth Symphonies project opposite moods: the Fourth in B-flat Major (1806) is jovial, while the *Fifth Symphony* in C Minor (1807–8) portrays struggle and final triumph. The Sixth Symphony in F Major, named the *Pastoral* (1808), is in five movements and evokes country scenes. The Seventh Symphony in A Major (1811–12) is expansive, while the Eighth in F Major (1812) is quite condensed. Beethoven also wrote several overtures, which resemble in form the first movement of a symphony (without the repetition of the exposition).

F. Piano Sonatas and Concertos
Many of Beethoven's piano sonatas show individual features. For example, the *Waldstein* Sonata in C Major, Op. 53 (1803–4), uses traditional forms with intense themes, unusual key relations, and strongly contrasting textures. His first three piano concertos belong to his first period and the Fourth in G Major (1805–6) and Fifth ("Emperor") in E-flat Major (1809) to his middle period, along with his one Violin Concerto (1806).

IV. Third Period (HWM 533–39, NAWM 104)

A. Career and Life
Although Beethoven was famous across Europe and well supported by patrons and publishers, his deafness led to greater social isolation. His music became more abstract and introspective, with extremes from the meditative to the grotesque conjoined in works that referred to classical conventions without being constrained by them.

B. Characteristics of Beethoven's Late Style
Beethoven's late compositions work out the full potential of themes and motives. The *Diabelli Variations, Op.* 120 (1819–23), do not simply embellish the theme as do earlier variations but rework material from it to create a new design, mood, and character in each variation. Several individual movements, especially slow movements, also use this kind of variation technique. Beethoven's late style is also marked by changes in other areas:

1. He creates a new sense of continuity by blurring phrase and section divisions and deemphasizing cadences.
2. He includes passages that have an improvisatory character or use instrumental recitative.
3. He often uses fugal textures in developments, and several movements or large sections are fugues.
4. He uses new sonorities, including wide spacings and unusually dense textures.
5. He often uses an unusual number of movements and unusual kinds of movements.

The *String Quartet in C-sharp Minor,* Op. 131 (1826), exemplifies all of these characteristics.　**Music: NAWM 104**

C. The *Missa solemnis*

The *Missa solemnis* (1819–23) or Mass in D is a grandiose work that recalls the choral style of Handel while resembling the symphonic conception and mix of chorus and soloists typical of Haydn's late Masses.

D. The Ninth Symphony

Beethoven's Ninth Symphony is longer than his others. Its finale is novel in recalling themes from the earlier movements and introducing soloists and chorus to sing stanzas from Friedrich von Schiller's *Ode to Joy.*

E. Beethoven and the Romantics

Beethoven's middle-period works were the most influential on later composers, particularly for their concept of music as a vehicle to express the composer's own feelings and experiences. (This was the most novel aspect of Beethoven's music; this idea became so influential that modern listeners often assume that this is what all composers have had in mind, when earlier composers sought only to convey the feelings in a text or represent the generalized affections.) Through this and his innovations in form and procedure, he became a revolutionary force in music history.

STUDY QUESTIONS

The Composer and His Music (HWM 513–16)

1. What are some reasons that Beethoven wrote fewer symphonies than Haydn or Mozart? (For a reason he could afford to do so, see question 4 below.)

2. What is the *Heiligenstadt Testament*? What does it discuss, and what attitudes does Beethoven express? What does Beethoven say in it about his relations with other people and about the role of his art in his life?

3. Beethoven's career is often divided into three periods. Provide the dates for each period and a brief characterization of each.

   First period:

   Second period:

   Third period:

First Period (HWM 516–22, NAWM 101–2)

4. How did Beethoven make a living in Vienna? How was his situation different from that of Haydn?

Music to Study
> **NAWM 101:** Ludwig van Beethoven, *Sonate pathétique* for piano, Op. 13 (1797–98), Rondo, Allegro (third movement)
> CD 8.33–42 (Concise 3.29–38)
> **NAWM 102:** Muzio Clementi, Piano Sonata in G Minor, Op. 34, No. 2 (1795), Largo e sostenuto / Allegro con fuoco (first movement)
> CD 8.43–51

5. In what ways is the finale of Beethoven's *Pathétique* Sonata (NAWM 101) like traditional rondos?

In what ways is it different?

6. What are some of the effects Beethoven uses to make this rondo dramatic?

---

7. Compare the later repetitions of the rondo refrain to its initial presentation. What changes are made? How do these changes contribute to the dramatic quality of the music?

8. Compare the rondo's first episode (mm. 25–61) to the reprise of this episode near the movement's end (mm. 134–69). In the reprise, how is it changed from its initial presentation? How does this reflect the influence of sonata form?

9. In the first movement of Clementi's Sonata in G Minor, Op. 34, No. 2 (NAWM 102), the exposition may be diagrammed as follows (P = first theme, T= transition, S = second theme, K = closing theme):

Measure:	1	10	23	41	48	63
	Intro	P	T	S	Extension	K
Key:	g	g	mod	B♭		b♭

Diagram the rest of the movement. Where does the recapitulation begin? How are the elements of the exposition changed in the recapitulation?

10. Describe the motivic relationship between the slow introduction and the first and second themes (P and S).

11. Both the first movement of Clementi's Sonata in G Minor and the finale of Beethoven's *Pathétique* Sonata use sudden changes in harmony, texture, or dynamic level for dramatic effect or to demarcate the form. Find and describe two such moments of sudden change in each movement.

12. Name the string quartets and symphonies Beethoven wrote during his first period, and give a date and a brief description for each. What composer served as his primary model for these works?

13. What else was played on the concert in 1800 on which Beethoven's First Symphony was premiered? How does this program differ from a modern symphony orchestra concert program?

Second Period (HWM 522–33, NAWM 103)

14. What was Beethoven's reputation as a pianist and composer by the early 1800s? How did he relate to his patrons and publishers?

Music to Study
    NAWM 103: Ludwig van Beethoven, Symphony No. 3 in E-flat Major
           (*Eroica,* 1803), Allegro con brio (first movement)
    CD 8.52–66

15. What are some of the unusual features of the first movement of Beethoven's *Eroica* Symphony (NAWM 103)?

16. What in the sketches (shown in NAWM, pp. 268–73) suggests that the second theme of the first movement is to be heard as arriving in m. 83 rather than at m. 57, when the key of the dominant is first reached?

17. What in the sketches (shown in HWM, p. 524, and in NAWM, pp. 273–74) suggests that the "new theme" in the oboe at m. 284 is only a counterpoint to a variant of the main theme?

18. According to HWM and NAWM, the principal theme is treated as a person in a drama, struggling against other players and triumphing in the end. How does Beethoven use changes in the principal motive (mm. 3-8) to convey struggle and triumph? (Hint: Look at the versions of this idea in the development, at mm. 408 and 424 in the recapitulation, and at mm. 639ff. in the coda.)

19. What other devices does Beethoven use in this movement to suggest a heroic struggle ending in triumph? How do the very long development and coda contribute to this effect?

20. What do Beethoven's *Eroica* Symphony and his opera *Fidelio* owe to the arts and politics of France in the Revolutionary period?

21. When were the *Rasumovsky* Quartets composed? _____

What elements distinguish them from earlier quartets?

22. How does Beethoven's Fifth Symphony portray the progress from struggle to triumph?

23. How does the music of Beethoven's Sixth Symphony (the *Pastoral*) suggest scenes from life in the country?

24. For each of Beethoven's first eight symphonies, what key is it in and when was it completed?

    1. _____ _____   5. _____ _____

    2. _____ _____   6. _____ _____

    3. _____ _____   7. _____ _____

    4. _____ _____   8. _____ _____

25. In the excerpts from the *Waldstein* Sonata shown in HWM, p. 532, how does Beethoven use contrasts of texture for dramatic effect?

Third Period (HWM 533–39, NAWM 104)

26. According to HWM, how did Beethoven's growing deafness affect his personality and his music?

27. For each of the following aspects of music, how does Beethoven's late style differ from Haydn, Mozart, and his own earlier style?

   a. juxtaposition of disparate elements

   b. variation technique

   c. delineation of phrases and sections

   d. evocation of improvisation and recitative

   e. use of fugue

   f. sonority

   g. number of movements

Music to Study
   NAWM 104: Ludwig van Beethoven, String Quartet in C-sharp Minor, Op.
        131 (1826), excerpts
   104a: Adagio ma non troppo e molto espressivo (first movement)
      CD 8.67–69 (Concise 3.39–41)
   104b: Allegro molto vivace (second movement)
      CD 8.70 (Concise 3.42)

28. Beethoven's String Quartet in C-sharp Minor, Op. 131, is in seven move-
    ments. Give the tempo marking, meter, key, and form for each movement.

	Tempo	Meter	Key	Form
1.	_____	_____	_____	_____
2.	_____	_____	_____	_____
3.	_____	_____	_____	_____
4.	_____	_____	_____	_____
5.	_____	_____	_____	_____
6.	_____	_____	_____	_____
7.	_____	_____	_____	_____

   How can this sequence of movements be reconciled with the traditional
   four-movement plan of a string quartet?

29. The key scheme of the quartet is unusual, and there is a correspondence
    between the keys used for each movement and the important pitches of the
    subject of the opening fugue (NAWM 104a). Write out the following notes
    for the subject in violin I (mm. 1–4) and the answer in violin II (mm. 4–8):

	first note (same as last note)	highest note	lowest note	longest and loudest note
subject in violin I	_____	_____	_____	_____
answer in violin II	_____	_____	_____	_____

   Of these notes, circle the ones that are used as the key of one of the movements in the quartet, as you listed them in question 28.

30. From the evidence in the previous question, can you suggest a reason that Beethoven might have chosen to have the answer in the the subdominant, rather than in the dominant as expected?

31. What traditional fugal techniques does Beethoven use in the first movement, and where is each one used?

32. What aspects of the music give the second movement (NAWM 104b) its particularly light and folklike character?

33. Where in the first movement is there a suggestion of the key of the second movement?

Where in the second movement is there a recollection of the key of the first movement?

34. In what ways does this quartet exemplify the characteristics of Beethoven's late style as you described them in question 27 above? (Hint: Answers for part d. of question 27 will be found in HWM and for parts e. and g. in the questions above. For parts a., b., c., and f., look both in HWM and at the two movements in NAWM 104.)

a. juxtaposition of disparate elements

b. variation technique

c. delineation of phrases and sections

d. evocation of improvisation and recitative

e. use of fugue

f. sonority

g. number of movements

35. What does Beethoven's *Missa solemnis* owe to Handel, and what does it owe to Haydn?

36. What is unusual about Beethoven's Ninth Symphony? Describe the sequence of events in the finale.

37. What was Beethoven's impact on later composers? In what ways was he "one of the great disruptive forces in the history of music"?

TERMS TO KNOW

Beethoven's sketchbooks   Beethoven's three periods

NAMES TO KNOW

Ludwig van Beethoven   *Pastoral* Symphony
Heiligenstadt Testament   *Waldstein* sonata
Muzio Clementi   *Diabelli* Variations, Op. 120
Jan Ladislav Dussek   String Quartet in C-sharp Minor,
Eroica Symphony   Op. 131
Fidelio   *Missa solemnis*
Rasumovsky Quartets, Op. 59   Beethoven's Ninth Symphony
Beethoven's Fifth Symphony   *Ode to Joy*

REVIEW QUESTIONS

1. Write an essay in which you recount Beethoven's career, including the changing circumstances of his life, his three major style periods, and major compositions of each period.

2. What other composers particularly influenced Beethoven's music, and what did he absorb from each?

3. You have examples in NAWM 101, 103, and 104 of movements from each of Beethoven's three periods. For each of these works, describe the form and other significant features of the movements in NAWM and explain what makes this work characteristic of its period.

4. Take the first eight measures of either of the Haydn string quartet movements you have studied (NAWM 97 and 98) and recompose it to feature one or more of the characteristics of Beethoven's late style. You can change as many notes and rhythms as you wish, as well as dynamics, articulations, registration, and any other aspect. You may recast it for piano or for another ensemble if you prefer. Try to make it sound as much like Beethoven as possible. Then write a short statement explaining what aspects of Beethoven's late style you have tried to imitate and how you have done so.

ROMANTICISM AND NINETEENTH-CENTURY ORCHESTRAL MUSIC

16

CHAPTER OBJECTIVES

After you complete the reading, study of the music, and study questions for this chapter, you should be able to

1. describe some of the differences between music of the Classic and Romantic periods, particularly in their aesthetic orientation;
2. explain how nineteenth-century symphonic composers responded to the example and influence of Beethoven;
3. identify some of the most important symphonic composers in the nineteenth century and suggest what makes each composer individual; and
4. briefly describe one or more characteristic works for each one.

CHAPTER OUTLINE

I. Romanticism (HWM 542–45)

There is more historical continuity than contrast between the Classic and Romantic periods. Most music between 1770 and 1900 uses a common set of conventions. The main differences are of attitude and degree: *Romanticism* is more a state of mind than a set of style traits, and Romantic music is more individual than Classic-era music in expressing feelings and transcending conventions. Some writers saw instrumental music as the ideal Romantic art, since it could convey emotion without words and feelings inexpressible in words. But music was also closely identified with literature, particularly in the *art song* and in *program music*.

II. Orchestral Music (HWM 545–65, NAWM 105)

A. The Place of Orchestral Music
Orchestral music increasingly centered on public concerts for middle-class audiences. Such concerts were rare in comparison to other kinds of music-making, but orchestral music was considered of great importance by audiences, critics, and composers. Beethoven cast a long shadow, and later composers sought to differentiate their music from his, typically by extending some elements of his music while rejecting others.

B. Franz Schubert (1797–1828)

Franz Schubert composed almost 1,000 works in his short life, including more than 600 lieder and nine symphonies. His *Unfinished Symphony* features song-like themes, harmonic excursions, and striking orchestration, traits also true of his *"Great" Symphony in C major.*

C. Hector Berlioz (1803–1869)

Hector Berlioz found precedents in Beethoven's symphonies for both the programmaticism and the thematic dramatization of his *Symphonie fantastique* (1830). This is a musical drama whose words are not spoken or sung but are written in a program handed out to the audience. The main theme or *idée fixe* (fixed idea or fixation) stands for the artist's beloved and appears in every movement, sometimes transformed; this procedure helped to initiate the *cyclic symphony. Harold en Italie* (Harold in Italy, 1834) is also a cyclic program symphony, with a solo viola portraying the protagonist. *Roméo et Juliette* (1839) is a "dramatic symphony" for orchestra, vocal soloists, and chorus, extending Beethoven's example in the Ninth Symphony into what is almost an unstaged opera. These innovative works influenced all later program music and began a new era of colorful orchestration.   **Music: NAWM 105**

D. Felix Mendelssohn (1809–1847)

Felix Mendelssohn combined adherence to Classical forms with themes reminiscent of foreign lands in his *Italian Symphony* (No. 4, 1833) and *Scottish* Symphony (No. 3, 1842). Among his other important orchestral works are his Violin Concerto, his *concert overtures* (independent one-movement works that are usually descriptive or programmatic), and his incidental music for Shakespeare's *A Midsummer Night's Dream.*

E. Robert Schumann (1810–1856)

Robert Schumann composed his first symphonies (published as No. 1 and No. 4) in 1841. The four movements of Symphony No. 4 are played without a break and linked by thematical recall. His principal models for the symphony were Schubert and Mendelssohn, but from Beethoven he acquired a view of the symphony as a prestigious genre and as a rite of passage for an ambitious composer.

F. Franz Liszt (1811–1886)

Franz Liszt wrote twelve *symphonic poems* between 1848 and 1858 and another in 1881–82. He was the first to use the term, which designates a programmatic work in one movement that evokes ideas and feelings associated with its subject and may follow the course of a poem or narrative with a similar sequence of moods and events. Liszt used *thematic transformation,* a process of transforming a single theme or motive into new themes and thus providing both motivic unity and variety of mood, as in the symphonic poem *Les Préludes* (1854). Many later composers wrote symphonic poems, and Liszt's harmonies and thematic transformation influenced Wagner and others. His two symphonies are also programmatic, on characters and episodes drawn from literature.

G. Johannes Brahms (1833–1897)

Johannes Brahms felt Beethoven as an almost overwhelming influence and waited to write symphonies until he could create something fresh within the Classic four-movement structure. The slow introductions to the first and last movements of his First Symphony (1876) foreshadow the themes of the following Allegros. His middle movements are often in keys a third away from the main key of the symphony, instead of in the dominant or subdominant. His textures are often contrapuntal, with active melodic basses that develop their own motives. His music is marked by *developing variation,* in which a musical idea is varied to create a string of interrelated but different ideas, producing both unity and variety. Brahms often superimposes duple and triple divisions of the beat or creates rhythmic conflicts between parts. He wrote four symphonies, four concertos, two overtures, two serenades, and a set of orchestral variations.

H. Anton Bruckner (1824–1896)

Anton Bruckner was an organist, and his symphonies show that influence in his orchestration and in their serious, religious spirit. Their length, harmony, use of sequence, and massive orchestra show the influence of Wagner. They often begin like Beethoven's Ninth Symphony, with the gradual emergence of a theme, and end with chorale-like themes. While outwardly conforming to Classic structures, his symphonies depend upon the continuous development of musical ideas.

I. Piotr Il'yich Tchaikovsky (1840–1893)

Piotr Il'yich Tchaikovsky wrote six symphonies, of which the last three are the best known. The Fourth has a private program about relentless fate, depicted in the opening horn theme that returns in the first and fourth movements. The key structure of the first movement is unusual, moving around the circle of minor thirds. The opening theme of the Fifth recurs in all movements. The Sixth (the *Pathétique*) has as its second movement a waltz in 5/4 (and is most unusual in ending with a slow movement). Tchaikovsky's ballets are well known.

J. Antonín Dvořák (1841–1904)

Antonín Dvořák is best known for his Symphony No. 9 (*From the New World,* 1893), written during his sojourn in the United States.

STUDY QUESTIONS

Romanticism (HWM 542–45)

1. What are some of the differences between music in the Classic era and music in the Romantic period? What are some of the similarities?

2. According to Liszt and Schopenhauer, what is special about music as an art?

3. What are some of the connections between music and literature in the nineteenth century?

Orchestral Music (HWM 545–65, NAWM 105)

4. What was the role of orchestral music in the nineteenth century? Who was its audience, and what was its status?

5. How do Schubert's symphonies differ in approach from those of Beethoven?

6. What does Schumann praise in Schubert's "Great" Symphony in C major (see the passage in HWM, p. 547)?

Music to Study

NAWM 105: Hector Berlioz, *Symphonie fantastique* (1830), excerpts
   III. *Scène aux champs* (Scene in the Country)
      not on recordings
   IV. *Marche au supplice* (March to the Scaffold)
      CD 9.1–6 (Concise 3.43–48)

7. What devices of orchestration, melody, and rhythm does Berlioz use to suggest that the third movement of his *Symphonie fantastique* (NAWM 105) is set in the country? (One device not mentioned in the commentary is the dotted siciliano rhythm, long associated with pastoral settings, first introduced in mm. 28–30.)

8. Where does the *idée fixe* (shown in NAWM, p. 327, and in HWM, Example 16.2, p. 549) appear in this movement? How is it transformed, and how is it introduced and developed, to fit the program (in NAWM, pp. 327–28)?

9. Chart the form of the fourth movement, *March au supplice,* including repetitions.

10. How does Berlioz develop and vary the theme introduced by the cellos and basses in mm. 17–25 over the course of the movement?

11. Where does the *idée fixe* appear in this movement? How is it treated, and how do its treatment and the surrounding music fit the program for the movement (given in NAWM, p. 328)?

12. What special instrumental effects does Berlioz use, and how do they suit the program? What other aspects of the music help to support the program?

13. What was Berlioz's significance for later generations?

14. What is "Italian" in Mendelssohn's *Italian* Symphony (No. 4)? What is "Scottish" in his *Scottish* Symphony (No. 3)?

15. How did Beethoven influence Schumann's view of the symphony?

16. What is a *symphonic poem*? Who invented it, and when?

17. How did Liszt use thematic transformation in his *Les Préludes*? What did this procedure allow him to accomplish?

18. In what ways do the Brahms symphonies continue the Classic tradition, and in what ways are they Romantic? What are some distinctive traits of Brahms's music?

19. Who coined the term *developing variation*? _____

    Define and describe this procedure. How does Brahms's music exemplify it?

20. What are the distinctive features of Bruckner's symphonies? What did he draw from Beethoven?

21. How does Tchaikovsky link the movements together thematically in his Fourth and Fifth Symphonies? What other symphonies discussed in this chapter are unified in this way? What is the term for this procedure?

TERMS TO KNOW

Romanticism
art song
program music
idée fixe
cyclic symphony
cyclical method (of thematic recurrence)

concert overture (nineteenth-century)
symphonic poem
thematic transformation
developing variation

NAMES TO KNOW

Franz Schubert
Unfinished Symphony
"Great" Symphony in C major
Hector Berlioz
Symphonie fantastique
Harold en Italie
Roméo et Juliette
Felix Mendelssohn

Italian Symphony
Scottish Symphony
Franz Liszt
Les Préludes
Johannes Brahms
Anton Bruckner
Piotr Il'yich Tchaikovsky
Antonín Dvořák

REVIEW QUESTIONS

1. Make a time-line for the nineteenth century, and place on it the composers and most significant pieces discussed in this chapter. Add to it the three periods of Beethoven's career and his most important works, as discussed in chapter 15. Make your time-line large enough to allow further additions, as you will be adding to it in chapters 17–19.

2. How are Classic and Romantic orchestral music similar, and how are they different? Use examples from the orchestral works you know by Haydn (NAWM 94–96) and Berlioz (NAWM 105) to illustrate these similarities and differences. Include consideration of the size and composition of the orchestra, forms and genres used, the artistic aims of the composers, and matters of style and procedure.

3. HWM sums up more than a century of music history in two succinct sentences (p. 546): "Composers who followed Beethoven had to come to terms somehow with how this towering figure of the immediate past had transformed the symphony. They accepted or rejected his legacy in different ways, according to their personalities and talents." Describe the symphonic works of Schubert, Berlioz, Mendelssohn, Schumann, Liszt, Brahms, Bruckner, and Tchaikovsky, and explain how each of them confronted the influence of Beethoven's symphonies and found an individual path. For each composer, what aspects of Beethoven's music did he continue, what did he reject, and what did he do that was innovative or distinctive?

SOLO, CHAMBER, AND VOCAL MUSIC IN THE NINETEENTH CENTURY

17

CHAPTER OBJECTIVES

After you complete the reading, study of the music, and study questions for this chapter, you should be able to

1. name some of the principal nineteenth-century composers of piano music and chamber music, characterize their styles, trace influences upon them, and describe representative works for piano by Mendelssohn, Schumann, Chopin, and Liszt;
2. describe the nineteenth-century German lied as practiced by Schubert, Robert Schumann, Clara Schumann, and Brahms; and
3. describe the social roles for and varieties of choral music in the nineteenth century and describe examples by Bruckner and Brahms.

CHAPTER OUTLINE

I. The Piano (HWM 571–72)

The nineteenth-century piano had a larger range, more varied dynamics, and faster response than the eighteenth-century piano, allowing greater expressivity and virtuosity and making it an attractive medium. (It was also now mass-produced and thus widely available and affordable.) It became the most common household instrument and heightened the demand for music that amateurs could play at home. There were two schools of piano playing in the early nineteenth century, one emphasizing clarity and fluency, the other large sound and dramatic orchestral effects. Many piano virtuosos gave concerts, toured, and wrote for piano.

II. Music for Piano (HWM 572–87, NAWM 106–10)

A. Romantic Piano Music
In order to sustain lyrical melodies with an active accompaniment, pianists often used a three-layer texture of melody, bass, and figuration shared between the hands. The new, more resonant piano also invited chordal textures.

B. The Early Romantic Composers
Composers of piano music included Carl Maria von Weber (discussed further in chapter 18) and a number of Bohemian composers.

C. Schubert
Schubert wrote marches, dances, and lyrical works that create a distinctive mood. His longer works include eleven sonatas and the *Wanderer Fantasy* (1822), which uses a theme from his song *The Wanderer.* His sonatas often present three keys in the exposition, rather than two, and while following Classic form use lyrical themes that resist development.

D. Mendelssohn
Mendelssohn wrote in a variety of piano genres, including preludes and fugues that show his interest in J. S. Bach. His most popular piano works are his *Lieder ohne Worte* (Songs without Words), which capture the lyrical quality of the lied in works for piano alone. He also wrote important music for organ, including three sonatas and six preludes and fugues.   **Music: NAWM 106**

E. Robert Schumann
Schumann aimed to be a concert pianist, but after injuring his right hand he turned to composition and to writing about music in the journal he founded, the *Neue Zeitschrift für Musik* (New Journal of Music). All his published music before 1840 was for piano. In addition to several longer works, he specialized in short character pieces, often grouped into collections such as *Phantasiestücke* (Fantasy Pieces). His pieces carry titles that suggest extramusical associations. In his criticism and his music, he used the imaginary characters Florestan, Eusebius, and Raro to reflect different sides of his own character. He also wrote fugues and fugal passages that pay homage to Bach.   **Music: NAWM 107**

F. Fryderyk Chopin (1810–1849)
Fryderyk Chopin wrote almost exclusively for piano. He was born in Poland and lived in Paris from 1831. His *mazurkas* and *polonaises* are stylized Polish dances and are among the first nationalist works of the nineteenth century. His playing style was more personal than theatrical, and his music is accordingly introspective. He used *tempo rubato,* in which the right hand pushes forward or holds back the tempo while the left hand accompanies in stricter time. He followed *John Field* (1782–1837) in composing *nocturnes,* slow works with embellished melodies over wide-ranging accompaniments. Chopin also wrote preludes, under the influence of Bach; *ballades* (a term he apparently coined); scherzos; fantasias; sonatas; and concertos. His *études* are studies in piano technique, but are unusual for études in that they are also for concert performance.   **Music: NAWM 108–9**

G. Liszt
Born in Hungary and trained in Vienna, Liszt was a touring virtuoso from a young age. Liszt ceased touring in 1848 and became court music director at Weimar, later moving to Rome. His style combines influences from Hungary, Vienna, and Paris. As performer and composer, he sought to

match on the piano the dazzling virtuosity of the violinist *Nicolò Paganini* (1782–1840). He made many transcriptions for piano of other music. His original works for piano include Hungarian Rhapsodies, études, and many short descriptive pieces, and his works for piano and orchestra include two concertos. His Piano Concerto No. 1 in E♭ Major and his one-movement Piano Sonata in B Minor exemplify his use of thematic transformation, as in his symphonic poems. Liszt experimented with chromatic harmony, especially in his late works. He also wrote for organ, using Baroque forms and styles. **Music: NAWM 110**

H. Brahms
Brahms avoided pianistic display but achieved a great variety of textures by combining simple ideas. He often used broken-chord accompaniments, cross-rhythms, and melodies doubled in octaves, thirds, or sixths. He wrote three early sonatas, variation sets in mid-career, and numerous small, lyrical piano pieces in later life, when he also composed a set of chorale preludes for organ in emulation of J. S. Bach.

I. Other Composers
César Franck (1822–1890) blended Romantic harmonies with Classic structures in his pieces for piano and organ. *Fanny Hensel* (1805–1847), sister of Felix Mendelssohn, wrote hundreds of piano pieces and songs that she performed in private concerts, although few were published in her lifetime. *Clara Wieck Schumann* (1819–1896) was a child prodigy on the piano and became an important soloist and composer. Her marriage to Robert Schumann and raising a family limited her touring, but she continued to perform, compose, and teach. Her works include a piano concerto, a piano trio, pieces for piano solo, and lieder.

III. Chamber Music (HWM 587–93)

The best chamber music of the Romantic period came from composers who felt closest to the Classic tradition.

A. Schubert
Schubert wrote several significant chamber works, notably the Trout Quintet, three late string quartets, an octet for strings and winds, and the String Quintet in C Major, widely regarded as his best chamber work.

B. Mendelssohn
Mendelssohn wrote an octet, six string quartets, two piano trios, and other chamber works.

C. Brahms
Brahms is Beethoven's true successor in the realm of chamber music, with many works of high quality spanning his entire career, including three piano trios, two string sextets, three string quartets, and sonatas for solo instrument with piano (three for violin, two for cello, and two for clarinet). Like most of Brahms's music, the well-known Piano Quintet in F Minor, Op. 34 (1864), uses developing variation. His chamber works with clarinet and with natural horn are peaks of the literature for those instruments.

D. Franck

Franck wrote several chamber works united by the cyclical use of themes, recalling themes in two or more movements.

IV. The Lied (HWM 593–98, NAWM 111–14)

A. The Ballad

Ballads were long narrative poems written in imitation of folk ballads. They required more variety and drama in the musical setting than did a lyrical strophic poem. In response, the piano became equal with the voice in conveying the meaning of the poetry.

B. Schubert

Schubert's song melodies were both beautiful in themselves and perfectly suited to the text. He often used chromaticism and harmonic contrast to create drama or highlight the meaning of the words. Many songs are strophic; others use recurring themes and a clear tonal structure. The accompaniments often include figuration that conveys an image or feeling in the text. He set dozens of poems by Goethe and composed two *song cycles* (groups of songs intended to be performed in sequence and often implying a story) to poems by Wilhelm Müller, *Die schöne Müllerin* (The Lovely Miller's Daughter, 1823) and *Winterreise* (Winter's Journey, 1827). **Music: NAWM 111–12**

C. Robert Schumann

In Schumann's lieder, the piano is equal to the voice in interest and expressivity and often has preludes before and postludes after the voice sings. The mood is often restless and intense. Schumann wrote more than one hundred songs in 1840, the year of his marriage, including the song cycle *Dichterliebe* (A Poet's Love) on poems by Heinrich Heine.   **Music: NAWM 113**

D. Clara Schumann

Clara Schumann's lieder also capture poetic imagery in music in subtle and original ways.   **Music: NAWM 114**

E. Brahms

Among Brahms's 260 songs, many are in a folk-like style over simple accompaniment, such as the famous "Brahms lullaby." He also arranged German folk songs. His principal model in song composition was Schubert. His usual tone is serious and reflective. His piano parts seldom depict an image in the poem, and they are quite varied in texture (unlike the Schumanns, who often use the same figuration throughout a song).

V. Choral Music (HWM 598–602, NAWM 115–16)

A. Types of Choral Music

The nineteenth century saw a revival of choral works from earlier centuries, such as Palestrina and Bach. (Partly as a result, new choral music tended to be relatively conservative or to hearken back to earlier eras; it was not the trailblazer of new styles it had been in the Renaissance.) There were three main types of choral music composed in the nineteenth century:

1. *Part-songs* on secular texts, usually short and mostly homophonic;
2. Music on liturgical texts, for church or home performance; and
3. Concert works for chorus and orchestra, often with soloists.

B. Part-Songs and Cantatas

Singing societies (amateur choruses who sang together for their own pleasure) were very popular in the nineteenth century, and composers produced hundreds of part-songs, cantatas, and other works for these amateur men's, women's, or mixed choirs. Brahms especially was a master of choral music of all types.

C. Church Music

The Cecilian movement, named after St. Cecilia, the patron saint of music, worked within the Catholic church to revive the a cappella style of Palestrina and restore Gregorian chant to purer form. Other composers continued to write church music with orchestra or organ, including Catholic Masses and English anthems. In St. Petersburg, *Dmitri Bortnyansky* (1751–1825) helped to found a new choral style of Russian church music inspired by traditional Orthodox chant.

D. Other Music on Liturgical Texts

Some composers wrote large works on liturgical texts, intended for special occasions or performance in concert rather than in church. Berlioz's *Requiem* (1837) and *Te Deum* (1855) are dramatic symphonies with voices, scored for large orchestras with interesting instrumental effects. Several of Liszt's works are on a similarly large scale, and Rossini and Verdi wrote choral works in operatic style. Bruckner was a church organist; his Masses share qualities and some themes with his symphonies, and his motets show the influence of the Cecilian movement. Several German, French, and English composers composed oratorios, most notably Mendelssohn. Brahms's *Ein deutsches Requiem* (A German Requiem, 1868) uses Biblical passages rather than the liturgical Requiem text, and combines evocations of Baroque procedures with rich Romantic harmonies.
Music: NAWM 115–16

STUDY QUESTIONS

The Piano (HWM 571–72)

1. How did the nineteenth-century piano differ from earlier keyboard instruments, including eighteenth-century pianos?

2. Describe the variety of approaches to piano playing in the nineteenth century.

Music for Piano (HWM 572–87, NAWM 106–10)

3. What were some ways composers for piano imitated textures from vocal and orchestral music?

4. How do Schubert's sonatas differ from Beethoven's?

Music to Study
> **NAWM 106:** Felix Mendelssohn, *Lieder ohne Worte* (Songs without Words), excerpts
>> 106a: Op. 85, No. 4 in D major (1845)   CD 9.7–8
>> 106b: Op. 67, No. 4 in C major (1845)   CD 9.9–11
> **NAWM 107:** Robert Schumann, *Phantasiestücke* (Fantasy Pieces), Op. 12 (1837), excerpts
>> 107a: No. 4, *Grillen* (Whims)   CD 9.12–14 (Concise 3.49–51)
>> 107b: No. 5, *In der Nacht* (In the Night) CD 9.15–17

5. In what ways do the examples from Mendelssohn's *Songs without Words* in NAWM 106 resemble songs?

6. Describe the figuration and textures in these pieces. How do they exploit the capabilities of the nineteenth-century piano? How does the figuration here differ from or resemble the keyboard figuration used by eighteenth-century composers such as Domenico Scarlatti (NAWM 89), C. P. E. Bach (NAWM 91), J. C. Bach (NAWM 93), or Mozart (NAWM 99)?

7. Diagram the form of Schumann's *Grillen* (NAWM 107a).

How does it compare to a traditional ABA form?

How does this piece, titled "Whims," convey a sense of whims or whimsy?

8. Diagram the form of Schumann's *In der Nacht* (NAWM 107b).

How does this piece convey passionate emotions? How does its form resemble a narrative—that is, how does it suggest that it is relating a story?

9. What textures and figuration does Schumann use in these piano pieces that are different from those used by Classic-era composers such as Domenico Scarlatti (NAWM 89), C. P. E. Bach (NAWM 91), J. C. Bach (NAWM 93), or Mozart (NAWM 99)?

10. What was Chopin's national heritage, and how is this reflected in his music?

11. What genres of piano music did Chopin use?

Music to Study
   NAWM 108: John Field, Nocturne in A Major, No. 8 (1815)
      CD 9.18
   NAWM 109: Fryderyk Chopin, Nocturne in E-flat Major, Op. 9, No. 2
      (1830–31)
      CD 9.19 (Concise 3.52)

12. In what ways does Field embellish the melodic line in his Nocturne in A
   Major (NAWM 108)? How do his melodies resemble the style of opera?

13. How does Chopin embellish the melodic line of his Nocturne in E-flat
   Major (NAWM 109)? How is it like operatic singing? How is it like Field's
   nocturne?

14. How is chromaticism used in the Field? How is it used in the Chopin?

15. What elements of style, sound, and texture distinguish Chopin's Nocturne
   from Schumann's *Phantasiestücke* (NAWM 107) and from earlier keyboard styles? Describe Chopin's style, based on this example.

16. Who was Nicolò Paganini? What was his significance for Liszt's career?

Music to Study
   NAWM 110: Franz Liszt, *Trois études de concert* (Three Concert Études),
        for piano (1849), excerpt: No. 3, *Un sospiro* (A Sigh)
   CD 9.20–24 (Concise 3.53–57)

17. What technical problem for the player is the focus of Liszt's étude *Un sospiro* (NAWM 110)? How is it addressed at the outset? How does the texture change over the course of the piece, to raise new problems for the performer?

18. What elements of style, sound, and texture distinguish Liszt's étude from Chopin's Nocturne (NAWM 109), from Schumann's *Phantasiestücke* (NAWM 107), and from earlier keyboard styles? Describe Liszt's approach to the piano, based on this example.

---

19. What genres of keyboard music did Liszt cultivate?

20. What is Brahms's approach to texture on the piano, and how does it differ from that of Chopin or Liszt?

21. Briefly describe the careers of Fanny Hensel and Clara Schumann. What genres did each cultivate, and what outlets did each find for her music?

Chamber Music (HWM 587–93)

22. How do Schubert's chamber works relate to his songs and theatrical music?

23. In what senses was Brahms "the true successor to Beethoven" in the realm of chamber music (HWM, p. 590)? How did he continue or extend the genres and approaches Beethoven cultivated, and what did he do that was new?

The Lied (HWM 593–98, NAWM 111–14)

24. What is a *ballad*? Why did ballads call for greater variety and expressivity from composers? What effect did this have on the piano accompaniments to art songs?

Music to Study

NAWM 111: Franz Schubert, *Gretchen am Spinnrade* (Gretchen at the Spinning Wheel), D. 118, lied (1814)
  CD 9.25–29 (Concise 3.58–62)

NAWM 112: Franz Schubert, *Winterreise* (Winter's Journey), D. 911, song cycle (1827), excerpt: *Der Lindenbaum* (The Linden Tree), lied
  CD 9.30–33

NAWM 113: Robert Schumann, *Dichterliebe* (A Poet's Love), Op. 48, song cycle (1840), excerpts
  113a: *Im wunderschönen Monat Mai* CD 9.34
  113b: *Ich grolle nicht* CD 9.35

NAWM 114: Clara Wieck Schumann, *Geheimes Flüstern hier und dort,* Op. 23, No. 3, lied (1853)
  CD 9.36

---

25. Schubert's *Gretchen am Spinnrade* (NAWM 111) sets a scene from Goethe's *Faust* in which Gretchen sits spinning thread while thinking of Faust. How is the spinning wheel depicted in this song? Why is this an effective device for depicting the spinning wheel?

How does this device also capture Gretchen's mood?

Where does the wheel suddenly stop, and then gradually start again? What does this suggest about Gretchen's feelings at this point?

26. Diagram the form of this song. How does Schubert use changes in melody, harmony, and key to portray Gretchen's changing emotions?

27. How does Schubert alter or repeat Goethe's words as given in NAWM? How does this help to convey Gretchen's feelings?

28. In *Der Lindenbaum* (NAWM 112), how does Schubert use figuration in the piano and contrasts between major and minor to suggest the images and meaning of the poem?

29. The text of *Im wunderschönen Monat Mai* (NAWM 113a) speaks of new love. How does Schumann's music imply, through melody and harmony, that this love is unrequited—as yet all "longing and desire" and no fulfillment? How are the opening piano prelude and closing postlude crucial in conveying this meaning?

30. What is the key of this song? Where does the tonic chord appear? What is unusual about the beginning and ending harmonies?

31. How does Schumann alter Heine's poetry in his setting of *Ich grolle nicht* (NAWM 113b)?

32. In what way is the setting ironic, with the emotional tone of the music contradicting what the words claim? What musical means does Schumann use to convey this emotional tone?

33. In Clara Schumann's song *Geheimes Flüstern hier und dort* (NAWM 114), how does the figuration in the piano capture the imagery in the poem?

   Where is there metric conflict between piano and voice, or melody and accompaniment? How does this convey the poetic imagery?

34. Where are there unusual or unexpected harmonic progressions? How do these suggest the mood of the poet?

   In what other ways does the music suit the poetry?

35. What are some characteristics of Brahms's songs? How do his lieder differ from those of Robert and Clara Schumann?

Choral Music (HWM 598–602, NAWM 115–16)

36. What types of choral music were written in the nineteenth century? What was the social function of each type?

37. What are *singing societies*? What effect did they have on the composition of choral music in the nineteenth century?

38. What was the *Cecilian movement,* and what were its goals?

39. Who was Dmitri Bortnyansky, when was he active, and what did he accomplish?

40. How do Berlioz's *Requiem* and *Te Deum* differ from traditional church music of the previous hundred years?

Music to Study
　　NAWM 115: Anton Bruckner, *Virga Jesse,* motet (1885)
　　　　CD 9.37
　　NAWM 116: Johannes Brahms, *Ein deutsches Requiem* (A German Requiem), Op. 45 (1868), No. 4: *Wie lieblich sind deine Wohnungen*
　　　　CD 9.38–42

41. How does Bruckner evoke or suggest sixteenth-century polyphony in his motet *Virga Jesse* (NAWM 115)?

42. What aspects of the music make clear that this Bruckner motet could not have been written earlier than the nineteenth century?

43. What traits in the fourth movement of Brahms's *German Requiem* (NAWM 116) are reminiscent of Baroque music? What contrapuntal devices are used?

    What elements in this movement are typical of nineteenth-century music, or of Brahms in particular?

    How do these Baroque and Romantic style traits help to depict the text and convey the emotions suggested in the text?

44. Choral singers often find this work particularly enjoyable to sing. What in the music do you think makes it so fun to sing? Given what you know about the social roles of choral music in the nineteenth century, why might Brahms have taken special care to make this a pleasure to perform?

TERMS TO KNOW

mazurka
polonaise
tempo rubato
nocturne
ballade (for piano)

étude
ballad
song cycle
part-song
singing societies

NAMES TO KNOW

Wanderer Fantasy
Lieder ohne Worte (Songs
  without Words)
Neue Zeitschrift für Musik
Phantasiestücke
Fryderyk Chopin
John Field
Nicolò Paganini
César Franck
Fanny (Mendelssohn) Hensel

Clara Wieck Schumann
Die schöne Müllerin
Winterreise
Dichterliebe
the Cecilian movement
Dmitri Bortnyansky
Berlioz's *Requiem* and *Te
  Deum*
Ein deutsches Requiem (A
  German Requiem)

REVIEW QUESTIONS

1. Add the composers and major works discussed in this chapter to the time-line you made for chapter 16.

2. Trace the history of piano music in the nineteenth century. Include in your discussion the changed character of the piano and the genres composers used, as well as describing the styles and works of the most prominent composers for the instrument.

3. What are the distinctive features of chamber music in the nineteenth century?

4. Trace the development of the German Lied from the turn of the nineteenth century through Brahms.

5. Name the varieties of choral music composed in the nineteenth century and describe one or more examples of each type. What were the social roles and contexts for choral music in the nineteenth century. How did this affect the types and styles used by choral composers? What roles did amateurs play in choral performance, and how might this have affected the relative prestige of choral music in comparison to orchestral music?

6. Choose two composers of choral music in the nineteenth century (such as Berlioz and Bruckner) and contrast their approaches. As part of your answer, describe at least one work by each composer.

Opera and Music Drama in the Nineteenth Century

18

Chapter Objectives

After you complete the reading, study of the music, and study questions for this chapter, you should be able to

1. trace the history of opera in France, Italy, and Germany in the nineteenth century and distinguish between the characteristics of each national tradition;
2. define and use terminology associated with nineteenth-century opera;
3. name the most significant composers in each nation and describe the style and approach of each of them; and
4. describe characteristic excerpts from operas by Rossini, Bellini, Verdi, Weber, and Wagner.

Chapter Outline

I. Italy (HWM 603–8, NAWM 117–18)

A. General

The eighteenth-century reforms of Jommelli and Traetta affected Italy in the nineteenth century, including a blend of Italian and French influences, more continuous dramatic flow, more important roles for chorus and orchestra, and more use of winds and horns.

B. Rossini

Gioachino Rossini (1792–1868) was the most successful opera composer of the early nineteenth century. He wrote both comic and serious operas but is best known today for his comic operas, such as *Il barbiere di Siviglia* (The Barber of Seville, 1816). Instead of consigning the plot to dry recitative interspersed between arias, Rossini and his librettists made the action more continuous. They developed a new pattern for scenes, typically including orchestral introduction, *scena* ("scene," in accompanied recitative), *primo tempo* ("first movement," a slow, cantabile song), *tempo di mezzo* ("middle movement"), and *cabaletta* (a lively and brilliant solo). The primo tempo and cabaletta together comprise the aria, called *cavatina* if it marks the character's entrance. Duets and finales have similar structures. His style emphasizes shapely, ornamented melody over spare accompaniment. Rossini often combines repetition of an idea with a crescendo to build excitement. After composing many operas for Italian opera houses, Rossini moved to Paris in 1824, wrote some operas in French, and then wrote smaller vocal and piano works. *Guillaume Tell* (William Tell, 1829), his most successful serious opera, mixed Italian and French conventions and foreshadowed later French opera.   **Music: NAWM 117**

C. Vincenzo Bellini (1801–1835)
Vincenzo Bellini wrote ten serious operas in a refined style marked by sweeping, elegantly embellished melody. French opera influenced the plots of Italian opera; *opera semiseria* featured a serious plot with Romantic sentimentality, as in French lyric opera.   **Music: NAWM 118**

D. Gaetano Donizetti (1797–1848)
Gaetano Donizetti composed about seventy serious and comic operas as well as many songs, oratorios, cantatas, religious works, symphonies, and chamber works. He made both the action and the music more continuous by disguising beginnings and endings of formal units.

II. France (HWM 608–13)

A. Background
Paris was a center for opera in the nineteenth century, with governmental support that varied through changes of regime.

B. Grand Opera
Grand opera was a new kind of opera on historical subjects that combined spectacle and Romantic elements and appealed to a wide audience. The genre was established by the librettist *Eugène Scribe* (1791–1861) and the composer *Giacomo Meyerbeer* (1791–1864). Their opera *Les Huguenots* (1836) dramatized the sixteenth-century religious wars in France. Typical of grand opera are massed choruses, soaring melodies, and strong contrasts.

C. Opéra Comique
Opéra comique used spoken dialogue rather than recitative and featured a smaller cast and simpler music than grand opera. Its plots were comic or romantic rather than historical. After the 1851 declaration of the Second Empire under Napoleon III, the satiric genre of *opéra bouffe* emerged with *Jacques Offenbach* (1819–1880). His comic style influenced the later operettas of Gilbert and Sullivan in England and of Johann Strauss and others in Vienna.

D. Berlioz
Berlioz's *La Damnation de Faust* (1846) is not an opera, but a series of scenes from Goethe's *Faust* set for concert performance by soloists, chorus, and orchestra. *Les Troyens* (The Trojans, 1856–58) is his operatic masterpiece, whose music in the tradition of Lully, Rameau, and Gluck matches the heroic epic plot in its serious, classic tone.

E. French Lyric Opera
Lyric opera developed from romantic comic operas, with similar romantic plots and a focus on melody, but on a somewhat larger scale. A famous example is *Faust* (1859) by *Charles Gounod* (1818–1893).

F. Georges Bizet (1838–1875)
Carmen (1875) by *Georges Bizet* was classed as an opéra comique because it had spoken dialogue, but is a drama that reflects *exoticism* and a late-nineteenth-century taste for *realism*.

III. Giuseppe Verdi (HWM 614–17, NAWM 119)

A. General
Giuseppe Verdi (1813–1901) was the major figure in Italian opera after Donizetti. He continued the Italian operatic tradition and was a strong nationalist. His operas focus on human drama conveyed through song, and his librettos, drawn mostly from Romantic authors, provide high emotions, strong contrasts, and quickly moving plots.

B. Early Works
Verdi's early operas adapt and expand the conventions of his predecessors and are especially notable for their choruses. From 1849 to 1853 (the year of *La traviata*), he intensified the drama and heightened the sense of characterization. He often mixed a variety of musical forces in a single scene to create a more compelling drama. After 1853, his operas appeared less frequently, as he experimented with French grand opera, daring harmonies, comic roles, *reminiscence motives,* and other new elements, culminating in *Aida* (1871).   **Music: NAWM 119**

C. Late Works
After a long hiatus, Verdi returned to opera with *Otello* (1884–87), responding to intervening developments in German and French opera by making the music more continuous and by using several unifying motives. The conclusion of the drama unfolds without pause, contrasting lyrical aria with dialogue and interludes to carry the action. *Falstaff* (1893) takes to a new level the elements of comic opera, particularly the ensemble.

IV. Germany (HWM 618–21, NAWM 120)

A. Background
German opera derived from Singspiel, absorbed French Romantic features, and was linked to German Romantic literature.

B. Carl Maria von Weber (1786–1826)
Carl Maria von Weber was director of the opera at Prague and later at Dresden. His *Der Freischütz* (1821) established the tradition of German Romantic opera. Plots draw from medieval history, legend, or fairy tale, and involve supernatural beings and events in a rural or wilderness setting. Characters stand for good or evil forces, and good triumphs in a kind of spiritual deliverance. These traits and some musical elements such as use of

folklike style, chromatic harmony, and emphasis on the inner voices as well as the main melody distinguish German from French or Italian opera, despite similarities in genre and musical style. The famous Wolf's Glen Scene uses *melodrama* (spoken dialogue over music), startling chromatic harmony, and unusual orchestral effects to create an eerie scene. Weber often used recurring themes for dramatic effect and to unify the drama. **Music: NAWM 120**

C. Other German Opera Composers
German composers after Weber wrote comic, lyric, and dramatic operas.

V. Richard Wagner and the Music Drama (HWM 621–28, NAWM 121)

A. Career and Music
Richard Wagner (1813–1883) was the most important German opera composer and a pivotal figure for music since the mid-nineteenth century. He (1) brought German Romantic opera to its peak, (2) invented the *music drama,* and (3) developed a harmonic idiom whose greater chromaticism and freer modulation influenced later composers. His legacy is marred by his antisemitism, as expressed in his notorious essay *Das Judentum in der Musik* (Judaism in Music, 1850), and by his later appropriation by the Nazi regime in mid-twentieth-century Germany.

For Wagner, the function of music was to serve dramatic expression. His opera *Die fliegende Holländer* (The Flying Dutchman, 1843) set the pattern for his later works with a libretto by the composer himself, a plot based on a legend, the use of recurring themes, and the hero's redemption through the loving sacrifice of the heroine. *Tannhäuser* (1845) combines German Romantic opera with grand opera and introduces a new declamatory vocal style. *Lohengrin* (1850) is more continuous, with less division into numbers, more use of recurring themes, and the association of keys with characters.

The 1848 Revolution forced Wagner into exile in Switzerland, where he wrote a series of essays on his musical theories and the librettos to his cycle of music dramas, *Der Ring des Nibelungen* (The Ring of the Nibelungs), whose music he completed over two decades: *Das Rheingold* (The Rhine Gold, 1853–54), *Die Walküre* (The Valkyrie, 1854–56), *Siegfried* (1856–71), and *Götterdämmerung* (The Twilight of the Gods, 1869–74). They are linked by a continuous story, common characters, and shared motives. His other music dramas are *Tristan und Isolde* (1857–59), *Die Meistersinger von Nürnberg* (The Mastersingers of Nuremberg, 1862–67), and *Parsifal* (1882). Wagner's notion of music drama links drama and music in the service of a single dramatic idea. Together with scenery, staging, and action, they comprise a *Gesamtkunstwerk* (total artwork). Vocal lines are only part of a complete texture in which the orchestra plays a leading role, and music is continuous throughout an act rather than being broken into separate numbers, despite echoes of earlier types such as recitative, arioso, aria, and scene.

B. The Leitmotif

In Wagner's music dramas, a person, thing, or idea may be associated with a motive called a *Leitmotif.* By recalling and developing these motives, Wagner creates unity, draws connections, and makes the music itself the locus of dramatic action. These differ from the reminiscence motives of Verdi and Weber by being briefer, more numerous, and more pervasive in the music and by acquiring new meanings as they are developed and joined with others. By linking leitmotifs and connecting passages in an unbroken stream, Wagner sought to create an endless melody, a *musical prose* in place of the "poetic" four-square phrases of other composers. **Music: NAWM 121**

C. Wagner's Influence

The complex chromatic chords, constant modulation, and evasion of resolutions that characterize Wagner's harmony in *Tristan und Isolde* created a novel, ambiguous approach to tonality. His concept of opera as a combination of many arts and his notions of continuous music and of musical prose strongly influenced later composers.

STUDY QUESTIONS

Italy (HWM 603–8, NAWM 117–18)

1. Briefly trace Rossini's career.

2. Who were the most important composers of Italian opera in the 1830s? What types of opera did each compose?

Music to Study
> **NAWM 117:** Gioachino Rossini, *Il barbiere di Siviglia* (The Barber of Seville), opera (1816), Act II, Scene 5: Cavatina, *Una voce poco fa*
> CD 9.43–46
> **NAWM 118:** Vincenzo Bellini, *Norma,* opera (1831), Act I, Scene 4: Scena and Cavatina, *Casta diva*
> CD 10.1–6

3. What was a *cavatina* in Rossini's time? How does *Una voce poco fa,* from Rossini's *Il barbiere di Siviglia* (NAWM 117), exemplify it?

4. At the beginning of this excerpt, what is the relationship between the instrumental introduction and the vocal melody that follows?

   At the Moderato (m. 43), what is the relationship between the instrumental passage and the following vocal melody?

5. Diagram the form of the whole scene, including indications of instrumental and vocal sections and changes of tempo, style, and figuration. How does this compare to the typical structure of a solo scene in a Rossini opera? How do the changes of style, tempo, and figuration in the different sections correspond to and help to convey what Rosina is saying and feeling?

6. How does Rossini's style compare to the operatic styles of Pergolesi (NAWM 85), Hasse (NAWM 86), Gluck (NAWM 88), and Mozart (NAWM 100)? Pay particular attention to the forms used, the melodic style, and the way the voice is accompanied.

7. Diagram the scene from *Norma* (NAWM 118), showing changes of tempo, performing forces, and type. How does this fit the standard pattern for a scene in Italian opera at this time? How do the contrasts between elements convey Norma's inner conflict?

8. Compare the melodic writing of Bellini's Andante section to that in the Andante section of Rossini's *Una voce poco fa* (NAWM 117). What differences and similarities do you see? What characteristics mark the styles of Rossini and Bellini in their slow arias?

9. Now compare both to the melodic writing in Chopin's Nocturne in E-flat Major (NAWM 109). What does Chopin's melodic style have in common with Rossini's? With Bellini's?

France (HWM 608–13)

10. How did political and economic changes affect opera and musical theater in France from the early to middle nineteenth century?

11. What is *grand opera*? In what ways does *Les Huguenots* exemplify the style?

    Who were the librettist and composer for *Les Huguenots*?

    librettist: _____   composer: _____

    What theater was associated with grand opera, and who was its director?

    theater: _____   director: _____

12. What is *opéra bouffe,* and when and why did it come into existence?

    Who was a major composer of *opéras bouffes*? _____

    Who were major composers of comic opera or operetta in England and Vienna?

    England: _____   Vienna: _____

13. What is *lyric opera*? How does it differ from grand opera and opéra bouffe?

14. Who wrote the following operas, and when?

    Carmen _____   *Les Troyens* _____

    What are the special qualities of each of these operas?

Giuseppe Verdi (HWM 614–17, NAWM 119)

15. In what ways was Verdi a nationalist composer? How was his name used as a nationalist emblem?

16. Describe the following periods of Verdi's career and the main features of each: (1) to 1853, (2) 1854–71, and (3) after 1871. Name and describe at least one opera from each period, highlighting the aspects that are typical for his operas around that time.

Music to Study
   NAWM 119: Giuseppe Verdi, *La traviata* (The Fallen Woman), opera
         (1853), excerpt from Act III: Scena and Duet
      CD 10.7–10 (Concise 3.63–66)

17. Compare the dialogue in the opening part (mm. 1–34) of this scene from
    Verdi's *La traviata* (NAWM 119) to the dialogue in recitative in the excerpt
    from Mozart's *Don Giovanni* in NAWM 100. What procedures does Verdi
    use to convey the sense of a spontaneous dialogue, without resorting to
    recitative? What does the orchestral backing provide?

18. How does Verdi use various musical forces, textures, and types to further the
    drama in this scene? How does this compare with the textures and types used
    in the excerpts from Rossini's *Il barbiere di Siviglia* (NAWM 117) and
    Bellini's *Norma* (NAWM 118)? (Note that the final cabaletta of the Verdi is
    omitted from the excerpt in NAWM.)

19. In the Andante section of the scene, *Parigi, o cara,* how does Verdi's melodic style compare to that of the slow arias in the excerpts from Rossini and Bellini (NAWM 117–18, and see question 8 above)?

Germany (HWM 618–21, NAWM 120)

Music to Study
> **NAWM 120:** Carl Maria von Weber, *Der Freischütz* (The Free Shot), opera (1821), Act II, Finale (Wolf's Glen Scene)
> CD 10.11–21

20. What are the distinguishing characteristics of German Romantic opera plots in the early nineteenth century? How are they exemplified in Weber's *Der Freischütz* as a whole and in the Wolf's Glen Scene (NAWM 120)?

21. What is *melodrama*? How is it used in the Wolf's Glen Scene from Weber's *Der Freischütz*? Why do you think it might be more effective here than recitative?

22. What supernatural events happen in the Wolf's Glen Scene? For each one, how does Weber depict it in the music? How does he use tritones, diminished or augmented harmonies, orchestration, sudden dynamic change, or other effects to create a feeling of the supernatural or spooky? (Note: In examining the harmony, remember that the clarinets in A sound a minor third lower than written; the horns in D a minor seventh lower than written; and the trumpets in D a whole step higher than written.)

Richard Wagner and the Music Drama (HWM 621–28, NAWM 121)

23. Who wrote the librettos for Wagner's operas? _____

24. What does *Gesamtkunstwerk* mean? What is its importance for Wagner?

25. Name (in English or German) and give the dates for Wagner's last three Romantic operas:

_____   _____

_____

Name (in English or German) and give the dates for his seven music dramas and indicate by (R) which are part of his cycle *The Ring of the Nibelungs*:

_____   _____

_____   _____

_____   _____

_____

26. What is a *music drama*? How does a music drama such as *Tristan und Isolde* differ from a Romantic opera?

Music to Study
    NAWM 121: Richard Wagner, *Tristan und Isolde* (1857–59), excerpt from
          Act I, Scene 5
    CD 10.22–30 (Concise 4.1–9)

27. How do text, action, scenery, and music reinforce each other in this scene from *Tristan und Isolde* (NAWM 121)? How is this like, and how is it different from, the scene from Verdi's *La traviata* in NAWM 119?

28. In the section from m. 132 to 188, how do the singers' melodies relate to the melodies in the orchestra? Where does the musical continuity lie, with the singers or with the orchestra, and how is continuity achieved?

How does this compare to the scene from *La traviata*?

How does it compare to the excerpts from operas by Rossini and Bellini in NAWM 117–18?

29. How do Wagner's vocal melodies here and throughout the scene compare to those of Rossini, Bellini, and Verdi in NAWM 117–19? Include observations on phrasing and overall shape as well as on vocal embellishment. What are the main characteristics of Wagner's vocal style?

30. What is a *leitmotif*? Where do leitmotifs appear in this scene from *Tristan und Isolde,* and how are they used? (Note: Several appeared earlier, in the overture, and will recur in Acts II and III.)

31. How does the harmonic language used for the sailors (e.g., at mm. 196–203, "Hail! King Mark, hail!") differ from that used for Tristan and Isolde after they have drunk the love potion? Why is this contrast appropriate, and how does it heighten the drama?

32. What aspects of Wagner's music were especially influential on later composers?

33. Why did Wagner attack "Judaism in music"? How have his antisemitic views interacted with wider German culture and history? How have they affected his reputation?

TERMS TO KNOW

scena
primo tempo
tempo di mezzo
cabaletta
cavatina
opera semiseria
grand opera
opéra comique
opéra bouffe

lyric opera
exoticism
realism
reminiscence motive
melodrama
music drama
Gesamtkunstwerk
Leitmotif
musical prose

NAMES TO KNOW

Names Related to Italian Opera

Gioachino Rossini
Il barbiere di Siviglia (The
    Barber of Seville)
Guillaume Tell (William Tell)
Vincenzo Bellini
Gaetano Donizetti

Giuseppe Verdi
La traviata
Aida
Otello
Falstaff

Names Related to French Opera

Eugène Scribe
Giacomo Meyerbeer
Les Huguenots
Jacques Offenbach
La Damnation de Faust

Les Troyens
Faust
Charles Gounod
Carmen
Georges Bizet

Names Related to German Opera and Music Drama

Carl Maria von Weber
Der Freischütz
Richard Wagner
Das Judentum in der Musik
    (Judaism in Music)
Der fliegende Holländer (The
    Flying Dutchman)
Tannhäuser
Lohengrin
Der Ring des Nibelungen (The
    Ring of the Nibelungs)

Das Rheingold (The Rhine
    Gold)
Die Walküre (The Valkyrie)
Siegfried
Götterdämmerung (The Twilight
    Twilight of the Gods)
Tristan und Isolde
Die Meistersinger von Nürnberg
    (The Mastersingers of
    Nuremberg)
Parsifal

REVIEW QUESTIONS

1. Add the composers and major works discussed in this chapter to the time-line you made for chapter 16.

2. What types of opera were written for production in Paris in the nineteenth century? Trace the emergence of the new types of opera, name a significant composer and opera for each type, and briefly describe what makes each type distinctive.

3. How were Italian and German composers influenced by French opera? Include in your answer some discussion of Italian and German composers who wrote operas for Paris, and name those operas.

4. Describe the operas and operatic styles of Rossini, Bellini, and Verdi, noting the similarities and differences among them. Use examples from NAWM 117–19 to illustrate your points.

5. Trace the development of Verdi's operas. What changed, and what remained constant?

6. How does the German Romantic opera of Weber and early Wagner differ from Italian and French opera in the first half of the nineteenth century? Use examples from the works excerpted in NAWM or described in HWM to support your answer.

7. Describe the mature style of Wagner in his music dramas, using the scene from *Tristan und Isolde* in NAWM 121 as an example. At the end of your essay, explain the elements of this style that were particularly influential on later composers.

EUROPEAN MUSIC FROM THE 1870s TO WORLD WAR I

19

CHAPTER OBJECTIVES

After you complete the reading, study of the music, and study questions for this chapter, you should be able to

1. name some of the most prominent European composers active in the late nineteenth and early twentieth centuries, characterize their styles, and describe some of their music;
2. describe the varieties of musical nationalism that were prominent at this time;
3. define and describe impressionism and related trends in music of this period.

CHAPTER OUTLINE

I. The German Tradition (HWM 631–44, NAWM 122–24)

A. Overview

After Wagner, the search for an individual voice led composers in many different directions, undermining the shared conventions of the Classic and Romantic eras, including tonality.

B. Wolf

Hugo Wolf (1860–1903) is best known for his 250 lieder, which brought to the art song Wagner's harmony and fusion of voice and instrument. Wolf sought an equality between words and music, choosing only excellent poets and writing collections of lieder on poems by a single poet or group as if to keep poet and composer on an equal basis. The musical continuity is often in the piano, while the voice has a speechlike arioso.   **Music: NAWM 122**

C. Mahler

Gustav Mahler (1860–1911) made a career as a conductor, directing the Vienna Opera (1897–1907) and the New York Philharmonic (1907–11). He completed nine symphonies and five song cycles with orchestra.

D. Mahler's Symphonies

Mahler's symphonies are long and often programmatic. He uses a large orchestra but often creates delicate effects with unusual instruments and combinations. Several symphonies are based in part on his songs, and four include voices. Mahler included a greater diversity of elements and styles than did earlier symphonists, seeking to suggest a world in all its variety, as in the diverse movements and sharp contrasts of his Fourth Symphony. His music often suggests irony or parody. Four symphonies begin and end in different keys.

E. Mahler's Lieder with Orchestra
The orchestral song cycle *Kindertotenlieder* (Songs on the Death of Children, 1901–4) uses the large orchestra and chromatic harmony of Wagner in a spare, haunting style. *Das Lied von der Erde* (The Song of the Earth, 1908), on poems translated from Chinese, alternates between ecstasy and resignation. Heir to the nineteenth-century symphony and the Viennese tradition, Mahler was a prime influence on Schoenberg, Berg, and Webern in the next generation.   **Music: NAWM 123**

F. Richard Strauss
Richard Strauss (1864–1949) is renowned for his symphonic poems, most written before 1900, and operas, most written after 1900. Like Mahler, he also wrote lieder and was well known as a conductor.

G. Strauss's Symphonic Poems
Symphonic poems may have a philosophical program, as do Strauss's *Tod und Verklärung* (Death and Transfiguration, 1889) and *Also sprach Zarathustra* (So Spoke Zoroaster, 1896, after a prose-poem by Friedrich Nietzsche), or a descriptive program that narrates a series of events, like his *Till Eulenspiegels lustige Streiche* (Till Eulenspiegel's Merry Pranks, 1889) and *Don Quixote* (1897).   **Music: NAWM 124**

H. Operas
Strauss achieved new fame as an opera composer with *Salome* (1905), whose decadent subject he captured with heightened dissonance and contrast. *Elektra* (1908) uses sharp, apparently unresolved dissonance contrasted with diatonic passages to tell the tragic story, along with leitmotifs and the association of certain keys with characters. *Der Rosenkavalier* (The Cavalier of the Rose, 1911) has a lighter setting and plot and is thus much less dissonant and more melodious. *Ariadne auf Naxos* (Ariadne at Naxos, 1912, rev. 1916) hearkens back to the sounds and conventions of the Classic era.

I. Humperdinck, Reger, and Pfitzner
Engelbert Humperdinck's fairy-tale opera *Hänsel und Gretel* (1893) combined Wagnerian orchestration and leitmotifs with folklike melodies. Max Reger (1873–1916) united Brahms's interest in form and counterpoint with Wagner's chromatic and modulatory harmony. Hans Pfitzner is best known for his operas.

II. National Trends (HWM 644–60, NAWM 125–26)

A. General

Nationalism in culture and music was evident in the eighteenth century in the choice of the vernacular for writings about music (instead of using Latin) and for musical theater (instead of Italian). Many in the nineteenth century sought to unify their nation (identified by a common language), as in the case of Italy and Germany, or liberate it from foreign rule. In this, pride in a language, its literature, and the nation's art was a key element. German nationalism was a strong force behind the revival of Bach, Handel, and other German-speaking composers. Composers contributed to the cultural definition of their nations by choosing patriotic subjects or topics drawn from national literature; using national, folk, or folklike melodies or rhythms; or setting texts in the national language. Composers in Russia, eastern Europe, England, France, and the United States especially sought a national style.

B. Russia

Mikhail Glinka (1804–1857) was the first Russian composer recognized for a distinctively Russian style, notably in his operas *A Life for the Tsar* (1836) and *Ruslan and Lyudmila* (1842). Tchaikovsky was more a cosmopolitan than a nationalist, but he chose Russian subjects for his operas. *The Mighty Handful* (or Mighty Five) was a group of five composers who sought a fresh Russian style founded on folk music and exoticism. César Cui is the least well known today. *Mily Balakirev* (1837–1910) collected folk songs and used folk melodies in a Romantic style. *Alexander Borodin* (1833–1887) was a chemist best known for symphonic works, quartets, and an opera. He seldom used folk tunes, but his melodies have some of their flavor.

C. Musorgsky

Modest Musorgsky (1839–1881) was the most original of the Five. In his opera *Boris Godunov* (premiered 1874) and his songs, his vocal melodies follow Russian speech accents closely and imitate Russian folk songs, which move in a narrow range, repeat rhythmic and melodic motives, and are modal rather than tonal. Musorgsky's harmony is innovative and his music depicts physical gestures realistically. His music creates its effects by repeating and accumulating ideas, not by developing themes.   **Music: NAWM 125**

D. Rimsky-Korsakov and Others

Nikolay Rimsky-Korsakov (1844–1908) was one of the Five but later developed a broader, still national idiom. He taught at the St. Petersburg Conservatory and was a master of orchestration. His principal works are symphonic poems and operas, which often render human characters in a diatonic, modal style and supernatural characters and events in a chromatic, fanciful style marked by *whole-tone* and *octatonic scales* (respectively, scales composed of all whole tones or whole and half steps in strict alternation). He taught Alexander Glazunov, Igor Stravinsky (discussed in chapter 20), and many others. *Sergei Rakhmaninov* (1873–

1943), a virtuoso pianist, wrote passionate, melodious piano concertos and other works in a style that was not deliberately nationalist.

E. Skryabin

Alexander Skryabin (1872–1915) wrote mostly for the piano, beginning in a style derived from Chopin and evolving to an individual idiom that was no longer tonal but used a complex chord or collection of notes as a reference point akin to a tonic chord. He sought a synthesis of the arts and intended his orchestral work *Prometheus* (1910) to be performed with changing colored lights.   **Music: NAWM 126**

F. Central Europe

Bedřich Smetana (1824–1884) and Antonin Dvořák, the main nineteenth-century Czech composers, chose national subjects for program music and operas and used national dance rhythms and folklike tunes. *Leoš Janáček* (1854–1928) collected folk music and cultivated a style based on Moravian peasant speech and song. He is best known for operas, in addition to choral works, chamber music, and symphonic works.

G. Norway

Edvard Grieg (1843–1907) was a nationalist who incorporated Norwegian national traits particularly in his short piano pieces and vocal works.

H. Other Countries

Nationalist composers were also active in Poland, Denmark, and the Netherlands.

I. Finland

Finnish composer *Jean Sibelius* (1865–1957) drew programs and song texts from the literature of Finland, especially the national epic, the *Kalevala*. He did not use or imitate folk songs. He is best known for symphonic poems, seven symphonies, and the Violin Concerto. Sibelius is most original in his themes, his treatment of form, and the way his themes grow, develop, and interact.

J. England

Edward Elgar (1857–1934) wrote in a style derived from Brahms and Wagner rather from English folk song.

K. Spain

Spanish nationalism was sparked by the operas of Felipe Pedrell (1841–1922) and the piano music of Isaac Albéniz (1860–1909). The principal Spanish composer of the early twentieth century was *Manuel de Falla* (1876–1946), who used rhythms and melodic turns from Spanish popular music.

III. New Currents in France (HWM 660–70, NAWM 127–29)

A. General

The *National Society for French Music,* founded in 1871 at the end of the Franco-Prussian War, performed music of living French composers and revived French music of the sixteenth through eighteenth centuries, helping to strengthen an independent French musical tradition. Three traditions coexisted in French music after 1871: a cosmopolitan tradition around Franck and d'Indy, a French tradition around Saint-Saëns and Fauré, and a new style developed by Debussy.

B. The Cosmopolitan Tradition

César Franck and his student *Vincent d'Indy* (1851–1931) represent a cosmopolitan tradition in France influenced by Wagner. Franck worked in instrumental genres and oratorio, enriching a restrained, traditional idiom with counterpoint and cyclic form. D'Indy also used cyclic transformation of themes.

C. The French Tradition

French music from Couperin to Gounod is typified by emotional reserve, lyricism, economy, refinement, and interest in well-ordered form rather than self-expression. The works of Camille Saint-Saëns (1835–1921) and the operas of Jules Massenet (1842–1912) combine this tradition with Romantic touches. *Gabriel Fauré* (1845–1924) studied with Saint-Saëns, worked as an organist, helped to found the National Society for French Music, taught composition at the Paris Conservatoire, and became its director. His refined songs, piano pieces, and chamber works are marked by lyrical melodies, lack of virtuosic display, and harmony that does not drive toward a tonic resolution, but instead suggests repose. His students included Ravel and *Nadia Boulanger* (1887–1979), who taught many later composers. **Music: NAWM 127**

D. Debussy

Claude Debussy (1862–1918) exercised a major influence on twentieth-century music. His style, called *impressionism* (a term he disliked) by analogy with the impressionist painters, suggested a mood or atmosphere rather than expressing the deep emotions of Romanticism. He absorbed influences from many composers, including Wagner, Liszt, Musorgsky, and French composers from Couperin to Ravel. Although his music usually has a tonal center, the harmony is often coloristic and the strong pull to resolution is missing, creating a sense of movement without direction and of pleasure without urgency. His orchestration features a great variety of sounds and colors. His most important music includes orchestral pieces, many songs and piano works, and the opera *Pelléas et Mélisande* (1902). He was a seminal force in music history, influencing almost every significant composer of the early and middle twentieth century. **Music: NAWM 128**

E. Satie

Erik Satie (1865–1925) was an avant-garde iconoclast who changed his style but consistently opposed sentimentality. His early piano pieces challenged Romantic pretension through deliberate simplicity and a modal, nonfunctional harmony that paved the way for impressionism. His later piano works mocked impressionism with parodistic music, surreal titles, and satirical commentary printed in the score. *Socrate* (1920) for singers and chamber orchestra is strangely moving in its austere simplicity, stylistic monotony, and avoidance of emotion.

F. Ravel

Maurice Ravel (1875–1937) looked back to the eighteenth-century French tradition in *Le Tombeau de Couperin* (for piano 1917, orchestrated 1919) and other works. His music features clear classic forms, functional harmonies, and colorful orchestration. He also wrote several impressionist works for piano or orchestra. Some of his music, such as the famous *Bolero* (1928), uses Spanish idioms.   **Music: NAWM 129**

G. Other French Composers

Other French composers of the early twentieth century include Paul Dukas, Florent Schmitt, and Albert Roussel.

IV. Italian Opera (HWM 670–71)

One trend in Italian opera in the late nineteenth century is *verismo* (realism or naturalism), which sought a realistic depiction of everyday people in extreme dramatic situations. *Giacomo Puccini* (1858–1924) was an eclectic composer who combined realism and exoticism with intense emotion through a style focused on melody over spare but harmonically enriched accompaniment.

STUDY QUESTIONS

The German Tradition (HWM 631–44, NAWM 122–24)

1. What texts did Wolf choose for his songs? What was his approach to the relationship of music and poetry?

Music to Study
   NAWM 122: Hugo Wolf, *Kennst du das Land,* lied (1888)
      CD 10.31–38

2. Diagram and describe the form of Wolf's *Kennst du das Land* (NAWM 122).

3. Compare Wolf's vocal style in this song to that of Schubert's lieder (NAWM 111–12) and to that of Wagner's *Tristan und Isolde* (NAWM 121). What are the similarities and differences in each comparison? Which earlier composer does Wolf's style resemble most?

4. What is the relationship in Wolf's song between the voice and the piano? Which part carries the musical continuity?

5. How does the piano part in Wolf's song compare to the piano parts in Schubert's lieder? What aspects of Wagner's operatic style does it incorporate?

6. Describe the characteristics of Mahler's symphonies that distinguish them from other nineteenth-century symphonies. How are these characteristics exemplified in the Fourth Symphony, as excerpted and discussed in HWM, pp. 635–37? How does Mahler suggest a varied world in this work?

Music to Study
   NAWM 123: Gustav Mahler, *Kindertotenlieder,* song cycle with orchestra
      (1901–4), No. 1: *Nun will die Sonn' so hell aufgeh'n*
   CD 10.39–40 (Concise 4.10–11)

7. Mahler's setting of *Nun will die Sonn' so hell aufgeh'n* (NAWM 123) high-lights the irony in the poem. In the poem, the tragedy that has befallen the speaker—the death of his child during the night—is ignored by the sun, which rises as if nothing bad has happened. Mahler heightens the irony by mismatching sad, lonely music to the bright, warm images in the first line of the poem, and bright, warm music to the sadness of the second line. Later repetition or reworking of these contrasting musical ideas is also ironic.

a. How is the effect of sadness and loneliness achieved in the music for the first line? How does the contour of the vocal line negate the poetic image of a rising sun?

b. How does the music of the second line suggest the rising sun and the warming earth?

c. How does the varied repetition of this opening section in mm. 22–40 con-tinue or expand upon the ironic setting of the first two lines of the poem?

d. How does the music in mm. 40–63 work against the apparently comfort-ing message of the text?

e. What indication is there in the music at the end of the song that the protagonist utters the final line, "Blessed be the joyous light of the world," with irony rather than with sincerity?

8. How does Mahler use the orchestra in this song? How is it different from Wagner's use of the orchestra in the excerpt from *Tristan und Isolde* (NAWM 121)?

9. What two kinds of program did Richard Strauss use in his symphonic poems? Name and describe two works of each type.

Music to Study
NAWM 124: Richard Strauss, *Don Quixote,* symphonic poem (1897), excerpts: Themes and Variations 1 and 2
CD 10.41–46 (Concise 4.12–17)

10. How does Strauss characterize Don Quixote and Sancho Panza in the themes of his *Don Quixote* (NAWM 124)? What musical devices does he use to depict their personalities?

11. How are these themes treated and varied in the first two variations, given in NAWM 124? What does this suggest, in terms of the story? Why is variation form appropriate to the tale?

12. What instrumental effects does Strauss use to suggest the bleating sheep and piping shepherds in the second variation? (Hint: The three strokes through the stems indicate tremolo on the strings or fluttertonguing on brass or wind instruments, a very rapid motion of the tongue that creates a blatty or buzzy sound; "mit Dämpfer" means "with a mute.")

13. Based on the descriptions of *Salome, Elektra, Der Rosenkavalier,* and *Ariadne auf Naxos* in HWM, pp. 641–43, what is distinctive about each of these operas?

National Trends (HWM 644–60, NAWM 125–26)

14. Briefly recount the political and cultural background to nationalism and describe the ways it was manifested in music from the eighteenth century through the early twentieth century.

15. What was the role of Glinka in the creation of a Russian national music?

16. What was *the Mighty Handful*? Who took part? What were their goals?

17. Briefly describe the styles and contributions of Rimsky-Korsakov and Rakhmaninov.

Music to Study
>   **NAWM 125:** Modest Musorgsky, *Bez solntsa* (Sunless), song cycle (1874),
>   No. 3, *Okonchen prazdnyi, shumnyi* (The idle, noisy day is over)
>   CD 11.1–2
>   **NAWM 126:** Alexander Skryabin, *Vers la flamme* (Toward the flame),
>   poem for piano, Op. 72 (1914)
>   CD 11.3–5

18. What is unusual about the harmony in Musorgsky's *Okonchen prazdnyi,
    shumnyi* (NAWM 125)? Cite and describe some unusual progressions.

19. How does the vocal line in Musorgsky's song compare to that of the other
    nineteenth-century songs you have studied, by Schubert, Robert Schumann,
    Clara Schumann, and Wolf (NAWM 111–14 and 122)?

20. How does the vocal line in mm. 31–34 of Musorgsky's song show the
    influence of Russian folk melody (see HWM, pp. 648–49)? Are there folk
    influences elsewhere in the song, and if so, where?

21. *Vers la flamme* (NAWM 126) is not tonal in a traditional sense. What kinds of chords does Skryabin use? How does he create a sense of tonal motion? What chord progressions (or root progressions) does he use most often?

22. What is the relationship between the opening passage of the piece and the closing passage (mm. 107–37) in terms of theme, rhythm, and harmony? How is a sense achieved of ending on a kind of tonic chord?

23. Describe the rhythm of this piece. Does it suggest a strong forward motion, or a static hovering? How is the effect achieved?

24. Name nationalist composers active in Czech regions, Norway, Finland, and Spain in the late nineteenth and early twentieth centuries and briefly describe what made their music nationalist.

New Currents in France (HWM 660–70, NAWM 127–29)

25. What was the National Society for French Music? When was it founded, what did it do, and what was its importance?

26. According to HWM, what are the three most significant tendencies in French music in the late nineteenth and early twentieth centuries? Describe the music of at least one composer associated with each.

Music to Study
   NAWM 127: Gabriel Fauré, *La bonne chanson* (The Good Song), Op. 61, song cycle (1891), No. 6, *Avant que tu ne t'en ailles*
      CD 11.6–10
   NAWM 128: Claude Debussy, *Trois Nocturnes,* tone poem suite (1899), No. 1: *Nuages* (Clouds)
      CD 11.11–16 (Concise 4.18–23)

27. What are the characteristics of Fauré's melodic and harmonic style, and how are they exemplified in *Avant que tu ne t'en ailles* (NAWM 127)?

28. How do the changes of texture, harmonic color, piano figuration, melodic style, tempo, and meter highlight the form, moods, and images of the poem?

29. How does Debussy use harmony and other factors in *Nuages* (NAWM 128) to create a sense of movement without direction, like clouds?

30. The motive in the English horn uses a fragment of an octatonic scale (alternating half and whole steps, here notated *C–B–A–G#–F#* and sounding a fifth lower) is never played by another instrument, while the English horn never plays anything else. It is never transposed, and it is changed only by omitting notes until all that remains is *B–A–F#* (as notated). How does this treatment of a motive differ from motivic development as practiced in the nineteenth century? If motivic development suggests a drama or story, with the motives as characters, in what ways does Debussy's approach suggest a visual impression, rather than a plot?

31. How does the section at mm. 64–79 imitate a Javanese gamelan?

32. If the form is ABA', what is the relationship of the final A' (mm. 80–102) to the first A section (mm. 1–63)? What happened to the clouds?

33. How does Debussy use the orchestra? How does this reinforce the sense of a visual impression moving without direction, rather than a drama with conflict and resolution? Take Strauss's use of the orchestra in *Don Quixote* (NAWM 124) as a point of comparison.

34. Briefly describe Satie's musical aesthetic and style.

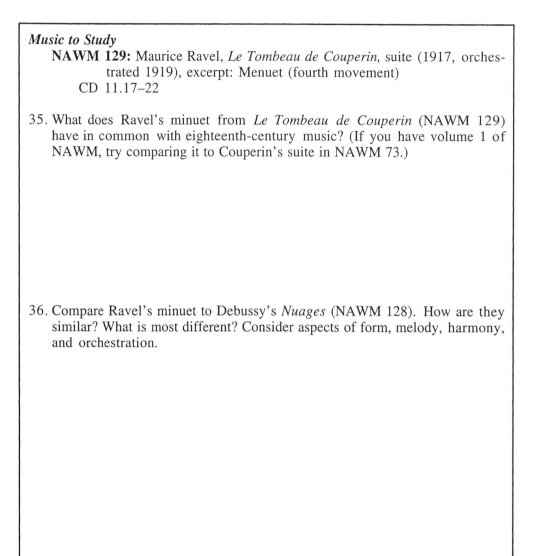

Music to Study
    NAWM 129: Maurice Ravel, *Le Tombeau de Couperin,* suite (1917, orches-
        trated 1919), excerpt: Menuet (fourth movement)
    CD 11.17–22

35. What does Ravel's minuet from *Le Tombeau de Couperin* (NAWM 129)
    have in common with eighteenth-century music? (If you have volume 1 of
    NAWM, try comparing it to Couperin's suite in NAWM 73.)

36. Compare Ravel's minuet to Debussy's *Nuages* (NAWM 128). How are they
    similar? What is most different? Consider aspects of form, melody, harmony,
    and orchestration.

Italian Opera (HWM 670–71)

37. What is *verismo*? What are some notable examples of it?

TERMS TO KNOW

nationalism
whole-tone scale
octatonic scale

impressionism
verismo

NAMES TO KNOW

Names Related to the German Tradition

Hugo Wolf
Gustav Mahler
Kindertotenlieder
Das Lied von der Erde (The
   Song of the Earth)
Richard Strauss
Tod und Verklärung (Death
   and Transfiguration)
Also sprach Zarathustra

Till Eulenspiegels lustige Streiche
   (Till Eulenspiegel's Merry
   Pranks)
Don Quixote
Salome
Elektra
Der Rosenkavalier
Ariadne auf Naxos
Hänsel und Gretel

Names Related to Nationalism in Eastern and Northern Europe and Spain

Mikhail Glinka
A Life for the Tsar
Ruslan and Lyudmila
The Mighty Handful
Mily Balakirev
Alexander Borodin
Modest Musorgsky
Boris Godunov
Nikolay Rimsky–Korsakov

Sergei Rakhmaninov
Alexander Skryabin
Prometheus
Bedřich Smetana
Leoš Janáček
Edvard Grieg
Jean Sibelius
Edward Elgar
Manuel de Falla

Names Related to French and Italian Music

National Society for French
   Music
Vincent d'Indy
Gabriel Fauré
Nadia Boulanger
Claude Debussy

Pelléas et Mélisande
Erik Satie
Socrate
Maurice Ravel
Le Tombeau de Couperin
Giacomo Puccini

REVIEW QUESTIONS

1. Add the composers and major works from the nineteenth century discussed
   in this chapter to the time-line you made for chapter 16. Make a new time-
   line for the entire twentieth century, and place on it the twentieth-century
   composers and major works discussed here. Leave plenty of space, as you
   will be adding to it in chapters 20–22. (Some composers, such as Strauss, will
   appear on both time-lines.)

2. How did Wolf, Mahler, and Strauss respond to the German Romantic tradition from Beethoven through Wagner? What elements did they continue in their music, what aspects did they further intensify or develop, and what did they introduce that was new and individual?

3. What is nationalism, and how is it manifested in music of the nineteenth and early twentieth centuries?

4. Beethoven's music conveys a sense of drama and forward motion toward a goal, as in the first movement of his *Eroica* Symphony (NAWM 103). Some of the music studied in this chapter conveys a different sense, of harmonic and rhythmic stasis, or of movement that is not directed toward a goal. Compare the works you have studied by Musorgsky, Skryabin, Fauré, and Debussy (NAWM 125–28) with Beethoven and with each other, seeking to show what musical techniques these later composers use to avoid tension, negate forward momentum, and create a musical experience of being present in the moment, rather than striving toward a goal.

5. For the following pairs of composers, compare and contrast their musical styles and aesthetics, showing what they have in common as composers from the same nation and what is individual about each: Mahler and Strauss; Musorgsky and Skryabin; Debussy and Ravel.

THE EUROPEAN MAINSTREAM IN THE TWENTIETH CENTURY

20

CHAPTER OBJECTIVES

After you complete the reading, study of the music, and study questions for this chapter, you should be able to

1. identify some of the factors that have led to a diversity of musical style and technique in the twentieth century that is greater than in any previous era;
2. name some of the most significant composers active after World War I in Hungary, Russia, England, Germany, and France and describe what makes their music individual;
3. describe the synthesis of folk and classical elements in the music of Bartók;
4. describe the music of Shostakovich and his circumstances under the Soviet regime;
5. summarize the careers and describe the musical styles of Hindemith and Stravinsky.

CHAPTER OUTLINE

I. Introduction (HWM 676–79)

After World War I, the division of the former Austro-Hungarian Empire, the rise of totalitarian regimes in Russia, Italy, Germany, and Spain, and a worldwide economic depression in the 1930s reduced cultural interaction between nations and led to a growing diversity in musical trends. Some composers abandoned common-practice tonality, goal-directed harmony, or thematic development. Folk and traditional music from Eastern Europe and Asia offered new possibilities in rhythm and pitch organization. Neo-Classic music evoked forms and styles of the eighteenth century. Composers of film music and of *Gebrauchsmusik* (workaday or utility music) for schools and amateurs sought more accessible idioms. The Soviet and Nazi regimes controlled music in Russia and Germany and condemned most modern music. After World War II, many composers turned to aleatoric and serial music, which found few avid listeners. In reaction, the desire to reach a wider audience led to new approaches after about 1970, such as minimalism, neo-Romanticism, and blends of popular music with the classical tradition. Throughout the century, recordings, radio, and television furthered the spread of both popular music and art music around the world. The diversity of music in the twentieth century was unprecedented, as composers sought individual paths even within wider trends.

II. Ethnic Contexts (HWM 680–84, NAWM 130)

A. Collecting Ethnic Musics
New recording technologies aided the collection and study of the music of traditional peoples, and the new scholarly discipline of ethnomusicology led to greater understanding of it. Rather than changing this music to fit art music, as had been done in the previous century, composers used it and elements from it to create new styles.

B. Bartók
Béla Bartók (1881–1945) collected and published folk tunes from his native Hungary, Romania, and elsewhere. Besides arranging folk tunes or incorporating them in his music, he synthesized a personal style that united folk and art music. He was also a pianist and a piano teacher, and his *Mikrokosmos* (1926–37) is a series of graded piano pieces that encapsulates his style. He used traditional forms, producing a distinguished series of six string quartets, two violin concertos, a piano sonata, three piano concertos, the Concerto for Orchestra (1943), and other works. From the Western tradition he took imitative and fugal techniques, sonata and other forms, and thematic development; from eastern Europe, modal and other scales, irregular meters, harmonic seconds and fourths, and certain melodic types. Most of his music has a tonal center, but this is established in novel ways. His *Music for Strings, Percussion, and Celesta* (1936) has a tonal center on A, with a secondary center a tritone away. The middle movements also feature a tritone relationship, between C and F-sharp. The piece shows Bartók's fondness for mirror form and his incorporation of elements of folk style.   **Music: NAWM 130**

C. Kodály
Zoltán Kodály (1882–1967) also collected Hungarian folk tunes and developed a strongly nationalist style. He was well known as a music educator and developed an influential method of teaching music to children.

III. The Soviet Orbit (HWM 684–89, NAWM 131–32)

A. Prokofiev
Sergey Prokofiev (1891–1953) left his native Russia after the 1917 Bolshevik Revolution, toured as a pianist, and composed on commission. He returned to the Soviet Union in 1934 and wrote some of his most popular music there. Soviet authorities demanded that composers adhere to the concept of *socialist realism* and attacked Prokofiev for *formalism*.

B. Shostakovich
Dmitri Shostakovich (1906–1975) was the most prominent composer to spend his entire career under the Soviet state, which both supported him and sought to control him. His opera *Lady Macbeth of Mtsensk* (1932, pre-

miered 1934) was an international success until it was condemned by the official newspaper *Pravda* in 1936. His popular Fifth Symphony was written in part to win back favor from the authorities. Several of his works use his musical signature *D–E♭–C–B* (*D–Es–C–H* in German, for Dmitri SCHostakovich).   **Music: NAWM 131**

C. Post-Soviet Music
The relaxation of state control in the 1970s allowed younger composers to learn more about music in the West and to experiment with new ideas, and exchanges have intensified since the dissolution of the Soviet Union in 1991. *Alfred Schnittke* (1934–1998) often incorporated existing music or refers to Baroque and popular styles to produce music that he called *polystylistic. Sofia Gubaidulina* (b. 1931) writes music with a spiritual dimension, often inspired by Christian themes.   **Music: NAWM 132**

IV. England (HWM 689–93, NAWM 133)

A. Vaughan Williams
Ralph Vaughan Williams (1872–1958), the leading English composer of the early twentieth century, drew inspiration from English folk song, hymnody, and earlier English composers. (His first name is pronounced "Rafe," and his last name is "Vaughan Williams," not "Williams.") He wrote hymns, choral music for amateur singers, operas, nine symphonies, and other orchestral music in a mixed tonal and modal style.

B. Holst and Walton
Gustav Holst (1874–1934) and *William Walton* (1902–1982) are also significant English composers.

C. Britten
Benjamin Britten (1913–1976), the most important English composer of the century, is known for his choral works, especially the *War Requiem* (1962), and his operas, inaugurated with *Peter Grimes* (1945). His music uses simple means to convey deep human emotions. It is marked by lyrical melodies often accompanied by drones or sustained chords and by mixtures of diatonic tonality with modal and chromatic effects.   **Music: NAWM 133**

D. Tippett
Michael Tippett (1905–1998) incorporated into his music elements of historical styles, African-American music, and Javanese gamelan music. He frequently uses modal melodies in a diatonic setting.

E. More Recent Composers
Harrison Birtwistle (b. 1934) uses music in a theatrical manner—for example, giving each instrument a unique personality in a voiceless drama.

V. Germany (HWM 693–99)

A. The Nazi Regime
Nazi policies in the 1930s, especially the persecution of Jews, hindered music in Germany and led many musicians to leave.

B. Hindemith

Paul Hindemith (1895–1963) was important as a composer and teacher. His music from the 1920s is thoroughly modernist, but in the late 1920s and 1930s he began to compose *Gebrauchsmusik* in an accessible style and to give his art music a more Romantic quality. His best-known work is his symphony *Mathis der Maler* (Matthias the Painter, 1934), drawn from his opera of the same name, which examines the role of the artist in a time of political turmoil. Hindemith used a procedure he called *harmonic fluctuation,* in which phrases start with relative consonance, move toward greater dissonance, and return to consonance.

C. Orff

Carl Orff (1895–1982) is best known for his choral work *Carmina burana* (1936) and for a method for teaching music to children in schools.

D. Weill

Kurt Weill (1900–1950) composed operas in Germany on librettos by Bertolt Brecht, notably *Die Dreigroschenoper* (The Threepenny Opera, 1928), adapted from John Gay's *The Beggar's Opera.* Brecht and Weill sought to promote a social ideology, and Weill used an easily understood musical language that parodied American popular music. After the Nazis rose to power in 1933, Weill emigrated to the United States and had a second career writing Broadway musicals.

VI. Latin America (HWM 699)

Major Latin American composers of the twentieth century include *Heitor Villa-Lobos* (1887–1959) of Brazil, *Carlos Chávez* (1899–1978) of Mexico, and *Alberto Ginastera* (1916–83) of Argentina.

VII. Neo-Classicism in France (HWM 699–701)

A. Neo-Classicism

Neo-Classicism was a broad movement from the 1910s to the 1950s in which composers imitated or evoked pre-Romantic styles, genres, and forms, especially from the eighteenth century. (When the reference is to the early eighteenth century, the term neo-Baroque is now often used, and neo-Renaissance and neo-Medieval music was also written.) Much other twentieth-century music refers back to earlier periods in less obvious ways.

B. Honegger

Arthur Honegger (1892–1955) is best known for *Pacific 231* (1923), an orchestral impression of a train, and for his opera-oratorio *King David* (premiered 1923).

C. Milhaud

Darius Milhaud (1892–1974) was prolific in almost every genre. He absorbed a variety of influences, including earlier French composers, Brazilian music, ragtime, and blues. Like others of his time, Milhaud frequently used *polytonality,* in which two or more streams of music, each implying a different key, are superimposed.

D. Poulenc
Francis Poulenc (1899–1963) wrote in an engaging style influenced by French popular song and eighteenth-century French composers.

VIII. Stravinsky (HWM 702–9, NAWM 134)

A. Career
Igor Stravinsky (1882–1971) took part in most important compositional trends during his lifetime. He made his reputation with three early ballets commissioned by Sergei Diaghilev for the Ballet Russes (Russian Ballet) in Paris.

B. Early Works
All three ballets feature plots from Russian culture and use Russian folk melodies. *The Firebird* (1910) continues the exoticism and colorful orchestration of Rimsky-Korsakov, Stravinsky's teacher. Some of Stravinsky's distinctive stylistic traits emerge in the second ballet, *Petrushka* (1911), including ostinatos or repetitive melodies and rhythms over static harmony; blocks of sound that alternate without transitions; independent layers of sound that are superimposed on one another; and octatonic and polytonal sonorities. *Le Sacre du printemps* (The Rite of Spring, 1913) adds to this new orchestral effects; a greater level of dissonance, often octatonic or derived from superimposed triads; and rhythm that, through changing meters and unexpected accents and silences, negates regular meter and emphasizes instead the basic indivisible pulse, suggesting a musical *primitivism.* The ballet precipitated a riot at its premiere (although this apparently had more to do with the dance than with the music). All three ballets have since become Stravinsky's most popular works and among the most popular in the entire century.   **Music: NAWM 134**

C. 1913–1923
Partly due to economic necessity, Stravinsky's works during and just after World War I are for smaller ensembles.

D. Stravinsky's Neo-Classicism
From the 1920s to the opera *The Rake's Progress* (1951), Stravinsky adopted a neo-Classic approach that abandoned the Russian tunes and extramusical concerns of his earlier works and sought to create absolute, objective music based on historical models. This was inaugurated by his reworkings of eighteenth-century music by Pergolesi and others in the ballet *Pulcinella* (1919) and continued in a series of works that revived genres and alluded to (but never directly imitated) styles of previous eras from Machaut to Tchaikovsky. The most frequent target is the Classic era, as in the *Symphony in C* (1940), modeled after Haydn and Beethoven symphonies, and *The Rake's Progress,* modeled after Mozart operas. Despite Stravinsky's evocations of earlier styles, his music continued to show the personal characteristics listed above and exemplified in *Le Sacre du printemps.* In works of the 1950s and 1960s, he adapted the serial techniques of Schoenberg and Webern.

STUDY QUESTIONS

Introduction (HWM 676–79)

1. What were some of the factors that led to the diversity of musical aesthetics, styles, and procedures in the twentieth century?

Ethnic Contexts (HWM 680–84, NAWM 130)

2. What were Bartók's activities in music, in addition to composing?

Music to Study
    NAWM 130: Béla Bartók, *Music for Strings, Percussion, and Celesta,* suite
        (1936), Adagio (third movement)
    CD 11.23–28 (Concise 4.24–29)

3. In the Adagio movement from *Music for Strings, Percussion, and Celesta* (NAWM 130), how does Bartók use mirrors, retrogrades, and palindromes? (A palindrome is its own retrograde, as in the palindrome about Napoleon, "Able was I ere I saw Elba.")

4. What elements of east European folk music are used in this movement?

5. This movement also uses techniques derived from Western art music, in addition to the use of traditional orchestral instruments and a complex arch form. Find instances of the following (indicate by measure number):

imitation and canon _____

ostinato _____

inversion of melodic material _____

rhythmic diminution of material _____

(Note also that the entire *Music for Strings, Percussion, and Celesta* uses cyclic recurrence of the fugue theme from the first movement. The four phrases of this theme occur in the Adagio in the original order and transposition but rhythmically altered, in mm. 18–19, 33–35, 60–64, and 73–74.)

6. Bartók's synthesis of the folk and art music traditions creates something new within the realm of the orchestral repertory. List the ways in which this movement offers new sounds and ideas, in comparison with nineteenth-century symphonic music. (You may use NAWM 103, 105, and 124 as points of comparison.)

7. How are pitch centers established in this movement? On what pitch does the movement close, and what is its opposite pole? How does this fit into the key scheme of the entire work? (Hint: See HWM, p. 682.)

The Soviet Orbit (HWM 684–89, NAWM 131–32)

8. As used by Soviet authorities, what is *socialist realism*? What is *formalism*? How did Prokofiev and Shostakovich attempt to conform to the demand for socialist realism?

Music to Study
   NAWM 131: Dmitri Shostakovich, *Lady Macbeth of Mtsensk,* opera (1932): Act IV, Scene 9 (excerpt)
   CD 11.29–33

9. What characteristics of Shostakovich's *Lady Macbeth of Mtsensk* displeased the Soviet authorities? Once you translate the negative words of the *Pravda* article (quoted in NAWM) into neutral or positive ones, which of these traits, if any, appear in the excerpt in NAWM 131?

10. The *Pravda* critic accused Shostakovich of "naturalism." In what ways is the music in this excerpt from the final scene naturalistic? How does it capture the inflections and emotions of the characters?

11. Describe the main elements of Shostakovich's style in this excerpt. How does it compare to the operatic style of Wagner (see NAWM 121) and Verdi (see NAWM 119)? How does it differ from Bartók's style in *Music for Strings, Percussion, and Celesta* (NAWM 130), written about the same time?

12. What is characteristic of the music of Alfred Schnittke? Describe a typical example.

Music to Study

NAWM 132: Sofia Gubaidulina, *Rejoice!* Sonata for Violin and Violoncello (1981): *Listen to the still small voice within* (fifth movement)
CD 11.34–37 (Concise 4.30–33)

13. What spiritual lesson does Sofia Gubaidulina seek to convey in the movement from *Rejoice!* (NAWM 132)? How is it conveyed in the music?

14. Measures 1–33 introduce a basic sequence of ideas, which is then varied and added to over the course of the movement. Chart the form of the violin part, using the following code, using the prime sign (') for variants, and introducing new letters as needed for new material. Start each repetition of the basic sequence on a new line.

Motive	A	B1	C1	B2	C2	B3	D	E
Measure	1	7	10	13	16	20	25	29

Motive	A
Measure	32

Motive	A
Measure	

Motive	A
Measure	

How does Gubaidulina use repetition, variation, and contrast in this movement? How is this like traditional eighteenth- and nineteenth-century procedures, and how is it different?

England (HWM 689–93, NAWM 133)

15. Briefly describe the music of Vaughan Williams and Tippett. How does their music contrast with that of Bartók (NAWM 130) in its relation to tonality and diatonicism? In what other ways is their music similar to Bartók's?

Music to Study
> **NAWM 133:** Benjamin Britten, *Peter Grimes,* opera (1945), excerpt from Act III, Scene 2: *To hell with all your mercy!*
> CD 11.38–40

16. In the concluding scene of *Peter Grimes* (NAWM 133), how does Britten portray Grimes's madness through musical means? (Note that the passage at mm. 22–33 is a reminiscence of an earlier, more hopeful scene, but now trails off at the end.)

---

17. What musical elements (including motives, chords, keys or collections of pitches, timbres, and so on) are associated with the townspeople (the chorus) and with the sea (the figuration in the orchestra)? How does Britten create the effect of events happening simultaneously, but remaining separate from one another?

Germany (HWM 693–99)

18. Briefly summarize Hindemith's career.

19. What is the procedure Hindemith called *harmonic fluctuation*? Describe how it works in the phrase from *Mathis der Maler* excerpted in HWM, p. 695, Example 20.8b. How does it help to delineate the phrase?

20. What were Kurt Weill's "two careers"? What were his musical and dramatic aims? Describe his musical style, and explain how it suited his aims and the types of music he composed.

Latin America (HWM 699)

21. Name three significant Latin American composers and their countries of origin.

_____	_____
_____	_____
_____	_____

Neo-Classicism in France (HWM 699–701)

22. If a work is *neo-Classic,* what are some characteristics one might expect to find in it?

23. Describe the music and musical style of Milhaud.

Stravinsky (HWM 702–9, NAWM 134)

> *Music to Study*
> **NAWM 134:** Igor Stravinsky, *Le Sacre du printemps* (The Rite of Spring),
>   ballet (1913), excerpt from Part I: *Danse des adolescentes* (Dance
>   of the Adolescent Girls)
>   CD 11.41–44 (Concise 4.34–37)

24. For each of the following traits of Stravinsky's style, find two passages that
    exemplify it in *Danse des adolescentes* (NAWM 134). Indicate each passage
    by measure numbers and describe it briefly.

    ostinatos

    repetitive melodies over static harmony

    blocks of sound that succeed each other without transitions

    independent layers of sound that are superimposed on one another

    unexpected accents that negate regular meter and emphasize pulsation

    novel orchestral effects

    Note: Here is a guide to some of Stravinsky's orchestral markings:
    • In m. 1 he asks the strings to play each beat with a down-bow instead of
    bowing up and down; this will create a forceful, detached effect.
    • "Con sord." (m. 18) means "with mute," which on the trumpet yields
    a thin, metallic sound.
    • "Flttzg." (mm. 27–31) means fluttertonguing, creating a buzzy effect.
    • The cellos in mm. 78–81 have a harmonic glissando, an effect Stravin-
    sky discovered; bowing the C string while moving the finger rapidly along it
    without touching the string to the fingerboard creates this effect by allowing
    only certain overtones to sound.
    • "Col legno" (m. 82) means to hit the string with the stick of the bow.

25. Within this essentially static texture of repeating figuration and almost constant pulsation, how does Stravinsky achieve variety?

26. How does Stravinsky create the effect of building intensity toward the end of the excerpt?

27. Summarize Stravinsky's career, including where he lived, his major compositions, and the main elements of his style in each period.

28. In the excerpts from Stravinsky's Symphony in C, *The Rake's Progress,* and *Symphony of Psalms* shown in Examples 20.15–17 in HWM, pp. 706–9, what elements recall Classic or Baroque music? Which of the characteristics of Stravinsky's style listed above in question 24 do you find in one or more of these excerpts?

TERMS TO KNOW

Gebrauchsmusik   harmonic fluctuation
socialist realism   neo-Classicism
formalism   polytonality
polystylistic music   primitivism

NAMES TO KNOW

Names Related to Music in Eastern Europe and Russia

Béla Bartók   Sergey Prokofiev
Mikrokosmos   Dmitri Shostakovich
Music for Strings, Percussion,   *Lady Macbeth of Mtsensk*
  and Celesta   Alfred Schnittke
Zoltán Kodály   Sofia Gubaidulina

Names Related to Music in England and Germany

Ralph Vaughan Williams   Harrison Birtwistle
Gustav Holst   Paul Hindemith
William Walton   *Mathis der Maler*
Benjamin Britten   Carl Orff
War Requiem   Kurt Weill
Peter Grimes   *Die Dreigroschenoper* (The
Michael Tippett   Threepenny Opera)

Names Related to Music in Latin America and France

Heitor Villa-Lobos   *The Firebird*
Carlos Chávez   *Petrushka*
Alberto Ginastera   *Le Sacre du printemps* (The Rite
Arthur Honegger   of Spring)
Darius Milhaud   *Pulcinella*
Francis Poulenc   Symphony in C
Igor Stravinsky   *The Rake's Progress*

REVIEW QUESTIONS

1. Add the composers and major works discussed in this chapter to the twenti-eth-century time-line you made for chapter 19.

2. Write an essay in which you summarize the major trends in European music between about 1915 and 1950 (excepting the atonal and twelve-tone music of Schoenberg and his associates, treated in chapter 21).

3. How does Bartók achieve an individual style within the Western art music tradition by integrating traditional procedures with elements abstracted from East European folk music? Describe how this synthesis works in *Music for Strings, Percussion, and Celesta.*

4. Compare the music of Shostakovich and Gubaidulina, using the excerpts in NAWM 131–32 as examples. What was each trying to achieve in these works, and what musical procedures or traditions did each find useful in achieving these aims? What did Soviet authorities ask of composers in the Soviet Union, and how did Shostakovich and Gubaidulina relate to the Soviet state?

5. Trace the career of Igor Stravinsky, naming major pieces and describing the changes in his style. What distinctive characteristics of his music, established in *Petrushka* and *Le Sacre du printemps,* continued throughout his career, and how are these traits embodied in his neo-Classical music?

ATONALITY, SERIALISM, AND RECENT DEVELOPMENTS IN TWENTIETH-CENTURY EUROPE

21

CHAPTER OBJECTIVES

After you complete the reading, study of the music, and study questions for this chapter, you should be able to

1. describe the music and innovations of Schoenberg, Berg, and Webern;
2. describe in simple terms how twelve-tone music works and analyze a brief passage;
3. describe the style of Messiaen and some of his characteristic devices; and
4. define expressionism, total serialism, electronic music, musique concrète, and indeterminacy and name and describe at least one work representing each trend.

CHAPTER OUTLINE

I. Schoenberg and His Followers (HWM 713–25, NAWM 135–38)

A. Schoenberg's Development
Arnold Schoenberg (1874–1951) was born in Vienna and first composed in a late Romantic style derived from Wagner, Mahler, and Strauss. Around 1905, he turned to smaller ensembles and a more concentrated language with complex rhythms and counterpoint and angular melodies.

B. Atonality
In about 1908, Schoenberg began to write music that was *atonal,* meaning that it avoided any sense of a tonal center (whether through traditional tonal harmony or any new way of establishing a central pitch). His own term for it was *"composing with the tones of a motive,"* as he varied the notes and intervals of a motive in any order, transposition, or inversion to form melodies and harmonies, suffusing the music with a consistent sound. (A *pitch-class set* is a group of notes treated in this way.) He tended to use all twelve chromatic notes within a phrase or section, so that the last of

them to appear completes a harmonic unit, analogous to a cadence in tonal music. Atonality grew out of the tendency among late-Romantic German composers and in his own early works to obscure the key through chromaticism and extensive modulation. Instead of treating each pitch and chord in terms of its function within a key and requiring dissonant notes and chords to resolve, all notes were equal and all sonorities possible. Schoenberg called this *"the emancipation of the dissonance,"* since dissonance was freed of its need to resolve to consonance. *Pierrot lunaire* (Moonstruck Pierrot), Op. 21 (1912), for female voice and chamber ensemble, is his best known atonal piece. In addition to atonality, it uses *Sprechstimme* (speech-voice or speech-song) and creates unity through canons, motivic devices, and reliance on the text.   **Music: NAWM 135**

C. Expressionism

Pierrot Lunaire is an example of *expressionism,* which portrayed extreme inner feelings such as anxiety, fear, and despair through extreme musical means. Expressionist music typically features dissonance, rhythmic and melodic fragmentation, and avoidance of the pretty and the familiar.

D. Twelve-Tone Method

Seeking a way to compose unified longer works without a tonal center and without depending on a text, Schoenberg by 1923 devised the *twelve-tone method.* The twelve chromatic notes are ordered in a *series* or *row.* Tones from the series, or from a contiguous segment of three or more pitches from the series, may be sounded in succession as a melody or simultaneously as a chord, in any octave and rhythm. The series may be used in its original (*prime*) form, in *inversion* (upside down), in *retrograde* (backward), in *retrograde inversion* (upside down and backward), or in any *transposition* of these four forms. Each statement of a row includes all twelve notes, but different statements can appear simultaneously. (The method systematized two traits of his atonal style: accompanying melodic motives with harmonies derived from the same group of notes, and using all twelve chromatic notes in almost every phrase or unit. The order of notes in the row is not arbitrary, but is based on the motives and chords the composer plans to use in the piece, which are embedded in the row.) Schoenberg wrote many twelve-tone works in standard forms. He fled Nazi Germany in 1933 and settled in the United States. Most of his late music is twelve-tone, but some works are tonal or blend aspects of tonal and atonal or twelve-tone music.   **Music: NAWM 136**

E. *Moses und Aron*

In Schoenberg's unfinished twelve-tone opera *Moses und Aron* (1930–32), Moses speaks in Sprechstimme to symbolize his inability to communicate his vision of God.

F. Alban Berg

Alban Berg (1885–1935) was Schoenberg's student and used many of his techniques. Berg's expressionist opera *Wozzeck* (1917–21) is atonal (not twelve-tone) but looks back to earlier music in several ways: by using leitmotifs and continuous music, as did Wagner; by imitating in atonal style the rhythms and sounds of folk tunes, dances, marches, and other familiar musical types; and by casting each scene as a traditional form, such as suite, passacaglia, sonata, or rondo. In his Violin Concerto (1935), Berg used the twelve-tone method in a way that allowed him to introduce elements of tonal music, such as triads and quoted melodies. The use of tonal effects and familiar types of music helped him to convey strong emotions in a language listeners could understand.   **Music: NAWM 137**

G. Anton Webern
Anton Webern (1883–1945) also studied with Schoenberg and adopted his atonal and twelve-tone methods. But Webern's works are usually brief, extremely spare, often canonic, and without tonal references. His melodies may change tone color as well as pitch, so that a single line may pass from one instrument to others in turn. The effect of Webern's very spare texture is often one of individual points of sound, called *pointillism*.   **Music: NAWM 138**

II. After Webern (HWM 725–29, NAWM 139)

A. The Spread of Twelve-Tone Methods
After World War II, several younger composers (as well as Stravinsky) took up the twelve-tone system. Those associated with the *Darmstadt* summer courses usually looked to Webern as a model.

B. Serialism
By 1950, composers began to apply the serial procedures of twelve-tone music to aspects other than pitch, such as duration and dynamics, resulting in *total serialism*. Such works can seem random, since pitch, rhythm, and other parameters are not being used to define and develop themes or to establish goals and create momentum, but instead produce a succession of unique and unpredictable events. *Pierre Boulez* (b. 1925), the most important European exponent of total serialism, moved beyond it to a more flexible but still pointillistic language in works such as *Le Marteau sans maître* (The Hammer without a Master, 1954).

C. Messiaen
Olivier Messiaen (1908–1992) was an organist, composer, and teacher (Boulez was his student). His music often has religious subjects. He devised his own musical system, incorporating transcribed birdsongs, modal and octatonic scales, repeated rhythmic series (related to medieval isorhythm and music theory of India), *non-retrogradable rhythms* (durational patterns that are the same forward and backward), avoidance of regular meter, and other devices designed to create music that suggests mystical contemplation.   **Music: NAWM 139**

III. Recent Developments (HWM 729–37)

A. New Timbres
Throughout the twentieth century, composers introduced new sounds into music. *Edgard Varèse* (1883–1965) wrote music that used many novel timbres and juxtaposed contrasting masses of sound.

B. Electronic Resources

Electronic music introduced new sonic resources through electronically generated sound. *Musique concrète* used recorded natural sounds that were transformed through tape and electronic procedures. Unlike music for live performers, music on tape allowed composers total control and an unlimited range of sounds.

C. New Technology

Technology developed quickly, from oscillators, to *synthesizers,* to computers and digital encoding of music. Since the invention of portable synthesizers, and especially since the rise of portable computers and the MIDI interface, it has become possible to create electronic music in real time, rather than solely on tape.

D. Influence of Electronic Music

Electronic music in turn suggested new sounds for traditional instruments and voices and brought a renewed interest in the spatial effects of locating performers in different places around a performing space. Varèse's *Poème électronique* was a tape piece created for the 1958 World's Fair in Brussels; played from 425 loudspeakers throughout the Philips Pavilion while colored lights and slides were projected on the walls, it gave a sense of sounds moving through space.

E. The Pitch Continuum

Partly influenced by electronic music, some composers used the entire continuum of pitch, not only the discrete pitches of the chromatic scale. *Threnody for the Victims of Hiroshima* for string orchestra (1960) by *Krzysztof Penderecki* (b. 1933) uses traditional instruments to make electronic-sounding sounds through such means as glissandi, extremely high notes, and bands of pitch within which every quarter-tone is played simultaneously. Penderecki's more recent music is more Romantic in style. *György Ligeti* (b. 1923) also used quasi-electronic sounds in such works as *Atmosphères* for orchestra (1961).

F. Indeterminacy

Throughout the history of notated music, performers have made choices or filled in what is not specified in the notation. In the twentieth century, some composers tried to exercise greater control over performance through very specific indications in the score. Others have explored *indeterminacy,* in which certain aspects of the music, such as the order of events or the precise coordination of parts, are not determined by the composer. *Karlheinz Stockhausen* (b. 1928) has used this in *Klavierstück XI* (Piano Piece No. 11, 1956) and other works. Several of his works use fragments of existing music. *Witold Lutosławski* (1913–1994) used indeterminacy to allow individual players to play at varying speeds or create a cadenza-like elaboration on a figure within controlled boundaries. Indeterminacy has brought new systems of notation and a new concept of a piece as the sum of its possible performances.

STUDY QUESTIONS

Schoenberg and His Followers (HWM 713–25, NAWM 135–38)

1. What was Schoenberg's early music like, and which composers most influenced it?

2. What is *atonal* music? What did Schoenberg mean by *"composing with the tones of a motive"* and *"the emancipation of the dissonance"*?

Music to Study
   NAWM 135: Arnold Schoenberg, *Pierrot lunaire,* Op. 21, song cycle for
            female speech-song voice and chamber ensemble (1912), excerpts
      135a: No. 8, *Nacht* (Night)   CD 11.45–46
      135b: No. 13, *Enthauptung* (Decapitation)
                                              CD 11.47–50

3. What is *Sprechstimme*? How is it notated, and how is it performed?

How is Sprechstimme used in the two numbers from *Pierrot lunaire* in NAWM 135? Where is it *not* used by the voice?

4. In *Nacht* (NAWM 135a), how is the three-note motive *E–G–E♭* (presented in the piano in m. 1 and treated in imitation in all three instruments in mm. 4–7) used during the course of the piece? Where does it appear in original, transposed, or otherwise adapted form? Where does it *not* appear in some form?

5. In addition to this unifying motive, how else do *Nacht* and *Enthauptung* (NAWM 135b) create a sense of unity and form, without tonality?

6. What musical gestures does Schoenberg use to express or illustrate the text in these two songs?

7. What is *expressionism*? What characteristics of these two songs mark them as expressionist works?

Music to Study
    NAWM 136: Arnold Schoenberg, *Variationen für Orchester* [Variations for
        Orchestra], Op. 31 (1926–28), excerpts
      136a: Theme   CD 11.51 (Concise 4.38)
      136b: Variation VI   CD 11.52 (Concise 4.39)

(Note: This score is at sounding pitch. Transposing instruments like clarinet
and horn are written as they *sound,* and not according to the former practice
of writing them in the score as they are notated for the player. Twelve-tone
music always assumes enharmonic equivalence, so *A♭* equals *G♯.*)

8. As shown in Example 21.1 in HWM, p. 718 (also in NAWM, p. 755), the
first half of the theme of Schoenberg's *Variations for Orchestra* (NAWM
136a, mm. 34–45) presents the row in the cello, first in the untransposed
prime form (P–0, meaning prime transposed up zero semitones), then in the
retrograde inversion transposed up nine semitones (RI–9). These are accompanied by chords drawn from I–9 (the inversion transposed up nine
semitones) and R-0 (the untransposed retrograde), respectively. With the
first half of the theme as an example, the following questions will help you
figure out what happens in the second half of the theme (mm. 46–57).

a. Before we begin, what does the harp do in the first half of the theme (mm.
34–45)? Where do its notes come from? (Hint: See the reduction in Example 21.1.)

b. What form of the row appears in the cello in mm. 46–50? _____
(Hint: Notice that the cello is in tenor clef, in which the second line from the
top is middle *C,* and see the diagram of row forms in Example 21.1. Which
form of the row begins with the notes the cello plays in m. 46?)

c. What form of the row is used for the accompanying chords? _____
(Hint: Look at the three-note chord in m. 46. Which form of the row as
shown in Example 21.1 begins with those three notes, in some order?)

d. Measures 46–47 include all twelve tones of the chromatic scale, six in the
melody, and the other six in the accompaniment. What is the relationship
between these two forms of the row that makes this possible? (Hint: Look at
the row chart in Example 21.1, and compare the first six notes and last six
notes in each row to the same groupings in the other row.)

e. What form of the row appears in Violin I (marked "I. Gg" for Geige) in mm. 51–57? What row form appears in the accompanying chords in the winds and horn?

in Violin I _____   in winds and horn   _____

What is the relationship between these two forms of the row? (Hint: See section d. above.)

f. A new transposition of the prime form of the row appears in the cello in mm. 52–57. By how many semitones up is it transposed, in comparison to P–0? If P–0 is the prime form transposed up zero semitones, what would you call this form of the row?

number of semitones by which it is transposed up: _____   name: _____

There, that wasn't so hard, was it? The point of Schoenberg's twelve-tone music is neither to be the musical equivalent of crossword puzzles nor to create completely arbitrary music, but to create logical, unified music based on motives that are developed and accompanied by harmonies derived from them. In that respect, twelve-tone pieces continue the nineteenth-century tradition of thematic development.

Since that's true, we should be able to follow that development without counting notes in the row. Indeed we can, as the next question shows.

9. In the theme (mm. 34–57), as we have seen, the main melodic line is in the cello, later joined by violin I. Just considering these melodies, what rhythmic and melodic motives does Schoenberg introduce, and how are these motives varied as the melodies unfold?

10. At the beginning of Variation VI (NAWM 136b), Schoenberg cleverly derives two new melodic ideas, a clarinet theme and its countermelody in other wind instruments, from alternating notes in a transposition of the inverted form of the row:

I–3	D♭	G	F	A♭	F♯	D	A	B♭	E	E♭	C	B
Clarinet I	D♭		F		F♯		A		E	E♭		
Flute I, English Horn, and Bassoon I		G		A♭		D		B♭			C	B

How are these melodic ideas treated in the rest of the variation?

In what sense is Variation VI a variation of the theme? What stays the same, and what is changed?

11. In what ways is Berg's *Wozzeck* similar to a Wagnerian opera? How does it use forms adapted from instrumental music? What other aspects of this music are likely to sound familiar to listeners?

Music to Study
    NAWM 137: Alban Berg, *Wozzeck,* Op. 7, opera (1917–21), Act III, Scene 3
        CD 11.53–55 (Concise 4.40–42)

12. Berg called Act III, Scene 3, of *Wozzeck* (NAWM 137) "Invention on a
    Rhythm." The rhythmic idea is presented in the right hand of the piano at
    the beginning of the scene (mm. 122–25) and immediately repeated. Woz-
    zeck then states it in augmentation and with a new melody (mm. 130–36).
    (Notice that the attacks are in the same rhythm, even though one note is
    sustained through what was originally a rest.) List below the appearances of
    this rhythm in mm. 138–54, by the measure in which each statement begins
    and the instrument(s) or voice that carry it.

    Measure   Instrument(s) or Voice   Measure   Instrument(s) or Voice

    1._____   _____   6._____   _____

    2._____   _____   7._____   _____

    3._____   _____   8._____   _____

    4._____   _____   9._____   _____

    5._____   _____   10._____ _____

    How does the constant reiteration of this rhythm convey the dramatic situa-
    tion?

13. Where does Berg imitate a polka? A folk song? How does he suggest these
    types of tonal music, despite using an atonal language?

14. Where do major and minor triads occur in the row for Berg's twelve-tone Violin Concerto (shown in Example 21.4 in HWM, p. 721)? Why did Berg introduce triads into a twelve-tone work?

Music to Study
    NAWM 138: Anton Webern, *Symphonie* [Symphony], Op. 21, for nine solo
         instruments (1928), Ruhig schreitend (first movement)
    CD 11.56–60

(Note: This score is written at sounding pitch.)

15. Which characteristics of Webern's style, as described in HWM, pp. 722–25, are evident in the first movement of his Symphony (NAWM 138)?

16. What is *pointillism*? In what way is this movement pointillistic?

17. The opening section of this movement is a double canon. The leading voice of the first canon begins in horn 2, passes to the clarinet, and continues in the cello (see the example in NAWM, p. 782). The canonic answer is in inversion and begins in horn 1. In what instruments does the answer continue?

18. Looking through the exposition of this movement (mm. 1–25a), find all occurrences of the note *A*. In what octave(s) do they appear? On the grand staff below, write *A* in all the octaves in which it occurs in the exposition.

Next, do the same for *E♭/D♯*, writing those that occur in the treble clef to the left of the *A*(s), and those that occur in the bass clef to the right.

Now, do the same for *D, G, C, F*, and *B♭*, writing them as a chord vertically aligned with the *E♭*(s) in the treble clef.

Finally, do the same for *E, B, F♯, C♯*, and *G♯/A♭*, writing them as a chord vertically aligned with the *E♭*(s) in the bass clef. (Note: Harp harmonics, marked with a little circle above or below the note, sound an octave higher than written, and the viola harmonic in m. 19 sounds on *E* a tenth above middle *C*.)

What do you discover? If all the notes played during the exposition sounded simultaneously, what would you have?

The collection of pitches you have discovered is symmetrical, in the sense that it can be inverted around a central pitch and the result will be precisely the same set of pitches, in precisely the same octaves.

What is that central pitch? _____

Where in the movement does it first appear? _____

From the listener's perspective, what is the effect of this type of harmonic structure?

After Webern (HWM 725–29, NAWM 139)

19. What is the importance of Darmstadt for composition in the decade after World War II? Which composer became most influential there?

20. What is *total serialism*? Name a composer and work influenced by total serialism.

Music to Study

NAWM 139: Olivier Messiaen, *Méditations sur le mystère de la Sainte Trinité* (Meditations on the Mystery of the Holy Trinity) for organ (1969), Vif (fourth movement)

CD 12.1–5 (Concise 4.43–47)

21. The fourth movement of Messiaen's *Méditations sur le mystère de la Sainte Trinité* (NAWM 139) features numerous birdsongs that are labeled in the score. What birdsongs are used, and where do they appear? How does Messiaen imitate these birdsongs on the organ?

22. How does Messiaen use his musical material? What happens to it over the course of the movement? How is it repeated or varied?

---

23. Describe Messiaen's use of rhythm. Is there a regular meter? Is there a sense of momentum toward a goal?

24. How do the musical material, the form, and the treatment of rhythm suggest mystical contemplation?

Recent Developments (HWM 729–37)

25. What have been some important developments in electronic and tape music since 1945?

26. How did Penderecki and Ligeti use traditional instruments to create novel sounds and textures in *Threnody for the Victims of Hiroshima* and *Atmosphères*?

27. What is *indeterminacy*? How has it been used in composition? Name two European composers who have used it, and describe a piece by each.

TERMS TO KNOW

atonal music, atonality
"composing with the tones
  of a motive"
pitch-class set
"the emancipation of the
  dissonance"
Sprechstimme
expressionism
twelve-tone method
row, series

prime, inversion, retrograde,
  retrograde inversion
pointillism
total serialism
non-retrogradable rhythms
electronic music
musique concrète
synthesizer
indeterminacy

NAMES TO KNOW

Arnold Schoenberg
Pierrot lunaire
Moses und Aron
Alban Berg
Wozzeck
Anton Webern
Darmstadt
Pierre Boulez
Le Marteau sans maître
Olivier Messiaen

Edgard Varèse
Poème électronique
Krzysztof Penderecki
*Threnody for the Victims of
  Hiroshima*
György Ligeti
Atmosphères
Karlheinz Stockhausen
Klavierstück XI
Witold Lutosławski

REVIEW QUESTIONS

1. Add the composers and major works discussed in this chapter to the twentieth-century time-line you made for chapter 19.

2. Compare the atonal music of Schoenberg's *Pierrot lunaire* (NAWM 135) to the music you know by Wagner, Wolf, Mahler, and Strauss (NAWM 121–24). How does Schoenberg continue the late-Romantic German tradition, and what does he introduce that is new?

3. How does Schoenberg's twelve-tone music, as exemplified in the *Variations for Orchestra* (NAWM 136), continue and extend nineteenth-century procedures?

4. How does Berg's music resemble that of Schoenberg, and how does it differ? How does it compare to the music you know by Wagner, Mahler, and Strauss?

5. How does Webern's twelve-tone music differ from that of Schoenberg?

6. List the predominant characteristics of Messiaen's style and explain how they are exemplified in the organ work in NAWM 139.

7. What are some of the trends in European art music since 1945? Describe an example of each trend you describe.

THE AMERICAN TWENTIETH CENTURY

22

CHAPTER OBJECTIVES

After you complete the reading, study of the music, and study questions for this chapter, you should be able to

1. summarize the historical background for art music in the United States;
2. outline the history of vernacular music in the United States from ragtime to rock; and
3. name the most significant composers of and trends in art music in the United States during the twentieth century, explain what is individual about each one, and describe pieces by some of the major composers of the century.

CHAPTER OUTLINE

I. Introduction (HWM 740–41)

The United States became the center for new music in the classical tradition after World War II. American music grew out of the European tradition, as European composers emigrated to or visited the United States and many Americans studied with Nadia Boulanger in Paris or with other European teachers at summer festivals. But American music also drew from its many ethnic and popular traditions.

II. The Historical Background (HWM 741–48, NAWM 140)

A. Music in the Colonies

New England colonists sang psalms, and singing schools were established in the eighteenth century to teach singing in parts from notation. *William Billings* (1746–1800) wrote psalms, hymns, anthems, and canons. Most of his hymns were simple harmonizations, but many were *fuging tunes,* which include a middle section in free imitation. Billings did not follow the rules of "correct" counterpoint, but allowed parallel octaves and fifths and often used chords without thirds.

B. Immigration and Its Influences

Other immigrants brought their musical cultures. The Moravians, German-speaking Protestants from Czech and Slovak regions, encouraged music in church, including arias and motets. Bohemian-born *Anthony Philip Heinrich* (1781–1861) wrote programmatic works, some of which use popular tunes or Native American themes. German immigrants were prominent as music teachers, conductors, and performers, and American composers often studied in Germany. *Lowell Mason* (1792–1872), trained by a German immigrant, introduced music into the public school curriculum and sought to replace the music of Billings and others with hymns harmonized in the "correct" European style. Several of Mason's hymns are still in use. The Yankee tunes remained in use in the *shape-note hymnals* in the South. The folk tradition of African-American *spirituals* was popularized after the Civil War by the *Fisk Jubilee Singers.* New England was a center for art music in the late nineteenth and early twentieth centuries. *Amy Cheney Beach* (1867–1944) wrote songs, chamber music, and orchestral music in a style influenced by Brahms and late-Romantic chromatic harmony. **Music: NAWM 140**

C. Brass and Wind Bands

In the nineteenth century, almost every town and city had an amateur *wind* or *brass band,* and in the twentieth century almost every high school and college had one. The nineteenth-century repertory included marches, dances, song arrangements, and solo display pieces. *John Philip Sousa* (1854–1932) wrote more than 100 marches. Brass bands and dance orchestras played an important role in African-American social life and provided training for black musicians.

III. Vernacular Music (HWM 748–55)

A. Ragtime

Ragtime developed from joining the march with elements of African music. A typical *rag,* such as *Maple Leaf Rag* (1899) by *Scott Joplin* (1868–1917), uses march form in duple meter and presents a syncopated melody over a steady bass.

B. Blues

Black laments evolved in the early twentieth century into a style called *blues.* Blues feature a text in rhymed couplets, the first line repeated; *blue notes,* lowering the third, seventh, or fifth degree of the major scale; a standard twelve-bar harmonic framework; and improvised instrumental "breaks" between lines of the song.

C. Jazz

Jazz is a form of group or solo improvisation over a blues or popular tune. The basic procedures, from uneven rhythms and anticipated beats to trading solos, were developed by black musicians and imitated by white bands by 1915. A leading band was *King Oliver's Creole Jazz Band,* which used the typical instrumentation of cornet, clarinet, trombone, piano, banjo, and drums.

D. Big Bands

The popularity of jazz brought larger performing spaces, leading in the 1920s to the *big bands* of *Duke Ellington* (1899–1974) and others, which had trumpets, trombones, saxophones, and clarinets in sections and a *rhythm section* of string bass, piano, guitar, and drums. Big bands performed from an arrangement or *chart,* which still provided some opportunities for improvised solos. This style is also called *swing,* from the swinging uneven rhythms.

E. Modern Jazz

Bebop (or *bop*) of the 1940s and 1950s and new jazz idioms that followed it used smaller groups, more improvisation, and new techniques, some borrowed from modern classical music, to create a serious art music in the jazz tradition.

F. Country Music

Country-and-western or *country music* blended traditional music of the Appalachian and Ozark Mountain regions, derived from Anglo-American ballads and fiddle tunes, with cowboy music of the West and some jazz elements. Singers accompanied themselves on guitar or were backed by a band featuring violins and guitars.

G. Rhythm-and-Blues

Rhythm-and-blues was a black urban blues-based style with an unrelenting rhythm emphasizing the offbeats and often using electric guitar and bass.

H. Rock-and-Roll

Rock-and-roll or *rock* emerged in the mid-1950s from a blending of white country and black rhythm-and-blues styles. (Like those two styles, it was promoted and virtually created by the recording industry and radio.) *Elvis Presley* (1935–1977) in the 1950s and *The Beatles* in the 1960s were both enormously popular.

I. Musical Comedy

The *Broadway musical* (or *musical comedy*) is the main genre of musical theater in the United States. Many popular songs by Cole Porter, Jerome Kern, Irving Berlin, and *George Gershwin* (1898–1937) were written for Broadway shows. Gershwin also wrote works that blend popular with classical traditions, such as his blend of jazz with the Romantic piano concerto in *Rhapsody in Blue* (1924) and his folk opera *Porgy and Bess* (1935).

IV. Foundations for an American Art Music (HWM 755–64, NAWM 141–44)

A. Charles Ives

Charles Ives (1874–1954) had an unusual career, making his living in insurance while composing in many diverse styles from Romanticism to radical experiments. Trained in American band and church music and in European art music, he blended these two traditions in his symphonies, symphonic poems, chamber music, and art songs, evoking nineteenth-century America through modernist techniques. He often used existing music, especially American tunes, as a basis for his own, reworking borrowed material in a variety of ways and with various meanings. His music was not published or performed until 1920 and later, starting with his *Second Piano Sonata, "Concord, Mass., 1840–60"* (known as the *Concord Sonata*). His independence of mind, innovations, use of popular materials, and multilayered textures inspired many younger composers to seek their own paths. **Music: NAWM 141**

B. Carl Ruggles
Carl Ruggles (1876–1971) wrote atonal, very original works.

C. Henry Cowell
Henry Cowell (1897–1965) explored new effects on the piano, including *tone clusters,* collections of notes separated by seconds, and strumming or playing directly on the strings. His later music used folk and non-Western elements. Cowell was also a promoter and publisher of new music.

D. Ruth Crawford Seeger
Ruth Crawford Seeger (1901–1953) composed in a modern atonal style, creating a series of very individual works, before changing her interests to transcribing and arranging American folk songs. **Music: NAWM 142**

E. Edgard Varèse
Edgard Varèse (discussed in chapter 21) was born and trained in France and moved to New York in 1915. Rather than using themes, harmony, or conventional rhythm, his works use pitch, duration, dynamics, and timbre, including many percussion instruments, to create *sound masses* that move and interact in musical space.

F. Aaron Copland
Aaron Copland (1900–1990) studied in France with Nadia Boulanger. His early works use jazz elements and dissonance. In the mid-1930s he turned to a more popular style of simple textures, diatonic writing, and folk tunes, as in *Appalachian Spring* (1944). In the 1950s, his music became more abstract, and he adopted some twelve-tone methods. **Music: NAWM 143**

G. Other National Idioms
Roy Harris (1898–1979) is best known for symphonic music that evokes the American West through modal themes and open textures. Critic and composer *Virgil Thomson* (1896–1989) studied with Boulanger but emulated the playfulness and simplicity of Satie. His two operas on texts by Gertrude Stein, *Four Saints in Three Acts* (1928) and *The Mother of Us All* (1947), draw on the styles of American hymns, songs, and dance music. *William Grant Still* (1895–1978), composer of the *Afro-American Symphony* (1931), and *Florence Price* (1888–1953) are among the best-known African-American composers of art music; both incorporated elements from African-American musical styles. Many American composers in the first half of the twentieth century composed music that was more cosmopolitan than nationalist. Other prominent American composers were William Schuman (1910–92), Ulysses Kay (b. 1917), Howard Hanson (1896–1981), and Walter Piston (1894–1976). **Music: NAWM 144**

V. Since 1945 (HWM 764–84, NAWM 145–50)

A. Abstract Idioms

Roger Sessions (1896–1985) wrote dissonant, complex music in an individual style based on continuous development. *Elliott Carter* (b. 1908) is noted for using *metric modulation,* in which the meter and tempo change in such a way that a fraction of the beat in the old meter becomes the beat in the new meter (for example, a dotted eighth in 4/4 becomes a quarter note in 4/4 at a proportionally faster tempo). Inspired by Ives's layered textures, Carter often gives each instrument a different rhythmic and melodic character to create a counterpoint of thoroughly independent lines, as in his String Quartet No. 2 (1959).   **Music: NAWM 145**

B. The University as Patron

In the United States and Canada, composers of music in the classical tradition have been supported during the twentieth century largely through teaching positions in universities and colleges. This has sometimes encouraged avant-garde experimentation, but has isolated composers from the public. (It has also become the major way younger composers are trained.) Important universities for composers have included Harvard (where Piston taught), Yale (Hindemith), the University of California at Berkeley, Mills College (Milhaud), the University of California at Los Angeles (Schoenberg), Princeton (Sessions and Milton Babbitt), the University of Illinois, the University of Michigan, Stanford, and the Eastman School (Hanson).

C. The Post-Webern Vogue

Webern influenced composers in the universities who sought an objective approach free from Americanism and the influence of popular music. *Milton Babbitt* (b. 1916) extended twelve-tone music in new directions and was the first to apply serial principles to duration and other parameters.

D. New Sounds and Textures

Conlon Nancarrow (1912–1997) anticipated the precision of electronic and computer music by using player-piano rolls to play pieces whose complex rhythmic relationships and rapid gestures were beyond human performers. *Harry Partch* (1901–1974) rejected equal temperament, formulated a scale of 43 unequal steps using only the pure harmonic ratios of just intonation, and built new instruments that used this scale. His works typically use these instruments to accompany dancing, singing, and theater. *Ben Johnston* (b. 1926) applies just intonation to traditional instruments, such as piano or string quartet. *George Crumb* (b. 1929) draws new sounds from traditional instruments and uses unusual instruments to create emotionally powerful music in an eclectic style, as in *Black Angels* (1970) for amplified string quartet.   **Music: NAWM 146**

E. Electronic Music

Lacking performers, electronic music is less often played in concert than heard in recording. But several composers have combined live performers with electronic music, as in Babbitt's moving *Philomel* (1964), a twelve-tone work for soprano and a tape with electronic and electronically altered vocal sounds. Recent developments include computer-driven synthesizers and pianos.   **Music: NAWM 147**

F. Third Stream
Many twentieth-century composers have used jazz elements in classical works, and Duke Ellington used symphonic techniques in extended jazz compositions. *Gunther Schuller* (b. 1925) merged jazz and classical traits in music he called *third stream. William Bolcom* (b. 1938) invokes ragtime and blues in classical genres. University-trained jazz pianist *Anthony Davis* (b. 1951) juxtaposed jazz and classical elements in his opera *X: The Life and Times of Malcolm X* (1984).   **Music: NAWM 148**

G. John Cage and Indeterminacy
In his music after 1950, *John Cage* (1912–1992) used both indeterminacy, in which some aspect of the music is left unspecified by the composer, and *chance,* in which some aspect of the music is determined, not by the composer's will or intentions, but by chance operations. An example of the first is the silent piece *4'33"* (Four Minutes and Thirty-Three Seconds, 1952), in which the music is the ambient sounds one hears during the duration of the piece; an example of the second is *Music of Changes* (1951), in which all pitches were determined by chance. The two procedures are often confused with each other, but are distinct; if something is determined by chance operations, it is not indeterminate. Cage's aim, inspired by Zen Buddhism, was to allow listeners to hear sounds as sounds in themselves, not as means by which a composer communicates a feeling or idea.

H. Minimalism
The approach called *minimalism* uses a deliberately restricted set of notes or sounds and a large amount of repetition. It was inspired in part by repetitive music of Asia and Africa and in part by a desire to make musical processes audible to listeners, in contrast to serial music. *Steve Reich* (b. 1936) has used small repeated units that begin in unison and gradually move out of phase with each other. *Philip Glass* (b. 1937) has written operas and works for his own ensemble using a very repetitive style. *John Adams* (b. 1947) has written operas and orchestral music using repeated ideas that evolve and shift in alignment with each other.   **Music: NAWM 149**

I. The Mainstream
Many American composers continue to write music accessible to a wide public. Three composers are particularly noted for their vocal music: *Ned Rorem* (b. 1923) for his songs, *Gian Carlo Menotti* (b. 1911) for his operas, and *Samuel Barber* (1910–1981) for both. *Joan Tower* (b. 1938) draws from a wide range of idioms. *Ellen Taaffe Zwilich* (b. 1939) was the first woman to win the Pulitzer Prize in music. Her Concerto Grosso (1985), written for the 300th anniversary of Handel's birth, incorporates music from one of his sonatas and other sounds and procedures of Baroque music.   **Music: NAWM 150**

J. Post-Modern Styles

Recent post-modern architects have incorporated elements of earlier styles into their designs, and so do a number of composers, who have abandoned the notion of continual progress in musical style and see all styles of all eras as available for use. *George Rochberg* (b. 1918) revisits and deconstructs the style of J. S. Bach in *Nach Bach* (After or According to Bach, 1966). *Sinfonia* (1968) by *Luciano Berio* (b. 1925) incorporates virtually an entire Mahler symphony movement and superimposes upon it more than 100 quotations from other works and verbal commentary from eight speakers, creating the impression of a stream of consciousness. *David Del Tredici* (b. 1937) has written a number of works based on parts of *Alice in Wonderland* and *Through the Looking Glass,* using a style derived from Wagner and Strauss in order to communicate with an audience and match the innocence and whimsy of the stories.

VI. Conclusions (HWM 784–85)

Four characteristics that have defined Western music since the Middle Ages have been challenged in the twentieth century. Composition has been augmented in some music by chance procedures or improvisation. Notation has expanded to include graphic and other notation. Principles of order do not always rule in chance or indeterminate music and are not always perceptible in serial music. Polyphony and harmony continue in novel forms. "Serious" music has found only a small audience, and radical experimentation a still smaller one. Recent composers have sought ways to please a broader public, often by incorporating ideas from popular music, non-Western music, or music of the past.

STUDY QUESTIONS

Introduction (HWM 740–41)

1. What were some of the ways in which twentieth-century European composers interacted with and influenced American composers of art music?

The Historical Background (HWM 741–48, NAWM 140)

2. When did William Billings live? What kinds of music did he write? What was his significance for American music?

3. What is a *fuging tune*? Explain what characteristics make *Washington-Street* (printed in HWM, p. 743) a fuging tune.

4. What were Lowell Mason's contributions to music in the United States?

Music to Study
   NAWM 140: Amy Cheney Beach, Quintet for Piano and Strings in F-sharp
         Minor, Op. 67 (1908), Allegro agitato (third movement)
      CD 12.6–10

5. Diagram or describe the form of the finale of Beach's Piano Quintet
   (NAWM 140). How does it relate to standard forms of nineteenth-century
   European instrumental music?

6. Describe the melodic material and figuration. What elements and characteristics reveal the influence of Brahms? What traits suggest other influences or
   Beach's individual voice?

7. What was the importance of brass and wind bands in the United States? What
   was their repertory? What was their significance for African Americans?

Vernacular Music (HWM 748–55)

8. What is *ragtime*? From what traditions did it derive? How is Scott Joplin's *Maple Leaf Rag* (excerpted in HWM, pp. 748-49, Example 22.2) typical of the style?

9. Describe the style and form of the *blues*. How is the tune of W. C. Handy's *St. Louis Blues* (in HWM, p. 749, Example 22.3) typical of a blues song?

10. Briefly trace the evolution of *jazz* from early jazz through big bands to modern jazz.

11. Describe the characteristics of *country music*. From what traditions did it derive?

12. Describe the origins and style of *rhythm-and-blues.*

13. Describe the origins and style of *rock-and-roll.*

14. Describe the Broadway musical. How does it compare to opera and operetta? What are its links to popular music?

Foundations for an American Art Music (HWM 755–64, NAWM 141–44)

15. What was Charles Ives's musical background and training? What are some prominent characteristics of his music? What was his significance for American music?

Music to Study
NAWM 141: Charles Ives, *They Are There!: A War Song March,* for unison chorus and orchestra (adapted in 1942 from Ives's 1917 song *He Is There!*)
CD 12.11–13 (Concise 4.48–50)

Most of Ives's mature works are in European genres and use modernist techniques to evoke nineteenth-century America. *They Are There!* (NAWM 141) is unusual, for it uses the verse-chorus format and ragtime-like melodic style of a Tin Pan Alley tune. But it illustrates several traits of Ives's music.

Tin Pan Alley composers often quoted existing tunes. Ives intensifies this practice, quoting or paraphrasing fragments of the following tunes. Most are Civil War songs, used to link what Ives considered the idealism of the fight to end slavery with the cause of fighting tyranny in World War I and II.

Measures	Parts	Tune
1–2	brass, piano, clarinets	*Country Band March,* by Ives
8–9	voices, trumpets, violin 1 & 2	*Country Band March*
12–14	voices, trumpets, violin 1 & 2	*Marching through Georgia*
18–19	voices, trumpets, violin 1	*Tenting on the Old Camp Ground*
19–21	voices, trumpets, violin 1	*Columbia, the Gem of the Ocean*
20–23	trombones	*The Battle Hymn of the Republic*
21–22	winds	*Dixie*
23	winds	*Marching through Georgia*
23–25	voices, trumpets, trombones, violin 1	*Tramp, Tramp, Tramp*
24	winds	*Yankee Doodle*
25–26	winds	*Marching through Georgia*
27–30	voices, trumpet 1, viola 1	*Columbia, the Gem of the Ocean*
29–30	winds	*Maryland, My Maryland*
31–35	winds	*La Marseillaise*
32–33	voices, brass, viola 1	*Columbia, the Gem of the Ocean*
34–38	voices and brass	*Tenting on the Old Camp Ground*
40–44	voices and brass	*Tenting on the Old Camp Ground*
43–47	winds	*The Battle Cry of Freedom*
44–48	voices, trumpet 1, violin 1	*The Battle Cry of Freedom*
48–50	winds and brass	*The Star-Spangled Banner*
51–53	flutes and trumpets	*Reveille* (bugle call)

16. In the voice part throughout and the upper winds from m. 21 to the end, how does Ives join these fragments of tunes into a coherent melody?

17. Ives harmonizes his vocal melody with the expected tonal harmonies, in most cases. But he also adds many elements that one would not expect to find in a Tin Pan Alley song, or in a traditional tonal work. What are some of these added elements?

How do these added elements affect your experience of the work? In your opinion, how do they affect the work's meaning?

18. Ives often superimposed layers of music, each with its own rhythm, melodic or harmonic character, and instrumental timbre. In mm. 28–29, what rhythmically independent layers are sounding simultaneously? For each layer, name the instruments or voices that are performing it and describe its rhythmic and melodic character.

19. What new musical resources did Henry Cowell introduce in his piano music? For each one, name at least one piece that uses it.

Music to Study
    NAWM 142: Ruth Crawford Seeger, Violin Sonata (1926), Bouyant (second movement)
    CD 12.14–16

(Note: In this work, accidentals apply only to the note to which they are affixed. For example, the fifth note of the piece is A♮, not A♭.)

20. The second movement of Ruth Crawford Seeger's Violin Sonata (NAWM 142) is built on a bass ostinato. How is this figure treated during this movement? Where is it repeated, where and how is it varied, and where (if ever) does it not appear?

21. How is the theme introduced by the violin varied and developed over the course of the movement?

---

22. Describe the music of Edgard Varèse. What resources does he use, and how does he deploy them? How does the excerpt from *Intégrales* in HWM, p. 760, Example 22.4, illustrate his approach? (Note: In addition to pp. 759–60, Varèse is also discussed in HWM on pp. 729 and 731 in chapter 21.)

23. Outline Aaron Copland's career, indicating distinctive aspects of his style in each period.

Music to Study
NAWM 143a: *'Tis the gift to be simple,* Shaker hymn
  not on recordings
NAWM 143b: Aaron Copland, *Appalachian Spring,* ballet (1944), excerpt,
  including variations on *'Tis the gift to be simple*
CD 12.17–24 (second part of excerpt on Concise 4.51–55)

24. How does Copland vary the Shaker tune *'Tis the gift to be simple* in the excerpt from *Appalachian Spring* in NAWM 143b?

---

25. What kinds of harmonies does Copland use in this excerpt? What traits of his harmonies and melodies convey an "American sound"?

26. What aspects of this excerpt suggest the influence of Stravinsky? What traits distinguish Copland's style from Stravinsky's? Use the excerpt from *Le sacre du printemps* in NAWM 134 (see chapter 20 above, questions 24–26) and the works treated in chapter 20, question 28, as points of comparison.

27. Name two operas by Virgil Thomson on librettos by Gertrude Stein.

_____   _____

What are the characteristics of Thomson's music for these operas? How are they exemplified in the passage in Example 22.5 in HWM, p. 762?

Music to Study
  NAWM 144: William Grant Still, *Afro-American Symphony* (1931), Ani-
      mato (third movement)
    CD 12.25–27 (Concise 4.56–58)

28. William Grant Still's *Afro-American Symphony* unites the symphonic and
    African-American traditions. What elements from the African-American tra-
    ditions (including spirituals, ragtime, blues, and jazz) does Still incorporate
    in the third movement (NAWM 144)? Refer back to pp. 746 and 748–52 in
    HWM for a discussion of these types of music. (Two elements not men-
    tioned there, both from jazz, are the trumpets with Harmon mutes starting at
    m. 58 and the wire brush used to play the drum starting at m. 69.)

29. What does this movement draw from the symphonic tradition? What does it
    have in common with symphonic works such as Beethoven's *Eroica* Sym-
    phony, first movement (NAWM 103)?

30. How does Still introduce and develop his themes in this movement?

Since 1945 (HWM 764–84, NAWM 145–50)

Music to Study
 NAWM 145: Elliott Carter, String Quartet No. 2 (1959), Introduction and
  Allegro fantastico
 CD 12.28–30

31. What are some of the ways in which Elliott Carter gives each of the four
 instruments a distinctive rhythmic and melodic character in his String Quartet No. 2 (NAWM 145)?

32. What is *metric modulation,* and how does Carter use it in the opening passage of this work (mm. 1–14)?

---

33. What has been the role of North American colleges and universities in sup-
 porting composition of new music? How does this differ from the situation in
 Europe?

34. What is Milton Babbitt saying in the excerpt from his article "Who Cares if You Listen" in HWM, p. 771? What is his view of contemporary music and its relationship to the wider musical public? How does his view relate to the employment of composers as college and university teachers?

Do you agree with his views? Why or why not?

35. Describe Babbitt's approach to composition. How does it correlate with the views expressed in his article?

36. Briefly describe the distinctive approach to music of each of the following composers:

Conlon Nancarrow

Harry Partch

Ben Johnston

Music to Study
> **NAWM 146:** George Crumb, *Black Angels: Thirteen Images from the Dark Land,* for electric string quartet (1970), excerpts
>
> 146a: Image 4. *Devil-Music*   CD 12.31
> 146b: Image 5. *Danse macabre*   CD 12.32
> 146c: Image 6. *Pavana lachrymae*   CD 12.33
> 146d: Image 7. *Threnody II: Black Angels!*   CD 12.34
> 146e: Image 8. *Sarabanda de la muerte oscura*   CD 12.35
> 146f: Image 9. *Lost Bells*   CD 12.36
>
> **NAWM 147:** Milton Babbitt, *Philomel,* for soprano, recorded soprano, and synthesized sound (1964), opening section
>   CD 12.37–41 (Concise 4.59–63)
>
> **NAWM 148:** Gunther Schuller, *Seven Studies on Themes of Paul Klee* for orchestra (1959), excerpts
>
> 148a: 3. *Kleiner blauer Teufel* (Little Blue Devil)   CD 12.42–43
> 148b: 5. *Arabische Stadt* (Arab Village) CD 12.44–46

37. What new playing techniques for string instruments does George Crumb use in these six movements from *Black Angels* (NAWM 146)? (Hint: Check the footnotes that explain how to perform certain effects; these footnotes sometimes appear on a different page.) What additional instruments and sounds does he call for, beyond the four instruments of the string quartet? List all the new playing techniques, instruments, and other sounds you can find. For each one, put down one or a few words that describe how the device sounds and what emotional effect it conveys.

38. Crumb quotes or refers to earlier music several times. *Danse macabre* (NAWM 146b) refers to the piece of the same name by Camille Saint-Saëns and—like Saint-Saëns—quotes the famous chant *Dies irae* from the Gregorian Mass for the Dead. *Pavana lachrymae* (NAWM 146c) uses the title of a William Byrd keyboard transcription of a John Dowland song (see NAWM 44 and 46), but Crumb instead quotes Schubert's song *Death and the Maiden,* which Schubert himself used in a string quartet. *Sarabanda de la muerte oscura* (NAWM 146e) presents a sarabande that is apparently not borrowed but written in fifteenth-century style, with double-leading tone cadences, a Landini cadence, and appropriate ornamentation. What is the effect of these references to earlier music within the context of Crumb's music? In your opinion, what might these references mean?

39. What are the programmatic ideas in this work, and how are they conveyed? How does music like this compare to earlier program music?

40. How does Milton Babbitt use the singer, taped vocal sounds, and electronic sounds in *Philomel* (NAWM 147)? What is each component like? How do they relate? And how do they work together to suggest the story and the feelings of Philomel?

41. What is *third stream*? How is it exemplified in *Kleiner blauer Teufel,* the third movement of Gunther Schuller's *Seven Studies on Themes of Paul Klee* (NAWM 148a)?

42. How does this movement compare to the third movement of Still's *Afro-American Symphony* (NAWM 144) in its use of jazz elements?

43. How does Schuller evoke Arab music in *Arabische Stadt,* the fifth movement of his *Seven Studies on Themes of Paul Klee* (NAWM 148b)?

44. Why did John Cage use indeterminacy and chance operations in his music? How did he use them?

Music to Study
   NAWM 149: John Adams, *Phrygian Gates,* for piano (1977–78), opening
         section
   CD 12.47–52 (Concise 4.64–69)

45. How does John Adams use repetition in *Phrygian Gates* (NAWM 149)?
    How does he vary the material?

46. In Adams's terminology, what is a "gate"? Where do gates occur? What
    changes at each one? And how do they relate to the work's title?

47. What is *minimalism*? In what sense is this work minimalist? In what sense is it
    complex?

48. How can you follow this music? In your opinion, what should you listen
    for?

49. What does *Phrygian Gates* have in common with a piece by Beethoven (such as NAWM 101, 103, or 104) or any other nineteenth-century composer, and what is different?

50. How are the minimalist works of Philip Glass and John Adams different from Reich's *Violin Phase* and from each other?

Music to Study
    NAWM 150: Ellen Taaffe Zwilich, *Concerto Grosso 1985* (1985), excerpts
      Presto (fourth movement)   CD 12.53
      Maestoso (fifth movement)   CD 12.54

51. How does Ellen Taaffe Zwilich evoke the sounds and procedures of Baroque music in the last two movements of her *Concerto Grosso 1985* (NAWM 150)?

52. What other means does Zwilich use to create a piece that is immediately accessible to a listener, yet fresh and individual?

53. How does Luciano Berio use existing music in his *Sinfonia* (1968)?

54. What is David Del Tredici's attitude toward communication with the audience, as summarized in his statement on p. 784 of HWM? How does his music reflect his concerns? How does this contrast with Milton Babbitt's point of view and music (see questions 34–35, above)?

Conclusions (HWM 784–85)

55. How have the four characteristics that have defined Western music since the Middle Ages (composition, notation, principles of order, and polyphony) fared in the twentieth century?

TERMS TO KNOW

Terms Related to American Music before 1900 and to Vernacular Music

fuging tunes
shape-note hymnals
spirituals
wind band, brass band
ragtime
rag
blues
blue notes
jazz
big bands

rhythm section
chart
swing
bebop (bop)
country music (country-and-western music)
rhythm-and-blues
rock (rock-and-roll)
Broadway musical (musical comedy)

Terms Related to 20th-Century American Art Music

tone clusters
sound masses
metric modulation
third stream

indeterminacy
chance
minimalism

NAMES TO KNOW

Names Related to American Music before 1900 and to Vernacular Music

William Billings
Anthony Philip Heinrich
Lowell Mason
Fisk Jubilee Singers
Amy Cheney Beach
John Philip Sousa
Scott Joplin
Maple Leaf Rag

King Oliver's Creole Jazz Band
Duke Ellington
Elvis Presley
The Beatles
George Gershwin
Rhapsody in Blue
Porgy and Bess

Names Related to American Art Music 1900–1945

Charles Ives
Concord Sonata (Second Piano Sonata)
Carl Ruggles
Henry Cowell
Ruth Crawford Seeger
Aaron Copland
Appalachian Spring

Roy Harris
Virgil Thomson
Four Saints in Three Acts
The Mother of Us All
William Grant Still
Afro-American Symphony
Florence Price

Names Related to American Art Music since 1945

Roger Sessions

Elliott Carter

Milton Babbitt

Conlon Nancarrow

Harry Partch

Ben Johnston

George Crumb

Black Angels

Philomel

Gunther Schuller

William Bolcom

Anthony Davis

X: The Life and Times of

   Malcolm X

John Cage

4'33"

Music of Changes

Steve Reich

Philip Glass

John Adams

Ned Rorem

Gian Carlo Menotti

Samuel Barber

Joan Tower

Ellen Taaffe Zwilich

George Rochberg, *Nach Bach*

Luciano Berio, *Sinfonia*

David Del Tredici

REVIEW QUESTIONS

1. Add the composers and major works discussed in this chapter to the twentieth-century time-line you made for chapter 19, or to the earlier time-lines you made for chapters 13 and 16, as appropriate.

2. Summarize the eighteenth- and nineteenth-century historical background for music in the United States.

3. What were the major forms of popular music in the United States between the 1890s and the 1960s? Describe each kind, and explain how each relates to the others in historical succession.

4. Trace the course of American art music in the first half of the twentieth century, naming the most important composers and describing their music.

5. What are some of the main trends in American art music since World War II? Define each trend, and describe at least one composer and piece associated with each.

6. Write a brief essay in which you defend or reject the position Milton Babbitt articulates in his statement on p. 771 of HWM. Whichever position you take, use examples from at least two twentieth-century works in NAWM to support your point of view about the relationship between a composer and his or her listeners.

7. Of the eight pieces in NAWM composed since 1950 (NAWM 132, 139, and 145–50), which one or two do you like the best? Which one or two do you like the least? Write an essay in which you explain what is especially good about the piece(s) you like and what is unappealing about the piece(s) you like less, as if you were writing a review or trying to persuade a friend about which CD to purchase. Explain what it is you find most valuable in music and how your judgments are based on those values.

CURSO AVANZADO DE
WORD

MP Ediciones S.A., Moreno 2062, 1094 Buenos Aires, Argentina
Tel. 4954-1884, Fax 4954-1791

ISBN 987-526-012-6

Primera edición impresa en agostode 1999, en Sociedad Impresora Américana.
Lavardén 153/157, Capital Federal.

Todas las marcas mencionadas en este libro son propiedad de sus respectivos dueños.

Agradecimientos

Las siguientes personas colaboraron directa
o indirectamente en este Manual.
A todos ellos mi enorme agradecimiento.

- *Jorge Sanchez Serantes*
- *Agnette*
- *Polok*
- *Daniel Faller*
- *Laura Bertero*
- *Claudia Soler*

Dedicatoria
A la memoria de Víctor Ramos.
En reconocimiento por su labor
como deportista y educador.

SOBRE LA AUTORA

Verónica Sanchez Serantes es técnica en electrónica digital egresada del Instituto Bunker Hill College de Boston, MA(USA). Estudiante de Análisis de Sistemas en la UTN (Universidad Tecnológica Nacional) se dedica a la docencia a nivel secundario y terciario. Actualmente está desarrollando productos de software para abogados y su carrera está orientada hacia el mantenimiento de sistemas y los servicios de soporte a usuarios.

Sobre la Editorial

MP Ediciones S.A. es una editorial argentina especializada en temas de tecnología
(Computación, IT, Telecomunicaciones).
Entre nuestros productos encontrará:
revistas, libros, fascículos, CD-ROMs, Sitios en Internet y Eventos.
Nuestras principales marcas son:
PC Users, PC Juegos, INSIDER, Aprendiendo PC y COMPUMAGAZINE.
Si desea más información, puede contactarnos de las siguientes maneras:
Web: www.mp.com.ar;
e-mail: libros@mponline.com.ar;
correo: Moreno 2062, (1094)
Capital Federal, Argentina.
Fax: 54-11-4954-1791; Tel: 54-11-4954-1884

SUMARIO

Lección 2. Objetos

Lección 3. Herramientas

Apéndice A. Lo nuevo en Word 2000

INTRODUCCIÓN

Este Curso Completo de Word está diseñado para trabajar frente a la computadora, siguiendo paso a paso las indicaciones que se dan a lo largo de las doce lecciones.

La entrega está dividida en dos tomos que se complementan brindando toda la información necesaria para dominar a fondo el programa.

Está diseñado en un formato de preguntas y respuestas de modo que, siguiendo el Indice, el lector también puede utilizarlo como guía de consulta mientras trabaja en Word.

Al final de cada capítulo hay Problemas resueltos, personalizados y alusivos al material desarrollado en ese capítulo. Los mismos tienen, por finalidad, realizar un repaso ameno del material estudiado y plantear problemas concretos y frecuentes relacionados con lo que se acaba de leer.

Verónica Sanchez Serantes
Serantes@impsat1.com.ar

EN ESTE LIBRO

De acuerdo con el modo en que están desarrollados los temas, puede considerarse dividido en cuatro etapas.

TOMO 1	Primera etapa	
	Cap,1, 2 y 3	La constituyen los tres primeros capítulos. En ellos aprenderemos lo básico del Procesador de texto: manejar el teclado y el Mouse, familiarizarnos con el entorno de la aplicación, corregir errores y guardar o abrir archivos.
	Segunda etapa	
	Cap. 4, 5, 6 y 7	Con ella podremos mejorar el aspecto del documento: modificando la letra, la apariencia de los párrafos, el formato de las páginas y trabajando con tablas. Se recomienda al lector no avanzar hasta aquí hasta no dominar ampliamente la primera etapa.

TOMO 2	Tercera etapa	
	Cap. 1 y 2	En estos capítulos se nos enseñará a trabajar con elementos distintos del texto y las tablas, como pueden ser los objetos, las imágenes, los sonidos, los esquemas, etc., de modo de romper la rutina de una línea detrás de otra y un párrafo debajo de otro.
	Cuarta etapa	
	Cap. 3, 4 y 5	Finalmente la última etapa corresponde a los capítulos 10, 11 y 12, que nos enseñan a automatizar tareas utilizando herramientas como, por ejemplo, el Envío masivo de correspondencia (también conocido como Mail Merge o Mailing), las Macros, las funciones Autotexto y Autoformato, la Revisión Automática de Ortografía, etc.

Por último, encontrará una serie de apéndices que complementarán la información vertida en el libro.

El **Apéndice** del **tomo 1** introduce a quienes no poseen los conocimientos suficientes acerca del manejo del teclado y cada una de sus funciones.

Para estar actualizado al máximo, el **Apéndice** del **tomo 2** capacita en las mejoras de la nueva versión *Word 2000* para quienes dudan en adoptarla.

Para ir más allá de lo que todos saben, nuestra sección **Información útil** muestra los atajos de teclado que permiten acelerar su trabajo sin sacar las manos del teclado y provee de un valiosísimo Índice alfabético que garantiza la posibilidad de profundizar el aprendizaje.

ELEMENTOS DE TRABAJO I

1

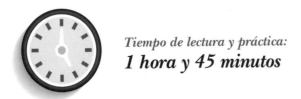

Tiempo de lectura y práctica:
1 hora y 45 minutos

Objetivo de la lección

Lección

1

■ Familiarizarse con el uso de Listas Numeradas y con Viñetas.
■ Trabajar con Cuadros de Texto.
■ Incluir Imágenes a un documento.

1. LISTAS NUMERADAS Y LISTAS CON VIÑETAS

Es muy común encontrar en documentos de *Word* Listas Numeradas o Listas con Viñetas, dado que son elementos fáciles de crear y que, por sus características, llaman mucho la atención. Las listas facilitan la lectura de una secuencia de elementos que están relacionados entre sí o que pertenecen a un mismo conjunto.

Existen dos tipos importantes de listas, las Listas simples y los Esquemas.

En la **Figura 1** se muestra una lista en la que la información está clasificada por rubros y existen niveles de jerarquía.

Figura 1. Un ejemplo de lista mixta (numerada y con viñetas).

Tanto las Listas Numeradas como las Listas con Viñetas se crean y eliminan haciendo un clic en un simple botón.

Si bien el procedimiento es sencillo, pueden aparecer algunas dificultades. El problema más típico se presenta cuando damos por terminada la lista y *Word* sigue poniendo números o viñetas después del último elemento, o cuando ponemos un número delante del texto sin intención de hacer una lista, y *Word* pone automáticamente los números consecutivos entendiendo que queremos crear una lista. Estos dos problemas se solucionan pulsando *ENTER* cuando el cursor está en la misma línea que el Número o la Viñeta no deseada.

Otro problema que surge con frecuencia es cuando el usuario quiere agregar renglones vacíos a una lista y *Word* entiende que se trata de más elementos y pone Números o Viñetas en el o los renglones que deberían quedar vacíos. En este caso la solución consiste en agregar los renglones vacíos antes de presionar el botón Viñetas o el botón Numeración.

1.1. ¿Qué características tienen las listas?

Las listas consisten en una secuencia de elementos distribuidos uno debajo de otro precedidos por una Viñeta o un Número y seguidos de un Marcador de Fin de Párrafo. Esto quiere decir que para *Word* cada elemento tiene que estar en un párrafo diferente para ser considerado un ítem de la lista. Recordemos que al pulsar *ENTER* damos por terminado un párrafo y empezamos otro, de modo que si queremos crear elementos independientes de una lista tenemos que separarlos con un *ENTER*.

De acuerdo al nivel de complejidad, las listas se clasifican en:

♦ Listas Simples, Numeradas o con Viñetas.
♦ Esquemas, Numerados o con Viñetas.

A continuación se explica el uso de cada una de estas listas.

1.1.1. Listas Simples

Pueden ser Numeradas, con Viñetas, o una combinación de las dos. Tienen todos los ítems a la misma distancia del margen izquierdo, es decir, en una única columna, por lo que no existen distintos niveles de jerarquía.

Listas Simples con Viñetas

Las Listas Simples con Viñetas se usan para diferenciar fácilmente un ítem de otro, pero no muestran un orden o una secuencia. Si alteramos el orden de los elementos no se modifica el sentido de la lista. La **Figura** *2* muestra un ejemplo de este tipo de listas:

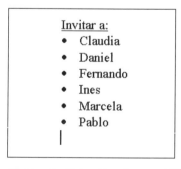

Figura 2. *Listas Simples con Viñetas.*

Elementos de trabajo I   1

Listas Simples Numeradas

Los elementos están alineados en la misma columna y siguen una secuencia. Si alteramos el orden, pierde sentido la secuencia. Un ejemplo de este tipo de listas se observa en la **Figura 3.**

Antes de encender la computadora realice los siguientes pasos:
1. Despeje el área de trabajo.
2. Saque de la caja CPU y Monitor.
3. Ubique en un lugar adecuado CPU y Monitor.
4. Conecte los cables como se indica en las primera páginas del Manual.
5. Controle que la llave de tensión se encuentre en 220v.
6. Conecte los cables de CPU y Monitor en el filtro de tensión.
7. Pulse el botón de encendido.

Figura 3. *Listas Simples Numeradas.*

1.1.2. Esquemas

Pueden ser Numerados, con Viñetas, o una combinación de los dos. En este tipo de listas los ítems de igual jerarquía están alineados en la misma columna. A menor jerarquía, mayor distancia del margen izquierdo.

Esquemas con Viñetas

Los Esquemas con Viñetas se utilizan para clasificar elementos en rubros. En este tipo de listas existen jerarquías, pero no hay una secuencia. Esto significa que si modificamos el orden de los elementos respetando las jerarquías, la lista sigue teniendo sentido. Un ejemplo de este tipo de esquemas se muestra en la **Figura 4.**

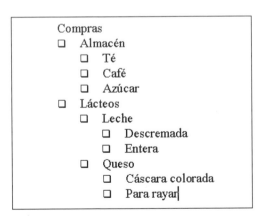

Figura 4. *Esquemas con Viñetas.*

Esquemas Numerados

En los Esquemas Numerados el texto está alineado por niveles de jerarquía y existe una secuencia. Si variamos el orden de los elementos deja de tener sentido la lista. La **Figura 5** nos da un ejemplo de un Esquema Numerado.

Secuencia de Trabjos de Pintura

1	Preparación de Pared		
	1.1	Rasquetear	
		1.1.1	Pintura Vieja.
		1.1.2	Reboques Viejos.
	1.2	Reboque	
		1.2.1	Grueso.
		1.2.2	Fino.
	1.3	Enduido	
		1.3.1	Una mano
		1.3.2	Lijado

Figura 5. *Esquema Numerado.*

1.2. ¿Cómo creamos Listas Simples?

Para crear una lista simple ubicamos el cursor en donde aparecerá el primer ítem y hacemos un clic en el botón **Viñetas** o en el botón **Numeración**, de la barra de Herramientas **Formato** que se muestra en la **Figura 6**. Luego realizamos los ingresos separando un ítem de otro con un *ENTER*. En el último elemento pulsamos dos veces *ENTER* para dar por terminada la lista.

Figura 6. *El botón Viñetas se usa para crear una lista.*

1.3. Esquemas Numerados y Viñetas

Al igual que en el caso anterior, ubicamos el cursor en donde aparecerá el primer elemento de la lista y luego procedemos así:

♦ En el menú **Formato** elegimos **Numeraciones y Viñetas**.
♦ En el Cuadro de Diálogo que aparece, en la ficha **Esquemas Numerados** que se muestra en la **Figura 7** seleccionamos un modelo de los que figuran allí y salimos aceptando.

Figura 7. *Ingresamos aquí para crear un Esquema.*

◆ Ingresamos el primer elemento de la lista y pulsamos *ENTER*.
◆ Si el segundo ítem es de menor jerarquía que el anterior, antes de ingresarlo presionamos la tecla *TAB* o el botón **Aumentar Sangría** para desplazarlo a la derecha y que adquiera la numeración adecuada.
◆ Procedemos así hasta ingresar todos los elementos de la lista.
◆ En el último elemento presionamos dos veces *ENTER* para dar por terminada la lista.

La **Figura 8** muestra los botones **Aumentar Sangría** y **Disminuir Sangría** que, junto con la tecla *TAB*, establece la jerarquía de los elementos del Esquema.

Figura 8. *Un clic en este botón y establecemos el nivel de cada elemento del Esquema.*

1.4. ¿Cómo quitamos elementos de una lista ?

Para sacar uno o más elementos de una lista hay que seleccionarlos y pulsar el botón **Viñetas** o el botón **Numeración**. *Word* reacomodará la numeración de la lista saltando el o los ítems seleccionados.

1.5. ¿Podemos cambiar Viñetas por Números y viceversa?

Sí, podemos hacerlo seleccionando la lista y haciendo un clic en el botón **Números** o el botón **Viñetas**, según si se quiere permutar Viñetas por Números o viceversa.

1.6. ¿Podemos ordenar una lista?

Las listas se ordenan del mismo modo que el texto Tabulado. Recordemos que el orden puede ser Alfabético, Numérico o por Fechas. También puede ser ascendente o descendente, etc.

A continuación, los pasos a seguir para ordenar una lista:

♦ Seleccionamos la lista a ordenar.
♦ En el menú **Tabla** elegimos **Ordenar Texto**.
♦ En el casillero **Primero Ordenar por** del Cuadro de Diálogo **Ordenar Texto** que mostramos en la **Figura 9**, seleccionamos la opción **Párrafo**.

Figura 9. *En esta ventana se ordenan las listas.*

En el casillero **Tipo** habilitamos la opción **Texto** y la opción **Ascendente.** *Word* ordenará cada línea desde la ¨A¨ a la ¨Z¨.

2. CUADROS DE TEXTO

Los Cuadros de Texto son unidades flexibles y atractivas que se utilizan mucho en *Word* por el aspecto que le proporcionan a la presentación. Son marcos con texto que pueden moverse a cualquier lugar de la hoja como si fueran objetos. En los Cuadros de Texto generalmente incluimos una porción del escrito que queremos destacar. En la **Figura 10** se ve un documento con un Cuadro de Texto.

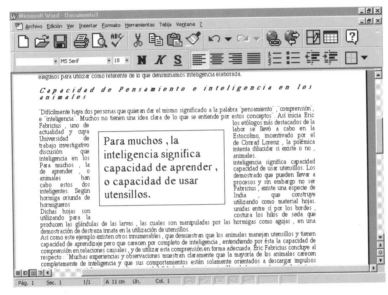

Figura 10. *Un ejemplo de Cuadros de Texto.*

Los Cuadros de Texto tienen, entre otras, las siguientes características:

- ◆ El formato del texto que está adentro es independiente del resto del escrito: Esto significa que cuando movemos un Cuadro de Texto a un entorno con formatos diferentes, el Cuadro de Texto no perderá sus propias características.
- ◆ Dos o más Cuadros de Texto pueden vincularse, es decir, podemos hacer que el texto empiece en uno de ellos y fluya hacia el segundo a medida que se va llenando.
- ◆ Los Cuadros de Texto pueden agruparse para que al cambiar la alineación o distribución de uno de ellos, se modifique automáticamente todo el grupo.
- ◆ También podemos agregarle bordes y fondo con colores, efectos 3D, sombras, tramas, imágenes, etc.

2.1. ¿Cómo insertamos un Cuadro de Texto en un documento?

Para insertar un Cuadro de Texto en un documento seguimos las siguientes instrucciones:

♦ Ubicamos el cursor en donde aparecerá el Cuadro de Texto.
♦ Hacemos un clic en el botón **Cuadro de Texto** de la barra **Dibujo,** que tiene el aspecto de la **Figura 11.**

Figura 11. *Un clic en este botón e inmediatamente aparece el Cuadro de texto.*

♦ Cuando el puntero toma forma de cruz, mantenemos pulsado el botón izquierdo del *Mouse* y trazamos a lo largo de la diagonal el Cuadrado de Texto.

Al soltar el botón izquierdo del *Mouse* aparece el marco gris rodeado de Controladores de Tamaño que se muestra en la **Figura 12**. Para ingresar texto adentro hacemos un clic en el interior y escribimos.

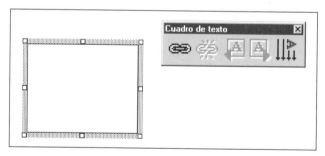

Figura 12. *Marco gris que caracteriza a los Cuadros de Texto.*

2.2. ¿Cómo seleccionamos y eliminamos un Cuadro de Texto?

Para seleccionar un Cuadro de Texto ubicamos el puntero arriba del marco y, cuando el puntero toma forma de flecha de cuatro cabezas, hacemos dos clics.

Para eliminarlo hay que seleccionarlo y luego presionar la tecla *DEL* (SUPRIMIR).

2.3. Modificar el tamaño de un Cuadro de Texto

La variación del tamaño se hace arrastrando con el *Mouse* alguno de los Controladores de Tamaño de las esquinas como se observa en la **Figura 13**.

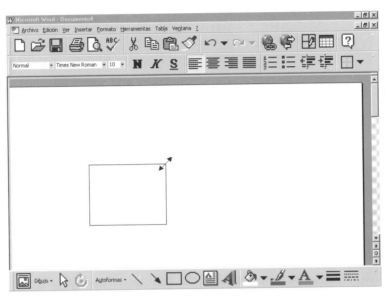

***Figura 13.** Variación del tamaño de un Cuadro de Texto.*

Si queremos llevarlo a un tamaño específico, o establecer un porcentaje de aumento o disminución sin que se pierdan las proporciones originales procedemos así:

◆ Hacemos doble clic sobre el contorno del Cuadro de Texto.

◆ En la ficha **Tamaño** que aparece y que se muestra en la **Figura 14**, ingresamos un porcentaje en el casillero **Alto** del recuadro **Escala**. Si, por ejemplo, queremos reducirlo a $1/4$ del tamaño original ingresamos 25%.

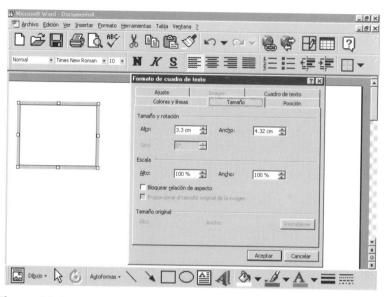

Figura 14. *Ingresamos en esta ventana para establecer un tamaño específico.*

2.4. Ajuste de un Cuadro de Texto.

El ajuste de un Cuadro de Texto es el modo como se distribuye el texto del documento alrededor del Cuadro de Texto. La **Figura 15** muestra un Cuadro de texto con ajuste Cuadrado.

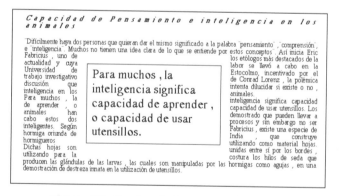

Figura 15. *Cuadro de Texto con ajuste cuadrado.*

Para modificar el ajuste de un Cuadro de texto seguimos las siguientes instrucciones:

◆ Seleccionamos el Cuadro de Texto.
◆ Hacemos un clic con el botón derecho del *Mouse*.
◆ En el Menú Contextual que aparece en la **Figura 16**, seleccionamos la opción **Formato de Cuadro de Texto**.

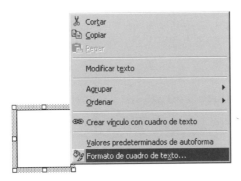

Figura 16. *Un clic en el botón derecho sobre el marco y aparece este menú desde donde modificamos el aspecto del Cuadro de Texto.*

En la ficha **Ajuste**, de la **Figura 17** elegimos alguno de los siguientes:

Figura 17. *Aquí elegimos el ajuste deseado.*

- **Cuadrado**: El texto se ajustará equitativamente alrededor de todos los bordes del Marco.
- **Estrecho**: El texto se ajustará alrededor de los bordes de la imagen real, en vez de ajustarse alrededor del marco. Este tipo de ajuste se usa en imágenes.
- **Ninguno**: Texto y Objeto aparecerán superpuestos.
- **Superior e Inferior**: El texto aparecerá arriba y abajo.
- **Transparente**: Es similar a Estrecho.

Es importante recordar que todos los ajustes anteriores se llevan a cabo siempre que el espacio entre el Cuadro de Texto y el margen sea como mínimo de 2,54 cm.

2.5. ¿Cómo centramos un Cuadro de Texto?

Para centrar un Cuadro de Texto seguimos los siguientes pasos:

- Pasamos a Presentación Diseño de Página y verificamos que está visible la barra de Herramientas **Dibujo**.
- Seleccionamos el Cuadro de Texto a centrar.
- Hacemos un clic en el botón **Dibujo** y elegimos la opción **Alinear o Distribuir,** como lo muestra la **Figura 18.**

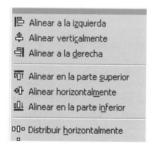

Figura 18. *Botón Dibujar, mostrando los comandos para centrar un Cuadro de Texto.*

- Seleccionamos **Distribuir Horizontalmente** y luego **Distribuir Verticalmente.**

2.6. Modificar la dirección de un texto

Sí, podemos. Un Cuadro de Texto en el que se cambió la dirección se ve como el de la **Figura 19.**

Figura 19. *Cuadro de Texto en el que se varió la dirección de su contenido.*

Para modificar la dirección de un Cuadro de Texto lo seleccionamos y, cuando aparece la barra **Cuadro de Texto** que se muestra en la **Figura 20,** usamos el botón **Cambiar dirección de Texto**.

Figura 20. *Un clic en este botón y el texto cambia de dirección.*

2.7. ¿Y si ya tenemos el texto y queremos incluirlo dentro de un Cuadro de Texto?

En este caso primero seleccionamos el texto y luego hacemos un clic en el botón **Cuadro de Texto** de la barra **Dibujo**.

2.8. ¿Cómo agregamos Bordes de colores y Fondo a un Cuadro de Texto?

Para agregarle cualquiera de estos elementos hay que seleccionar el Cuadro de Texto y utilizar los botones **Color de Línea**, **Tipo de Línea**, **Estilo de Línea** y **Color de relleno** de la barra de Herramientas **Dibujo,** que se ven en la **Figura 21.**

Figura 21. *Aspecto que tienen las herramientas para trabajar con bordes.*

Los Cuadros de Texto sin bordes o fondo no se ven. El texto aparece distribuido como si estuviese dentro de un marco pero no vemos el contorno. Los dos botones con forma de cubo verde que aparecen en la Figura anterior permiten agregarle sombras y efectos 3D al marco.

3. IMÁGENES

Incorporar imágenes en un documento *Word* es tan simple que los documentos "Sólo texto" se limitan a contratos, escrituras y documento formales. Las imágenes que se incorporan a un documento van desde el simple dibujo hasta aquellas imágenes escaneadas retocadas en programas especiales, pasando por los gráficos, las marcas de agua y las imágenes prediseñadas.

Las imágenes que insertamos en un documento pueden tener diferentes orígenes. A continuación analizaremos cada caso.

3.1. Insertar imágenes a un documento Word.

Figura 22. *El Clipart es la librería de imágenes del Office.*

El modo más simple, fácil y directo de incorporar una imagen a un documento es utilizando la librería de Imágenes Prediseñadas *Clipart*. Todos los utilitarios de *Office* acceden a esta librería de Imágenes Prediseñadas guardadas en la carpeta ARCHIVOS DE PROGRAMA/*MSOFFICE*/*CLIPART*.

Una vez incorporada la imagen podemos dibujar sobre ella, o modificarla utilizando las herramientas de dibujo, como se verá en otro capítulo. En la **Figura 22**, un ejemplo de una imagen dibujada.

A continuación, una serie de instrucciones para insertar una Imagen Prediseñada:

♦ Ubicar el cursor en donde aparecerá la imagen.
♦ En el menú **Insertar** elegir **Imagen** y luego seleccionar la opción **Prediseñadas,** como se muestra en la **Figura 23.**

Figura 23. *Primer paso a seguir para insertar una imagen.*

♦ En el Cuadro de Diálogo de la **Figura 24**, elegir el rubro que queremos y luego la imagen. Podemos elegir el rubro **Animales**, luego el burro y hacer un clic en el botón **Insertar**.

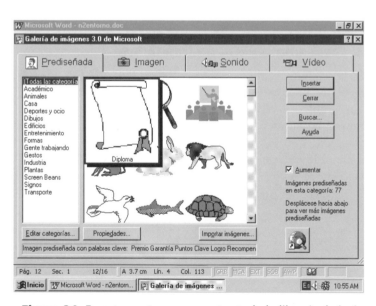

Figura 24. *En esta ventana se muestra toda la librería de imágenes.*

3.2. Incorporar Imágenes desde un Archivo

Otro modo de incorporar imágenes al documento es importándolas de un archivo ubicado en un disquete, en el disco rígido, en un CD, etc. El procedimiento es el siguiente:

◆ En el menú **Insertar** elegimos **Imagen** y luego **Desde Archivo**, como se muestra en la **Figura 25.**

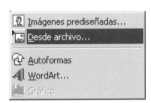

Figura 25. Primer paso a seguir para insertar una imagen desde un archivo.

◆ En el Cuadro de Diálogo que aparece ingresamos la ruta de acceso y nombre del archivo. Podemos ingresar ¨a:\pochoclo. jpg¨ y pulsar **Aceptar**.

Si al realizar adecuadamente este procedimiento aparece un mensaje de error, es posible que no tengamos instalado el filtro para abrir imágenes con ese formato. En este caso corremos el programa instalador de *Office*, instalamos el filtro adecuado e intentamos nuevamente.

3.3. Crear una galería de Imágenes.

Cada vez que abrimos una imagen desde un archivo, además de incorporarla al documento, podemos guardarla en una librería personal para tenerla disponible en el futuro. Para insertar una imagen a un documento y además guardarla en la librería personal procedemos del siguiente modo:

◆ En el menú **Insertar** elegimos **Imagen** y luego **Prediseñada**.
◆ Seleccionamos la ficha **Imágenes** que se muestra en la **Figura 26.**

Elementos de trabajo I

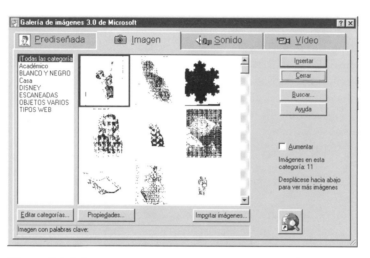

***Figura 26.** Primer paso para crear nuestra propia galería de imágenes.*

◆ Hacemos un clic en el botón **Importar Imagen**, y en el Cuadro de Diálogo que aparece y que mostramos en la **Figura 27** ingresamos el nombre del archivo y la ruta de acceso.
◆ En el casillero **Categoría** elegimos el rubro para la nueva imagen.
◆ En el casillero **Palabra Clave** ingresamos un nombre para la imagen.
◆ Pulsamos **Insertar** para incorporarla al documento.

***Figura 27.** Esta ventana nos permite construir nuestra librería personal.*

La imagen quedará disponible en la librería personal para futuros usos.

3.4. ¿ Cómo incorporamos Imágenes de Internet?

Capturar imágenes de Internet es tan sencillo como abrirlas desde un archivo. Para hacerlo necesitamos tener instalado un Navegador, como por ejemplo el Explorador de Internet o el Netscape. Por supuesto, el sistema debe estar configurado para acceder a Internet.

El procedimiento consiste en copiar al Portapapeles las imágenes capturadas en Internet y luego pegarlas en el documento de acuerdo a las siguientes instrucciones:

♦ Verificar que el documento al que vamos a agregarle las imágenes está abierto y activo.
♦ En el menú **Insertar** elegir **Imagen**.
♦ Seleccionar la opción **Desde Archivo**.
♦ En el Cuadro de Diálogo que aparece pulsar el botón con el símbolo del **Explorador de Internet**, que se muestra en la **Figura 28**.

Figura 28. Botón que representa el acceso a Internet.

♦ Verificar que se inicia el Navegador y que accedemos a Internet.
♦ Navegar por Internet hasta encontrar una imagen adecuada. Hacer un clic con el botón derecho del *Mouse* sobre la imagen.
♦ Seleccionar el comando **Copiar**.
♦ Pulsar *ALT*+TAB para pasar a *Word*.
♦ Ubicar el cursor en el lugar en donde aparecerá la imagen.
♦ Pulsar CTRL+V.
♦ Proceder así hasta copiar todas las imágenes.
♦ Cerrar el Explorador de Internet.

3.5. ¿Qué es una Imagen Compuesta?

Una imagen compuesta es una imagen dibujada. Las imágenes compuestas son tratadas como objetos. A continuación se indica cómo proceder para crear una imagen compuesta:

♦ Verificar que la barra **Dibujo** está visible.
♦ Hacer un clic en el botón **Imagen de *Word***, de la **Figura 29**.

Figura 29. Un clic aquí y empezamos a crear una imagen compuesta.

♦ En el marco que aparece insertar una imagen como se indicó antes, y luego dibujar arriba. Más adelante, en este Manual, se indicará cómo utilizar las herramientas de la barra **Dibujo**.

Una vez concluido el dibujo, es indispensable restablecer los nuevos límites de la imagen para no cortar lo que se agregó o para que no quede un marco excesivamente grande. Los límites de una imagen se restablecen haciendo un clic en el botón **Restablecer límites**, de la Barra de Herramientas **Modificar Imagen** que aparece automáticamente cuando creamos una imagen compuesta. Esta barra de Herramientas tiene dos botones, el de la izquierda es el que se usa para restablecer los límites. Es importante destacar que esta Barra de Herramientas sólo aparece cuando está abierta la imagen. Si la cerramos accidentalmente y luego queremos usarla, tenemos que hacer un clic con el botón derecho del *Mouse* arriba de cualquier barra de Herramientas y elegirla de la lista. Para que la Barra de Herramientas **Modificar Imagen**, de la **Figura 30,** aparezca en la lista tiene que estar abierta la imagen.

Figura 30. Un clic en el primer botón evita que parte de la imagen quede afuera.

3.6. Ajuste de una imagen.

Una imagen puede ajustarse del mismo modo que un Cuadro de Texto.
La **Figura 31** muestra texto escrito en dos columnas con una imagen en el medio. En este ejemplo se definió un ajuste Cuadrado.

Figura 31. *En el Ajuste Cuadrado el texto forma un marco alrededor de la imagen.*

Para que el texto se ajuste a una forma diferente de la que tiene el contorno de la imagen, seleccionamos la imagen y modificamos el contorno de ajuste utilizando la herramienta **Modificar puntos de Ajuste.** Esta herramienta se encuentra en el botón **Ajuste de Texto**, de la Barra de Herramientas **Imagen** que se muestra en la en la **Figura 32.** Si esta barra no está visible, hacemos un clic con el botón derecho del *Mouse* arriba de cualquier Barra de Herramientas y la elegimos de la lista.

Figura 32. *Podemos cambiar la forma del texto alrededor de la imagen utilizando este botón.*

3.7. ¿Qué son las Marcas de Agua y cómo las creamos?

Las Marcas de Agua son texturas, imágenes u objetos que aparecen impresos de forma tenue detrás del texto y que generalmente se usan para mejorar el aspecto de la presentación o para informarnos sobre algo especial. Podemos agregar una Marca de Agua con nuestro logo personal de fondo. En este caso el lector sabrá inmediatamente quién creó el documento y a su vez, lo que está leyendo le resultará agradable.

Para crear e imprimir una Marca de Agua, es necesario insertarla dentro de un Encabezado o Pie de Página y luego llevarla al medio de la hoja. El procedimiento es el siguiente:

- En el menú **Ver** seleccionar **Encabezado y Pie de Página**.
- Verificar que aparece un recuadro y la barra de Herramientas **Encabezado y Pie** que se muestra en la **Figura 33**.

Figura 33. *Abrir el recuadro del Encabezado es el primer paso para crear una Marca de Agua.*

- Ubicar el cursor adentro del recuadro del Encabezado e insertar la imagen eligiendo **Insertar** y luego **Prediseñada**.
- Verificar que la imagen aparece adentro del recuadro del Encabezado de la página.
- Arrastrarla con el *Mouse* al medio de la hoja.
- Seleccionar la imagen y hacer un clic en el botón derecho del *Mouse*.
- En el menú contextual que aparece en la **Figura 34**, seleccionar la opción **Formato de Imagen**.

Figura 34. *Un clic con el botón derecho del Mouse nos permite definir la Marca de Agua.*

◆ En el casillero **Color,** de la ficha **Imagen,** seleccionar la opción **Marca de Agua** como vemos en la **Figura 35.**

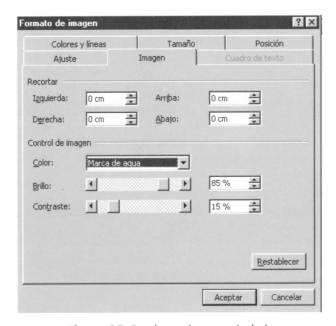

Figura 35. *Desde aquí se atenúa la imagen.*

◆ En la ficha **Ajuste** seleccionar la opción **Ninguno**.
◆ Pulsar **Aceptar**.
◆ Hacer un clic en el botón **Cerrar** de la barra de Herramientas **Encabezado y Pie de Página**.
◆ Verificar los resultados en Presentación Diseño de página o Preliminar.

3.8. ¿Cómo modificamos brillo y contraste de una imagen?

Estas modificaciones se hacen seleccionando la imagen y usando los botones **Más Contraste** y **Menos Contraste**, y los botones **Más Brillo** y **Menos Brillo**, de la Barra de Herramientas **Imagen** que se muestra en la **Figura 36.**

Figura 36. *Un clic aquí para modificar brillo y contraste.*

3.9. Recortar una imagen

Para recortar una imagen procedemos así:

◆ Seleccionamos la imagen.

◆ En la barra **Imagen** elegimos la herramienta **Recortar**, que es la primera de la izquierda (Ver **Figura 37**).

Figura 37. Herramienta para recortar imágenes.

◆ Cuando el puntero cambia de forma mantenemos pulsado el botón izquierdo del *Mouse* y arrastramos los controladores de tamaño hasta la nueva posición.

3.10. Más sobre imágenes

Las imágenes que se incorporan a un documento importándolas desde un archivo pueden vincularse. Esto se hace para reducir la cantidad de memoria que ocupan dentro del documento. Cuando insertamos una imagen vinculada, guardamos un bosquejo de la misma y no la representación completa. Esta última queda guardada en otra parte del sistema y *Word* la consulta en diferentes situaciones, como, por ejemplo, antes de imprimir.

En los documentos que contienen muchas imágenes, éstas generalmente se vinculan porque la diferencia de tamaño es enorme en uno u otro caso. Por ejemplo, un documento de 125Kb que contiene una sola imagen escaneada no vinculada, ocupa sólo 19 Kb cuando vinculamos la imagen.

Las imágenes vinculadas de un documento *Word* tienen menos posibilidades de quedar desactualizadas que aquellas no vinculadas. Esto es así porque *Word* las actualiza permanentemente cuando detecta cambios en los archivos originales.

En el capítulo siguiente, cuando trabajemos con objetos, analizaremos con más detalles el tema de los archivos vinculados.

Para vincular una imagen es necesario habilitar el casillero correspondiente al momento de importarla desde el archivo. La **Figura 38** muestra el Cuadro de Diálogo que nos permite vincular una imagen cuando la importamos de un archivo.

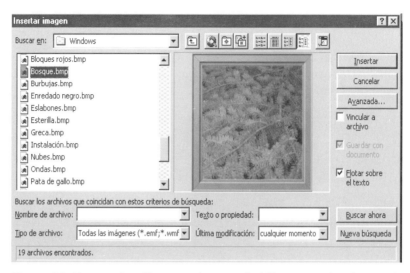

Figura 38. *Este es el casillero que hay que habilitar para vincular una imagen.*

3.10.1. ¿Qué tipos de imágenes podemos incorporar a un documento Word?

Si bien existen diferentes formatos de imágenes, todas se ven similares en pantalla, y no podemos distinguir entre un tipo y otro. La diferencia sí se ve en el tamaño que ocupan dentro del documento y en la nitidez al momento de imprimirlas.

Existen diferentes tipos de formatos de imágenes, dependiendo del grado de compresión de los mismos y del modo como se tratan sus pixeles (puntos de la imagen). En algunas un pixel es un byte, mientras que en otras un pixel es una fórmula matemática, un vector, etc. Analizaremos cuatro tipos principales de imágenes, sus características y sus usos.

Imágenes tipo Vectorial

Generalmente se crean en programas de dibujo. Cada punto de la imagen es un vector que se archiva como una fórmula matemática. Esto hace que ocupen poca memoria y sean fáciles de imprimir. En *Word*, podemos desagrupar las imágenes de tipo vectorial y utilizar sus componentes para crear otras imágenes. Las imágenes prediseñadas de la carpeta *Clipart* son ejemplos de imágenes tipo Vectorial. Estas imágenes pueden desagruparse utilizando la herramienta **Desagrupar**, de la barra de **Dibujo**, y con sus partes podemos crear nuevos diseños.

Algunas extensiones de imágenes Vectoriales son:

- WMF(Metarchivo mejorado de *Windows*)
- GDI (*Window Graphic Device Interface*)
- EMF (Metarchivo mejorado)

Imágenes de tipo Mapa de Bits.

Se crean en los programas para pintar del tipo *Microsoft Paint*. La imagen se forma a partir de un diagrama de puntos. En general son muy voluminosas ya que no llevan ningún tipo de compresión. En *Word*, las imágenes de tipo *Bitmap* se comportan como verdaderos bloques, no podemos separarlas en sus componentes y sólo podemos dibujar sobre ellas. Respecto de las de tipo Vectorial, son consideradas de inferior calidad y son más engorrosas para imprimir. Algunas de las extensiones típicas son: BMP, RLE, DIB, PCX (Archivo PC *Paintbrush*).

Imágenes Escaneadas

Son de tipo *Bit-mapped* pero pueden guardarse a mayor resolución. Aparecen difusas en el monitor, pero al imprimirlas tienen la fidelidad de una foto. El formato típico de este tipo de imágenes es TIFF. Las imágenes TIFF *(Tag Image File Format)* pueden tener dos tipos de compresión, Normal y Laurenciana. En este último caso se resigna algo de información a cambio de la reducción del archivo.

Las Imágenes Escaneadas no pueden editarse en *Word*. Para realizar cambios recurrimos a aquellos programas especiales que permiten editar este tipo de imágenes, como por ejemplo *Photoshop*, y luego volvemos a insertarla en nuestra presentación.

Imágenes Encapsuladas

Son imágenes que están codificadas en lenguaje binario o ASCII. La codificación se realiza automáticamente en programas de dibujo o directamente ingresando los códigos en el lenguaje de programación. Este tipo de imágenes es ideal para redimensionar porque el tamaño se transfiere por parámetros. La extensión típica es EPS (*Encapsulated Postcript*) y en *Word* podemos desagruparlas e utilizar sus componentes.

Elementos de trabajo I

Imágenes JPG Y GIF

Las imágenes JPG y GIF se usan mucho en Internet porque son los formatos que más se comprimen.

Dependiendo del nivel de compresión pierden más o menos información, por ejemplo, un archivo de 10 MB puede llevarse a 100KB.

El formato GIF incluye dos formatos específicos, GIF 87 y GIF 89a, mejorados para transparencias y entrelazados. Los archivos GIF están indicados para logotipos, íconos e imágenes de líneas, ya que como el formato se limita a 256 colores, no resulta el más indicado para fotografías detalladas.

PROBLEMAS

1. A Raúl le molesta que cuando coloca un número delante de un párrafo, *Word* continúe colocando números como si se tratara de una lista.

2. Mariana quiere hacer un Esquema Numerado realizando los siguientes pasos: Crea una Lista Simple, la selecciona y luego elige la opción **Esquemas Numerados** del Cuadro de Diálogo **Números y Viñetas** (menú **Formato**).

3. Ricardo ubica el cursor a la derecha de una viñeta y pulsa la tecla *BACKSPACE*, pero no puede borrarla.

4. Matías crea una lista numerada que tiene diez elementos. Cuando la termina se da cuenta de que el quinto elemento era en realidad una parte del cuarto. Intenta varias cosas pero no puede corregir el error.

5. Anibal quiere insertar un Cuadro de Texto, pero no tiene visible la barra de Herramientas **Dibujo** y no sabe cómo mostrarla.

6. Roberto quiere ubicar una imagen entre dos columnas pero no puede arrastrarla con el *Mouse*.

7. María creó una imagen como Marca de Agua, ahora quiere eliminarla pero no puede.

8. Roman eligió ajuste **Ninguno** para su imagen. Ahora el texto pasa por arriba de la imagen y no pude seleccionarla para modificar su tamaño.

9. Natalia quiere capturar imágenes de Internet: Para ello abre el Navegador junto con el procesador de texto, pero luego no sabe cómo proceder.

10. Arturo recibe un disquete que supuestamente contiene el logo de su Facultad para pegarlo en un informe. Abre el documento *Word* y cuando selecciona **Insertar Imagen/ Desde Archivo**, el disquete está vacío.

SOLUCIONES

1. Raúl pudo interrumpir la lista pulsando dos veces *ENTER* a la altura del número "Intruso". También puede resolver definitivamente el problema deshabilitando las opciones **Lista Automática con Números** y **Lista Automática con Viñetas**, en el menú **Herramientas** opción **Autocorrección**, ficha **Autoformato**.

2. A Mariana le falta aumentar la sangría de menor jerarquía. La Lista Simple se convertirá automáticamente en un verdadero Esquema Numerado.

3. Las viñetas y los números de una lista no se borran como cualquier carácter. Para eliminarlos hay que ubicar el cursor en la línea en la que se encuentran y volver a pulsar el botón **Viñetas** o el botón **Numeración** según se trate de una Lista con Viñetas o una Lista Numerada.

4. Matías tiene que ubicar el cursor al final del párrafo del cuarto elemento y pulsar la tecla *DEL*. Al borrarse la marca de Fin de Párrafo, el elemento cinco pasará automáticamente a formar parte del cuatro. Toda la lista se reacomodará para adaptarse al cambio.

5. Como toda barra de Herramientas, la de **Dibujo** se muestra haciendo un clic con el botón derecho del *Mouse* sobre cualquier barra y eligiéndola de la lista.

6. Las imágenes, al igual que los objetos, pueden estar ubicadas en una capa encima del texto (configuradas para flotar sobre el texto), o pueden estar a la par del texto (configuradas como un párrafo más). Cuando se establecen como un párrafo más no podemos moverlas de un lado a otro de la hoja como lo haríamos si flotaran. Para variar de una configuración a otra es necesario seleccionar la imagen y pulsar el botón derecho del *Mouse*. En el menú contextual elegir **Formato de Imagen** y seleccionar la ficha **Posición**. Allí hay un casillero denominado **Flotar sobre Texto**, que permite pasar de una configuración a otra.

7. Para modificar o eliminar una Marca de Agua hay que abrir el **Encabezado** en el que se encuentra, seleccionarla y pulsar *DEL*. Recordemos que si bien la imagen está en el medio de la hoja, en realidad fue insertada dentro del Encabezado.

8. Roman tienen que mostrar la barra **Dibujo**. Allí hay una herramienta con forma de flecha blanca que se usa para seleccionar objetos. Con esa herramienta podrá seleccionar fácilmente la imagen. Si todavía no puede hacerlo puede ser porque la imagen está detrás del texto. Lo que tiene que hacer en este caso es elegir, en el botón **Dibujo**, la opción **Ordenar** y luego **Delante de Texto**. Esto obligará a la imagen a salir de atrás del texto.

9. Natalia tiene que navegar por Internet y cuando vea una imagen que le guste hacer un clic con el botón derecho del *Mouse* sobre ella y elegir la opción **Copiar**. Luego pasar a *Word* utilizando el atajo de teclado *ALT*+TAB y pegarla con la Herramienta **Pegar** de la barra **Estándar** o bien utilizando el atajo de teclado CTRL+V.

10. Cuando intentamos importar una imagen se abre la ventana **Abrir,** para que ingresemos la ruta de acceso y el nombre del archivo. Arturo tiene que verificar que el casillero **Tipo de Archivo,** del Cuadro de Diálogo **Abrir**, tenga habilitada la opción **Todos los Archivos**, de lo contrario, sólo verá los archivos con el formato habilitado allí.

OBJETOS 2

Tiempo de lectura y práctica:
1 hora y 15 minutos

Lección

2

Objetivo de la lección

- ■ Aprender a crear, modificar y eliminar objetos.
- ■ Trabajar con objetos de Dibujos, Autoformas y Objetos *WordArt*.
- ■ Importar, modificar y analizar Gráficos.
- ■ Incorporar sonidos a un documento.
- ■ Analizar la diferencia entre objetos Incrustados y Vinculados.

1. OBJETOS

En términos generales, un objeto es un gráfico, diagrama, ecuación, sonido o cualquier otra información que aparezca en un documento y que no sea Texto. Los objetos, al igual que las imágenes y los Cuadros de Texto, pueden arrastrarse de un lugar a otro de la hoja utilizando el *Mouse*. Antes de mover un objeto es necesario seleccionarlo haciendo un clic encima de él. Cuando un objeto está seleccionado, aparece rodeado por un marco y varios Controladores de Tamaño. Los Controladores de Tamaño son los cuadraditos que aparecen sobre el contorno del objeto, y que usamos para redimensionarlo. En la **Figura 1** se ve un objeto en movimiento.

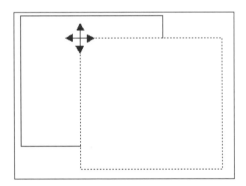

Figura 1. *Objeto en movimiento.*

Actualmente, las tecnologías OLE y DDE desarrolladas para compartir información entre aplicaciones facilitan tanto el intercambio de objetos e imágenes, que es difícil no tentarse a incluir objetos en todos los documentos. Ahora todo está al alcance de la mano, disponible en librerías o flotando en el sistema para que, pulsando un simple botón y sin preocuparnos por los filtros que tanto dolor de cabeza nos daban antes, aparezca una o varias veces donde más nos guste.

En este capítulo prestaremos atención a los objetos de Dibujo, Gráficos y Sonido, que son los más utilizados por los usuarios de *Word*.

1.1. ¿Qué función cumplen los objetos en un documento?

Podría decirse que los objetos en *Word* cumplen, entre otras, alguna de las siguientes funciones:

♦ Aportan información relevante: Esta es la función más común, si eliminamos el objeto, el texto pierde sentido.
♦ Completan la información existente: este es el caso de las ilustraciones, dibujos, esquemas, etc., que sintetizan o completan la información del texto que las precede.
♦ Cumplen funciones estéticas: un documento que sólo contiene texto muchas veces resulta tedioso.
♦ Cumplen funciones recreativas: es más atractivo leer un documento que contiene sonidos o un video, que uno que no contiene ninguno de estos dos elementos.

1.2. Crear objetos en Word.

Lo primero que hay que hacer para crear un objeto en *Word*, es elegir una aplicación en donde diseñarlo. Esto es así porque los objetos en *Word* siempre se crean en aplicaciones independientes que se abren dentro del Procesador de Texto. Son ejemplo de aplicaciones independientes, *MicrosoftGraph*, *Microsoft Equation*, etc.

Cuando una aplicación se abre dentro de *Word*, su interfase reemplaza total o parcialmente la Ventana Principal de *Word*. Durante la creación de un objeto, las barras de Herramientas de la aplicación Independiente reemplazan parcial o totalmente a las Barras de *Word* y no podemos hacer otra cosa que diseñar el objeto.

Un ejemplo de esto es el siguiente: Para incorporar una pintura a un documento, no es necesario pasar a *Paint* sino que simplemente insertamos un objeto y elegimos como aplicación independiente *Microsoft Paint*. *Word* abrirá automáticamente esta aplicación y las herramientas del *Paint* reemplazarán a las barras de *Word*. Para volver al documento, el usuario tiene que hacer un clic fuera del objeto o en el menú **Archivo** (de la aplicación Independiente), seleccionar **Cerrar Objeto** y volver a *Word*.

Los objetos creados sin salir de *Word* se denominan Incrustados y tienen la siguiente característica: Si hacemos doble clic sobre ellos, abrimos automáticamente la Aplicación que les dio origen.

Para crear un objeto sin salir de *Word* hay que seguir las siguientes instrucciones:

♦ Verificar que el documento *Word* que recibirá el objeto esté abierto y activo.
♦ Ubicar el cursor donde aparecerá el objeto.

◆ En el menú **Insertar**, elegir **Objeto**.

◆ En el Cuadro de Diálogo de la **Figura 2**, seleccionar alguna aplicación de las que figuran en la lista. Entre otras están *Microsoft Excel, Microsoft PowerPoint, Microsoft Equation*, etc. El contenido de la lista dependerá del *software* instalado en el sistema.

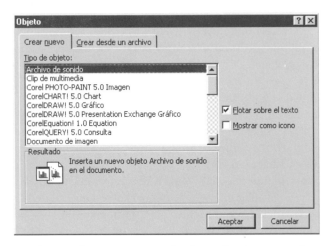

Figura 2. *En esta lista aparecen todas las aplicaciones con las que se podrá crear un objeto.*

◆ Habilitar el casillero **Flotar sobre Texto** para establecer el objeto como Flotante (Ver más adelante).

◆ Verificar que se abre la aplicación elegida y que las barras de Herramientas de la misma reemplazan a las barras de Herramientas de *Word*.

◆ Trabajar en el objeto utilizando las herramientas de la Aplicación Independiente que reemplazaron a las herramientas de *Word*.

◆ Una vez creado el objeto, para volver al documento hay que pulsar fuera del mismo, o bien seleccionar en el menú **Archivo** la opción **Cerrar Objeto**, y volver al documento *Word*.

La **Figura 3** muestra una fórmula creada utilizando la Aplicación Independiente *Microsoft Equation*.

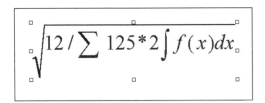

Figura 3. *Una fórmula puede ser un objeto.*

1.3. ¿Porqué cuando hacemos doble clic sobre un objeto, se abre una aplicación distinta de Word?

Los Objetos Incrustados contienen, además del objeto propiamente dicho, las instrucciones necesarias para volver a la aplicación que les dio origen. Cuando hacemos doble clic sobre un Objeto creado sin salir de *Word*, se abre automáticamente la ventana Principal de la aplicación en la que se generó el objeto, y las herramientas de *Word* se ocultan temporalmente. Los objetos creados sin salir de *Word* se comportan de ese modo, hacemos doble clic sobre ellos y accedemos a la aplicación en la que fueron creados. Cuando esto no ocurre, pueden pasar dos cosas: que la aplicación que les dio origen no esté instalada en el sistema, o que nosotros mismos hayamos eliminado la conexión a fin de reducir el tamaño del documento. Recordemos que tanto el objeto como las instrucciones para llegar a su aplicación pasan a ser parte del documento, por lo que un objeto Incrustado ocupa mucho más memoria que uno no Incrustado.

Si profundizamos más en el tema veremos que el Objeto y las instrucciones de cómo volver a la aplicación que le dio origen son en realidad Campos. El formato Campo es ideal para elementos que varían una y otra vez, porque los campos son fácilmente actualizados, sin embargo los campos ocupan mucha memoria.

Si incrustamos un objeto y sabemos que no vamos a modificarlo más, conviene romper la conexión con su aplicación. En este caso el objeto se verá exactamente igual que antes, pero no podremos abrir la aplicación haciendo doble clic sobre él. Para romper la conexión entre un objeto y su aplicación hay que seleccionarlo y pulsar CTRL+*SHIFT*+F9. Antes, es necesario verificar que el mismo se comporte como objeto NO Flotante (ver a continuación)

1.4. ¿Cómo se comportan los objetos en un documento?

Word 97 tiene un manejo de los objetos distinto de las versiones anteriores. En esta versión existen varios niveles o capas superpuestas que pueden ser ocupadas por texto y/u objetos alternativamente. La existencia de estas capas hace posible colocar objetos detrás, delante, o a la par del texto. Si colocamos un objeto delante o detrás del texto decimos de él que se comporta como "Flotante". Los objetos configurados como "Flotantes" se arrastran con el *Mouse* a cualquier parte de la hoja (incluso podemos llevarlos fuera de la página y dejarlos allí hasta determinar su ubicación final), son libres, volátiles y pueden perder su ubicación fácilmente.

Los objetos definidos como "No Flotantes" tienen las características de un párrafo más de texto. Esto significa que no podemos arrastrarlos con el *Mouse* a cualquier lugar de la hoja, no podemos ubicarlos encima o debajo del texto, ni podemos sacarlos fuera de la página. Se comportan como si estuviesen anclados, es difícil moverlos de lugar, así como también es difícil que pierdan su ubicación cuando el texto se reordena.

En general se trabaja con el objeto configurado como "Flotante" hasta definir su posición final. Una vez determinada la misma, lo pasamos a "No Flotante" para evitar que se mueva o pierda su ubicación respecto del resto del texto.

Para establecer un objeto como "Flotante" o "No Flotante" procedemos del siguiente modo:

♦ Seleccionamos el objeto.
♦ Pulsamos el botón derecho del *Mouse*.
♦ En el menú contextual que se muestra en la **Figura 4** seleccionamos **Formato de Objeto**.

Figura 4. *Un clic aquí es el primer paso para definir un objeto como flotante.*

♦ En la ficha de la **Figura 5** habilitamos o deshabilitamos el casillero **Flotar sobre el Texto**.

Figura 5. *Los objetos flotantes son muy fáciles de manejar con el Mouse.*

1.4.1. Características de los objetos "No Flotantes"

◆ Cuando están seleccionados, los Controladores de Tamaño son de color negro.
◆ Se ven en todas las presentaciones, incluso en presentación Normal.
◆ Su posición en la hoja se determina utilizando las mismas herramientas que para el texto. Por ejemplo, podemos centrarlos pulsando el botón **Centrar** de la barra de Herramientas **Formato**, podemos tabularlos o sangrarlos usando TAB, etc.
◆ Conservan la ubicación respecto de su entorno, si el texto baja, el objeto también baja.
◆ Es difícil modificar su posición utilizando el *Mouse*.
◆ No podemos especificarles una posición precisa en la página.
◆ No podemos superponerlo al texto.

1.4.2. Características de los Objetos "Flotantes"

◆ Podemos superponerlos con el texto.
◆ Los Controladores de Tamaño son blancos.
◆ No pueden verse en presentación Normal.
◆ La posición del objeto se determina utilizando el *Mouse*.
◆ Es posible especificarles una posición precisa en la página.
◆ Podemos determinar que el objeto se mueva o no junto con su entorno.

1.5. ¿Cómo seleccionamos un objeto?

Los objetos se seleccionan ubicando el puntero encima y haciendo un clic (¡Ojo! un doble clic los abre). Cuando un objeto está seleccionado aparece rodeado por un marco con varios cuadrados que se denominan Controladores de Tamaño y se utilizan para redimensionar el objeto. La **Figura 6** muestra el aspecto que tiene un objeto seleccionado.

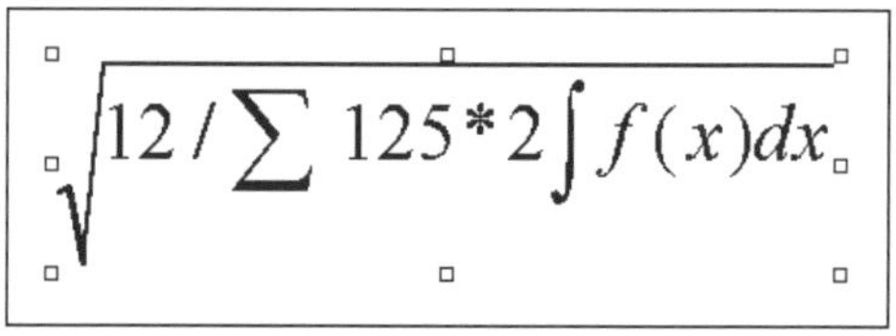

$$\sqrt{12 / \sum 125*2 \int f(x)dx}$$

Figura 6. *Para seleccionar un objeto hay que hacer un clic sobre él.*

1.6. ¿Cómo eliminamos un Objeto?

Para eliminar un objeto hay que seleccionarlo haciendo clic sobre él y, cuando aparecen los Controladores de Tamaño, pulsar la tecla SUPRIMIR (del).

2

Objetos

1.7. ¿Cómo modificamos el Tamaño de un Objeto?

El tamaño de un Objeto se modifica arrastrando con el *Mouse* alguno de los Controladores de Tamaño de las esquinas en la dirección correspondiente, como muestra la **Figura 7.**

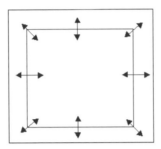

Figura 7. *Así se ve un objeto que está siendo redimensionado.*

Al elegir los Controladores de las esquinas la figura cambia de tamaño sin perder las proporciones originales. Si elegimos alguno de los Controladores laterales, la figura "crece" en la dimensión en la que se encuentra dicho controlador. En este caso, además de cambiar de tamaño, se deforma. Si modificamos accidentalmente la forma de un objeto, recordemos que podemos anular la última acción utilizando el atajo de teclado CTRL+Z.

1.8. Ajustar Objetos respecto del Texto

Ajustar un objeto respecto del texto significa determinar cómo se distribuirá el texto del documento alrededor del Objeto. El texto puede bordearlo, puede aparecer arriba, abajo, etc. Para ajustar texto respecto de un objeto hay que proceder del siguiente modo:

♦ Seleccionar el objeto.
♦ Pulsar el botón derecho del *Mouse*.
♦ En el Menú Contextual que se muestra en la **Figura 8** seleccionar la opción **Formato de Objeto**.

Figura 8. *Este es el primer paso para ajustar texto alrededor de un objeto.*

◆ En la ficha **Ajuste**, de la **Figura 9**, elegir alguno de los siguientes ajustes:

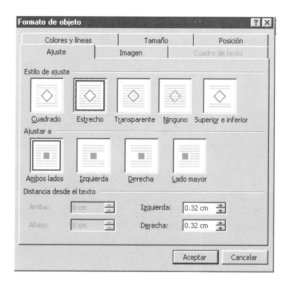

Figura 9. *En esta ventana se configura el aspecto del texto alrededor de un objeto.*

◆ **Cuadrado:** El texto se ajustará equitativamente alrededor de todos los bordes del Objeto, como lo muestra la **Figura 10.**

Figura 10. *El ajuste cuadrado es un marco de texto alrededor del objeto.*

- **Estrecho:** El texto se ajustará alrededor de los bordes de la imagen real, en vez de ajustarse alrededor del marco, como se ve en la **Figura 11.**

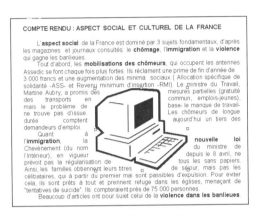

Figura 11. El texto sigue la silueta de la imagen.

- **Ninguno:** Texto y Objeto aparecerán en el mismo lugar.
- **Superior e Inferior:** El texto aparecerá en la parte superior e inferior del Objeto, como lo representa la **Figura 12.**

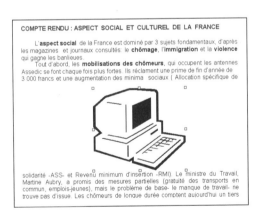

Figura 12. El texto está arriba y abajo en el ajuste Superior e Inferior.

- **Transparente:** Es similar a Estrecho, pero el ajuste se realizará en el interior de las partes del objeto que estén abiertas.

1.9. Importar Objetos de un Archivo

Otro modo de incorporar objetos a un documento es importarlos de un archivo. El procedimiento en este caso es el siguiente:

◆ Verificar que el documento que recibirá el objeto este abierto y activo.

◆ Ubicar el cursor en donde aparecerá el objeto y, en el menú **Insertar,** seleccionar **Objeto**.

◆ En el Cuadro de Diálogo que aparece, y que se muestra en la **Figura 13**, seleccionar la ficha **Desde Archivo** que tiene el siguiente aspecto**.**

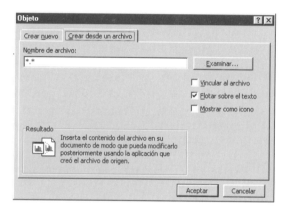

Figura 13. *Primer paso para importar un objeto.*

◆ En los casilleros correspondientes, ingresar la ruta de acceso y el nombre del archivo.

◆ Habilitar el casillero **Vincular Objeto** para que el objeto quede vinculado al original (Ver a continuación) y pulsar **Aceptar**.

1.10. ¿Qué significa Vincular Objetos?

Cuando hablamos de Objetos Vinculados, hablamos de objetos que existen por duplicado, una copia está en el documento *Word*, y la otra se encuentra en otra parte del sistema. El Objeto que está en el documento *Word* es en realidad un borrador. Borrador y original están vinculados, de modo que cualquier cambio en el original se refleja automáticamente en su copia ubicada en el documento *Word*. Un ejemplo de esto es el siguiente: Supongamos que en un informe de *Word* incrustamos y vinculamos la planilla "Salarios" creada en *Excel*. Cuando mensualmente modifiquemos la planilla en el archivo original, el objeto contenido en el informe de *Word* se actualizará automáticamente.

1.11. ¿Cuál es la ventaja de Vincular Objetos?

Vincular objetos tiene las siguientes ventajas:

◆ Cualquier modificación que se realice sobre un objeto vinculado podrá hacerse desde la aplicación en la que fue creado el objeto, sin necesidad de abrir *Word*.

♦ Los documentos con objetos vinculados ocupan mucho menos memoria que aquellos con objetos no vinculados.

♦ Los objetos del documento no corren el riesgo de quedar desactualizados por cambios de último momento que tengan lugar en los originales.

1.12. ¿Cómo vinculamos un Objeto?

Para vincular un objeto hay que habilitar el casillero **Vincular Objeto** al momento de importarlo desde un archivo. En la **Figura 14** se muestra la ventana que permite vincular objetos.

Los objetos vinculados contenidos en un documento se comportan igual que sus originales. Esto significa que podemos llevarlos de una parte de la hoja a otra, podemos redimensionarlos, etc. *Word* trabaja con ellos como si fuesen únicos y sólo consulta los originales para imprimir. Si vinculamos varios objetos y luego eliminamos los originales del sistema, cada vez que *Word* abra ese documento nos hará saber que no existen los originales. Como es de esperar, en estos casos, podremos trabajar con las copias, pero no podremos realizar una buena impresión porque no estará disponible toda la información necesaria.

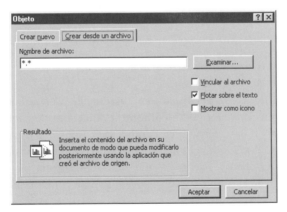

Figura 14. *Habilitar el casillero Vincular para "unir" el objeto con su archivo de origen.*

Si abrimos la aplicación en la que se encuentra el objeto simultáneamente con *Word* también podemos vincular un objeto utilizando el comando **Pegado Especial**. En este caso procedemos de la siguiente forma:

♦ Copiamos el objeto al Portapapeles utilizando el comando **Copiar**.

♦ Pasamos a *Word* y lo pegamos en el documento utilizando el comando **Pegado Especial**, del menú **Edición**. Una vez hecho esto aparecerá la ventana de la **Figura 15**, que nos permitirá vincularlo.

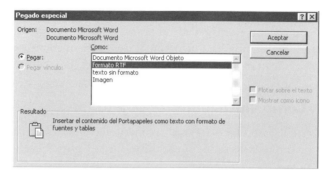

Figura 15. *Este es otro modo de vincular objetos.*

1.13. ¿Cómo actualizamos los objetos vinculados que existen en un documento?

La actualización de los objetos vinculados puede llevarse a cabo de tres formas distintas:

- De forma Automática.
- De forma Manual.
- Antes de la Impresión.

1.13.1. Actualización Automática

Este tipo de actualización tiene lugar cada vez que *Word* abre el documento que contiene el o los objetos vinculados. El procedimiento es el siguiente: cada vez que *Word* abre el documento evalúa si hubo cambios en los archivos originales. En caso afirmativo cambia las copias incrustadas en el documento *Word* por la versión actual. En caso contrario deja los objetos tal cual están.

Para activar la Actualización Automática de un vínculo procedemos del siguiente modo:

- Abrimos el documento que contiene el o los objetos vinculados.
- Seleccionamos el primer objeto cuya actualización queremos automatizar.
- En el menú **Edición** elegimos **Vínculos**.
- En el Cuadro de Diálogo de la **Figura 16** habilitamos el casillero **Vinculación Automática** y pulsamos **Aceptar**. Procedemos así con cada uno de los objetos del documento.

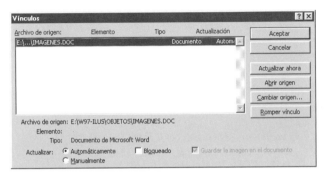

Figura 16. *La Actualización Automática se hace desde esta ventana.*

1.13.2. Actualización Manual

Cuando existen varios objetos vinculados y no queremos que *Word* los actualice automáticamente porque llevaría mucho tiempo, podemos determinar Actualizaciones Manuales sobre algunos de ellos. La Actualización la llevamos a cabo nosotros, en el momento más conveniente y obviamente cuando el original haya sufrido alguna modificación. Para actualizar un Vínculo de forma Manual hay que seleccionar el objeto vinculado, y en el Cuadro de Diálogo anterior habilitar el casillero **Manualmente**, luego pulsar el botón **Actualizar Ahora**.

1.13.3. Actualización de los Vínculos antes de la Impresión.

Existe una última alternativa, que es actualizar todos los vínculos de forma conjunta antes de la impresión. La actualización en este caso es general, todos los vínculos a la vez. Para actualizar los vínculos antes de la impresión necesitamos proceder del siguiente modo:

◆ Verificar que el documento está abierto y activo.
◆ En el menú **Archivo** elegir **Impresión**.
◆ En el Cuadro de Diálogo de la **Figura 17** pulsar el botón **Opciones**, y en la siguiente ventana habilitar el casillero **Actualizar Vínculos**.

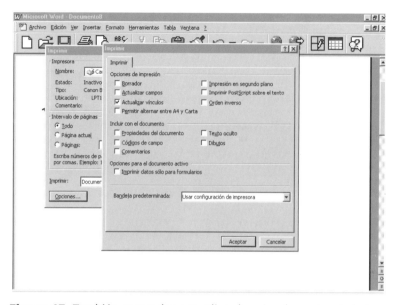

Figura 17. *También se pueden actualizar los vínculos antes de la impresión.*

2. OBJETO DIBUJO

Para dibujar en *Word* utilizamos la Barra de Herramientas **Dibujo**, que se muestra pulsando el botón derecho del *Mouse* sobre cualquier otra barra y seleccionándola de la lista. Esta barra tiene el aspecto que muestra la **Figura** 18.

Figura 18. *Barra de Herramientas Dibujo.*

El dibujo que se muestra en la **Figura 19** fue creado combinando alguno de los siguientes elementos:

- ◆ Círculos y Elipses.
- ◆ Polígonos Regulares e Irregulares.
- ◆ Líneas.
- ◆ Arcos.
- ◆ Figuras abiertas.

♦ Autoformas.
♦ Combinación de todos los anteriores.
♦ Figuras de Forma Libre.
♦ Otros.

Figura 19. *Dibujo hecho en Word.*

Si bien podemos dibujar en cualquier parte de la hoja, conviene hacerlo dentro de un marco de contención a fin de poder redimensionar, mover, copiar el dibujo seleccionando el marco y no cada una de las figuras, autoformas, líneas, etc. que componen el dibujo final. Además, un dibujo dentro de un marco se ve en todas las presentaciones, mientras que los dibujos "libres" no pueden verse en presentación Normal.

A continuación se explica el procedimiento para dibujar dentro de un marco:

♦ Hacer un clic en el botón **Imagen de** *Word* de la barra **Dibujo,** de la **Figura 20**.

Figura 20. *Un clic aquí inicia el dibujo.*

♦ Cuando aparece el marco, dibujar (aún sobrepasando los límites del marco) utilizando las herramientas de la barra **Dibujo** como se explica más adelante.

Al terminar de dibujar, hay que hacer un clic en el botón **Restablecer Límites,** de la barra **Modificar Imagen** que apareció automáticamente con el marco. El botón **Restablecer Imagen**, que aparece en la **Figura 21**, permite acomodar el marco a la dimensión final del dibujo, de modo que no aparezca nada cortado o que el marco original no quede demasiado grande. A continuación se muestra el aspecto que tiene la barra **Modificar Imagen**. Si la misma no aparece junto con el marco, es posible abrirla como cualquier Barra de Herramientas haciendo un clic con el botón derecho del *Mouse* y seleccionándola de la lista. Para que figure en la lista de barras de Herramientas tiene que estar abierto el marco.

Figura 21. *Este botón impide que quede afuera parte del dibujo.*

Si los dibujos ya existen y queremos incorporarlos adentro de un marco, lo que hacemos es seleccionarlos utilizando la herramienta con forma de flecha blanca de la barra **Dibujo**, como se muestra en la **Figura 22**. Cuando todos los componentes aparecen dentro del recuadro creado por esta herramienta recién pulsamos el botón **Imagen de *Word*** que mostramos arriba. Los elementos del dibujo quedarán automáticamente agrupados dentro de un marco de contención. Este marco permitirá que sean tratados como una sola imagen, podremos redimensionarlos todos juntos, moverlos, etc. A continuación se muestra cómo se seleccionan varios dibujos utilizando la herramienta con forma de flecha blanca de la barra **Dibujo**.

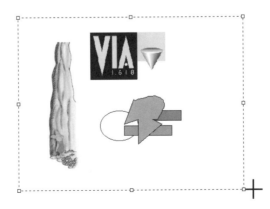

Figura 22. *Los dibujos primero se agrupan y luego se declaran como imágenes.*

2.1. Dibujar Círculos, Elipses, Cuadrados y Rectángulos

Para dibujar cualquiera de estas figuras utilizamos las herramientas **Rectángulo y Elipse**, que se muestran en la **Figura 23.**

Figura 23. Esta herramienta dibuja cuadrados, rectángulos, etc.

Los círculos y cuadrados se dibujan con estas mismas herramientas pero, además hay que presionar la tecla MAYUSCULA (*SHIFT*) mientras arrastramos el puntero.

2.2. Dibujar a mano alzada

Para crear una figura a mano alzada utilizamos la herramienta **Forma Libre,** del botón **Autoforma** que se muestra **Figura 24.**

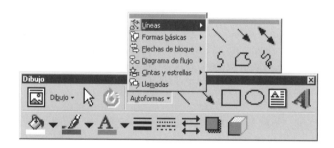

Figura 24. En Word se puede dibujar a mano alzada utilizando esta herramienta.

Cuando el puntero toma la forma de lápiz, mantenemos pulsado el botón izquierdo del *Mouse* y realizamos los trazos. Para incluir rectas a lo largo de la figura, hacemos un clic al comienzo de la línea y un clic al final. Si queremos cerrar la figura, hacemos un doble clic al final del dibujo.

Para modificar una figura creada con la herramienta **Forma Libre** utilizamos el botón **Modificar Puntos** de la herramienta **Dibujo**, que se muestra **Figura 25**.

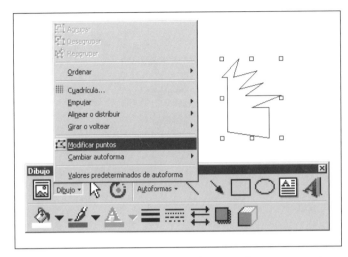

Figura 25. Una vez realizado el dibujo podemos retocarlo variando la posición de sus puntos.

Al mover los Controladores de Tamaño con esta herramienta cada uno responde de forma independiente, ubicándose donde el usuario los lleve. Si queremos crear Controladores de Tamaño adicionales que sirvan como nuevos puntos de inflexión utilizamos la herramienta **Modificar Puntos** y manteniendo presionada la tecla CTRL, hacemos un clic en el contorno de la figura donde aparecerá el nuevo Controlador de Tamaño.

2.3. ¿Qué son las Autoformas y cómo trabajamos con ellas?

Las Autoformas son figuras predeterminadas que aparecen en una lista como la que se ve en la **Figura 26**:

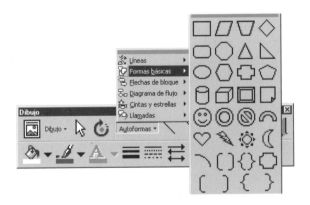

Figura 26. Así aparecen las formas preestablecidas.

Para dibujar una Autoforma hacemos un clic sobre ella y con el puntero en el Area de Trabajo realizamos los trazos manteniendo pulsado el botón izquierdo del *Mouse*. Si pulsamos la tecla CTRL y arrastramos los controladores de Tamaño de las Autoformas, aumentamos o disminuimos el tamaño sin alterar su aspecto.

Cuando terminamos de dibujar una Autoforma, en algunos casos aparecen Controladores de Tamaño amarillos como se muestra en la **Figura 27**, que permiten variar algunos aspectos de la Autoforma sin modificar el aspecto general de la misma. A continuación se muestra una Autoforma con un Controlador amarillo en la sonrisa que nos permite crear la misma cara pero con distintas expresiones.

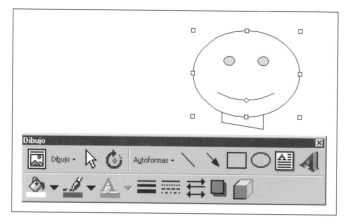

Figura 27. *Forma predeterminada.*

2.4. ¿Cómo agrupamos varias figuras?

Para agrupar varias figuras procedemos así:

♦ Elegimos la herramienta **Selección de objeto**, de la **Figura 28** (El botón con forma de flecha blanca).

Figura 28. *La flecha blanca se usa para seleccionar agrupando.*

♦ Manteniendo pulsado el botón del *Mouse* abarcamos el conjunto de objetos a agrupar. Esto se hace arrastrando el *Mouse* a lo largo de la diagonal del conjunto. La línea punteada indica el límite de la selección, como muestra la **Figura 29.**

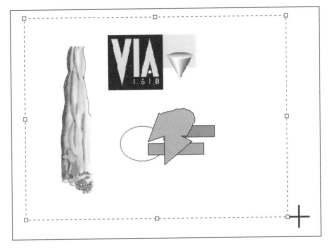

Figura 29. *Así se agrupan objetos.*

♦ Pulsamos el botón **Agrupar** que se muestra en la **Figura 30.**

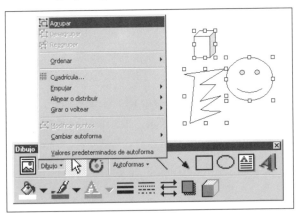

Figura 30. *Este es el último paso para agrupar objetos.*

Cuando agrupamos los Controladores de Tamaño desaparecen de cada una de las figuras y se ubican alrededor del grupo. Si movemos, reducimos o modificamos las proporciones de un dibujo agrupado, los cambios tendrán lugar en todo el conjunto. Para hacer modificaciones individuales hay que desagrupar nuevamente todo el dibujo hasta que cada uno de los elementos cuente con sus propios controladores de Tamaño.

En general se agrupan figuras que en su conjunto componen un dibujo, a fin de evitar que el cambio accidental de cualquiera de ellas altere la forma final del dibujo.

2.5. ¿Cómo variamos el contorno y el color de una Figura?

Primero hay que seleccionar la figura y luego utilizar los botones **Estilo de Línea**, **Tipo de Línea** y **Color de Línea**, de la barra de Herramientas **Dibujo** que se muestran en la **Figura 31**.

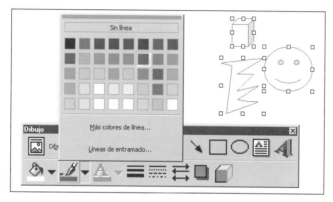

Figura 31. *Estos son los botones que usamos para variar el aspecto de los contornos de un dibujo.*

Para variar el relleno de un figura utilizamos el botón **Color de Relleno**, que se encuentra junto al grupo de botones anteriores y tiene forma de balde.

También podemos aplicarle efectos 3D y sombreado, utilizando los botones **3D** y **Sombra** que tienen el aspecto de la **Figura 32**.

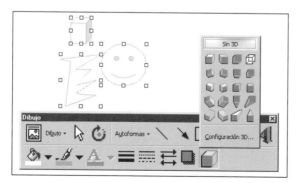

Figura 32. *Los efectos 3D y sombra se usan para realzar las figuras.*

2.6. ¿Cómo alineamos varias Figuras?

La alineación se hace respecto de una línea imaginaria que puede ser vertical u horizontal. Existen dos tipos de Alineación: Manual y Automática.

2.6.1. Alineación Manual

Para alinear de forma manual varias figuras hay que proceder del siguiente modo:

♦ Seleccionar las figuras a alinear.
♦ En el botón **Dibujo** elegir **Alinear o Distribuir**, como se muestra en la **Figura 33**, y luego la alineación deseada. Por ejemplo, la opción **Alinear en la Parte Inferior** unirá a todas las figuras por su base.

Figura 33. *Alinear varias figuras significa hacer que reposen en la misma línea imaginaria.*

2.6.2. Alineación Automática

Cuando creamos varias figuras y queremos que queden automáticamente alineadas activamos la Cuadrícula y arrastramos la figura hasta la línea más cercana para que quede ¨pegada¨ allí.

La Cuadrícula es una trama de líneas imaginarias que puede estar activada o no. Si lo está, no vemos nada especial en la pantalla, pero los bordes más cercanos de las figuras son atrapados por alguna de estas líneas imaginarias como si fueran imanes. Si todas las figuras son atrapadas por la misma línea entonces quedan alineadas.

Podemos modificar la cuadrícula cambiando las distancias entre las líneas. De forma predeterminada están a 0. 25 cm.

Para activar y modificar la Cuadrícula hay que pulsar el botón **Dibujo** y seleccionar la opción **Cuadrícula**, como se muestra en la **Figura 34.**

Objetos 2

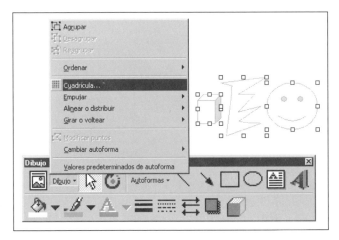

Figura 34. *Al desactivar la cuadrícula las figuras se mueven libremente.*

En el Cuadro de Diálogo de la **Figura 35** habilitar el casillero **Activar Cuadrícula**, y en los Casilleros **Espacio Vertical** y **Espacio Horizontal** ingresar un valor adecuado para el ancho y alto de la trama. Pulsar Aceptar.

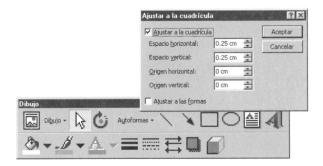

Figura 35. *Desde aquí se configura la cuadrícula.*

2.7. Girar y voltear Figuras

Los dibujos creados en *Word* pueden rotarse o voltearse. Se entiende por voltear el cambio de dirección del eje principal de la figura, por ejemplo si está parada y la acostamos. La **Figura 36** muestra las herramientas que se utilizan para estas operaciones.

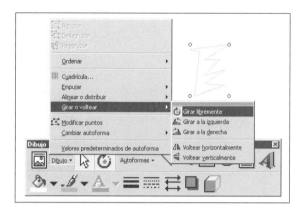

Figura 36. Herramientas para girar y voltear figuras.

Para girar libremente una figura hay que hacer un clic en la herramienta con forma de flecha curva y, cuando los controladores de tamaño se convierten en puntos de color verde, ubicar el puntero arriba de cualquiera de ellos, mantener pulsado el botón izquierdo del *Mouse* y girar. Toda la figura rotará en la dirección elegida.

2.8. ¿Qué pasa cuando una Figura tapa a otra?

Esto ocurre cuando las dos están en estratos diferentes, pero en el mismo lugar de la hoja. Cuando dos figuras están superpuestas no podemos acceder a la que se encuentra detrás. Para pasar adelante una figura que se encuentra oculta por otra hay que:

♦ Seleccionar la que se encuentra adelante.
♦ Pulsar el botón **Dibujo**.
♦ Seleccionar la opción **Ordenar**.
♦ En la lista de comandos que se muestra en la **Figura 37** seleccionar **Enviar atrás**.

Figura 37. Word tiene varias capas. Con este botón elegimos en qué capa queremos cada uno de los dibujos.

3. OBJETOS *WORDART*

WordArt es una aplicación para crear letreros. En versiones anteriores a *Word*, *Microsoft WordArt* se incluía como una Aplicación Independiente, sin embargo ahora se incorporó como una herramienta más de la barra **Dibujo**.

WordArt es tan amigable que para hacer un cartel tenemos que seguir sólo cuatro pasos:

♦ Elegir el botón *WordArt* de la barra **Dibujo**, que tiene el aspecto de la **Figura 38.**

Figura 38. *Un clic en este botón y arranca la aplicación para crear carteles.*

♦ En el muestrario de la **Figura 39** elegir un modelo predeterminado de cartel.

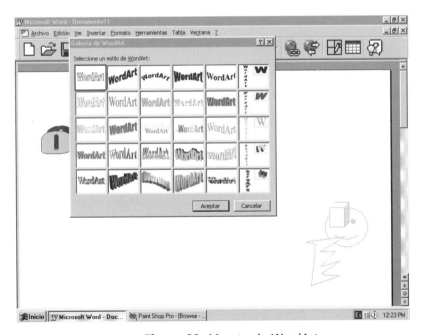

Figura 39. *Muestrario WordArt.*

♦ Verificar que aparece una ventana en donde escribir el texto.
♦ Una vez ingresado el texto, pulsar el botón **Aceptar** para que el cartel aparezca en el documento.

Los carteles creados en *WordArt* tienen el aspecto de la **Figura 40** y se comportan como cualquier dibujo. Podemos rotarlos, modificar su tamaño, su aspecto, etc. Muchos de ellos incluso aparecen con los Controladores de Tamaño amarillos típicos de las Autoformas para variar sus atributos sin modificar el aspecto general.

Figura 40. *Tirando del punto amarillo variamos el aspecto del cartel.*

4. OBJETOS GRÁFICOS

Los Gráficos son objetos que ilustran valores contenidos en una tabla. Los gráficos, como cualquier objeto, se incrustan desde un archivo o se crean desde cero sin salir de *Word*. Las aplicaciones más usadas para crear o importar gráficos son *Excel* y *Microsoft Graph*, esta última es una aplicación que trabaja como soporte de los utilitarios del *Office*.

4.1. ¿Cómo creamos un gráfico sin salir de Word?

Como todo objeto, lo primero que hacemos es seleccionar la aplicación Independiente en la que trabajaremos. El procedimiento es el siguiente:

♦ Ubicamos el cursor en donde queremos que aparezca el gráfico.
♦ En el menú **Insertar** elegimos **Imagen** y luego **Gráficos**, como se muestra en la **Figura 41.** Esta secuencia de acciones abre automáticamente *Microsoft Graph*, que es una aplicación Independiente utilizada para crear gráficos a partir de una planilla o tabla.

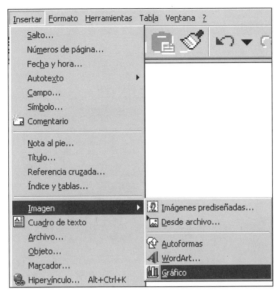

Figura 41. *Un clic aquí y arranca la aplicación para crear gráficos.*

◆ Una vez abierto *Microsoft Graph* aparece una tabla en donde ingresar los datos a graficar. A medida que vamos ingresando valores, la curva o el gráfico que aparece detrás se modifica, reflejando los cambios de la tabla.

La **Figura 42** muestra cómo las barras de Herramientas de *Microsoft Graph* reemplazaron a las de *Word*. Además se ve la tabla en donde ingresar los datos y, detrás, el gráfico correspondiente a la tabla. Dicho gráfico varía automáticamente a medida que cambiamos los datos en las celdas de la tabla. Si hacemos un clic fuera del gráfico o fuera de la tabla (en la parte de la hoja que está en blanco), volvemos automáticamente al documento *Word* y el gráfico aparece pegado en la posición en la que se encontraba el cursor antes de la inserción.

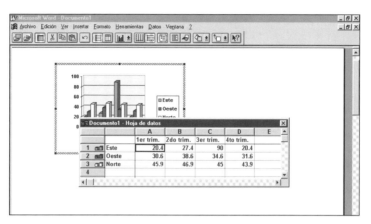

Figura 42. *Este es el aspecto de la pantalla cuando está abierto Microsoft Graph.*

4.2. ¿Y si ya tenemos la tabla y sólo queremos graficarla?

Si la tabla fue hecha en *Word* tenemos que seleccionarla antes de elegir los comandos **Insertar** y luego **Imagen y Gráficos**. *MicrosoftGraph* se abrirá mostrando nuestra tabla y su correspondiente gráfica.

4.3. ¿Cuáles son los principales elementos de un gráfico?

La **Figura 43** muestra los principales elementos de un gráfico.

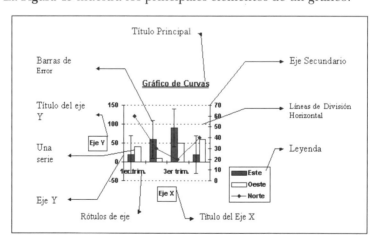

Figura 43. *Elementos de un gráfico.*

A continuación, una breve descripción de cada uno de ellos y de su función:

4.3.1. Ejes

Existen dos tipos de ejes: Principal y Secundario. Tanto los ejes Principales como los Secundarios pueden estar visibles o no. Según su orientación estos ejes se clasifican en Verticales y Horizontales, que corresponden a la Ordenada y Absisa respectivamente. Los ejes Secundarios están enfrentados a los ejes Principales y pueden tener escala y unidades distintas, permitiendo una doble lectura del gráfico. Los ejes Secundarios sólo pueden insertarse en aquellas gráficas combinadas.

4.3.2. Líneas de división

Es la cuadrícula que aparece al fondo del gráfico y que sirve como referente. En el gráfico que figura arriba sólo están visibles las líneas de División Horizontal y son punteadas.

4.3.3. Rótulo de datos

Es el valor numérico del punto que aparece escrito en las proximidades de éste. Si la gráfica no es suficientemente grande y los datos no se encuentran espaciados entre sí, no conviene mostrar el valor del punto porque creará mucha confusión.

4.3.4. Título del gráfico

Es el título Principal. En el ejemplo anterior "Exportación de Granos ˝

4.3.5. Título de los Ejes

Son los nombres de los ejes. Es importante no confundir Título de Eje con Rótulo de Eje, que son los nombres de las marcas de graduación. En el ejemplo anterior,

˝Y˝ y ˝X˝ son los Títulos de los Ejes mientras que "1er Trimestre", etc., son los Rótulos de Eje.

4.3.6. Series

Es el grupo de datos con el que se construye una gráfica. Una serie puede ser una barra en un gráfico de barras, una línea en un gráfico de Curvas o una porción en un gráfico de Sectores. Cada serie tiene un color diferente. En el ejemplo de la **Figura 44** hay dos series, la roja y la azul.

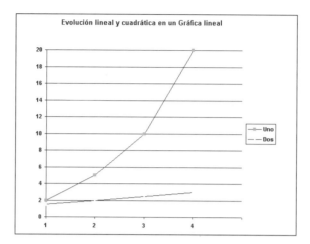

Figura 44. *Ejemplo de dos series.*

4.3.7. Barra de error

La Barra de Error es un segmento que se ubica en la proximidad del punto y marca el rango en el que se encuentra el valor real de ese punto. Es el área en donde se estima que se encuentra realmente el punto.

4.3.8. Marcas de Graduación

Es la escala de los ejes. Puede representar, por ejemplo, longitudes, litros, etc. Las marcas de graduación principales generalmente aparecen cada centímetro mientras que las secundarias cada milímetro.

4.3.9. Leyenda

Es la referencia que generalmente aparece al lado del gráfico y que nos indica a qué serie corresponde cada color.

4.4. ¿Cómo modificamos cualquiera de estos elementos?

Antes de modificar cualquiera de estos elementos, primero hay que mostrarlos. Esto quiere decir que primero hay que determinar que aparezcan en el gráfico. Esto se hace del siguiente modo:

♦ Ubicamos el puntero dentro del marco que contiene el gráfico, en cualquier parte en blanco (Area Principal) y hacemos un clic con el botón derecho.
♦ En el menú contextual que aparece, y que se muestra en la **Figura 45**, elegimos los elementos del gráfico que queremos agregar. Elegimos por ejemplo **Insertar Títulos, Insertar ejes,** etc.

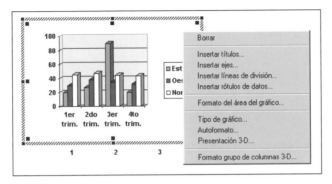

Figura 45. *Primero hay que agregar todos los elementos que queremos que aparezcan en el gráfico.*

♦ En la ventana que aparece y que mostramos en la **Figura 46**, seleccionamos el elemento que queremos agregar.

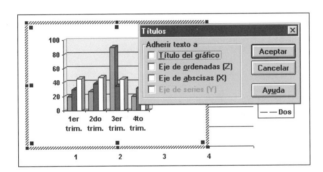

Figura 46. *Aquí se configura el elemento a agregar.*

♦ Una vez visible los elementos del gráfico, para modificar cualquiera de ellos hay que ubicar el puntero justo arriba del elemento a modificar y pulsar el botón derecho del *Mouse*. En el Menú Contextual que aparece seleccionar la opción **Formato** y luego realizar los cambios necesarios. Un ejemplo de esto es el siguiente: Supongamos que queremos modificar la leyenda. Si ubicamos el cursor arriba de la leyenda y hacemos un clic con el botón derecho del *Mouse*, aparecerá el Menú contextual **Formato leyenda del gráfico**, como se muestra en la **Figura 47.**

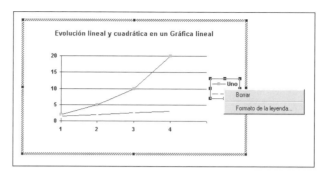

Figura 47. *Este es el primer paso para modificar el aspecto de la leyenda de un gráfico.*

Si hacemos un clic arriba de esta opción, se abre la ventana de la **Figura 48** desde donde podemos cambiar el aspecto de la leyenda.

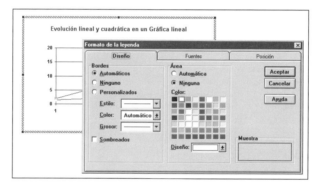

Figura 48. *Aquí modificamos el aspecto de la leyenda.*

Es importante destacar que para realizar cualquier cambio, el gráfico tiene que estar abierto. Un gráfico está abierto cuando está abierta la aplicación en la que fue creado. En el ejemplo anterior, para saber si el gráfico está o no abierto tenemos que observar si las barras de *MicrosoftGraph* reemplazaron a las de *Word*.

4.5. ¿Cómo pasamos de un tipo de gráfico a otro?

Pasar de un tipo de gráfico a otro significa utilizar la misma información de la tabla, pero crear diferentes representaciones con diferentes característi-cas. Ciertos datos serán más adecuados que otros para un determinado ti-po de gráfico. Un gráfico con más de una serie y en el que es relevante la evo-lución, se verá mejor en una curva que en un gráfico de sectores.

Para pasar de un tipo de gráfico a otro utilizamos la galería de Gráficos. El procedimiento es el siguiente:

◆ Verificamos que el gráfico está abierto. De no ser así lo abrimos haciendo doble clic sobre él.

◆ Ubicamos el puntero sobre el Area Principal y pulsamos el botón derecho del *Mouse*.

◆ En el menú contextual que aparece seleccionamos la opción **Tipo de Gráfico**.

◆ En la ventana de la **Figura 49** seleccionamos cualquiera de los tipos que figuran allí.

◆ Cuando pulsemos **Aceptar** el cambio tendrá lugar automáticamente en el gráfico.

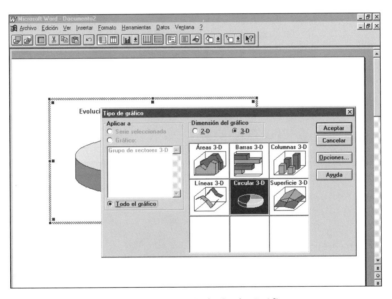

Figura 49. *Galería de Gráficos.*

4.6. Los gráficos más utilizados en Word

4.6.1. Gráfico de Curvas

La información está representada sobre dos ejes ¨Y¨ y ¨X¨, que se cortan en el punto 0. Este tipo de gráfico se usa para dar idea de evolución, ya que lo que importa es el recorrido de la línea, la pendiente, etc. Pueden confeccionarse varias series (curvas) en un mismo par de ejes para poder realizar comparaciones. La **Figura 50** muestra un Gráfico de Curvas con dos series.

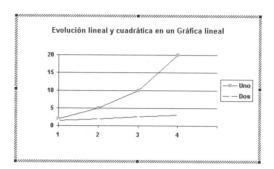

Figura 50. *Gráfico lineal y una curva.*

4.6.2. Gráfico de Areas

El gráfico de Areas que se muestra en la **Figura 51** es similar al anterior, pero además de indicar el ritmo de cambio indica la magnitud del mismo, que está representada por el área debajo de la curva.

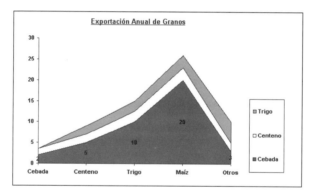

Figura 51. *Gráfico de Areas.*

4.6.3. Gráfico de Barras y de Columnas

El gráfico de Barras y Columnas, como el que se muestra en la **Figura 52**, se utiliza para comparar cantidades en períodos de tiempo fijos. Utilizamos este tipo de gráfico para representar ganancias en cada uno de los trimestres del año. A continuación se muestra un gráfico de columnas 3D.

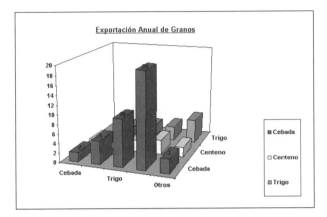

Figura 52. *Gráfico de Barras y Columnas.*

4.6.4. El gráfico de Sectores y Anillos

Los gráficos de sectores, como el que se muestra en la **Figura 53**, son muy útiles para mostrar una sola serie de datos. La siguiente imagen muestra la exportación de cereales a lo largo del 1º trimestre del año.

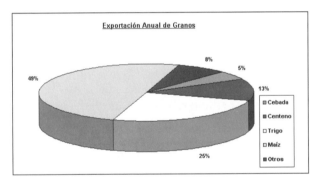

Figura 53. *Gráfico de Sectores.*

Si queremos mostrar más de una serie utilizamos un gráfico de Anillos como el que se ve en la **Figura 54**. En el gráfico de Anillos, el círculo representa los valores del eje X, y cada color es una serie. En el siguiente ejemplo se ve que se exportó prácticamente la misma cantidad de maíz en el primer y tercer cuatrimestre del año y que el maíz fue casi un 50% del total de granos exportados en esos dos cuatrimestres.

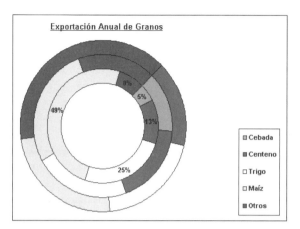

Figura 54. *Gráfico de Anillos.*

5. OBJETO SONIDO

Los objetos de sonido que se insertan en un documento pueden usarse para brindar al lector instrucciones, especificaciones, información adicional, o simplemente para saludarlo e introducirlo en lo que va a leer.

Si queremos escuchar un sonido incluido en un documento necesitamos tener instalada y configurada una tarjeta de sonido y por supuesto los parlantes. Si somos capaces de escuchar los sonidos que emite *Windows* significa que las configuraciones anteriores están hechas y podremos trabajar con sonidos dentro de *Word*.

Los sonidos incrustados en *Word* pueden provenir de archivos aportados por terceros o de archivos grabados en directo por nosotros mismos. Dos extensiones conocidas de archivos de sonido son *WAV* y *MIDI*.

Para grabar nuestros propios archivos de sonido e insertarlos en los documentos *Word* no necesitamos instalar ningún programa especial. Sólo hay que verificar que en el menú **Accesorios** de *Windows,* en la opción **Multimedia** aparece la **Grabadora de Sonido**, y que en la placa de sonido tenemos enchufado el micrófono en donde dice **Mic**.

Si no disponemos de un micrófono, igual podemos trabajar con sonidos, ya que podemos grabarlos de la lectora de CD, de un auxiliar conectado a la placa de sonido, o directamente usar los archivos de sonido con que cuenta *Windows*. En este último caso, tendremos que limitarnos a los sonidos existentes, que seguramente no tienen nada que ver con el contenido del documento al que queremos aplicarle el sonido.

Una vez incrustado un sonido en un documento, el mismo aparece representado con un ícono en forma de parlante como se muestra en la **Figura 55.**

Para escuchar lo que está guardado allí hay que pulsar dos veces sobre este ícono y verificar que el volumen de los parlantes es el adecuado.

Figura 55. Así se representa un sonido en Word.

5.1. Insertar un sonido desde la Grabadora de Sonidos

Para insertar un Sonido desde la Grabadora de Sonidos de *Windows* procedemos del siguiente modo:

♦ Abrimos tanto el documento de *Word* como la Grabadora de Sonidos. Esto último se hace seleccionando en el menú **Inicio** de *Windows*, **Accesorios** / **Multimedia** y luego **Grabadora de Sonido**, como se muestra en la **Figura 56.**

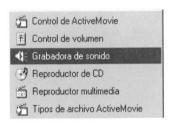

Figura 56. Antes de insertar un sonido hay que abrir la grabadora de sonido de Windows.

♦ Para crear un sonido nuevo seleccionamos, en el menú **Archivo** de la Grabadora de sonido, la opción **Nuevo**. Pulsamos el botón *Rec* y hablamos en el micrófono o ponemos *"Play"* en un auxiliar conectado a la placa de sonido o en el CD. Para detener la grabación usamos el botón *Stop*. Una vez grabado el sonido, guardamos este archivo con un nombre representativo y luego lo insertamos en el documento como se indica a continuación.

5.2. Insertar un archivo de sonido en un documento Word

Para insertar un archivo de sonido en un documento *Word* procedemos del siguiente modo:

♦ Elegimos **Abrir** del menú **Archivo** de la Grabadora de Sonido y seleccionamos el archivo a insertar.

♦ Pasamos a *Word* y elegimos **Pegar** en el menú **Edición**.

En donde está ubicado el cursor aparecerá el ícono del parlante que representa el sonido.

Si queremos que además de incrustado ese sonido quede vinculado, en vez de elegir el comando **Pegar**, seleccionamos **Pegado Especial** y en el Cuadro de Diálogo de la **Figura 57** habilitamos la opción **Pegar Vínculo.** En el casillero **Como** seleccionamos **Objeto de sonido**.

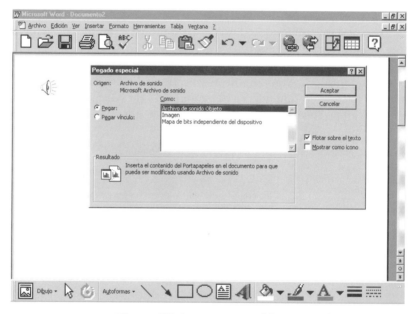

Figura 57. *Insertar un sonido en Word.*

Los archivos de sonido vinculados cambian automáticamente si cambia el archivo original guardado en otra parte del sistema. Tanto los archivos incrustados como los vinculados pueden editarse sin salir de *Word*. Cuando hacemos doble clic sobre ellos, además de sentir el sonido, se abre la Grabadora de Sonido que nos permite cortarlos, mezclarlos con otros sonidos, aumentar su volumen, su calidad, etc.

PROBLEMAS

1. Un informe mensual creado en Word contiene los siguientes elementos:

   ♦ Texto que no varía de mes a mes.
   ♦ Una tabla de gastos mensuales creada en Excel, que sí varía de mes a mes.
   ♦ El gráfico de la tabla anterior.

   Elena se pregunta cómo crear el informe de modo de cambiar la menor cantidad de elementos posibles todos los meses.

2. María quiere agrupar tres dibujos de modo de convertirlos en una misma imagen. Luego reducir el conjunto a un 60% del tamaño original e insertarlo alrededor del texto que ya está escrito.

3. Silvia aprendió a vincular objetos, pero tiene problemas porque en algunos casos los objetos vinculados aparecen recortados en la parte inferior y derecha aún cuando hay suficiente espacio en el documento para mostrarlos.

4. Omar quiere modificar una figura que quedó detrás de otra pero no puede seleccionarla.

5. Mirta no puede fijar un objeto en un lugar de la hoja, a los pocos segundos de hacerlo el objeto ya está en otro lado.

6. Tomás no sabe cómo alinear dos figuras que acaba de dibujar.

7. Esteban importó varios objetos a su documento. Cuando quiere guardar el trabajo en un disquete se da cuenta de que el archivo ocupa tanto lugar que no entra en el disquete.

SOLUCIONES

1. Lo más conveniente es insertar, en el documento *Word*, la tabla y el gráfico de *Excel* como objetos vinculados que se actualicen de forma automática. Cada mes, Elena tendrá que modificar en *Excel* la tabla. El gráfico se adaptará automáticamente a los nuevos valores, y ambos se actualizarán automáticamente al abrir el informe de *Word*.

2. María puede incluir los tres dibujos dentro de un marco, luego variar el tamaño del mismo y finalmente elegir el ajuste más adecuado en el menú **Formato de Objeto**. Uno de los modos de hacer todo esto es el siguiente:
    ♦ Seleccionar los tres dibujos y, en la barra **Dibujo,** hacer clic sobre el botón **Imagen de *Word*** que tiene el aspecto de la **Figura 58**.

Figura 58. *Botón Imagen de Word.*

♦ Una vez incluidos los tres elementos dentro del marco, hacer un clic en el botón **Restablecer Límites,** de la barra **Modificar Imagen** que apareció automáticamente junto con el marco.
♦ Hacer un clic en el botón **Cerrar Imagen** de la barra de Herramientas anterior, y verificar que el marco con los tres dibujos ahora aparece en el documento.

Para reducirlo al 60% de su tamaño y para ajustarlo al texto ya existente, hay que:

♦ Hacer un clic sobre el marco y, cuando aparecen los controladores de tamaño, hacer otro clic pero esta vez con el botón derecho del *Mouse*.
♦ Verificar que aparece un Menú Contextual. Elegir **Formato de Imagen** y corroborar que aparece un Cuadro de Diálogo que contiene varias fichas, entre ellas la ficha **Tamaño** y la ficha **Ajuste**.
♦ En la ficha **Tamaño**, en **Escala**, ingresar el 60% para el ancho y alto de la imagen.
♦ En la ficha **Ajuste** elegir la opción **Cuadrado** y salir aceptando.
♦ *Word* redimensionará el marco con los tres dibujos y distribuirá el texto existente en la página alrededor de la nueva imagen.

3. Esto se debe a que cuando vinculamos un objeto, *Word* lo convierte automáticamente en un formato especial que tiene un alto y ancho máximo, por lo que si el objeto supera esas medidas aparece recortado en el documento de *Word*. Para evitar que esto ocurra hay que volver a pegarlo siguiendo las siguientes instrucciones:

♦ Abrir la aplicación en la que se creó el objeto.

♦ Copiarlo al Portapapeles.

♦ Volver a *Word*.

♦ En el menú **Edición** seleccionar **Pegar** o **Pegar vínculo**, y a continuación hacer clic en **Texto con formato (RTF)** o **Texto sin formato.**

4. Omar tiene que pasar la figura que está delante atrás. Esto se hace seleccionándola y pulsando el botón **Dibujo** de la barra de Herramientas **Dibujo.** En el menú **Ordenar** elegir **Enviar al Fondo**. Una vez realizados estos pasos Omar podrá seleccionar la figura que estaba detrás. Si el problema se hubiese presentado porque había texto delante, el procedimiento hubiese sido el mismo, pero tendríamos que haber elegido la opción **Delante de texto**, para que la figura emplazada detrás del texto pasara adelante y pudiese ser seleccionada.

5. Mirta tiene que establecer el objeto como "No Flotante". Esto se hace seleccionándolo y pulsando el botón derecho del *Mouse*. En el Menú Contextual que aparece tiene que elegir **Formato de Objeto** y en el Cuadro de Diálogo **Posición** deshabilitar el casillero **Flotar sobre Texto**.

6. En el botón **Dibujo**, de la barra de Herramientas **Dibujo**, existe el menú **Alinear o Distribuir** que nos permite alinear dos o más figuras previamente seleccionadas.

7. Esteban puede aliviar la memoria que ocupa el documento vinculando los objetos contenidos en él. Para vincular un objeto hay que habilitar el casillero **Vincular** al momento de importarlo del archivo. Los objetos originales quedarán guardados en el disco rígido y el documento de *Word* sólo tendrá una "copia" que ocupará mucha menos memoria. Esta "copia" de objetos se comporta igual que los verdaderos objetos, pero *Word* tendrá que consultar el archivo original si el usuario quiere realizar una impresión de alta resolución.

HERRAMIENTAS 3

Tiempo de lectura y práctica:
1 hora

Objetivo de la lección

■ Editar un documento usuarios utilizando Marcas de Revisión y Comentarios.
■ Crear resúmenes con la función Autorresumen.
■ Insertar información de uso frecuente.
■ Realizar un Envío Masivo de Correspondencia.
■ Utilizar las Herramientas de Autocorrección y otras.

1. COMENTARIOS Y MARCAS DE REVISIÓN

Los Comentarios y las Marcas de Revisión son herramientas de edición que permiten que varios usuarios, que no están en contacto entre sí, discutan y decidan la forma final de un documento. El procedimiento es el siguiente: El documento va pasando de mano en mano y cada usuario agrega, en un color distinto, los cambios que le realizaría y su opinión sobre tal o cual parte del mismo. Los cambios y/o comentarios realizados se mantienen como sugerencias en un nivel superior al del texto y sólo pasan a formar parte del documento cuando la persona que decide la forma final así lo determina. Al final de la ronda, si un usuario quiere conocer los cambios sugeridos por otro o sus comentarios, no tiene que ir a preguntárselos a nadie, simplemente abre el documento y lee las Marcas de Revisión y los Comentarios de un determinado color. Si no recuerda el color vinculado con ese usuario o sus iniciales, ubica el puntero arriba de la sugerencia o arriba del comentario hasta que aparece el nombre del autor.

Las sugerencias de cambios se conocen en *Word* como Marcas de Revisión y, como dijimos antes, no son incorporadas directamente al escrito, sino que quedan flotando, resaltadas, para que la persona que se encarga de imprimir la versión final del documento las incorpore o no al documento teniendo en cuenta las propuestas de los demás y su propio criterio.

1.1. ¿Cuál es la diferencia entre una Marca de Revisión y un Comentario?

Las Marcas de Revisión sugieren cambios puntuales, como ser la inserción o eliminación de texto, la modificación del tamaño de Fuente, el agregado de un subrayado, etc. Los comentarios son opiniones sobre lo que dice el texto, sobre su contenido.

La sugerencia de eliminación de parte de un párrafo por ejemplo, puede incorporarse como una Marca de Revisión mientras que el comentario sobre el nivel de discurso de la escritura será incorporado como un Comentario. La Marca de Revisión se verá como un tachado de color arriba del texto mientras que el comentario aparecerá como un ¨parche¨ resaltado. En la **Figura 1** se muestran las Marcas de Revisión de dos usuarios. Los Comentarios aparecen resaltados y escritos en una ventana independiente.

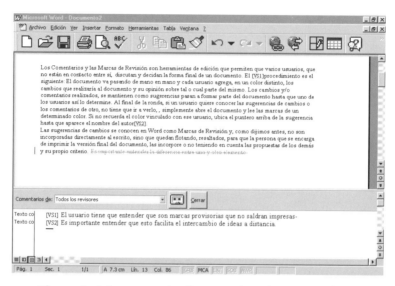

Figura 1. *Así aparecen los Comentarios y las Marcas de Revisión.*

1.2. ¿Cómo insertamos una Marca de Revisión?

Para insertar Marcas de Revisión en un documento hay que hacer doble clic sobre la abreviatura MCA de la Barra de Estado y luego corregir el documento como si se tratara de cualquier escrito. Cuando el modo MCA está activado, las correcciones se registran en un nivel distinto al de las correcciones reales. En el ejemplo anterior la eliminación de texto aparece como un tachado de color sobre la porción de texto a eliminar, pero de ninguna manera el texto desaparece. La persona que confecciona la versión final del documento interpreta la sugerencia de eliminación cuando ve el tachado y decide si da curso o no a la sugerencia. Si lo hace, con sólo pulsar un botón el texto quedará eliminado. De lo contrario, otro botón le permitirá eliminar el tachado y que ese texto quede libre de sugerencias. Una vez realizadas todas las sugerencias es necesario volver a hacer doble clic sobre la abreviatura MCA de la barra de Estado para desactivar el modo Revisión.

1.3. ¿Cómo elige cada usuario su color?

Antes de incorporar las sugerencias de cambios, el usuario tiene que elegir un color que lo represente y que quede vinculado con su nombre y sus iniciales. Esto se hace desde la ventana **Información del Usuario**, del menú **Herramientas** comando **Opciones**, que se muestra en la **Figura 2.** Los datos quedarán automáticamente registrados allí y vinculados a un color, que será el que aparezca en las Marcas de Revisión a partir del momento de la configuración.

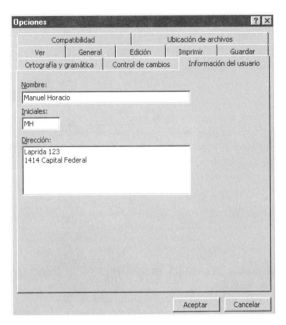

Figura 2. El usuario tiene que elegir un color antes de sentarse a corregir.

1.4. ¿Cómo aceptamos o rechazamos los cambios sugeridos por las Marcas de Revisión?

La aceptación o el rechazo se realizan utilizando el botón **Aceptar** o el botón **Eliminar** de la barra **Revisión**. La barra de **Revisión** aparece automáticamente cuando existen Marcas de Revisión en el escrito, y tiene el aspecto de la **Figura 3**.

Figura 3. Barra de Revisión.

Cuando se acepta una sugerencia de eliminación de texto, el tachado con color desaparece automáticamente, pero también desaparece el texto afectado por esa Marca de Revisión. Por el contrario, si la sugerencia se rechaza desaparece el color y el tachado, pero no el texto, el cual seguirá perteneciendo al documento.

1.5. ¿Existe otro modo de ingresar Marcas de Revisión?

Existe un modo de automatizar el ingreso de Marcas de Revisión, que consiste en comparar dos documentos distintos basados en un mismo original. Cuando *Word* complete la comparación mostrará como Marcas de Revisión, las diferencias que existen entre ambos. El procedimiento es el siguiente:

♦ Abrimos uno de los dos documentos y verificamos que esté activo.
♦ En el menú **Herramientas** seleccionamos **Comparar Documentos**.
♦ En el Cuadro de Diálogo **Abrir** ingresamos la ruta de acceso y el nombre del segundo documento, por ejemplo ¨C:\ Mis Documentos\ Carta2¨.

Al finalizar el proceso ambos documentos aparecerán con las Marcas de Revisión correspondientes.

1.6. ¿Qué pasa cuando las Marcas de Revisión no aparecen en pantalla?

Si las Marcas de Revisión no aparecen en pantalla, los cambios podrían estar en formato de texto oculto o en Códigos de Campo que no estén visibles. Para mostrar las Marcas de Revisión en pantalla procedemos del siguiente modo:

♦ En el menú **Herramientas** seleccionamos **Control de cambios**.
♦ Seleccionamos la opción **Resaltar Cambios**.
♦ En la ventana que se muestra en la **Figura 4** habilitamos el casillero **Resaltar los cambios en pantalla**.

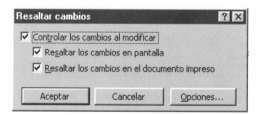

Figura 4. *Ingresamos a esta ventana cuando no se ven las Marcas de Revisión en la pantalla.*

1.7. ¿Cómo insertamos un comentario?

Cuando insertamos un Comentario, el lugar en donde estaba el cursor al momento de la inserción aparece resaltado y en la parte inferior de la pantalla se abre una ventana para escribir allí el comentario.

Cuando ubicamos el *Mouse* arriba de un Comentario, el puntero toma forma de sobre, aparece el nombre del autor y una parte del comentario. Si hacemos un clic abrimos la ventana para ver todo el Comentario.

Para insertar un comentario procedemos así:

♦ Abrimos el documento que recibirá los comentarios.
♦ Verificamos que se encuentra visible la barra de herramientas **Revisión**.
♦ Ubicamos el cursor en donde queremos que aparezca el comentario.
♦ Pulsamos el botón **Insertar Comentario** que se muestra en la **Figura 5**, y luego escribimos el comentario.

Figura 5. *Un clic aquí y se inserta un comentario.*

1.8. ¿Cómo eliminamos un comentario?

Para eliminar un comentario hay que seleccionarlo y luego utilizar el botón **Eliminar,** de la barra **Revisión,** que tiene el aspecto de la **Figura 6.**

Figura 6. *Un clic aquí y eliminamos un comentario.*

2. FUNCIÓN AUTORRESUMEN

La Función Autorresumen se usa para confeccionar automáticamente resúmenes con los principales puntos de un documento. Esta función analiza el documento según lo siguiente: Identifica títulos y subtítulos y los escribe en el resumen. Luego asigna una calificación a cada frase, por ejemplo, asigna una calificación más alta a las frases que contienen palabras utilizadas con mayor frecuencia en el documento. Una vez hecho ésto ubica las frases de acuerdo a la calificación que tienen, las mejor calificadas primero, y así sucesivamente. Finalmente, crea lo que podríamos llamar un principio de resumen, el cual abarcará más o menos detalles según un porcentaje de detalle ingresado por el usuario al momento de la creación del Autorresumen. El usuario deberá revisar este principio de resumen, completarlo, o directamente corregirlo en los puntos incompletos o incorrectos. La función Autorresumen no crea un resumen completo ni mucho menos, dado que el trabajo que realiza no se basa en una verdadera interpretación del texto sino en la evaluación de la jerarquía de las palabras, en la estadística de aparición de frases, etc. Sin embargo es importante tener en cuenta que esta función alcanza la mayor eficacia con documentos bien estructurados, por ejemplo, informes, artículos y documentos científicos.

2.1. ¿Cómo creamos un Autorresumen?

Para crear un Autorresumen hay que seguir las siguientes instrucciones:

♦ Abrir el documento a resumir.
♦ En el menú **Herramientas** seleccionar **Autorresumen**.
♦ En el Cuadro de Diálogo que aparece y que se muestra en la **Figura 7**, seleccionar la opción **Crear un documento nuevo para colocar el resumen**. En el casillero **Porcentaje** ingresar un valor porcentual relacionado con el nivel de detalle que queremos para nuestro resumen y luego pulsar **Aceptar**.

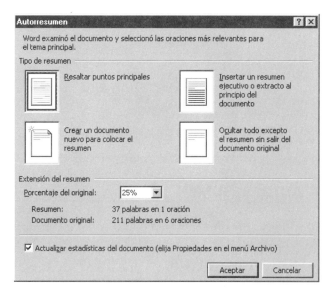

Figura 7. *Aquí le pedimos a la computadora que genere un resumen del documento.*

Cuando *Word* termine de resumir el trabajo, los puntos más resonantes del mismo aparecerán en una hoja nueva.

3. FUNCIÓN AUTOTEXTO

La función Autotexto se usa para almacenar texto, gráficos o cualquier otro elemento que usemos con frecuencia, e insertarlo rápidamente escribiendo un par de letras y pulsando F3. Nuestro logo personal, por ejemplo, puede guardarse como Autotexto a ser insertado cuantas veces necesitemos y en cualquier documento pulsando F3 y sin tener que ir a buscarlo en el archivo donde está guardado.

Además de los elementos que nosotros podemos definir como Autotexto, *Word* trae una lista con palabras y frases de uso común. En general, se trata de fórmulas para saludos, despedidas, etc.

3.1. ¿Cómo declaramos nuestros propios elementos como Autotexto?

Antes de declarar un elemento como Autotexto hay que tenerlo en pantalla. A partir de ese momento el procedimiento es el siguiente:

♦ Seleccionamos el o los elementos que serán incorporados como Autotexto.
♦ En la barra de Herramientas **Autotexto** pulsamos el botón **Nuevo**.
♦ En el Cuadro de Diálogo que se muestra en la **Figura 8** ingresamos un nombre o un par de letras con que se identificará el elemento declarado, por ejemplo ¨logo¨, y pulsamos Aceptar.

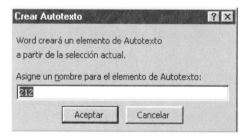

Figura 8. *Este ventana se usa para declarar un elemento seleccionado como Autotexto.*

Una vez declarado el elemento como Autotexto, para insertarlo hay que ingresar el nombre con el que fue identificado y luego presionar la tecla F3.

3.2. ¿Cómo modificamos un elemento de Autotexto?

Para modificar un elemento de Autotexto tenemos que insertarlo en el documento, realizar todos los cambios necesarios y volver a guardarlo bajo el mismo nombre, como se indicó arriba.

Herramientas 3

3.3. ¿Cómo eliminamos un elemento de Autotexto?

Para eliminar un elemento de Autotexto, pulsamos el botón **Autotexto** de la barra de Herramientas correspondiente, y en el Cuadro de Diálogo que aparece, seleccionamos de la lista el elemento a eliminar y pulsamos el botón **Eliminar** como se muestra en la **Figura 9.**

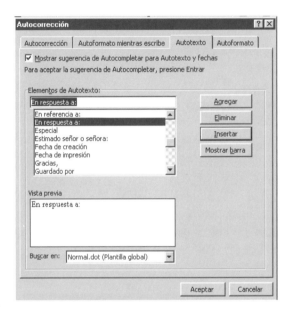

Figura 9. *Así eliminamos un Autotexto.*

3.4. ¿Y si queremos cambiar el nombre de un Autotexto?

Para cambiar el nombre de un Autotexto hay que proceder como si fuéramos a eliminarlo pero, cuando el nombre se muestra en el casillero, escribir el nuevo nombre y pulsar el botón Agregar.

3.5. ¿Podemos imprimir una lista con todos los elementos de Autotextos?

Sí, podemos hacerlo y hasta es conveniente para recordar todo lo que tenemos declarado como Autotexto y sus respectivos nombres.

Una lista de este tipo se imprime siguiendo las siguientes instrucciones:

◆ En el menú **Archivo** seleccionar **Imprimir**.

◆ En el Cuadro de Diálogo de la **Figura 10,** en el casillero **Imprimir,** pulsar la flecha descendente y seleccionar de la lista la opción **Autotexto**. Pulsar el botón **Aceptar**.

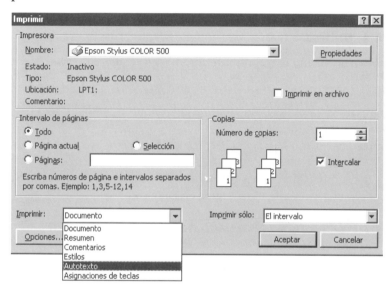

Figura 10. *Imprimir la lista de los elementos declarados como Autotexto nos sirve para tenerlos presentes y así poder utilizarlos.*

4. COMBINACIÓN DE CORRESPONDENCIA

La Combinación de Correspondencia es, sin duda, el recurso más poderoso con que cuenta *Word*. También conocido como *Mail Merge* o *Mailing*, se utiliza para realizar Envíos Masivos de Correspondencia. El *Mail Merge* o *Mailing* es una herramienta tan potente y fácil de manejar, que aún después de años de usarla, no dejamos de maravillarnos cada vez que, pulsando un sólo botón, vemos llenarse los cientos de cartas, sobres o etiquetas con los nombres y direcciones guardados en un archivo o en una tabla. Y hay más todavía para sorprenderse ya que con los filtros con que cuenta *Word*, además de escribir cientos de nombres y direcciones en pocos segundos podemos establecer a quién incluir en el envío y a quién no. Podemos incluir, por ejemplo, sólo a los habitantes de tal o cual ciudad o excluir a aquellos cuyo apellido empiece con tal o cual letra, una tarea que si fuese hecha manualmente requeriría de horas o hasta días.

A continuación analizaremos esta facilidad. El buen manejo de esta herramienta no sólo ahorra horas de trabajo, sino que nos permite realizar envíos prolijos, consistentes y hasta más económicos por la menor cantidad de errores que se producen al automatizar la tarea.

Dado que uno de los pasos de la Combinación de Correspondencia puede ser la confección de sobres y/o etiquetas, empezaremos analizando este tema.

4.1. Sobres

La confección de sobres utilizando *Word* requiere de las siguientes etapas:

♦ Determinar el tamaño del sobre (alto y ancho).
♦ Ingresar los datos del destinatario y del remitente, y establecer el aspecto y posición de esta información.
♦ Determinar cómo se cargará el sobre en la impresora.

A continuación desarrollaremos cada una de estas etapas, indicando paso a paso el procedimiento a seguir en cada caso.

4.1.1. Determinar el tamaño de sobre (alto y ancho).

El procedimiento en este caso es así:

♦ Medir el sobre que vamos a utilizar o averiguar cómo se llama.
♦ En el menú **Herramientas** elegir la opción **Sobres y Etiquetas**.
♦ En el Cuadro de Diálogo **Sobres**, que se muestra en la **Figura 11**, pulsar el botón **Opciones**.

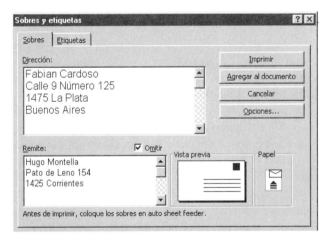

Figura 11. *Entramos aquí para confeccionar un sobre.*

♦ Verificar que aparece la ventana de la **Figura 12.**

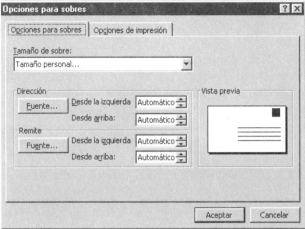

Figura 12. *El primer paso para confeccionar un sobre es elegir el tamaño del mismo.*

♦ En el casillero **Tamaño del Sobre** elegir el nombre del sobre. En caso de que éste no figure en la lista, seleccionar la opción **Personal** e ingresar alto y ancho en los casilleros correspondientes. Salir aceptando.

4.1.2. Ingresar los datos del destinatario y del remitente y establecer el aspecto y la posición que tendrán los mismos.

Los datos del destinatario y del remitente se ingresan en la ventana **Sobres** que mostramos en la **Figura 11.** Para que el remitente no aparezca en la parte de adelante del sobre hay que deshabilitar el Casillero **Omitir**. En el Cuadro de Diálogo de la **Figura 12** que utilizamos para establecer el tamaño del sobre hay un botón **Fuente** que permite determinar estilo, tipo y tamaño de letra de los datos del destinatario y del remitente. En esta misma ventana hay un casillero denominado **Desde la izquierda** y otro denominado **Desde arriba.** Pulsando las flechas de estos casilleros llevamos la dirección y el remitente a la posición deseada respecto del extremo izquierdo y superior del sobre. El cambio de posición aparecerá en el recuadro **Muestra**.

4.1.3. Establecer cómo será cargado el sobre en el alimentador.

Este es uno de los pasos más importantes en la configuración del sobre, dado que si el modo como cargamos el sobre en el alimentador no coincide con el modo como fue declarada la carga en *Word*, el texto puede aparecer atravesado. A continuación los pasos a seguir para establecer esta configuración:

♦ En el Cuadro de Diálogo **Opciones** (Ver **Figura 12**) que usamos para establecer el tamaño del sobre hay que seleccionar la ficha **Opciones para Impresión** que se muestra a continuación.

♦ Allí existen seis tipos de alimentación posibles que se muestran en la **Figura 13.** Elegir alguna.

♦ Habilitar el casillero **Mirando arriba** o **Mirando abajo**, dependiendo si vamos a colocar los datos del destinatario hacia arriba o hacia abajo.

Una vez establecido el modo de carga, es necesario respetarlo cuando coloquemos el sobre en el alimentador.

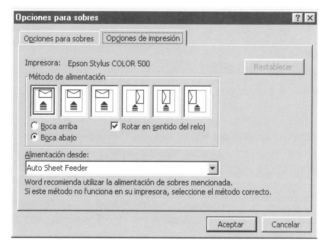

Figura 13. Aquí se decide cómo cargar el sobre en la bandeja de impresión.

4.2. Etiquetas

Las planchas de etiquetas pueden tener los mismos datos en todas las etiquetas o datos distintos en cada una de ellas. Aquí aprenderemos como escribir el mismo dato en toda la plancha. Cuando desarrollemos la Combinación de Correspondencia veremos cómo imprimir diferentes datos en cada una de las etiquetas. La **Figura 14** muestra cómo se ve en *Word* una plancha de etiquetas con los mismos datos en toda la plancha.

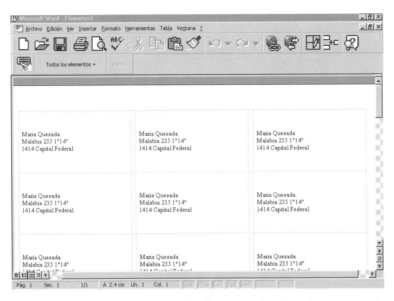

Figura 14. *Así se ve una plancha con todas las etiquetas iguales.*

Los pasos a seguir para crear etiquetas son los siguientes:

◆ Escribir los datos de la o las etiquetas.
◆ Determinar el rango de impresión.
◆ Elegir el tamaño de la etiqueta.

4.2.1. Escribir los datos de la o las etiquetas.

El procedimiento en este caso es el siguiente:

◆ En el menú **Herramientas** seleccionar **Sobres y Etiquetas** y luego la ficha **Etiquetas**.
◆ En el Cuadro de Diálogo que se muestra en la **Figura 15** escribir o seleccionar los datos de la o las etiquetas. Si habilitamos el casillero **Usar Remitente** las etiquetas irán dirigidas a la dirección que consta en el remitente de los sobres que confeccionamos antes.

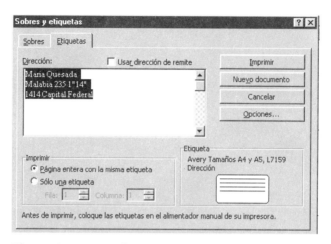

Figura 15. *Este es el primer paso para confeccionar etiquetas.*

4.2.2. Determinar el rango de impresión.

Determinar el rango de impresión significa decidir si se imprimirá toda la plancha o una sola etiqueta. Esto se hace habilitando, en la ventana que mostramos en la **Figura 15,** la opción **Una sola Etiqueta** o la opción **Toda la Plancha**. En el primer caso hay que ingresar la fila y columna en la que se encuentra la etiqueta, por ejemplo, podemos ingresar primera columna tercera fila por ser la única disponible de toda la plancha.

4.2.3. Elegir el tamaño de la Etiqueta.

Esto se hace del siguiente modo:

♦ En la ventana **Etiquetas** de la **Figura 15** hacer un clic en el botón **Opciones**.
♦ Verificar que aparece el Cuadro de Diálogo de la **Figura 16.**

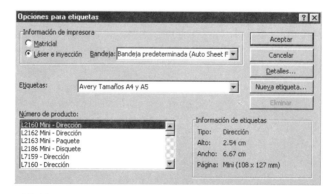

Figura 16. *Esta ventana se usa para elegir el tamaño y tipo de etiqueta que vamos a usar.*

♦ Seleccionar el tipo de impresora que estamos usando. Las opciones son Matricial, o Láser.

♦ En el casillero **Número de Producto** elegir el tipo de etiqueta a utilizar. Los diferentes tamaños aparecen clasificados en dos grupos: *Avery* Tamaño A4 /A5 y *Avery* Estándar EEUU. Si el tamaño deseado no aparece en ninguno de estos dos grupos habrá que seleccionar el tamaño **Otras** y luego pulsar el botón **Detalles**. El Cuadro de Diálogo **Detalles** se usa para personalizar el tamaño de las etiquetas y tiene el aspecto de la **Figura 17**.

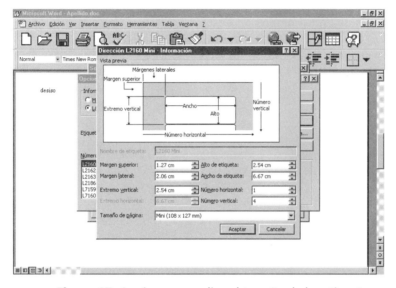

***Figura 17.** Aquí se personaliza el tamaño de las etiquetas.*

En cada uno de los casilleros de este Cuadro de Diálogo ingresamos las dimensiones de la etiqueta. Podemos ingresar, por ejemplo, un valor para la distancia entre las filas, otro para la distancia entre las columnas, etc. Esto se hace previa medición de la plancha. En el casillero **Nombre de Etiqueta** ingresamos el nombre que se nos ocurra. Al aceptar todas las opciones anteriores, y si hicimos las cosas bien aparecerá, en la lista de etiquetas, el nombre de la que acabamos de personalizar. Este nombre quedará disponible para que lo seleccionemos cada vez que sea necesario.

Ahora que sabemos cómo configurar Sobres y Etiquetas podemos pasar al siguiente tema, que es la Combinación de Correspondencia.

4.3. Mailing

Como dijimos antes, la Combinación de Correspondencia, *Mail Merge* o *Mailing* es un envío masivo de correspondencia que se realiza con la computadora utilizando *Word*. La Combinación de Correspondencia evita que escribamos uno por uno los sobres, las etiquetas o las cartas dirigidas a distintas personas cuyos datos están guardados en un archivo. El proceso consiste en fusionar un Documento Principal con un archivo o tabla (Base de Datos), que es el que tiene la información de cada una de las personas a las que queremos escribir.

El Documento Principal no es un documento común, sino que tiene lo que denominamos Campos de Combinación. Los Campos de Combinación no son otra cosa que los lugares en donde aparecerán los datos de la persona luego de la fusión. Podríamos compararlos con "envases" que se llenan con distintas cosas cada vez. Primero se llenarán con los datos de la primera fila de la Base de Datos, después con los datos de la segunda fila, etc. Es decir, durante la combinación o fusión, los datos de la primera persona se escribirán automáticamente en los Campos de Combinación del Documento Principal generando la primera correspondencia. Luego la máquina leerá la segunda fila de la Base de Datos y la escribirá en los Campos de Correspondencia del Documento Principal generando la segunda correspondencia y así sucesivamente hasta crear tantas cartas, etiquetas o sobres como datos figuren en la Base de Datos.

De lo anterior se desprende que para realizar un *Mail Merge* necesitamos:

♦ Crear un documento Principal.
♦ Crear una Base de Datos
♦ Realizar la fusión entre estos dos elementos.

A continuación se describe cómo proceder en cada caso.

4.3.1. El Documento Principal

El documento principal puede ser una carta, un sobre o una etiqueta. Generalmente contiene texto común y Campos de Combinación. Los Campos de Combinación aparecen escritos entre los signos "Mayor que" y "Menor que", como se muestra en la **Figura 18.** En el Campo de Combinación DIRECCION se escribirá automáticamente la dirección de la persona en el momento de la fusión, en el Campo de Combinación NOMBRE el nombre, etc.

<Apellido>:

Figura 18. Así se ve el campo Apellido.

Si el documento Principal es una carta, escribimos el texto común y cuando llegamos al lugar en donde tiene que aparecer el nombre del destinatario, en vez de ingresar un nombre común, insertamos el Campo de Combinación correspondiente. La **Figura 19** muestra cómo se ve el documento principal una vez insertados los Campos de Combinación Nombre y Apellido.

Estimado <Nombre> <Apellido>:

Nos dirigimos a Ud. para informarle que a partir del día de la fecha no será necesario que se presente personalmente en el banco ya que hemos iniciado nuestro programa de visitas a domicilio el cual consiste en comunicarse con todos los clientes y avisarles el dia y la hora a la cual con curriremos.

Figura 19. Así se ve una carta en la que conviven texto común y Campos de Combinación.

La Figura anterior puede ser el comienzo de una carta en la que un banco le comunica a sus cientos de clientes que no necesitan pasar a buscar personalmente su tarjeta de Crédito. Luego de la fusión o *Mail Merge*, los Campos de Combinación Nombre y Apellido desaparecerán y serán reemplazados, por ejemplo, por Eduardo Olmeida, Juan Pérez, María Nuñez, etc. Las cartas dirigidas a Eduardo Olmeida, Juan Pérez y María Nuñez serán algunas de las tantas obtenidas luego de la fusión entre *un único* Documento Principal y la Base de Datos. Para ser más precisos, habrá tantas cartas como personas registradas en la Base de Datos, y todas empezarán con el mismo ¨Estimado. . . ¨ pero el nombre y apellido será distinto para cada una de ellas.

4.3.2. Fuente de Datos o Base de Datos

La Base de Datos es el archivo que tiene la información de los destinatarios a quienes se envía las cartas, etiquetas o sobres. Esta información está distribuida en filas y en columnas. Cada registro o fila corresponde a una persona, y cada campo o columna es un tipo de información determinada. Un ejemplo de esto es el siguiente: la Base de Datos de la compañía M. S. contiene cien registros con información de sus clientes distribuida en los siguientes campos: Apellido, Nombres, Domicilio, Código Postal, Localidad.

4.3.3. ¿Cómo se realiza la Combinación de Correspondencia?

Para realizar la Combinación de Correspondencia los pasos a seguir son los siguientes:

1. Crear la Base de Datos.
2. Crear el Documento Principal.
3. Realizar la combinación.

A continuación desarrollaremos cada uno de estos pasos.

<u>Crear la Base de Datos o Fuente de Datos.</u>

Para crear la Base de Datos o Fuente de Datos hay que proceder del siguiente modo:

◆ Insertar o dibujar una tabla. En el ejemplo de la compañía M. S. S. A., cuando terminemos de ingresar los datos la tabla tendrá cien filas y cinco columnas.
◆ Ingresar los encabezados de la tabla (los nombres de cada columna), por ejemplo ¨Apellido¨, ¨Nombres¨, etc.
◆ Pulsar el botón derecho del *Mouse* sobre cualquier barra de Herramientas y seleccionar la opción **Base de Datos**.
◆ Verificar que aparece la barra de Herramientas Base de Datos que se muestra en la **Figura 20.**

Figura 20. *Barra de Herramientas Base de Datos.*

◆ Ubicar el cursor en la segunda fila de la tabla y pulsar el botón **Ficha de Datos**, que es el primero de la barra **Base de Datos**.
◆ Verificar que aparece una ficha como la que se muestra en la **Figura 21.** Esta ficha nos facilitará el ingreso de los datos en la tabla.

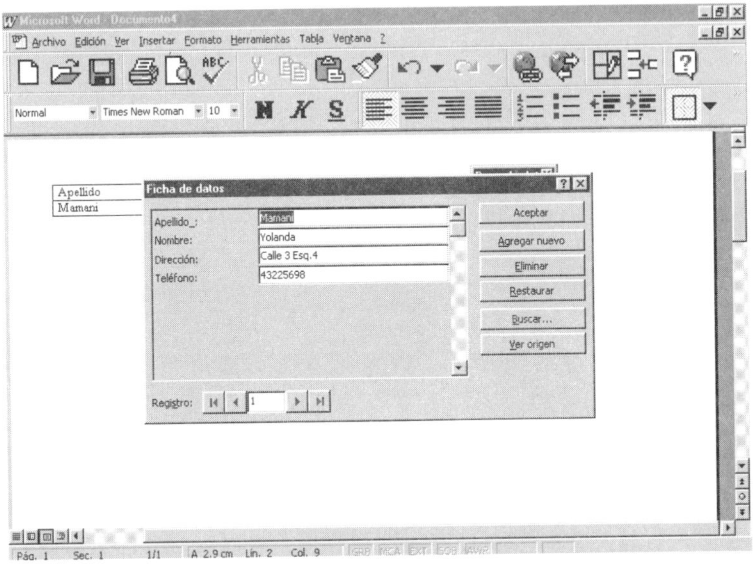

Figura 21. *Esta ficha trabaja igual que su equivalente en el papel. La vamos llenando con los datos de la persona.*

- Ingresar los datos del primer destinatario pulsando TAB para pasar de un campo al otro y *ENTER* para pasar al próximo registro.
- Proceder así hasta completar todos los registros.
- Hacer un clic en el botón **Aceptar** para que la tabla aparezca en el documento.
- Guardar el documento con un nombre representativo y cerrarlo.

La **Figura 22** muestra una tabla confeccionada según la explicación anterior.

Apellido	Nombre	Dirección	Teléfono
Mamani	Yolanda	Calle 3 Esq.4	43225698
Romero	Victor	Tomas de Aquino 5	4256-8965
Abrebaya	Hugo	Urquiza 54	4776-8965

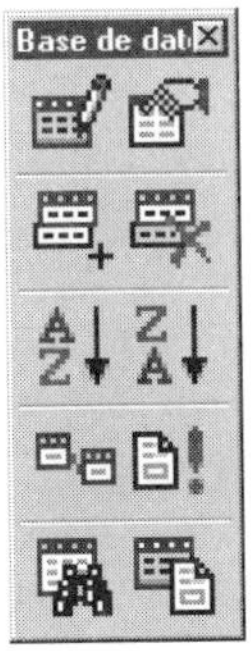

Figura 22. *Base de Datos vista como una tabla.*

<u>Crear el Documento Principal y Realizar la Combinación de Correspondencia.</u>
Para crear el Documento Principal y realizar la fusión debemos proceder así:

♦ En el menú **Herramientas** seleccionar **Combinar Correspondencia**.
♦ En el Cuadro de Diálogo que aparece y que se muestra en la **Figura 23**, pulsar el Botón **Crear** y seleccionar de la lista, un tipo de Documento Principal. Las opciones son: Carta, Sobres o Etiquetas.

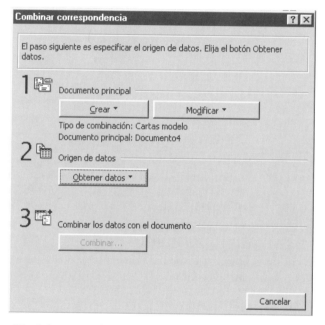

Figura 23. *Así se crea el Documento Principal (Documento Madre o Master) que es la base del Mail Merge.*

♦ Pulsar el botón **Fuente de Datos**, seleccionar la opción **Abrir** y en el Cuadro de Diálogo que aparece ingresar la ruta de acceso y el nombre del archivo que tiene la tabla que creamos con anterioridad.
♦ A esta altura *Word* pregunta si debe trabajar en la ventana activa (Ver **Figura 24**). Dado que la respuesta generalmente es afirmativa, cerramos esa ventana aceptando.

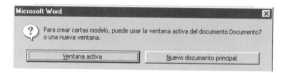

Figura 24. *En esta ventana, Word le pregunta al usuario si quiere trabajar en donde está o abrir otro documento.*

· ·

♦ Hacer un clic en el botón **Modificar el Documento Principal** de la **Figura 23** y verificar que aparece la barra de Herramientas **Combinar Correspondencia** que tiene el aspecto de la **Figura 25**.

Figura 25. Esta Barra de Herramientas es la que aparece durante la Combinación de Correspondencia.

♦ Si el documento principal es un sobre o una etiqueta, determinar los atributos adecuados como el tamaño, el Formato de Fuente, etc.
♦ Si el documento principal es una carta, escribir el texto que aparecerá en todas las cartas, por ejemplo la fecha, el encabezado, el saludo, etc.
♦ Ubicar el cursor en el lugar en donde aparecerá el primer Campo de Combinación y pulsar el botón **Insertar Campo de Combinación** de la barra de Herramientas **Combinar Correspondencia**, que se muestra en la **Figura 25**.

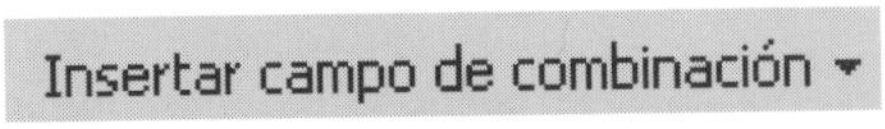

Insertar campo de combinación ▾

Figura 26. Botón Combinar Correspondencia.

♦ En la lista de Campos seleccionar uno, por ejemplo Apellido. Los Campos de Correspondencia que aparecen en la lista no son otra cosa que los nombres de los encabezados de la tabla que creamos al comienzo y que elegimos como Base de Datos. En la **Figura 27** se muestra el aspecto que tiene una lista con Campos de Combinación.

Figura 27. Aquí vemos la lista de los Campos de Combinación de la Base de Datos activa.

♦ Procedemos así hasta ingresar todos los Campos de Combinación en donde corresponda. La **Figura 28** muestra cómo se verá una carta conteniendo texto y Campos de Combinación.

Estimado <Nombre> <Apellido>:

Nos dirigimos a Ud.
para informarle que a partir del día de la fecha
no será necesario que se presente
personalmente en el banco ya que hemos
iniciado nuestro programa de visitas a domicilio
el cual consiste en comunicarse con todos los
clientes y avisarles el dia y la hora a la cual
con curriremos

Figura 28. *Carta conteniendo texto y Campos de Combinación.*

♦ Pulsar el botón **Combinar Correspondencia** de la **Figura 29.**

Figura 29. *Un clic en este botón y largamos la fusión.*

♦ Verificar que aparece el Cuadro de Diálogo de la **Figura 30.**

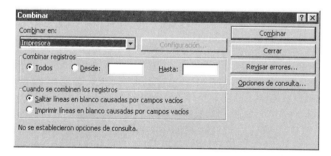

Figura 30. *En esta ventana se decide el soporte en el que aparecerán las cartas hijas. Puede ser en papel, o en un archivo.*

♦ En el casillero **Combinar en** seleccionar el lugar en donde se llevará a cabo la combinación. Las opciones son: en un documento nuevo o en la impresora. En este último caso no se creará un archivo con el resultado de la fusión sino que sólo saldrá impreso.

♦ En el casillero **Combinar Registros** decidir el rango de los registros a combinar, por ejemplo desde el registro Nº 1 al 50.

♦ Deshabilitar la opción **Imprimir líneas vacías** para evitar que queden líneas en blanco en aquellos registros que no estén completos.

♦ Pulsar el botón **Consultas**. En el Cuadro de Diálogo **Consultas,** que se muestra en la **Figura 31**, utilizar los filtros para determinar el rango del envío. Para incluir en el envío sólo los apellidos que empiecen con la letra "P", escribimos, en el casillero **Campo** la opción " Apellido, en el casillero **Comparación** "Igual a" y finalmente, en el casillero **Comparado con**, la letra"P". Luego de la fusión sólo aparecerán combinados los registros cuyos apellidos empiecen con "P".

Figura 31. *Estos son los filtros que permiten personalizar el Mailing.*

♦ Al salir de esta ventana volvemos a la ventana de la Figura 30 y hacemos un clic en el botón **Combinar** para que la combinación tenga lugar.

Si la combinación se realizó con éxito, aparecerán en pantalla tantas cartas, sobres o etiquetas como registros seleccionados.

El nuevo documento, resultado de la fusión, se comportará como cualquier otro documento, podremos guardarlo, editarlo o imprimirlo.

5. FUNCIÓN AUTOCORRECCIÓN

La función Autocorrección se encarga de corregir automáticamente aquellos errores de tipeo y de ortografía más frecuentes. El proceso se lleva a cabo del siguiente modo: a medida que ingresamos palabras *Word* controla si cada uno de los ingresos figura o no en una lista de errores frecuentes. Si la palabra ingresada está en esa lista, significa que se trata de un error. En este caso, la reemplaza inmediatamente por la palabra bien escrita, que está en una lista paralela a la anterior.

Word trae una lista de errores más frecuentes, pero el usuario puede agregar otros y sus respectivas enmiendas.

La Función Autocorrección además puede personalizarse para corregir las siguientes ocurrencias.

5.1. Dos mayúsculas seguidas.

Este error ocurre cuando no soltamos a tiempo la tecla *SHIFT* (Mayúscula). Si la función está activada y el casillero que controla esta ocurrencia está habilitado, la Función Autocorrección convertirá automáticamente la segunda mayúscula en una minúscula.

5.2. Bloqueo accidental del CAPSLOCK

Un error muy común es presionar la tecla *CAPSLOCK* (Bloqueador de mayúscula) en lugar de la tecla *SHIFT*(Mayúscula). Cuando esto ocurre la primera letra aparece en minúscula y el resto queda en mayúscula.

Si la Función Autocorrección está activada, detectará este tipo de ocurrencia y aquellas palabras que comiencen con minúscula y continúen en mayúscula serán corregidas automáticamente y desbloqueado el bloqueador de mayúscula.

5.3. Minúscula después del punto

Empezar una palabra con minúscula después de un punto generalmente es un error. *Word* contempla este tipo de errores en la Función Autocorrección. Si el casillero que controla este error está activado, la Función Autocorrección cambiará automáticamente la minúscula por una mayúscula. Para que esta función resulte verdaderamente útil hay que especificarle a *Word* las abreviaturas más frecuentes después de las cuales no poner mayúscula. Esto se hace del siguiente modo:

♦ En el menú **Herramientas** seleccionamos **Autocorrección**.
♦ En el Cuadro de Diálogo que aparece y que mostramos en la **Figura 32** pulsamos el botón **Excepciones**.

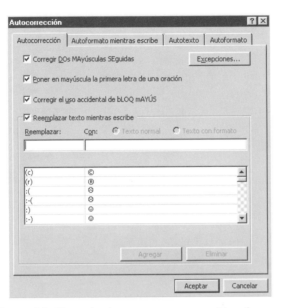

Figura 32. *No todos los puntos van seguidos de mayúsculas.*

◆ En la ventana **Excepciones**, de la **Figura 33,** agregamos las abreviaturas más usadas y luego pulsamos **Agregar** para que sean incorporadas.

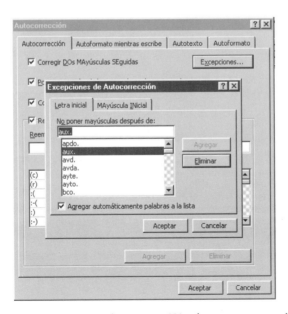

Figura 33. *Ingresamos aquí para que Word no ponga mayúscula luego de una abreviatura.*

5.4. ¿Cómo habilitamos o deshabilitamos la función Autocorrección?

En realidad, lo que habilitamos o no son los tipos de errores que puede corregir esta función. Por ejemplo, podemos dejar activo el casillero que corrige dos mayúsculas seguidas y desactivar el que corrige una minúscula después del punto. Esto se hace seleccionando, en el menú **Herramientas**, la opción **Autocorrección** y luego haciendo un clic en los respectivos casilleros como lo muestra **Figura 34.**

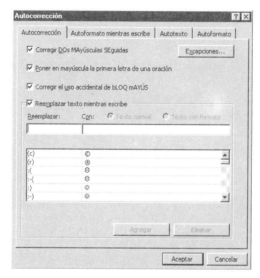

Figura 34. Ventana que permite personalizar la función Autocorrección.

5.5. ¿Qué otro uso tiene la función Autocorrección?

La función Autocorrección puede usarse, además de para enmendar errores, para ingresar símbolos especiales que no se encuentran en el teclado. En la tabla que se muestra a continuación, en la columna de la izquierda, aparece una lista con los caracteres que debemos ingresar desde el teclado para que Word inserte los símbolos de la columna derecha.

CARACTERES A INGRESAR	SÍMBOLO INSERTADO
(c)	©
(r)	®
:)	☺
:(	☹
:|	☺
1 / 2	½

6. REVISIÓN AUTOMÁTICA DE ORTOGRAFÍA

Es otra de las herramientas de Edición con que cuenta *Word*. La Revisión Automática de Ortografía se lleva a cabo del siguiente modo: *Word* recorre palabra por palabra el documento comparando cada ingreso con la información existente en uno o más diccionarios de ortografía y gramática del idioma definido. Cuando la palabra que figura en el documento no aparece en el diccionario, se detiene, la muestra como un error y sugiere una o más palabras con similitud fonética como posibles correcciones. Si ingresamos ¨oja¨, por ejemplo, las sugerencias serán las siguientes:

Ja
Hoja
Ojal
Ojea
Ojo

Si el error que encuentra es de tipo gramatical, lo explica, y generalmente sugiere el modo de corregirlo.

6.1. ¿Cómo iniciamos la Revisión Automática de Ortografía y Gramática?

Antes de iniciar la Revisión Automática de Ortografía y Gramática es necesario definir en qué idioma se llevará a cabo la corrección. Esto se hace seleccionando el documento y eligiendo el idioma en el menú **Herramientas**, opción **Idioma**. En el Cuadro de Diálogo de la **Figura 35** es posible predeterminar un idioma. Es importante destacar que el idioma quedará predeterminado si es también el elegido como predeterminado en la barra de Tareas de *Windows*.

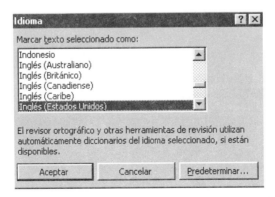

Figura 35. *En esta ventana se predetermina un idioma.*

Herramientas 3

Si un documento está definido en un idioma diferente del que está escrito, aparece lleno de errores indicados por subrayados rojos.

Para que *Word* corrija automáticamente un documento hay que ubicar el puntero al comienzo del mismo y pulsar el botón **Ortografía** de la barra **Estándar**, que tiene el aspecto de la **Figura 36.**

Figura 36. *Un clic aquí e iniciamos la Corrección Automática de Ortografía.*

Los errores van apareciendo en una ventana independiente, como la que se muestra en la **Figura 37,** en donde podemos aceptar o no las sugerencias hechas por *Word*. En el caso de aceptar la sugerencia pulsamos el botón **Cambiar**, de lo contrario usamos el botón **Omitir**.

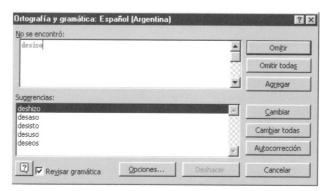

Figura 37. *Word nos muestra los errores y sus respectivas sugerencias. El usuario puede aceptarlas o no.*

6.2. ¿Qué diccionarios utiliza Word para la Revisión Automática de Ortografía?

Word utiliza los siguientes tipos de diccionarios para realizar la Revisión Automática de Ortografía:

♦ Diccionario Principal.
♦ Diccionarios Personalizados.

El Diccionario Principal es un archivo que contiene la mayoría de las palabras que usamos habitualmente en un determinado idioma. Existen varios Diccionarios Principales en distintos idiomas, que son instalados junto a *Word* en la carpeta ARCHIVOS DE PROGRAMAS subcarpetas ARCHIVOS COMUNES/ *MICROSOFT SHARED/ PROOF* y que tienen la extensión ˝*LEX* ˝. Los Diccionarios Principales no pueden accederse ni modificarse.

Los Diccionarios Personalizados son creados por el usuario como una lista de palabras. La idea es incorporar en este diccionario aquella terminología técnica o especial que pueda ser considerada como error durante la Revisión Automática de Ortografía. Después de agregar un determinado término a un Diccionario Personalizado, la próxima vez que *Word* ejecute la Revisión Automática de Ortografía, ese término no aparecerá más como un error salvo que esté mal escrito. El Diccionario Personalizado de un oculista, por ejemplo, contendrá términos como: ˝córnea˝, ˝iris˝, ˝conos˝, ˝bastoncillos˝, que pueden ser detectados como errores.

Los Diccionarios Personalizados poseen la extensión DIC, y se guardan en los mismos directorios y subdirectorios que los Diccionarios Principales, o bien en ˝c:*WINDOWS\MSAPPS\PROOF*˝.

Puede haber más de uno declarado y en uso. Además podemos accederlos, modificarlos y guardarlos cuantas veces sea necesario. Existe también la posibilidad de que en vez de crearlos los compremos ya que muchas veces se venden según las distintas disciplinas, por ejemplo Diccionarios Legales, Médicos etc.

6.3. ¿Cómo incorporamos a Word un Diccionario Personalizado?

Existen tres modos de hacerlo:

- Crearlo desde cero escribiendo la lista de las palabras.
- Crearlo incorporando términos cada vez que revisamos automáticamente la ortografía.
- Importándolo de un archivo.

A continuación analizaremos cada caso:

6.3.1. Crear un Diccionario Personalizado desde Cero

Este es el método más común. Para crear un Diccionario Personalizado hay que:

- En **Herramientas** elegir **Opciones** y luego **Ortografía y Gramática**, y verificar que aparece la ventana de la **Figura 38**.

(margen derecho) **3** Herramientas

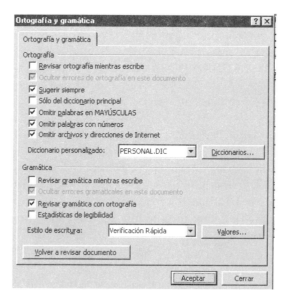

Figura 38. *Primer paso para crear un Diccionario Personalizado.*

♦ Hacer un clic en el botón **Diccionario**, y en el Cuadro de Diálogo que se muestra en la **Figura 39** hacer un clic en **Nuevo** e ingresar el nombre del nuevo diccionario, por ejemplo TECNICO.

Figura 39. *Segundo paso en la creación de un Diccionario Personalizado.*

♦ Guardarlo en el mismo directorio que el resto de los diccionarios, esto es en C:*WINDOWS\MSAPPS\PROOF,* cuidando de incluir después del nombre un punto y la extensión DIC.

♦ Cuando *Word* nos da la página en blanco escribir la primera palabra del diccionario y pulsar *ENTER.*

♦ Proceder así hasta ingresar todas las palabras deseadas.

♦ Al finalizar, volver a guardar todos los cambios realizados.

Para determinar que el diccionario que acabamos de crear participe en el proceso de Revisión Automática de Ortografía hay que habilitar el casillero correspondiente en el Cuadro de Diálogo **Diccionarios Personalizados**, del menú **Herramientas/Opciones** ficha **Ortografía y Gramática**, que mostramos en la **Figura 38.**

6.3.2. Crear un Diccionario Personalizado mientras corregimos un documento

Para crear un diccionario Personalizado mientras corregimos un documento hay que proceder del siguiente modo:

♦ En el menú **Herramientas** elegir **Opciones** y luego la ficha **Ortografía y Gramática**.

♦ En el Cuadro de Diálogo que aparece (Ver **Figura 40**), en el casillero **Diccionario Personalizado**, seleccionar el nombre del diccionario que queremos que participe en el proceso de Revisión.

♦ Salir aceptando.

Figura 40. *Un diccionario también puede construirse corrigiendo errores.*

La próxima vez que realicemos una revisión ortográfica y *Word* se detenga en un término específico, pulsamos el botón **Agregar** . La palabra se guardará automáticamente en el diccionario personalizado activado en el párrafo anterior. Volviendo al ejemplo del oculista, supongamos que este profesional está realizando una Revisión Automática de uno de sus informes y *Word* se detiene en la palabra ˝ fovea ˝. Puesto que se trata de un término técnico que no encuentra en ninguno de los dos diccionarios, el oculista puede aprovechar esta ocasión para actualizar su diccionario personalizado con esta palabra. Para ello tiene que hacer un clic en el botón **Agregar**. La palabra ˝ fovea ˝ se incorporará automáticamente a su diccionario Personalizado y *Word* no la considerará más un error.

6.3.3. Importar un Diccionario Personalizado de un archivo

Esto se hace, por ejemplo, cuando alguien que trabaja con el mismo léxico que nosotros nos de un diccionario ya confeccionado.

Para ingresarlo a *Word* procedemos del siguiente modo:

♦ En el Cuadro de Diccionarios con el que trabajamos antes pulsamos el botón **Agregar** de la **Figura 41.**

Figura 41. *Primer paso para importar un diccionario.*

♦ En el Cuadro de Diálogo que se abre ingresamos unidad de disco, carpeta y nombre del archivo a importar y pulsamos **Aceptar**. El nombre del nuevo diccionario tiene que aparecer en la lista junto con el resto.

6.4. Agregar elementos de Autocorrección mientras revisamos automáticamente la ortografía.

Durante el proceso de Revisión Automática de Ortografía, *Word* se detiene en aquellas palabras que están mal escritas o que no aparecen en los diccionarios de consulta. Antes de aceptar la sugerencia y seguir adelante podemos agregar este error y su correspondiente enmienda a la lista de errores comunes y enmiendas de la Función Autocorrección que vimos antes. Si la operación se lleva a cabo correctamente, la próxima vez que *Word* detecte ese mismo error lo corregirá automáticamente sin consultarnos y sin consultar en los diccionarios. Esto agilizará el proceso de corrección que generalmente es bastante lento.

Para agregar un error a la Función Autocorrección hay que proceder del siguiente modo:

◆ Iniciar la Revisión Automática de Ortografía.
◆ Cuando *Word* se detiene en un error que cometemos con frecuencia pulsar el botón **Autocorrección**.
◆ La palabra que se encuentra en el casillero **No se encuentra** será definida como elemento de Autocorrección, y aquella que se encuentra en el casillero **Sugerencia** será declarada como enmienda, como se muestra en la **Figura 42.**

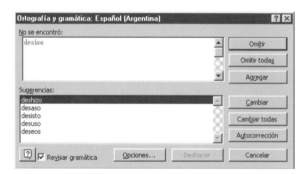

Figura 42. *Otro modo de agregar elementos de Autocorrección.*

7. HERRAMIENTA SINÓNIMOS

Word cuenta con un diccionario de sinónimos para ayudarnos con los términos que repetimos y para los que no encontramos rápidamente sustitutos. Con esta herramienta podemos reemplazar una palabra o toda una expresión que figure en nuestro documento, por un sinónimo que se encuentra en un diccionario especial que está incorporado al programa. Para reemplazar una palabra por su sinónimo procedemos del siguiente modo:

♦ Seleccionamos la palabra o grupo de palabras cuyo sinónimo queremos encontrar.

♦ En el menú **Herramientas** seleccionamos **Idioma** y luego **Sinónimo**.

♦ En el Cuadro de Diálogo que se muestra en la **Figura 43**, en el casillero **Significados**, aparecen las acepciones más comunes para la palabra o palabras seleccionadas. Si, por ejemplo, la palabra es ¨bajo¨, *Word* escribe en este casillero las acepciones ¨Sustantivo´ y ¨Adjetivo¨, dado que los sinónimos serán diferentes para cada caso (cuando existen varias acepciones para una misma palabra es necesario elegir la más apropiada).

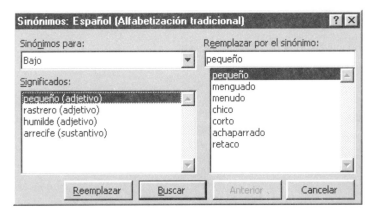

Figura 43. *Ventana de sinónimos.*

♦ En el casillero **Reemplazar por el sinónimo** aparece una lista con los posibles sinónimos, dependiendo de la acepción elegida. El usuario tendrá que elegir el adecuado y pulsar el botón **Reemplazar** para que el cambio tenga lugar en el documento. Si ejecutamos la Función Sinónimo sin seleccionar una o más palabras, el nombre del casillero **Reemplazar por el sinónimo** cambiará a **Insertar**, podremos escribir una palabra y luego iniciar una búsqueda de sinónimos pulsando el botón **Buscar**.

8. HERRAMIENTA CONTAR CARACTERES, PALABRAS, LÍNEAS, PÁGINAS O PÁRRAFOS EN UN DOCUMENTO

La herramienta para contar caracteres, palabras, etc. es una función que ahorra gran cantidad de trabajo, es simple de usar, rápida y precisa. Es sumamente útil para seguir consignas relacionadas con la cantidad de palabras, líneas, páginas, etc. como las que se piden en los concursos, traducciones, etc.

Para utilizar esta función hay ubicar el cursor en cualquier punto del documento o seleccionar una porción de éste, y en el menú **Herramientas**, seleccionar **Contar Palabras**. Aparecerá una ventana con todos los datos del recuento, como la de la **Figura 44.**

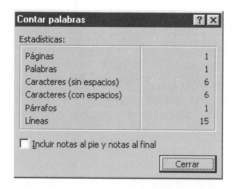

Figura 44. *Así nos muestra Word el recuento de palabras.*

PROBLEMAS

1. Raúl está cansado de escribir todos los días los datos de su empresa en los encabezados de las cartas.

2. Laura es traductora oficial. En muchos de sus trabajos tiene que incluir los símbolos de *Copyright* © y *Trademark*®, y como no sabe cómo ingresarlos con la computadora generalmente lo hace a mano.

3. Manuel tiene que hacer una lista con los puntos más relevantes de un informe que hizo en la computadora, y se pregunta cuál será el modo más rápido de hacerlo.

4. Mariana quiere mandar un *Mailing* usando los datos de la agenda que tiene instalada en su computadora, pero no sabe cómo proceder.

5. Julián terminó de imprimir varios sobres con los datos de sus clientes. Ahora quiere imprimir las etiquetas con los remitentes para pegarlas al dorso de los sobres, pero no sabe cómo hacerlo.

6. A Jorge le molesta que cuando escribe ciertas palabras, éstas aparezcan subrayadas en rojo o verde. En el *Word* que tenía antes eso no pasaba.

7. Elena está cansada de que *Word* considere palabras técnicas como errores.

8. Natalio escribe un documento en inglés y quiere aprovechar el corrector ortográfico para revisar los posibles errores que pudo haber cometido, pero no sabe cómo hacerlo.

9. Pablo y Marta trabajan juntos en un documento. La tarde en que tienen que presentarlo, a Marta se le ocurren algunos cambios pero Pablo no está para consultarlo. Marta piensa realizar los cambios con un lápiz y, si Pablo los aprueba, pasarlos al documento original. Como recuerda que Pablo vendrá con el tiempo justo para imprimir todo y llevárselo decide no hacer los cambios.

10. Osvaldo tiene cuatro estudiantes de medicina a su cargo. Cuando realizan informes en conjunto, cada uno le presenta a su jefe una versión del informe y éste le indica a la secretaria cómo compaginar todo en un sólo documento. Cuando la secretaria tiene mucho trabajo, los cuatro tienen que esperar varios días hasta tener el informe final.

SOLUCIONES

1. Raúl podría definir estos datos como Autotexto y darle un nombre, por ejemplo "Enca". La próxima vez que necesite ingresar estos datos, lo único que tiene que hacer es ubicar el cursor en donde aparecerán los datos, escribir "Enca" y presionar F3. Los datos de su empresa aparecerán automáticamente en la posición del cursor. Para definir el logo y los datos de la empresa como Autotexto, Raúl tiene que abrir una carta en donde figuren todos estos elementos, seleccionarlos y, en el menú **Insertar** elegir **Autotexto** y luego **Nuevo**. En la ventana que aparece, ingresar el nombre, por ejemplo, "Enca" y luego pulsar **Aceptar**.

2. Laura puede ingresarlos como elementos de Autocorrección. El procedimiento es el siguiente:

♦ En el menú **Insertar** seleccionar **Símbolo**.
♦ En el muestrario de símbolos que aparece, seleccionar por turno los símbolos *Copyright* y *Trademark*, y pulsar el botón **Autocorrección**.
♦ En la ventana que se abre, ingresar un par de letras con las que se identificará cada uno de estos símbolos.

La próxima vez que Laura tenga que ingresar el símbolo de *Trademark* o *Copyright* deberá ingresar el par de letras con que se identificó a cada uno de estos símbolos. *Word* reemplazará automáticamente el nombre por el indicador *Trademark* o *Copyright*.

3. Una posibilidad es abrir el informe y, en el menú **Herramientas** elegir la opción **Autorresumen**. En la ventana Autorresumen, Manuel puede elegir la opción **Crear un documento nuevo para colocar el resumen**, y elegir un porcentaje de detalle , por ejemplo 10% o 20%. Cuando *Word* procese el resumen podrá agregar o quitar ideas teniendo en cuenta la consigna establecida.

4. Mariana tiene que proceder como con cualquier *Mailing* pero, cuando *Word* le pregunte de dónde obtener los datos de los destinatarios, elegir la opción **Libreta de Direcciones**. *Word* abrirá una ventana sugiriendo las diferentes agendas que pueden estar instaladas en *Windows*, por ejemplo *Microsoft Schedule*, *Microsoft Outlook*, etc. Luego de elegir la que corresponda, Mariana dispondrá de todos los datos contenidos en la agenda para incluirlos como Campos de Combinación en el documento principal del *Mailing* (ver **Figura 45**).

Herramientas 3

Figura 45. *Estas son algunas de las agendas que pueden estar instaladas.*

5. Julián tiene que conseguir varias planchas de etiquetas y luego proceder así:

◆ En el menú **Herramientas** seleccionar **Sobres y Etiquetas**.
◆ En ficha **Sobres** ingresar el remitente a imprimir.
◆ En la ficha **Etiquetas** habilitar la opción **Usar dirección del Remitente** y la opción **Página entera con la misma etiqueta**.
◆ Pulsar el botón **Opciones** y seleccionar el tamaño de la etiqueta que va a utilizar. En el caso de que sus etiquetas no figuren en la lista, seleccionar la opción **Otras** y personalizar el tamaño desde **Detalles**.

6. Las palabras subrayadas con verde indican errores gramaticales, y las subrayadas con rojo errores de ortografía. Si Jorge ubica el puntero sobre la palabra subrayada y hace un clic en el botón derecho del *Mouse*, *Word* le ayudará a corregir cualquiera de estos errores.
Si no queremos ver los errores mientras escribimos podemos deshabilitar la función **Revisar ortografía mientras escribe**, o bien habilitar la función **Ocultar errores de ortografía en este documento**. Ambas opciones están en la ficha **Ortografía y Gramática** del Cuadro de Diálogo **Herramientas/Opciones**.

7. Elena puede solucionar el problema incorporando estas palabras a un Diccionario Personalizado. Esto se hace ubicando el puntero arriba de cada una de las palabras subrayadas con rojo y pulsando el botón derecho del *Mouse*. En el menú que aparece hay que elegir **Agregar**. *Word* ingresará esa palabra al diccionario Personalizado activado y, a partir de ese momento, no la considerará más un error.

8. Lo primero que tiene que hacer Natalio es abrir el documento, seleccionarlo y en **Herramientas/Idioma** elegir "Inglés Británico", o "Inglés Americano". Una vez definido el idioma iniciar la Revisión Automática de Ortografía pulsando el botón **Ortografía** de la barra **Estándar** o seleccionando **Revisar Ortografía** en el menú **Herramientas**. *Word* utilizará el diccionario Principal de Inglés para evaluar si existen o no errores.

9. Marta podría haber incorporado los cambios como Marcas de Revisión. Pablo podría haberlas incorporado o rechazado pulsando un sólo botón.

10. Osvaldo podría confeccionar el informe base y pasarle el disquete a sus alumnos, para que cada uno de ellos agregue su parte como Comentarios o Marcas de Revisión, activando en la barra de Estado la abreviatura MCA. Al final de la rueda, Osvaldo podría incorporar o no los comentarios y las sugerencias pulsando un solo botón. Esto evitaría el paso del informe por la secretaría.

ELEMENTOS DE TRABAJO II

4

Tiempo de lectura y práctica:
1 hora y 45 minutos

Lección

4

Objetivo de la lección

- Crear Indices y Tablas de Contenidos.
- Utilizar Macros para tareas repetitivas.
- Capturar información para una Base de Datos utilizando Formularios de llenado por pantalla.

1. TABLA DE CONTENIDOS

Una Tabla de Contenidos es un temario o índice que generalmente aparece al comienzo de una publicación, presentación, informe, etc. y que informa sobre los temas de esa publicación, el orden de aparición de los mismos, la o las páginas en las que se encuentran, la vinculación que tienen entre sí, bajo qué nombre o nombres aparecen, etc. La **Figura 1** muestra una Tabla de Contenidos.

Fracciones ———————	*1*
Trabajar con Fracciones ————	*2*
Fracciones Decimales ————	*3*
Convertir a la Unidad seguida de cero —	*4*
Fracciones Periódicas ———————	*5*

Figura 1. *Un ejemplo de Tabla de Contenidos.*

Word puede crear automáticamente Tablas de Contenidos utilizando las palabras o frases de los títulos de un documento. Cuando el usuario termina su presentación, si utilizó Estilos Predeterminados para dar formato a los Títulos y Subtítulos, lo único que tiene que hacer es ubicar el cursor en donde aparecerá la Tabla de Contenidos y seleccionar, en el menú **Insertar, Tablas e Indice.** En la ventana que se abre elegir un estilo de Tabla de Contenidos de los que figuran allí y pulsar **Aceptar**. *Word* demorará unos segundos durante los cuales procederá del siguiente modo:

♦ Buscará las palabras o frases del documento que lleven Estilos Predeterminados, y las escribirá una debajo de otra siguiendo el orden de aparición y el orden de jerarquía.
♦ Hará referencia a sus números de página y los escribirá a la derecha del título.
♦ Por último realizará los cambios de aspecto que correspondan según el estilo de Tabla elegido por el usuario. Por ejemplo, puede agregar sangría a los títulos de menor jerarquía, variar los tamaños de letra, insertar relleno entre los títulos y sus números de página, etc.

Elementos de trabajo II 4

♦ El resultado será en todos los casos el mismo: una lista con los títulos principales y secundarios y sus correspondientes números de página.

Una vez creada la Tabla de Contenidos podemos modificarla como si se tratara de texto común pero estas modificaciones se perderán si la actualizamos. Esto significa que si modificamos el aspecto de una Tabla de Contenidos y luego tenemos que actualizarla por cambios en el temario o en los números de página, perderemos todos los formatos agregados, como por ejemplo, el cambio de color de la fuente, los subrayados, etc.

1.1. ¿Podemos determinar qué títulos mostrar y cuáles no?

Sí podemos hacerlo. La **Figura 2** muestra la ventana **Tablas de Contenidos**, desde donde insertamos y configuramos el aspecto de una Tabla de Contenidos.

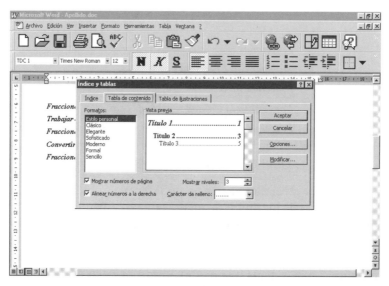

Figura 2. *Esta ventana es la que usamos para insertar una Tabla de Contenidos.*

Allí existe un casillero denominado **Mostrar Niveles** que es el que se utiliza para seleccionar el nivel de títulos que se mostrará en la Tabla de Contenidos. Si, por ejemplo, seleccionamos Nivel 3, la tabla quedará formada por los Títulos de nivel 1,2 y 3. Esto significa que podemos determinar el nivel de detalle de la Tabla de Contenidos, pero no discriminar entre títulos del mismo nivel. Si elegimos mostrar un nivel determinado se mostrará todo lo que exista a ese nivel, sin excepciones. Lo que podríamos hacer para ocultar ciertos temas es eliminarlos de la tabla cuando ésta aparezca en pantalla. Recordemos que una vez creada la Tabla de Contenidos, podemos tratarla como a una porción más de texto, seleccionarla, editarla, modificar su aspecto, etc.

El casillero **Carácter de Relleno** del Cuadro de Diálogo anterior se utiliza para determinar el tipo de carácter que aparecerá entre los Títulos y sus Números de Página, algunas opciones son: Línea punteada, Línea llena, etc.

1.2. ¿Qué pasa cuando en lugar de la Tabla aparece escrito {TDC}?

Cuando insertamos una Tabla de Contenidos, *Word* genera un campo y no una tabla común. Este campo puede aparecer de dos modos distintos: como {TDC}, que quiere decir CAMPO TABLA DE CONTENIDO, o como una Tabla de Contenidos propiamente dicha. En el caso de que aparezca el campo en lugar de la tabla, hay que seleccionarlo y pulsar *SHIFT*+F9. La Tabla de Contenidos reemplazará inmediatamente a la expresión {TDC}.

Recordemos que los campos son elementos que pueden variar su contenido fácilmente. De acuerdo a esta propiedad podríamos compararlos con recipientes que se llenan con diferentes cosas cada vez. El campo TCD se llena con los Títulos de la Presentación y sus Números de Página. Cuando un título o su posición cambia, el contenido de la Tabla puede cambiarse fácilmente pulsando F9. A este procedimiento se lo denomina Actualización y generalmente lo realizamos cuando la Tabla de Contenidos no refleja el verdadero estado del documento, ya sea porque hubo cambios en los títulos o en la ubicación de los mismos. Si cambiamos los títulos o reordenamos las páginas de un documento que ya tiene su Tabla de Contenidos, esos cambios no aparecerán en la Tabla de Contenidos a no ser que nosotros la actualicemos seleccionándola y pulsando F9.

También es necesario actualizar una tabla cuando aparece, en lugar de un número de página determinado, el mensaje "Error: marcador no definido". Esto ocurre cuando existe un desfazaje entre la ubicación de los títulos en la Tabla de Contenidos y su verdadera ubicación en el documento. Para eliminar este tipo de mensajes de error es necesario actualizar la tabla ubicando el cursor dentro de la misma y pulsando F9.

1.3. ¿Qué pasa cuando tenemos un mensaje "Error: marcador no definido" que no se corrige actualizando la Tabla?

En este caso puede que el documento contenga Saltos de Sección o de Página Ocultos, que provoquen que *Word* no pueda determinar la verdadera numeración de las páginas. La solución en este caso es hacer visibles todos los Saltos de Página o de Sección, aún los que puedan estar ocultos. El procedimiento es el siguiente:

Elementos de trabajo II 4

- Pulsar el botón **Mostrar u Ocultar** de la barra **Estándar**.
- Recorrer el documento en Presentación Normal, y cuando un salto que no estaba visible aparece en pantalla seleccionarlo.
- En el menú **Formato** seleccionar **Fuente** y deshabilitar allí el casillero **Texto Oculto**.
- Pulsar **Aceptar**.

Una vez visibles todos los Saltos de Sección y Página actualizamos la Tabla de Contenidos ubicando el cursor en su interior y pulsando el botón F9.

1.4. ¿Podemos modificar el Formato de una Tabla de Contenidos?

Existen dos modos de modificar el aspecto de una Tabla de Contenidos. El primero es seleccionar cada uno de los elementos de la tabla y agregarle colores, bordes, sombreados, cambiar la letra, etc. como lo haríamos con cualquier otro párrafo del escrito. Como dijimos antes, estas modificaciones se perderán si actualizamos la tabla. El otro modo es dar formato directamente al campo {TDC}. Esto se hace mostrando el campo con el atajo de teclado *SHIFT*+F9. Cuando desaparece la tabla y aparece la inscripción {TDC} hay que seleccionarla y modificar la fuente, el color, el tamaño, etc. de la misma. Los cambios de aspecto se aplicarán automáticamente a la Tabla de Contenidos y no se perderán en una actualización.

1.5. ¿Cómo eliminamos una Tabla de Contenidos?

Para eliminar una Tabla de Contenidos hay que seleccionarla y presionar *DEL*(SUPRIMIR).

2. INDICES

Teniendo en cuenta el grado de familiaridad y el origen que tienen, podríamos decir que los Indices son parientes de las Tablas de Contenidos, ya que ambos poseen una lista de los temas del documento y sus respectivas ubicaciones, y ambos se generan automáticamente tomando palabras o frases del documento que están marcadas o que son diferentes al resto. Los Indices, aunque parecidos a las Tablas de Contenidos son esencialmente distintos por lo siguiente:

- Se trata de una lista mucho más extensa que las Tablas de Contenidos que tiene, además de los títulos importantes, otros de menor jerarquía y palabras claves. Las palabras claves permiten que el lector encuentre rápidamente un tema aún cuando el mismo no sea troncal o medianamente importante.
- No están ordenados por orden de aparición sino por orden alfabético.
- En los Indices no importa tanto la jerarquía de los temas sino los nombres en sí. Es decir, no importa tanto que un tema esté dentro de tal o cual otro, sino que aparezca como palabra clave contribuyendo así a la búsqueda rápida.

2.1. ¿Cómo creamos un Indice?

Si las palabras o frases que van a aparecer en el índice fueron marcadas adecuadamente, la confección se realiza de modo similar al de una Tabla de Contenidos, es decir, ubicando el cursor en donde aparecerá el Indice, seleccionando los comandos **Tablas e Indices** y eligiendo un estilo. La ficha **Indice** tiene el aspecto de la **Figura 3**.

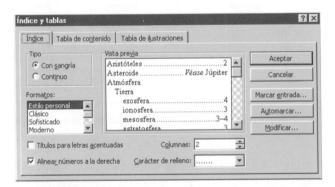

Figura 3. *Ventana desde donde se genera un Indice.*

Para crear automáticamente Indices y Tablas de Contenidos, *Word* necesita diferenciar las palabras del documento que aparecerán en la lista de las que no. En el caso de las Tablas de Contenidos, esta diferenciación existe naturalmente si el usuario dio formato a los Títulos y Subtítulos utilizando Estilos Predeterminados. Esto implica que el trabajo de preparación del documento para generar automáticamente una Tabla de Contenidos es prácticamente nulo.

En los Indices la cosa es diferente ya que, además de los Títulos y Subtítulos, deben aparecer otras palabras que si bien son especiales para el autor de la presentación, para *Word* son iguales al resto. Para distinguir estas "Palabras Claves" de las comunes, hay que aplicarles una marca. La aplicación de la marca se hace manualmente, a medida que escribimos, o bien utilizando un Archivo de Concordancia. Dado que la cantidad de "Palabras Claves" supera ampliamen-

Elementos de trabajo II   4

te la cantidad de Títulos y Subtítulos de un documento, es de esperar que el trabajo de preparación de un documento será mucho mayor para la confección automática de Indices que para la creación de Tablas de Contenidos.

2.2. ¿Cómo marcamos Palabras?

Desde el punto de vista técnico Marcar una palabra significa aplicarle un Campo denominado Entrada de Indice {Eí} o Subentrada de Indice {SI}. Esto significa que luego de la marcación, las palabras elegidas dejarán de ser texto común para convertirse en Campos. Estos campos a su vez tendrán jerarquías, de modo que las Subentradas de Indice estarán incluidas dentro de una Entrada de Indice. Si, por ejemplo, marcamos la palabra ˝Planeta˝ como Entrada de Indice y las palabras "Mercurio" y "Saturno" como Subentradas de Indice, cuando las mismas aparezcan en el Indice se verán de forma similar a la **Figura 4.**

```
Planetas ————————————— 1
            Mercurio ————— 2
            Tierra ————— 3
            Martes ————— 4
            Júpiter ————— 5
```

Figura 4. *Así se ven las entradas de Indice y subíndice.*

Los Campos {Eí} y {SI} tienen formato de Texto Oculto, por lo que sólo podemos distinguir si una palabra o frase está marcada seleccionándola (los campos se resaltan en gris cuando están seleccionados) o bien pulsando el botón **Mostrar u Ocultar..** de la barra **Estándar**, que tiene el aspecto de la **Figura 5.**

Figura 5. *Botón Mostrar/Ocular Códigos.*

Existen dos modos de marcar palabras o frases. Uno es aplicar las Entradas y Subentradas a medida que escribimos el documento. El otro modo es utilizar un Archivo de Concordancia. Los Archivos de Concordancia se recomiendan para incorporar un Indice a una Presentación que ya fue escrita y en la que no se marcaron las palabras Claves. A continuación analizaremos cada caso.

2.3. Marcar Palabras o Frases como Entradas o Subentradas a medida que escribimos.

Para marcar palabras o frases como Entradas o Subentradas procedemos del siguiente modo:

◆ Seleccionamos el texto a marcar.
◆ Presionamos las teclas *ALT*+MAYúS+E.
◆ En el Cuadro de Diálogo que aparece y que se muestra en la **Figura 6** verificamos que el texto seleccionado aparece en el casillero **Entrada**.

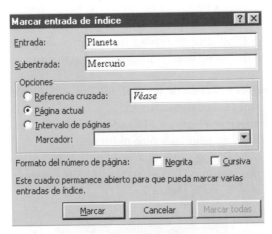

Figura 6. *El primer paso para crear un Indice es la marcación de palabras como Entradas o Subentradas de Indice.*

Para crear una Subentrada escribimos el texto correspondiente en el casillero Subentrada.

Para incluir una entrada de tercer nivel, después del texto de la Subentrada anterior, escribimos dos puntos y a continuación el texto de la entrada de tercer nivel.

Pulsamos el botón **Marcar**, para que sólo se marquen las palabras que acabamos de ingresar, o el botón **Marcar Todas** si queremos marcar todas las ocurrencias similares a lo largo del documento.

Si la Entrada de Indice seleccionada contiene el carácter dos puntos (:), *Word* insertará una barra inversa delante de los dos puntos para no confundir los dos puntos con una Entrada de Tercer Nivel.

Los símbolos del tipo @ no se marcan como una palabra común sino que debemos proceder del siguiente modo:

- Seleccionar el símbolo a marcar.
- Pulsar las teclas ALT+MAYúS+E.
- En el casillero **Entrada**, inmediatamente después del símbolo, escribir; # ¨ (Punto y coma seguido de Numeral).
- Pulsar el botón **Marcar** o **Marcar Todo**.

2.4. ¿Qué pasa si un tema ocupa varias páginas?

Esto quiere decir que en el Indice, ese tema tiene que aparecer vinculado a un rango de páginas y no a una sola hoja. Cuando un tema ocupa varias páginas, no podemos proceder como antes. No podemos seleccionar el título del tema y marcarlo, ya que *Word* le asignará el número de página en el que se encuentra la palabra marcada y no un rango de páginas. El modo de marcar un tema que ocupa varias páginas es el siguiente:

- Seleccionamos el intervalo de texto al que queremos hacer referencia en el Indice, por ejemplo las páginas 13 a 25.
- En el menú **Insertar** elegimos **Marcador**. *Word* insertará un Marcador al comienzo del rango de páginas y otro al final.
- En el Cuadro de Diálogo que aparece escribimos un nombre para estos dos marcadores, por ejemplo ¨Ribosomas¨ y pulsamos **Agregar**. A continuación se muestra como se ve en la **Figura 7**.

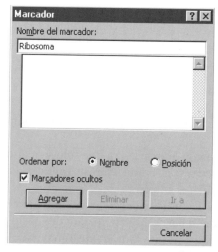

Figura 7. *Marcadores que se utilizan para delimitar rangos de página.*

- Ubicamos el cursor al final del segundo Marcador. En el ejemplo anterior lo ubicaríamos al final de la página 25, y presionamos las teclas *ALT*+MAYúS+E.
- En el Cuadro de Diálogo de la **Figura 8**, escribimos el nombre que aparecerá en el Indice vinculado a ese rango de páginas. Escribimos, por ejemplo, "La Célula".

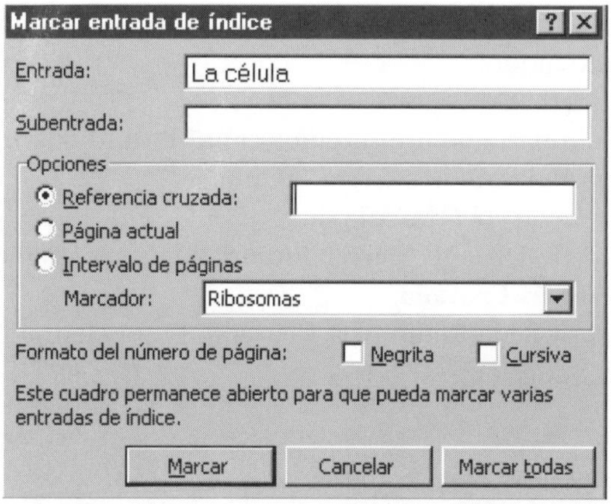

***Figura 8.** Aquí escribimos la Entrada de Indice relacionada con ese marcador.*

- En el casillero **Marcador** seleccionamos el nombre del Marcador insertado en los pasos anteriores y pulsamos **Marcar**.

Si hicimos todo bien, cuando *Word* confeccione el índice, escribirá "La Célula" y para asignarle el número de página se guiará por los marcadores asociados a esa palabra. El resultado será algo parecido a lo que muestra la **Figura 9.**

La Célula
    Ribosomas 13-25
    Lisosomas 16
    Centríolos 20

***Figura 9** . Así se verá en el Indice una referencia a un rango de páginas.*

2.5. ¿Qué son las Referencias Cruzadas y cómo se crean?

Las referencias cruzadas son aquellos temas del Indice que nos mandan a otros temas. Un ejemplo de esto es el caso que se muestra en la **Figura 10.**

Figura 10. *Esto es lo que denominamos Referencia Cruzada.*

Para que nuestro Indice contenga Referencias Cruzadas hay que proceder del siguiente modo:

♦ Seleccionar el texto que utilizaremos como Entrada de Indice, en el ejemplo anterior seleccionamos la palabra ¨Fémur¨.
♦ Presionar las teclas *ALT*+MAYúS+E.
♦ En el Cuadro de Diálogo **Marcar Entradas** que mostramos antes, habilitar la opción **Referencia Cruzada**.
♦ Escribir el texto de la Referencia Cruzada. En el ejemplo anterior escribimos ¨Extremidad Superior¨.
♦ Pulsar **Marcar**.

2.6. Marcar texto utilizando Archivos de Concordancia

Un archivo de Concordancia es un documento que creamos para automatizar el marcado de Entradas y Subentradas de Indice. Este documento consiste en una tabla de dos columnas: la primera columna tiene las palabras a marcar y la segunda los nombres con que aparecerán en el Indice. Supongamos que las ¨Palabras Claves¨ Húmero, Radio y Cúbito van a aparecer en el Indice como ¨Extremidad Superior¨; en este caso la tabla del Archivo de Concordancia tendrá entre otras las filas que muestra la **Figura 11.**

Humero	Extremidad Superior
Cúbito	Extremidad Superior
Radio	Extremidad Superior

Figura 11. *Tabla contenida en un Archivo de Concordancia.*

Word trabaja con el Archivo de Concordancia del siguiente modo:

♦ Lee la primera columna del Archivo de Concordancia.
♦ Busca en todo el documento las ocurrencias iguales y las marca como Entrada de Indice o Subentrada, dándoles el nombre de la segunda columna.
♦ Procede así hasta marcar todas las palabras del documento que coincidan con aquellas que figuran en la primera columna de la Tabla del Archivo de Concordancia.

Una vez marcadas todas las Entradas y Subentradas de Indice podemos generar el Indice de forma similar a como lo hicimos antes.

Para crear un Archivo de Concordancia hay que pedir una hoja en blanco e insertar una Tabla de dos columnas. En la primera columna ingresamos las palabras claves que *Word* va a buscar en el documento. Esto puede hacerse de dos modos distintos:

♦ Recordando palabras claves que figuren en la Presentación e ingresándolas una por una.
♦ Abriendo la presentación simultáneamente con el Archivo de Concordancia y copiando palabras claves de la Presentación a la primera columna del Archivo de Concordancia.

Es importante destacar que para asegurarnos de marcar todo el texto que queremos incluir en el índice, hay que escribir todas las formas posibles del texto. Podemos escribir, por ejemplo, jinete, cabalgar y cabalgata en tres celdas separadas de la columna izquierda y, a continuación, escribir Equitación en las celdas de la columna derecha. El lector que busque material relacionado con Equitación derivará en las páginas correspondientes a cabalgar, cabalgata y jinete.

A continuación, una serie de instrucciones para crear un Archivo de Concordancia:

♦ En el menú **Archivo** elegir **Nuevo**.
♦ Seleccionar la plantilla **Documento en Blanco**.
♦ Dibujar una tabla de dos columnas.
♦ En la primera columna, escribir el texto que queremos que *Word* busque y marque como Entrada de Indice. Es importante ingresar el texto exactamente como aparece en la Presentación, respetando mayúsculas y minúsculas.
♦ Presionar la tecla TAB.
♦ En la segunda columna, escribir el nombre que aparecerá en el Indice. En el ejemplo anterior escribiríamos ¨Equitación¨.
♦ Proceder así hasta llenar toda la tabla.
♦ Para crear una Subentrada escribir la entrada principal seguida por dos puntos y, a continuación, la Subentrada.
♦ Guardar el Archivo de Concordancia bajo un nombre apropiado.

Para crear un Indice utilizando el Archivo de Concordancia anterior procedemos del siguiente modo:

♦ Verificamos que el documento que llevará el índice esté abierto y activo.

Elementos de trabajo II

4

♦ En el Cuadro de Diálogo de la **Figura 12** pulsamos el botón **Automarcar** y luego abrimos el Archivo de Concordancia.

Figura 12. *Una vez creado el Archivo de Concordancia utilizamos esta ventana para iniciar la marcación.*

Word hará lo siguiente:

♦ Buscará en el documento las ocurrencias exactas a las de la primera columna del Archivo de Concordancia y las marcará.
♦ A continuación utilizará el texto de la segunda columna como Entrada de Indice para crear la lista de palabras correspondientes. En la Barra de Estado aparecerá un mensaje con la cantidad de palabras marcadas.

Una vez marcadas las Entradas de Indice el procedimiento es así:

♦ Ubicamos el cursor en donde aparecerá el Indice.
♦ En el menú **Insertar** seleccionamos Indice y Tablas.
♦ En el Cuadro de Diálogo **Indices y Tablas** que mostramos antes, seleccionamos un formato adecuado para el Indice, por ejemplo Clásico y pulsamos **Aceptar**.

La lista aparecerá en la posición del cursor y contendrá todas las palabras de la segunda columna de la tabla del archivo de Concordancia. Los números de páginas serán determinados por la ubicación de las palabras marcadas en el documento.

2.7. ¿Cómo actualizamos un Indice?

Cuando agregamos o modificamos la Presentación que contiene el Indice, es necesario actualizar tanto la Tabla de Contenidos como el Indice, a fin de incluir los nuevos elementos y sus correspondientes números de página. Recordemos que al actualizar un Indice se pierden los formatos agregados manualmente. La actualización se lleva a cabo ubicando el cursor dentro del Indice y pulsando F9.

Para aplicar un formato que no se pierda con las sucesivas actualizaciones debemos hacerlo sobre los campos de Entrada y Subentrada. Es decir, si damos formato al texto mientras el mismo se encuentra en el casillero **Entrada o Subentrada** ese formato se mostrará en el índice.

2.8. ¿Cómo eliminamos un Indice?

Para eliminar un Indice lo seleccionamos y presionamos *DEL*(SUPRIMIR).

3. MACROS

Una Macro es un grupo de instrucciones que se ejecutan pulsando un solo botón o presionando una combinación de teclas. Las Macros generalmente se utilizan para automatizar tareas rutinarias, que de hacerse manualmente llevarían mucho tiempo.

Si habitualmente realizamos tareas en las que se repite un grupo de acciones, en lugar de perder el tiempo haciendo siempre lo mismo, creamos una Macro con todas esas acciones juntas, una detrás de la otra, y la guardamos en la plantilla en la que trabajamos habitualmente (por ejemplo, en la plantilla ¨Normal. dot¨). Una vez creada la Macro, ésta podrá ser ejecutada una y otra vez cuando lo necesitemos, con sólo pulsar un botón o presionando una combinación de teclas elegida por nosotros. Cuando una Macro se ejecuta, *Word* se apodera de la computadora y realiza, paso a paso, la lista de instrucciones que tiene escritas en la Macro. El usuario actúa como un espectador, mira lo que hace *Word*, o aprovecha el tiempo para realizar otras tareas. Por ejemplo, podemos crear una Macro para iniciar una carta que habitualmente enviamos al mismo destino. La Macro ejecutará automáticamente el siguiente grupo instrucciones:

- Creará un documento nuevo utilizando la plantilla Carta Elegante.
- Insertará automáticamente la fecha del día.
- Ingresará los datos de Destinatario y Remitente.
- Creará un sobre con los datos anteriores y lo adicionará al documento
- Llevará el cursor al comienzo para que el usuario empiece a escribir.

3.1. ¿Cuál es la relación entre Macros y Plantillas?

Las Macros se almacenan en Plantillas. De forma predeterminada, *Word* guarda las Macros en la plantilla ¨Normal. *Dot*¨ para que estén disponibles en todos los documentos creados a partir de una hoja en blanco. Las Macros también pueden guardarse en un documento y no en una plantilla. En este caso sólo estarán disponibles para ese documento, sin embargo, lo más lógico es guardarlas en plantillas, porque si bien una Macro puede almacenarse en un documento, ¿para qué tomarse el trabajo de crear una Macro que sólo sirva para un sólo documento?.

Cuando generamos un documento a partir de una Plantilla que incluye una Macro, el botón de la Macro aparece en las barras de Herramientas que le designó el usuario al momento de crear la Macro, y queda disponible para que el usuario lo use cuando quiera. Pulsando este botón ejecutamos el paquete de instrucciones contenidas allí y que generalmente está vinculado al tipo de trabajo que habitualmente realizamos.

Si una Macro guardada en la plantilla ¨Normal. *Dot*¨ sólo es útil para determinados tipos de documentos, por ejemplo para faxes, podemos pasarla de la plantilla ¨Normal. *Dot*¨ a alguna de las plantillas para faxes. Más adelante veremos cómo copiar, eliminar o cambiar el nombre de una Macro utilizando el **Organizador**.

3.2. ¿Cómo creamos una Macro?

Word incluye tres métodos para crear macros, que son los siguientes:

- ◆ Utilizar la Grabadora de Macros.
- ◆ Trabajar con el Editor de *Visual Basic* para Aplicaciones.
- ◆ Utilizar una combinación de ambos.

3.2.1. Crear una Macro utilizando la Grabadora de Macros

Este método consiste en lo siguiente: el usuario asigna un botón o combinación de teclas para la Macro que va a grabar, pulsa en la Grabadora de Macro el botón *REC* y ejecuta una detrás de otra las acciones para que queden registradas en la Macro. Desde el momento en que pulsa *REC* procede como si estuviese trabajando en cualquier documento *Word*. Por ejemplo, en el menú **Archivo**, selecciona **Nuevo** y elige la plantilla **Carta Elegante,** en el menú **Insertar**, elige **Fecha y Hora,** escribe, subraya, etc.

Word graba las acciones que el usuario realiza y cuando éste detiene la grabación, traduce automáticamente todo lo grabado al lenguaje de programación *Visual Basic* para Aplicaciones, que es el que usan las Macros.

Una vez completada la tarea, y si todo salió bien, aparece en alguna de las barras de Herramientas (la que el usuario eligió), el botón de la Macro que queda disponible para servir de nexo entre la Macro recién creada y el usuario.

Crear Macros grabándolas tiene la ventaja de que el usuario no necesita saber programar, ni tampoco necesita conocer el lenguaje de programación para Macros. Lo único que hace es trabajar en *Word* mientras está activada la grabación: selecciona comandos, pulsa botones, escribe y realiza tareas de rutina. Un traductor interno pasará estas instrucciones al lenguaje *Visual Basic* para Aplicaciones, dándole así el formato adecuado para ser interpretada por *Word* cuando se la ejecute.

3.2.2. Editar Macros en el Editor de Visual Basic para Aplicaciones.

Este método es más complejo dado que consiste en ingresar manualmente las instrucciones en el lenguaje *Visual Basic* para Aplicaciones. Es un método que requiere conocimientos de programación y de lenguaje, y que generalmente se usa para crear Macros más flexibles y complejas como por ejemplo, asistentes que muestren ventanas para el ingreso de datos, etc.

En este capítulo no analizaremos cómo utilizar el Editor de *Visual Basic* para Aplicaciones. Para obtener información acerca del mismo conviene consultar las "Referencias de *Visual Basic* para *Microsoft Word*" que se encuentran en la ficha **Contenido** del menú **Ayuda de Word**. Para que esta ficha figure en la ayuda es necesario activar la casilla de verificación **Ayuda en pantalla para Visual Basic** durante la instalación de *Word*. Si no se hizo durante la instalación, podemos volver a ejecutar el programa instalador e instalarla como cualquier otro componente (ver apéndice al final del manual). La **Figura 13** muestra cómo se ve una Macro en el Editor de *Visual Basic* para Aplicaciones.

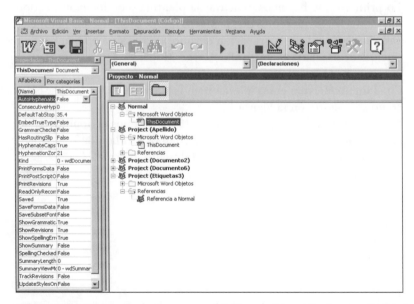

Figura 13. *Así se ve una macro en el Editor de Visual Basic para Aplicaciones*

3.2.3. Crear Macros utilizando una combinación de los dos métodos anteriores.

Las macros grabadas pueden abrirse y modificarse en el Editor. La idea es agregarle instrucciones que no pueden grabarse.

3.3. ¿Cómo grabamos una Macro?

Antes de grabar una Macro es necesario tener en cuenta los siguientes consejos:

♦ Planificar los pasos y comandos a ejecutar dado que si cometemos un error en el momento de la grabación, las correcciones también se grabarán.
♦ Anticiparnos a cualquier mensaje que *Word* pueda mostrar como consecuencia de las instrucciones elegidas. Un ejemplo de esto es el siguiente: si entre las instrucciones hay una que cierra el documento, prever que *Word* nos preguntará si queremos guardarlo o no, y no seguirá adelante hasta que no le demos una respuesta. En este caso, para evitar que la Macro se detenga esperando un ingreso, conviene anticiparse al hecho grabando la instrucción **Guardar** antes de **Cerrar**.
♦ Verificar que la Macro no quede asociada al contenido del documento actual sino que se guarde en la plantilla ¨Normal.*Dot*¨.

Grabar una Macro es más simple de lo que en general se cree. A continuación describimos los pasos a seguir:
♦ Lo primero que hacemos es activar la plantilla o el documento adonde guardar la Macro. Si queremos que la Macro quede asociada a la plantilla ¨Normal.*Dot*¨, antes de iniciar la grabación abrimos una página en blanco. Si queremos que quede asociada a la plantilla ¨Cartas Moderna.*Dot*¨ creamos un nuevo documento pero basado en dicha plantilla.
♦ En el menú **Herramientas** seleccionamos **Macros** y luego **Grabar Nueva Macro** como se muestra en la **Figura 14.**
♦ En el Cuadro de Diálogo de la **Figura 15** ingresamos el nombre de la Macro, y en el casillero **Guardar Macro** seleccionamos la Plantilla o el Documento al que quedará asociada la Macro, generalmente ¨Normal.*Dot*¨.

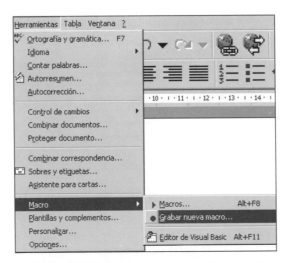

Figura 14. *Primer paso para grabar una Macro.*

♦ En el Cuadro de Diálogo de la **Figura 15** pulsamos el botón **Barras** para asignarle un botón a la Macro.

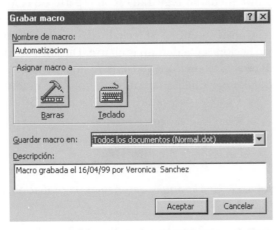

Figura 15. *Utilizamos esta ventana para designarle un botón a la Macro.*

♦ Se abrirá la ventana de la **Figura 16** mostrándonos, a la derecha, el botón que *Word* designó para la Macro. Para ubicar ese botón en alguna de las Barras de Herramientas hay que arrastrarlo con el *Mouse* hasta allí. Si la barra no está visible la mostramos antes de arrastrar el botón. También podemos crear una Barra especial que contenga sólo los botones de nuestras Macros. Esto se hace pulsando el botón **Nuevo** de la ficha **Barra de Herramientas,** que se encuentra en este mismo Cuadro de Diálogo.

Elementos de trabajo II

4

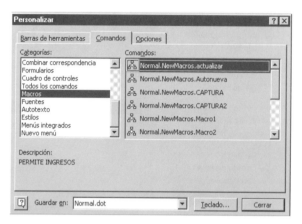

Figura 16 . Desde esta ventana arrastramos el botón de la Macro hasta la Barra de Herramientas elegida.

♦ Una vez asignado el botón, y cuando cerramos la ventana anterior, el puntero toma forma de cassette y aparece en la Barra de Estado la abreviatura "GRB", indicándonos que iniciamos la grabación. Todas las acciones realizadas a partir de ese momento quedarán registradas como parte de la Macro. Podemos, por ejemplo, pasar a Presentación Preliminar, modificar márgenes, escribir un encabezado, etc. Conviene utilizar el teclado, dado que si trabajamos con el *Mouse* algunas instrucciones pueden no grabarse. Durante la grabación aparecerán los botones **Pausa** y **Detener** que permiten parar temporalmente la grabación, reanudarla o darla por finalizada. Ambos botones se muestran en la **Figura 17.**

Figura 17. Un clic aquí y detenemos la grabación de la Macro.

3.4. ¿Cómo ejecutamos una Macro?

Las Macros se ejecutan desde el Botón o desde el Atajo de teclado asignado a tal fin al momento de grabarla. Si al grabarla no definimos ninguno de estos dos elementos, la ejecución se realiza eligiendo **Macro** en el menú **Herramientas** y haciendo doble clic sobre ella. Si, por ejemplo, grabamos una macro que inserte una tabla con determinadas características y le asignamos un botón, la próxima vez que necesitemos crear este tipo de tablas, pulsamos el botón de la Macro e inmediatamente aparece la tabla en pantalla.

Para modificar el aspecto del botón asignado a una Macro procedemos del siguiente modo:

◆ Mostramos la barra de Herramientas que contiene el botón a modificar, y con el puntero arriba de la barra, pulsamos el botón derecho del *Mouse* y seleccionamos la opción **Personalizar**.

◆ Aparece un Cuadro de Diálogo como el que se muestra en la **Figura 18.** Con el Cuadro de Diálogo abierto, ubicamos el puntero sobre el botón a modificar y hacemos un clic con el botón derecho del *Mouse*. Esto quiere decir que para poder modificar el botón necesitamos tener abierta la ventana **Personalizar** aún cuando no hagamos nada allí.

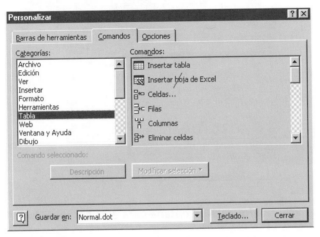

Figura 18. *Esta ventana tiene que estar abierta para modificar el botón de la Macro.*

◆ En el Menú Contextual que aparece y que se muestra en la **Figura 19,** elegimos **Cambiar Imagen del Botón** y seleccionamos la nueva imagen.

Figura 19. *Menú contextual que permite cambiar la imagen de un botón.*

155

3.5. ¿Cómo eliminamos una Macro?

Una Macro se elimina desde la ventana **Macro** que se muestra en la **Figura 20,** y que se encuentra en el menú **Herramientas.**

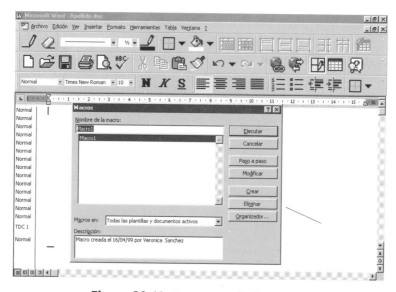

Figura 20. *Ventana para eliminar una Macro.*

En el casillero **Nombre de la Macro** hay que seleccionarla y pulsar el botón **Eliminar.** Si no aparece en la lista, buscamos otra lista de macros en el casillero **Macros en.**

3.6. ¿Qué son las Macros Predeterminadas por Word?

Son Macros que vienen con el *Office,* y que son suministradas por *Microsoft* para automatizar una serie de tareas, como por ejemplo las siguientes:

MACRO SUMINISTRADA POR WORD	FUNCION
Valor Ansi	Muestra el valor ANSI de cualquier carácter seleccionado.
Utilidad Autocorrección	Crea una copia de seguridad denominada "AutoCorrect Backup.doc" de los elementos de Autocorrección del documento activo. Este documento de seguridad puede utilizarse para copiar todos los elementos de Autocorrección en otro equipo.

MACRO SUMINISTRADA POR WORD	FUNCION
Copiar Especial	Funciona como el comando Especial, en el que se almacenan a la vez varios elementos en el Portapapeles, a excepción de que Copiar Especial copia en Especial en vez de cortar.
Buscar Símbolo	Agrega funcionalidad a los comandos Buscar y Reemplazar para facilitar la búsqueda de caracteres de símbolo en un documento.
Insertar Nota al Pie	Muestra un asistente que facilita la creación de notas al pie mediante la utilización de las instrucciones de la Modern Language Association (MLA) o The Chicago Manual of Style para varios tipos de publicaciones.
Vista Normal Encabezado Pie	Presenta los paneles del encabezado y pie de página en la vista Normal. En documentos grandes, es una forma más rápida de ver los encabezados y los pies de página.
Estadísticas Super Doc	Proporciona información acerca del formato utilizado en cada uno de los documentos y secciones, tal como fuentes, estilos, secciones, hipervínculos y marcadores.
Ayuda Celda Tabla	Muestra la columna y la fila de la celda de la tabla en la barra de estado, por ejemplo, F17. Resulta de gran utilidad para crear fórmulas complejas en las tablas.

Las Macros Predeterminadas no están presentes en el sistema si realizamos la instalación típica de *Word*, por lo general tenemos que agregarlas como un componente más (ver apéndice al final del manual).

Las Macros suministradas por *Word* son útiles para el trabajo diario o como base para crear nuestras propias Macros. Están contenidas en las plantillas ˝Macros8. *dot*˝ y ˝*Support8. dot*˝ pero podemos copiarlas a la plantilla ˝Normal. *dot*˝.

Si al abrir cualquiera de estas dos plantillas aparece el cuadro de diálogo **Advertencia**, debemos pulsar el botón **Abrir con Macros**.

3.7. ¿Cómo accedemos a las Macros Predeterminadas?

Para utilizar cualquiera de las Macros suministradas por *Word* tenemos que corroborar que estén instaladas en la carpeta **Macros** del *Office*. De no ser así habrá que correr el programa instalador e instalar el componente ¨Plantillas y Complementos¨. Una vez instaladas las plantillas con sus respectivas Macros podemos ejecutarlas procediendo del siguiente modo:

◆ Ingresamos a *Word*.
◆ En el menú **Archivo** elegimos **Abrir**.
◆ Seleccionamos la carpeta *Microsoft Office\Office\Macros*.
◆ En el casillero **Tipo de archivo** seleccionamos la opción **Todos los archivos**.
◆ Seleccionamos el nombre de la plantilla, por ejemplo ¨*Support8. dot*¨ y pulsamos el botón **Abrir**.

Si luego de ver funcionar las Macros, decidimos que son útiles para nuestro trabajo, podemos copiarlas a la Plantilla ¨Normal. *dot*¨ para que queden disponibles para cualquier documento que se cree a partir de una hoja en blanco. Este procedimiento se lleva a cabo desde el **Organizador**, como se explica a continuación

3.8. Copiar Macros entre plantillas

Para copiar Macros entre plantillas se usa el **Organizador** del menú **Herramientas**. Para ejemplificar este procedimiento copiaremos las Macros Predeterminadas por *Word* y que existen en las plantillas *Support8.dot* y Macros8.*dot* a la plantilla Normal. *dot*. Si todo sale bien, cuando terminemos de hacerlo, podremos utilizar todas estas macros para trabajar con cualquier documento nuevo basado en una hoja en blanco. El procedimiento es el siguiente:

◆ En el menú **Herramientas** seleccionar **Macros**.
◆ Pulsar el botón **Organizador**.
◆ En el Cuadro de Diálogo que se muestra en la **Figura 21** seleccionar la ficha **Elementos del Proyecto Macro**.

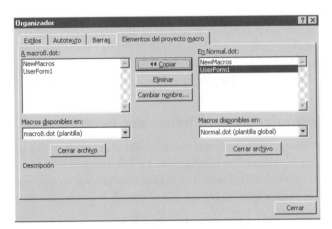

Figura 21. *Ventana para copiar, renombrar y eliminar Macros.*

Si la plantilla de la que queremos copiar no está visible pulsamos el botón **Cerrar Archivo** y luego abrimos la plantilla que tiene las macros que vamos a copiar. En el ejemplo anterior abrimos la plantilla Macro8. *dot* y en la otra mitad de la ventana abrimos la plantilla de destino.

Seleccionamos, de la lista de origen, las Macros a copiar y pulsamos el botón **Copiar**.

El Cuadro de Diálogo Organizador también nos permite renombrar una Macro.

4. FORMULARIOS

Existen dos tipos de formularios en *Word*:

♦ Formularios Impresos.
♦ Formularios que se completan por pantalla.

4.1. Formularios Impresos

Los Formularios Impresos son los que estamos acostumbrados a llenar cuando realizamos trámites rutinarios, encuestas, solicitudes de servicios, etc. El usuario los completa escribiendo y siguiendo una serie de consignas que aparecen como instrucciones y que le indican dónde marcar, tachar, hacer círculos, ingresar Verdadero o Falso, etc.

Elementos de trabajo II

4

En *Word*, un Formulario Impreso se crea como cualquier documento, pero tiene un diseño especial con tablas, casilleros para llenar, recuadros, elementos alineados, instrucciones, etc. que lo diferencian de otros documentos. En general, además de los elementos típicos aparecen dibujos, imágenes, colores, flechas, etc. que los hacen más atractivos a la lectura y al llenado.

4.2. Formularios para llenar por Pantalla

Los Formularios para llenar por Pantalla se completan desde la computadora. El usuario puede leer las instrucciones o escucharlas desde un objeto de sonido. De forma similar a los Formularios Impresos el usuario tiene que llenar Campos de Texto, tildar casilleros, elegir elementos de una lista desplegable, etc.

Los Formularios para llenar por Pantalla tienen las siguientes características:

♦ Pueden distribuirse y recogerse por Correo Electrónico u otro tipo de red. Por ejemplo, pueden utilizarse para encuestas a través de Internet. O, como en el caso de las páginas *Web* de las Universidades Americanas, para que el usuario solicite información.

♦ Están protegidos de modo que pueda modificarse sólo los campos, casilleros, etc. y no el formulario en sí.

♦ Se guardan y distribuyen como plantillas para usarse una y otra vez.

Algunas de las ventajas de los formularios que se llenan por pantalla son las siguientes:

♦ Podemos hacer que *Word* verifique automáticamente la entrada del usuario, rechazando formatos equivocados, como por ejemplo números de más o menos dígitos, texto en lugar de números, etc.

♦ Podemos asociar dos campos de modo que el segundo se actualice automáticamente con el primero. Un ejemplo de esto sería el caso de asociar ciudad y código postal.

♦ Los campos pueden mostrar mensajes de ayuda para que resulte más fácil rellenarlos.

♦ Al guardarlos como plantillas podemos utilizarlos varias veces.

4.3. ¿Cómo creamos un Formulario para ser llenado por Pantalla?

Podemos crearlo desde cero o utilizar un formulario existente como guía. En la carpeta Plantillas, que se encuentra dentro de la carpeta *Microsoft Office* o en la carpeta de *Word*, hay una serie de formularios comerciales disponibles. Si estas plantillas no aparecen habrá que instalar el componente **Plantillas y Complementos**.

Los siguientes elementos pueden aparecer en un formulario:

◆ **Texto que el usuario no puede modificar**: son las preguntas, comentarios, listas de opciones, tablas de información, instrucciones, etc. que guían el llenado.
◆ **Campos de Formulario**: son los lugares en donde se vuelcan los datos solicitados
◆ **Bordes, Colores, Sombreados**: delimitan zonas, organizan y clasifican de modo que sea más simple el llenado.
◆ **Objetos y otros elementos especiales**: tienen función estética, le dan al formulario un aspecto colorido, llamativo, agradable a la vista, que hace que el usuario se sienta atraído a leerlo y completarlo.

4.3.1. Campos de Formulario

En los formularios que se rellenan por pantalla podemos utilizar cualquiera de los siguientes Campos de Formulario:

◆ **Campos con Texto**: se rellenan sólo con texto.
◆ **Casillas de Verificación**: se pueden activar y desactivar. Es decir, tildarse o no.
◆ **Listas Desplegables**: muestran una lista para seleccionar una sola opción.

A continuación analizaremos cómo crear un Formulario de llenado por pantalla y trabajaremos con cada uno de estos Campos de Formulario.

4.3.2. Crear un Formulario desde cero

Para crear un formulario desde cero hay que:

◆ En **Archivo** elegir **Nuevo**.
◆ En la ficha **General** seleccionar **Documento en blanco** y habilitar la opción **Plantilla** que se encuentra abajo a la derecha, como se muestra en la **Figura 22**.

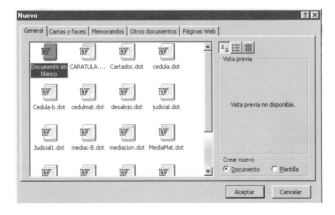

Figura 22. *Primer paso para crear un formulario.*

♦ Diseñar la tabla del formulario, delimitando con bordes gruesos el contorno externo y con bordes más finos la cuadrícula interna, agregar colores iguales a las celdas relacionadas entre sí, diferenciar entre una zona y otra del formulario cambiando el aspecto del fondo de la tabla, etc. Las celdas que piden datos familiares por ejemplo, pueden tener un color, mientras que las que piden datos laborales otro, etc.

♦ Escribir las preguntas a responder, los datos que se solicitan, las instrucciones y todo otro tipo de texto que el usuario debe leer como guía para llenar el formulario. En donde el usuario tiene que escribir la dirección podemos escribir ¨ Escriba aquí su dirección ¨ y al lado, con letra más pequeña (llenar sólo sí solicita respuesta por escrito).

♦ Ingresar y configurar los **Campos de Formularios,** que son los lugares donde el usuario volcará sus datos. El modo de hacer esto se explica en detalles más adelante.

♦ Ingresar otros elementos complementarios como Objetos, Marca de Agua, Sonido, etc.

♦ Proteger el formulario para que sólo puedan modificarse los Campos del Formulario. Esto se hace haciendo un clic en el botón **Proteger Formulario**, de la barra de herramientas **Formularios** (ver más adelante). Guardar la plantilla y salir.

4.4. ¿Cómo insertamos y configuramos Campos de Formulario?

A continuación se explica cómo crear y configurar cada Campos de Formulario. Antes, es importante tener en cuenta lo siguiente:

♦ En todos los campos podemos incluir un mensaje de ayuda para guiar al usuario, que puede aparecer en la barra de Estado o pulsando la tecla F1. Este tipo de mensajes se ingresan durante la configuración del campo, pulsando el botón **Agregar Ayuda**.

♦ Una vez terminada la configuración de todos los campos es necesario protegerlos pulsando el botón **Proteger** de la barra **Formulario**. Si no lo hacemos, el usuario no podrá llenarlos, lo que generará una gran confusión ya que donde supuestamente debería escribir no puede hacerlo. Es importante no proteger los campos durante el diseño porque no podremos variar su aspecto, su tamaño, etc.

♦ Para establecer el tipo de fuente, los colores, los bordes, etc. del texto que aparecerá en los Campos de Formulario cuando el usuario realice los ingresos, hay que dar formato directamente al Campo de Formulario utilizando las herramientas de la barra **Formato**.

4.4.1. Insertar y Configurar un Campo con Texto

Para insertar un Campo con Texto hay que proceder del siguiente modo:

♦ Ubicar el cursor en donde aparecerá el Campo con Texto.
♦ Verificar que el botón **Sombreado de Campo** de la barra **Formulario** que se muestra en la **Figura 25** esté pulsado para que podamos distinguir el campo del resto del texto.

Figura 23. *Botón sombreado de Campo.*

♦ Pulsar el botón **Campo con Texto**, de la barra **Formulario**, que tiene el aspecto que se muestra en la **Figura 24**.

Figura 24. *Este botón se usa para ingresar un Campo de Texto.*

♦ Observar que aparece una zona gris como la que se muestra en la **Figura 25.**

Figura 25. *Zona gris que identifica a los Campos de Texto.*

Para Configurar el Campo con Texto tenemos que:

♦ Verificar que el botón **Proteger** (botón con forma de candado) de la barra **Formulario** no esté pulsado, de lo contrario, no podremos configurarlo.
♦ Pulsar el botón derecho del *Mouse* sobre el campo y seleccionar la opción **Propiedades**.

En el Cuadro de Diálogo de la **Figura 26,** en el casillero **Texto Predeterminado,** escribimos el nombre o las indicaciones para el campo, en el ejemplo anterior escribimos¨ Escriba aquí su Apellido ¨.

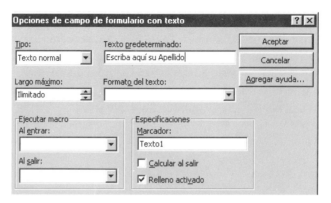

Figura 26. Ventana que se usa para configurar un Campo de Texto.

♦ En el casillero **Tipo** seleccionar el formato del texto de ese campo, por ejemplo **Formato Fecha**, **Formato Texto común**, etc.
♦ En el casillero **Largo Máximo** ingresar la longitud límite que podrá tener el texto a ingresar, por ejemplo diez caracteres.
♦ Pulsar **Aceptar**.

4.4.2. Insertar y Configurar un Campo con Casilla de Verificación
Para insertar y configurar un Campo con Casilla de Verificación hay que:

♦ Ubicar el cursor en donde aparecerá el campo.
♦ Pulsar el botón **Campo con Casilla de Verificación** de la barra **Formulario** que se muestra en la **Figura 27**.

Figura 27. Un clic en este botón y aparece un Campo de Verificación.

♦ Verificar que aparece la Casilla de Verificación que tiene el aspecto de la **Figura 28**.

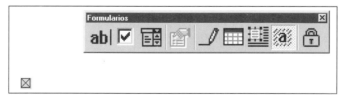

Figura 28. Un ejemplo de Casilla de Verificación.

♦ Verificar que el botón **Proteger**, de la barra **Formulario**, esté desactivado, hacer un clic con el botón derecho del *Mouse* arriba del campo y seleccionar la opción **Propiedades**.

♦ En Cuadro de Diálogo de la **Figura 29**, en el recuadro **Tamaño de Casilla,** ingresar un tamaño adecuado, y en el recuadro **Valor Predeterminado** determinar si la casilla aparecerá tildada o no. Salir aceptando.

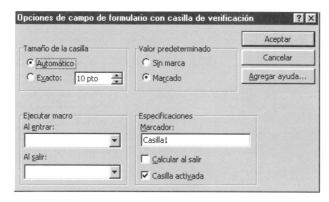

Figura 29. *Ventana que se usa para configurar los Campos Casilla de Verificación.*

4.4.3. Insertar y Configurar un Campo con Lista Desplegable

Para insertar y configurar un Campo con Lista Desplegable hay que:

♦ Ubicar el cursor en donde aparecerá la **Lista Desplegable**.

♦ Pulsar el botón **Campo con Lista Desplegable** de la barra **Formulario**, que se muestra en la **Figura 30**.

Figura 30. *Un clic aquí y aparece Campo con Lista Desplegable.*

♦ Verificar que aparece la **Lista Desplegable** que tiene el aspecto de la **Figura 31**.

Figura 31. *Un ejemplo de Lista Desplegable.*

♦ Corroborar que el botón **Proteger** no esté pulsado, hacer un clic con el botón derecho del *Mouse* arriba del campo y seleccionar la opción **Propiedades**.

♦ En el Cuadro de Diálogo de la **Figura 32**, en el recuadro **Tamaño de Casilla** ingresar un tamaño adecuado y luego ingresar los elementos de la lista. Utilizar los botones **Quitar** y **Mover,** para eliminar o cambiar los elementos de lugar. Salir aceptando.

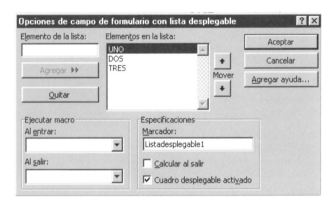

Figura 32.

♦ *Ventana desde donde configuramos las Listas Desplegables.*

4.5. ¿Qué significa automatizar un Formulario de llenado por pantalla?

Automatizar un Formulario significa asignarle una Macro a alguno de los campos del Formulario. Dicha Macro podrá ejecutarse cuando el usuario entre o salga del Campo al que está asignada. Un ejemplo de esto es el siguiente: si un usuario activa la Casilla de Verificación ¨Casado¨, la Macro de salida asignada a ese campo podría llevar el cursor automáticamente al Campo **Nombre del Cónyuge** estableciendo diferentes secuencias dependiendo de los datos ingresados.

Para asignar una Macro a un Campo de Formulario procedemos así:

♦ Abrimos la plantilla que contiene el formulario al que le asignaremos la Macro.

♦ Quitamos la protección desactivando el botón **Proteger Formulario** de la barra de herramientas **Formularios**.

♦ Creamos la Macro como se explicó en este capítulo y la guardamos vinculada a la plantilla de los formularios.

♦ Pulsamos dos veces el **Campo de Formulario** al que queremos asignarle la Macro. Si queremos que se ejecute cuando el punto de inserción entra al campo, seleccionamos **Al entrar**, del Cuadro **Propiedades** que se muestra en la **Figura 33**. De lo contrario elegimos la opción **Al Salir**.

Figura 33. *Ventana que se usa para asignarle una Macro a un Campo de Formulario.*

4.6. ¿Cómo imprimimos sólo los datos de un formulario?

Esto se hace cuando cargamos el formulario vacío en la impresora y sólo queremos imprimir los datos de los campos. Para imprimir sólo los datos de un formulario procedemos así:

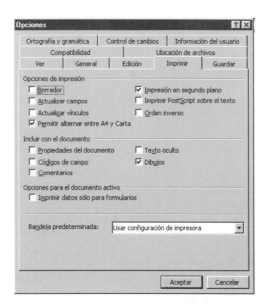

Figura 34. *Así se imprimen sólo los datos del formulario.*

167

♦ En el menú **Herramientas** elegimos **Opciones**.

♦ En el Cuadro de Diálogo de la **Figura 34**, en la ficha Imprimir activamos el casillero Imprimir sólo datos del formulario y pulsamos el botón Imprimir.

♦ *Word* imprimirá sólo los datos incluidos y no todo el formulario.

PROBLEMAS

1. Marina quiere incluir una Tabla de Contenidos a su presentación y no sabe cómo hacerlo.

2. Marcos borró algunos temas de su presentación y ahora no coincide lo que figura en la Tabla de Contenidos con lo que hay realmente en el documento. Como no tiene tiempo para crear otra Tabla de Contenidos entrega el trabajo sin el temario.

3. Alejandra no sabe qué tiene que hacer para crear un Indice. Alguien se lo explica pero no entiende qué significa Entrada y Subentrada de Indice.

4. Esteban ingresó una acción equivocada mientras intentaba grabar una Macro.

5. Clara no sabe cómo instalar las Macros que una amiga le entrega en un disquete.

6. Alicia no puede configurar los Campos de Formulario que acaba de insertar.

7. Pedro terminó de realizar un formulario y ahora quiere llenar los campos, pero algo no funciona bien ya que las Listas Desplegables no aparecen y los otros campos tampoco funcionan correctamente.

8. Amalia quiere cargar la impresora con un formulario en blanco e imprimir sólo los campos, pero alguien le dice que eso no puede hacerse.

Elementos de trabajo II 4

SOLUCIONES

1. Mariana tiene que proceder así:

   ♦ Ubicar el cursor en donde aparecerá la Tabla de Contenido y en el menú **Insertar** elegir **Indice y tablas**.
   ♦ En la ficha **Tablas de Contenidos** seleccionar un formato adecuado, por ejemplo Clásico y salir aceptando.
   ♦ Observar que aparece el campo {TCD} o directamente el temario con los principales títulos y sus respectivos números de página. En el primer caso presionar simultáneamente *ALT*+F9 para ver el temario.

2. Marcos podría haber solucionado este problema ubicando el cursor dentro de la Tabla de Contenidos y pulsando F9. La actualización hubiese sido automática.

3. Lo primero que hacemos antes de crear un Indice es poner una marca a las palabras que van a aparecer en él. A este proceso se lo denomina crear Entradas o Subentradas de Indice. Para crear un índice *Word* revisa el documento y cada vez que encuentra una palabra marcada la incluye en la lista. Luego se fija el número de página en la que está dicha palabra o frase y lo escribe al costado.

   Alejandra debe crear un Indice siguiendo estas instrucciones:

   ♦ Recorrer el documento marcando las palabras que figurarán en el índice. Esto se hace presionando simultáneamente las teclas *ALT*+*SHIFT*+E.
   ♦ Ubicar el cursor en donde aparecerá el Indice y ejecutar los comandos **Insertar/Indice.**
   ♦ Pulsar **Aceptar**.
   ♦ Antes de que pueda darse cuenta, *Word* habrá confeccionado una lista de palabras, frases, etc. y sus respectivas ubicaciones

4. Si el error es la última acción que realizó, puede hacer clic en el botón **Deshacer** del menú **Edición** y luego continuar grabando. Si el error se produjo antes, Esteban puede abrir la macro en el Editor de *Visual Basic*, identificar y quitar los pasos que no desee incluir. El procedimiento en este caso es el siguiente:

   ♦ En el menú **Herramientas** elegir **Macro**.
   ♦ En el casillero **Nombre de la Macro** seleccionar la Macro que desee modificar.
   ♦ Pulsar el botón **Modificar**.

   Finalmente, si no puede reconocer la o las acciones equivocadas, Esteban deberá eliminar la Macro y grabar otra.

5. Seguramente el disquete consta de una o más plantillas conteniendo las Macros creadas por su amiga, por lo que Clara tiene dos opciones:

♦ Copiar las plantillas tal cual están y utilizar las Macros sólo con estas plantillas.

♦ Transferir las Macros de las Plantillas de su amiga a la plantilla global "Normal.*dot*".

♦ En el primer caso, Clara tiene que copiarlas a la carpeta **Archivos de Programa**, subcarpeta *Microsoft Office*/Plantillas. Cuando quiera trabajar con estas plantillas, las mismas estarán disponibles en la ficha **General** del menú **Archivo/Nuevo** de *Word*.

Para transferir las Macros de las Plantillas de su amiga a la plantilla global "Normal.*dot*" Clara tiene que utilizar el **Organizador de Plantillas y Complementos** situado en el menú **Herramientas**. Una vez seleccionada la ficha **Elementos de proyectos de Macro,** que se muestra en la **Figura 35**.

♦ Pulsar el botón **Cerrar Archivo** y cuando se transforme en el botón **Abrir Archivo** pulsarlo nuevamente.

♦ Ingresar la ruta de acceso del disquete en donde se encuentran las plantillas de su amiga. Cuando las macros aparecen en pantalla seleccionarlas y copiarlas a la plantilla "Normal.*dot*" situada en la otra columna.

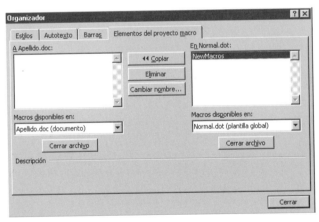

Figura 35. Ventana para transferir macros de una plantilla a otra.

6. Para poder configurar los Campos de Formulario sin problema, lo primero que tenemos que hacer es desactivar el botón **Proteger** que tiene forma de candado y que se encuentra en la barra de Herramientas **Formulario**.

7. Lo más probable es que el formulario siga en modo diseño. Para sacarlo de ese modo hay que desprotegerlo con el botón **Proteger** que tiene forma de candado y está ubicado en la barra de Herramientas **Formulario**.

8. Sí, puede hacerse. El modo de hacerlo es el siguiente:

    ♦ Cargar la impresora con el formulario.
    ♦ Mostrar el formulario en pantalla.
    ♦ En **Herramientas** elegir **Opciones**.
    ♦ En el Cuadro de Diálogo que aparece seleccionar la ficha **Impresión**.
    ♦ Habilitar la opción **Imprimir datos sólo para formulario**.
    ♦ Imprimir el formulario como cualquier documento.

LA WEB 5

Tiempo de lectura y práctica:
1 hora y 30 minutos

5

Objetivo de la lección

■ Utilizar las herramientas *Web* para incorporar información de Internet.

■ Crear páginas *Web*.

■ Utilizar Hipervínculos para navegar dentro y fuera del disco rígido.

1. INTRODUCCIÓN

Antes de aprender a utilizar las herramientas de *Word* para Internet analizaremos qué es y cómo funciona Internet.

Internet es una red mundial de más de miles de redes de computadoras que se comunican entre sí en forma satelital o por cable utilizando un Protocolo de Comunicación denominado *Internet Protocol* (IP).

Originalmente Internet tuvo un uso militar, luego se abrió a la comunidad científica y ahora es de orden público.

Las siguientes son algunas redes que componen Internet: *World Wide Web, Telnet, Usnet, Bitnet*, Red de servidores FTP, Red de servidores *Gopher*, etc. La más popular de todas estas redes que conforman Internet es la *World Wide Web*, más conocida como "la Web". Los servidores y computadoras de la *World Wide Web* se comunican entre sí utilizando un protocolo denominado *Hipertext Transfer Protocol*, por lo que todas las direcciones de sitios localizados en estos servidores están precedidas por la siglas "http:/".

1.1. ¿Qué necesitamos para acceder a Internet?

Para acceder a Internet necesitamos:

◆ Una PC con Módem.
◆ Una línea telefónica.
◆ Una conexión con un Proveedor de Internet.
◆ Un *Software* de simulación de red PPP (ver más adelante).
◆ Aplicaciones para el uso de la red: para recorrer la red y capturar información necesitamos un Navegador (los más conocidos son *Netscape* y *Explorer*), para enviar y recibir correspondencia necesitaremos un programa de Correo Electrónico como Eudora o la Bandeja de Intercambio de *Windows* 95/98, etc.

1.2. ¿Qué es un el Software de simulación de red PPP ?

En una conexión de red normal, la PC se conecta a la red a través de una Placa de Red que se instala dentro de la computadora y un cable. Si instalamos en nuestra computadora un *Software* especial denominado PPP (*Point to*

Point Protocol) y un Módem, el Módem se comportará como una Placa de Red y podremos utilizar la línea telefónica como el cable para conectarnos a Internet. La conexión es a través de nuestro Proveedor y se mantiene mientras dure la comunicación telefónica con él. Es nuestro Proveedor quien nos entrega el *software* PPP, y generalmente también las aplicaciones para utilizar Internet. Este último *Software* podrá ser actualizado por nosotros a medida que salen nuevas versiones o herramientas más modernas.

1.3. ¿Qué cosas podemos hacer utilizando Internet?

Internet se utiliza entre otras cosas para:

♦ Acceder a una gran cantidad de información muy actualizada, distribuida en las páginas de la *World Wide Web* o en servidores Ftp. Los servidores Ftp contienen generalmente documentos, artículos, listados, *papers* científicos, libros, etc.
♦ Escribir a otros usuarios utilizando el correo electrónico (*E-mail*). Los mensajes electrónicos quedan en el servidor al que estamos abonados. Si queremos saber si nos enviaron un mensaje tenemos que conectarnos a la red, ingresar nuestros datos y rescatar lo que pueda estar esperándonos. También es posible transferir archivos incorporándolos a un *E-mail*.
♦ Conversar con personas de todo el mundo utilizando alguno de los programas de charla en tiempo real (Chatear). En la pantalla vemos lo que el otro escribe e inmediatamente le respondemos. Las conversaciones *On-Line* también pueden tener incorporado Audio e Imagen, de modo de poder oír y ver a nuestro interlocutor.
♦ Consultar catálogos de libros, publicaciones, revistas, etc. utilizando las bases de datos conectadas a *Telnet*.
♦ Participar en *Forums* (Grupos de Noticias) sobre temas específicos. En los *Forums* se dejan mensajes relativos a un tema específico para que otros usuarios los lean y respondan. Hay miles de *Forums* en los que podemos participar, los más comunes son aquellos en los que los *fans* hablan de sus ídolos, pero hay otros técnicos, médicos, etc.
♦ Bajar programas para usar con la PC.

En Internet hay páginas en las que debemos abonar para consultar, participar, realizar una compra, etc. Cuando ingresamos allí, se nos solicita el número de tarjeta de Crédito, momento en el cual decidimos seguir adelante o no.

1.4. ¿Cómo está organizada la información en la World Wide Web?

La red más popular de Internet se llama *World Wide Web*, y se la conoce como la *Web*. En esta red la información está organizada en "Sitios", los cuales a su vez contienen una o más ¨Páginas¨. Los sitios de la W. W. W tienen las siguientes características:

♦ Están ubicados en direcciones específicas denominadas en inglés URL.

♦ Las páginas de estos sitios están escritas en un lenguaje que se conoce como HTML, y que ahora puede ser interpretado por *Word* o por cualquier aplicación de *Office*.

♦ La comunicación entre las páginas de un sitio utiliza un protocolo que se denomina Http (*Hyperlink Transfer Text Protocol*). Esto significa que para pasar de una página a otra dentro de un sitio, o de un sitio a otro, hay que hacer un clic en alguno de los Hipervínculos visibles en la pantalla.

♦ Existe una jerarquía entre las páginas de un sitio, hay una página Principal que da un pantallazo general de todo, y varias secundarias que profundizan lo que anuncia la Página Principal.

Para entender cómo funcionan los Sitios de la *Web* podríamos compararlos con los comercios: ambos tienen una determinada dirección y tienen una primera cara visible, que en los comercios es la vidriera y en los ¨*Sytes*¨ es la Página Principal . Así como una vidriera no contiene todo lo que hay en un negocio, la Página Principal de un Sitio tampoco muestra todo en una sola pantalla. El total de la información está distribuido en varias páginas vinculadas entre sí, y accesibles a través de Hipervínculos.

1.5. ¿Qué es un Hipervínculo?

Un hipervínculo es un texto, un ícono o una imagen que se destaca del resto porque cuando ubicamos el puntero encima éste toma forma de mano. Si hacemos un clic pasamos automáticamente a la página cuya dirección está contenida en ese hipervínculo. La página principal de *Microsoft*, por ejemplo, tiene entre sus numerosos hipervínculos uno denominado ¨Novedades ¨. Si pulsamos este hipervínculo, el Navegador abrirá automáticamente la página que contiene las últimas novedades de *Microsoft*.

Cuando saltamos de una dirección a otra utilizando hipervínculos decimos que estamos ¨navegando¨. Gracias a las herramientas *Web* del *Office*, ahora, podemos crear hipervínculos para navegar dentro de nuestro disco rígido, así como también ¨salir¨ a Internet directamente desde el documento en el que estamos trabajando. Por ejemplo, en un documento *Word* podemos insertar hipervínculos para saltar a otra posición dentro del mismo documento, a otro documento dentro de nuestro disco rígido, o directamente a una dirección dentro de Internet. Dada la importancia de los hipervínculos, más adelante analizaremos con profundidad como trabajar con ellos.

La Web 5

1.6. ¿Qué características tienen las direcciones de las páginas de la World Wide Web?

Las direcciones de una página de *Web* tienen las siguientes características:

♦ Están siempre precedidas por la sigla http:// , que indica el tipo de servidor en el que se encuentran.

♦ Empiezan con las siglas www.

♦ A esta sigla le sigue un punto y un nombre principal que está relacionado con la información de la página. Por ejemplo, los nombres principales *Microsoft, Le Figaro* y Clarín contendrán información relacionada con cada una de estas empresas.

♦ El nombre principal está seguido por un punto y una extensión relacionada con el tipo de actividad que desarrolla la entidad que publicó la página. Por ejemplo, la extensión ¨com¨ hace referencia a la actividad comercial, la extensión ¨gov¨ indica que se trata de un organismo gubernamental, la extensión ¨edu¨ se refiere a una institución con fines educativos, etc.

En el siguiente ejemplo, la URL http://www. *microsoft.* com es una dirección de la *Web* que contiene información relacionada con la empresa de *Software Microsoft.*

1.7. ¿Cuáles son las Herramientas Web con que cuenta Word?

Dada la gran utilidad de Internet, *Office* 97 incorporó una serie de herramientas para poder aprovechar al máximo las posibilidades de la red. Las herramientas *Web* no se instalan generalmente en la Instalación Típica, por lo que tenemos que instalarlas como un componente más. Estas herramientas son las siguientes.

1.7.1. Editor de Páginas Web

El Editor de Páginas Web es el programa que le permite a *Word* crear e interpretar páginas *Web.* Se trata de una interfase sencilla y sumamente eficiente que traduce texto, imágenes, etc. a códigos HTML de última generación. El Editor para páginas *Web* es la herramienta que permite que nosotros, los usuarios de *Microsoft Word*, podamos crear e interpretar páginas *Web* sin más conocimientos que aquellos que poseemos para manejar el procesador de texto, y sobre todo sin necesidad de aprender e ingresar manualmente los complicados códigos del lenguaje HTML.

Lo anterior no invalida la posibilidad de que si conocemos el lenguaje HTML y queremos utilizarlo directamente en el Editor de Páginas *Web* también podamos hacerlo. Para ello hay que elegir en **Ver** la opción **Codigos Html**, que muestra la página *Web* en el lenguaje de origen.

Con el Editor de Páginas *Web* podemos crear páginas desde cero ingresando los códigos HTML, o bien crearlas como documentos comunes y luego convertirlas al formato HTML. Esto último se hace en el momento de guardar , seleccionando **Archivo** y luego **Guardar como Html**. Recordemos que si no están instaladas las herramientas *Web*, esta opción de guardado no estará habilitada. Cuando trabajamos con formato HTML, las Barras de Herramientas **Formato y Estándar** son reemplazadas por otras similares.

1.7.2. Barra de Herramientas Web.

Figura 1. *Barra de Herramientas Web.*

Esta barra, que se muestra en la **Figura 1**, es la que nos permite trabajar con *Word* como si fuera un Navegador, saltar entre páginas vinculadas, detener el armado de un página, ir a la página Inicio etc.

Si abrimos una página de Internet utilizando *Word*, o si insertamos Hipervínculos en nuestros documentos, usamos esta barra para controlar el flujo de la información que vemos en pantalla.

A continuación se describe la función de los botones, que de izquierda a derecha son:

♦ **Botón Atrás:** permite retroceder a la página anterior a la activa.
♦ **Botón Adelante**: permite pasar a la página siguiente a la activa.
♦ **Botón Detener:** detiene la transferencia de un documento de la red a nuestra PC, o del disco rígido al documento activo.
♦ **Botón Actualizar**: vuelve a cargar la página seleccionada. Esto permite tener siempre la última versión de un página. Si deshabilitamos las imágenes podemos habilitarlas y luego actualizar la página para que se carguen las imágenes.
♦ **Botón Página de Inicio**: nos lleva a la página de Inicio configurada en *Word*. De forma predeterminada, la Página de Inicio contiene los principales buscadores de sitios *Web*.
♦ **Botón Buscar en la** *Web*: inicia el Navegador configurado en el sistema.
♦ **Botón Favorito**: permite acceder a la carpeta **Favoritos**, que contiene las direcciones de uso frecuente. Este botón también se usa para guardar la dirección de la página activa en la carpeta **Favoritos**.

La Web

5

♦ **Botón Ir a**: este botón permite abrir documentos ubicados en servidores *Web*, FTP, *Gopher*, etc. También encontramos aquí los comandos para configurar la página de Inicio, Búsqueda, etc.

♦ **Botón Mostrar Sólo la Barra de Herramientas** *Web*: lo pulsamos sólo cuando queremos Navegar y no vamos a utilizar los otros comandos o herramientas.

♦ **Casillero Dirección**: escribimos aquí la dirección a la que queremos acceder. La lista de Historial de este casillero muestra las últimas diez direcciones consultadas.

La **Figura 2** muestra cómo se ve una página de Internet en *Word* cuando usamos esta aplicación como si fuera un Navegador.

Figura 2. *Así se ve Word cuando actúa como un navegador.*

1.7.3. Botón Hipervínculo (ver **Figura 3**).

El Botón Hipervínculo está ubicado en la barra de Herramientas **Estándar**, y se usa para ingresar un Hipervínculo. Más adelante describiremos cómo trabajar con ellos.

Figura 3. *Un clic aquí e insertamos un Hipervínculo.*

1.7.4. Menú contextual Hipervínculos (ver **Figura 4**).

Sólo aparece cuando pulsamos el botón derecho del *Mouse* sobre un hipervínculo. Este botón nos permite modificar la dirección de un hipervínculo, abrirlo, copiarlo, seleccionarlo, etc. sin que la pantalla salte a la dirección contenida en ese hipervínculo.

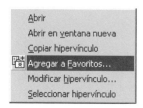

Figura 4. *Este menú contextual se usa para configurar los hipervínculos.*

1.8. Incorporar información existente en Internet a nuestro documento

Como dijimos antes, la mayoría de la información que está dando vueltas por Internet es pública, lo que significa que cualquiera puede capturarla, hacer una copia de ella y utilizarla para mejorar, completar, ampliar o modernizar un documento. Es muy común bajar documentos de servidores Ftp, como se verá más adelante, pero también se pueden aprovechar los dibujos, tablas, gráficos, mapas, etc. de las páginas *Web*.

Para bajar un documento o una página *Web* directamente a *Word* sin pasar por el Navegador, hay que ingresar, en el Cuadro de Diálogo **Abrir** del menú **Archivo** que se muestra en la **Figura 5**, el tipo de servidor, la dirección de la página y si se trata de un documento, el nombre del documento. Por ejemplo, el siguiente ingreso "http://*microsoft. com/soft*. doc" busca el documento "*Soft. doc*" en la página que *Microsoft* tiene en un servidor de la *World Wide Web,* y lo abre en *Word* sin pasar por el Navegador instalado en el sistema. A continuación se muestra el aspecto que tiene el Cuadro de Diálogo **Abrir** cuando, en lugar de elegir el nombre de un archivo de cualquiera de las unidades de disco, elegimos abrir información localizada en una computadora remota (servidor).

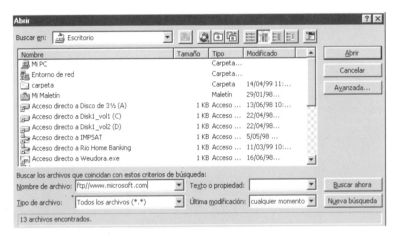

Figura 5. *Aquí empieza la tranferencia de un documento vía Internet.*

Cuando se inicia la transferencia del documento o de la página *Web*, vemos en pantalla una ventana como la que se muestra en la **Figura 6** indicándonos el volumen bajado y por bajar.

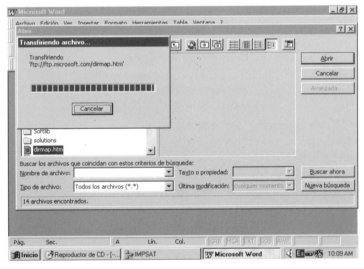

Figura 6. *Esta ventana indica que la tranferencia de un documento o una página vía Internet se está llevando a cabo.*

La operación anterior no es posible si no conocemos la dirección exacta de la página, o el nombre del documento. En estos casos será necesario abrir el Navegador instalado en nuestro sistema simultáneamente con *Word*, buscar la información necesaria, y cuando la tenemos en pantalla, transferirla a *Word* utilizando el botón **Editar**, que en el *Explorer* tiene el aspecto de la **Figura 7**.

Figura 7. *Un clic en este botón y pasamos a Word para editar la página abierta por el Navegador.*

1.8.1. ¿Qué son los sitios FTP ?

Los sitios Ftp están ubicados en Servidores Ftp y pueden ser accedidos desde *Word* para subir o bajar archivos. Cuando ingresamos desde *Word* a un sitio FTP, accedemos al disco rígido de una computadora remota y aparece en pantalla la lista de carpetas y subcarpetas guardadas allí. Una vez dentro de la computadora remota, elegimos el o los archivos a abrir, como si se tratara de nuestro disco rígido. La **Figura 8** muestra cómo accede desde *Word* el disco rígido de una PC remota del sitio Ftp. *Microsoft*. com.

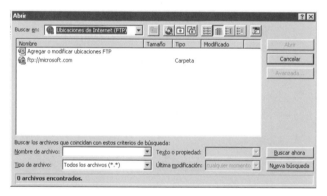

Figura 8. *Así se ingresa a un sitio FTP desde Word.*

1.8.2. ¿Cualquiera puede acceder a un sitio FTP y llevarse un archivo?

Si el sitio es Anónimo sí, ya que Anónimo significa público. Existen dos modos de acceder a un sitio FTP, un modo es como usuario regular de ese sistema, y otro, como un usuario anónimo. En el primer caso, para visitar el sitio necesitamos tener una cuenta en ese sitio FTP e ingresar la contraseña cuando sea solicitada. En el segundo caso no necesitamos tener ni cuenta ni conocer una contraseña, ya que se trata de sitios públicos creados para que la gente pueda compartir archivos. Los FTP anónimos generalmente contienen programas de actualización de *Software*, *Drivers*, aplicaciones para conversión de archivos, navegadores, programas para Correo Electrónico, archivos de sonido, etc.

1.8.3. ¿Cómo accedemos a un sitio FTP desde Word?

Para que *Word* pueda abrir un archivo que está guardado en un sitio FTP primero hay que agregar el sitio a la Lista de Servidores de Internet con que cuenta *Word*. Esto se hace del siguiente modo.

◆ En el menú **Archivo** seleccionamos **Abrir**, como se muestra en la **Figura 9.**
◆ En el casillero **Buscar en** elegimos la opción **Agregar o modificar ubicaciones FTP**.
◆ En el casillero **Nombre del sitio FTP**, escribimos el nombre del sitio FTP; por ejemplo ˝ftp://ftp. *microsoft.* com˝
◆ Habilitamos la opción **Anónimo** si el sitio es anónimo, por el contrario si estamos adheridos a ese sitio FTP habilitamos la opción **Usuario** y, a continuación, escribimos la contraseña.
◆ Pulsamos **Agregar**.

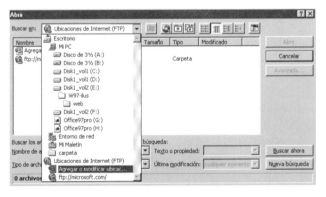

Figura 9. *Este es el primer paso para acceder a un sitio FTP.*

Una vez agregado el sitio FTP a la lista de sitios con que cuenta *Word* procedemos del siguiente modo:

◆ En el menú **Archivo** seleccionamos la opción **Abrir** .
◆ En el casillero **Buscar en** elegimos **Ubicaciones de Internet (FTP).**
◆ En la lista de sitios FTP seleccionamos el sitio al que queremos llegar, como se muestra en la **Figura 10.**

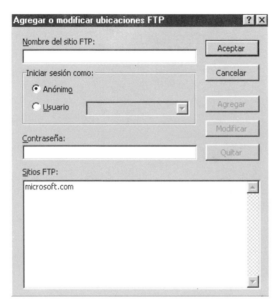

Figura 10. *Aquí aparecen todos los sitios FTP que tenemos registrados en Word para que podamos accederlos.*

♦ Verificamos que se establece la conexión con Internet y que *Word* muestra todas las carpetas y archivos guardados en ese sitio.

♦ Seleccionamos el documento a abrir.

♦ Pulsamos **Abrir**.

1.9. Trabajar con Hipervínculos

Como dijimos antes, *Word* 97 permite usar Hipervínculos para navegar, no sólo por Internet, sino también por nuestro disco rígido o por nuestro documento. Esto último es útil cuando queremos dirigir el flujo de información de aquellos documentos que van a ser leídos por pantalla, ya que los Hipervínculos guían al lector a los sitios de su interés, evitando la lectura de todo el documento.

Los Hipervínculos, en un documento *Word*, pueden llevarnos a sitios ubicados fuera del disco rígido. El secreto para que funcione bien esta conexión es que las direcciones sean las correctas y estén actualizadas.

1.9.1. ¿Cómo insertamos un Hipervínculo?

Para insertar un Hipervínculo en un documento o en una página *Web* procedemos del siguiente modo.

♦ Seleccionamos la palabra, frase o imagen que aparecerá como Hipervínculo.

♦ Pulsamos el botón **Insertar Hipervínculo**, de la barra de Herramientas **Estándar**, que se muestra en la **Figura 11.**

Figura 11. *Un clic aquí e ingresamos un Hipervínculo.*

♦ En el casillero **Vincular al archivo o dirección URL**, del Cuadro de Diálogo que se muestra en la **Figura 12,** escribimos la dirección a la que saltará el usuario al hacer un clic en el Hipervínculo. Las opciones son:

♦ Una dirección HTML en la *Web*.
♦ Una dirección HTML en una Intranet (Red local).
♦ Un sitio *Gopher*.
♦ Un sitio *Telnet*.
♦ Un grupo de debate.
♦ Un sitios FTP.
♦ Una archivo de nuestro disco rígido.

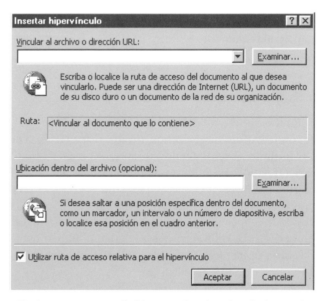

Figura 12. *Ingresamos aquí el lugar adonde saltará el usuario cuando haga clic en el Hipervínculo.*

♦ Pulsamos **Aceptar**
♦ Procedemos así hasta ingresar todos los Hipervínculos deseados.

Para ilustrar lo anterior tomemos el siguiente ejemplo: supongamos que tenemos que escribir un informe sobre "El lagarto overo de la Pampas Argentinas", y encontramos en Internet un documento muy completo sobre otros lagartos con costumbres similares. En una parte de nuestro informe podríamos hacer referencia a este hecho e incluir un Hipervínculo con la dirección del informe existente en Internet. El lector podría entonces leer sobre los lagartos overos y luego pulsar el Hipervínculo para pasar al informe de los otros lagartos contenido en Internet. En este último caso, *Word* iniciará automáticamente la conexión con la red y el Navegador abrirá la página correspondiente.

1.9.2. ¿Cómo creamos, modificamos y eliminamos Hipervínculos para navegar dentro de un documento?

Este tipo de Hipervínculos permite que el lector determine el curso de lectura de un documento según sus necesidades, saltando a la sección que le interesa sin necesidad de pasar por otras. El siguiente ejemplo ilustra lo anterior: Supongamos que en un informe encontramos la siguiente frase " Antes de tratar con el departamento de Compras hay que llenar las siguientes solicitudes. . . ". Si la palabra " Compras " es un Hipervínculo, el lector tiene dos alternativas de lectura, seguir leyendo sobre las solicitudes que tiene que llenar antes de tratar con el Dpto. de Compras, o hacer un clic sobre el Hipervínculo "Compras" para saltar a la sección del documento que profundiza sobre ese departamento.

Para crear Hipervínculos dentro de un mismo archivo procedemos del siguiente modo:

- Seleccionamos el texto, imagen, objeto, etc. adonde saltará *Word* cuando el usuario haga clic encima del Hipervínculo. En el ejemplo anterior seleccionaríamos el comienzo de la sección en donde se profundiza sobre el Departamento de Compras.
- En el menú **Insertar** seleccionamos el comando **Marcador**.
- En el Cuadro de Diálogo que aparece, y que mostramos en la **Figura 13**, escribimos un nombre para el marcador, por ejemplo "Compras", y salimos aceptando

Figura 13. *Los marcadores son referencias adonde puede saltar el usuario al hacer un clic en un Hipervínculo.*

♦ Seleccionamos el texto, frase o imagen que hará las veces de Hipervínculo y pulsamos el botón **Insertar Hipervínculo**, de la barra de Herramientas **Estándar**.

♦ En el Cuadro de Diálogo que se muestra en la **Figura 15**, en el casillero **Ubicación dentro del archivo**, escribimos el nombre del marcador de destino, en nuestro caso ¨Compras¨, y pulsamos **Aceptar** .

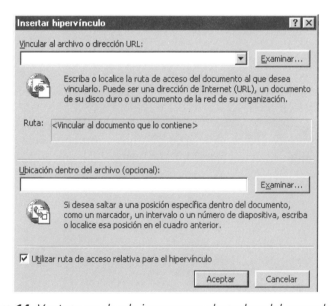

Figura 14. *Ventana en donde ingresamos el nombre del marcador para que quede registrado en el Hipervínculo.*

♦ Una vez creados los Hipervínculos, podemos modificar la dirección y el aspecto de los mismos ubicando el puntero arriba y pulsando el botón derecho del *Mouse*. El Menú Contextual de la **Figura 15** nos permite realizar los cambios necesarios.

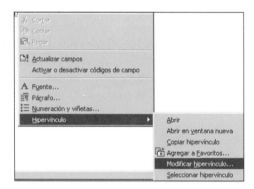

Figura 15. *Un clic en el botón derecho del Mouse y podemos configurar el Hipervínculo.*

Para borrar un Hipervínculo hay que seleccionarlo desde el teclado, o utilizando el menú Contextual anterior, y luego pulsar *DEL*.

Para eliminar la función Hipervínculo pero dejar el elemento, es necesario:

♦ Seleccionarlo.
♦ En el menú **Insertar** elegir la opción **Hipervínculo**, y en el Cuadro de Diálogo que mostramos arriba, pulsar el botón **Quitar vínculo**.

2. CREAR PÁGINAS *WEB*

El modo como está dispuesta la información en una página *Web* es muy importante, ya que el número de visitas que tendrá dicha página depende, entre otras cosas, del diseño de la misma.

A continuación analizaremos cuatro modos de crear y diseñar páginas *Web* utilizando *Word* 97. Una vez completado el diseño, las páginas se "suben" a la red siguiendo las instrucciones aportadas por nuestro proveedor. Cuando la página ya está en la red, es necesario declararla en los buscadores para que la gente pueda encontrarla.

Los modos de diseñar una página *Web* utilizando *Word* son los siguientes:

♦ Utilizar el Asistente para páginas *Web*.
♦ Utilizar una Plantilla.
♦ Convertir un documento *Word* en un archivo HTML.
♦ Utilizar una página ya existente como modelo.

2.1. Utilizar el Asistente para Páginas Web

El Asistente para páginas *Web* es una plataforma de lanzamiento que contiene distintas páginas, para usarlas como base de nuestra página. Existe, por ejemplo, un modelo para una Página Personal, otro para una Tabla de Contenidos, una Encuesta, un Formulario de Registro, etc. Estos modelos contienen la mayoría de los elementos que necesita una página *Web* de ese tipo, de modo que lo único que tenemos que hacer es adaptarla a nuestras necesidades modificando , por ejemplo, la dirección y el nombre de los Hipervínculos, el texto de las propuestas, la posición de las viñetas, etc. La idea es siempre la misma: adaptar el modelo a nuestras necesidades sin perder el diseño.

La **Figura 16** muestra uno de los modelos con que cuenta el Asistente para Páginas *Web*.

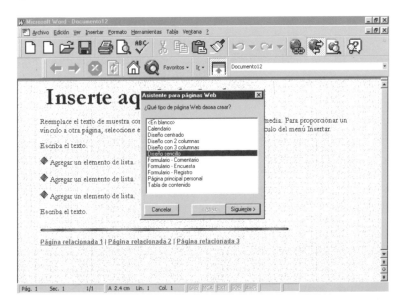

Figura 16. *Ejemplo de uno de los modelos que vienen en el Asistente de Páginas Web.*

Para crear una página *Web* utilizando el Asistente procedemos así:

- ◆ En el menú **Archivo** elegimos **Nuevo**.
- ◆ En el Cuadro de Diálogo que se muestra en la **Figura 17** seleccionamos la opción **Páginas** *Web*.

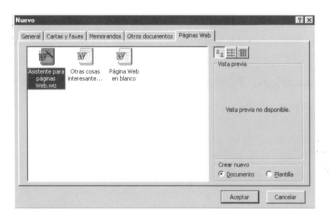

Figura 17. *Primer paso para crear una página Web.*

♦ Hacemos doble clic sobre la opción **Asistente para Páginas** *Web*.
♦ En el Cuadro de Diálogo que muestra la **Figura 18**, seleccionamos el modelo más adecuado para nuestra página, por ejemplo **Diseño Sencillo**, y luego pulsamos **Aceptar**.

Figura 18. *Aquí elegimos el tipo de página que queremos crear.*

♦ Junto con la página modelo aparece un Cuadro de Diálogo con diferentes estilos, por ejemplo¨ Cómico¨, ¨Elegante¨, etc. Seleccionamos uno y pulsamos el botón **Terminar**.
♦ Una vez elegido el modelo, hay que realizar las modificaciones necesarias para crear nuestra página. En general, lo que hacemos es cambiar las direcciones de los Hipervínculos, el contenido del texto, insertar nuevas imágenes, etc.

Una vez concluido el trabajo, guardamos la página como archivo HTML utilizando los comandos **Archivo/Guardar como HTML**.

2.2. Crear una Página Web a partir de una Plantilla

Este es otro modo de iniciar la creación de una página *Web*. La única plantilla que viene con *Word* se denomina Página *Web* en Blanco y se trata de una hoja en blanco a la que debemos agregarle Hipervínculos, imágenes, texto, viñetas y todo otro elemento necesario de acuerdo al tipo de página a crear.

Sin embargo, existen otras plantillas que pueden descargarse desde el sitio *World Wide Web* de *Word*. Al descargar estas plantillas, las mismas se instalan en la carpeta en la que se encuentra la plantilla en blanco, de modo de quedar disponible en el menú **Archivo** opción **Nuevo**, ficha **Páginas** *Web*, para ser utilizada cuantas veces sea necesario.

2.3. Convertir un documento Word en un archivo HTML.

Otro modo rápido de hacer una página *Web* consiste en crear un documento común con un diseño adecuado para que sea una página *Web* y, al momento de guardarlo, convertirlo en un archivo HTML. En este caso es posible que se pierdan algunos formatos del documento ¨Doc¨ que no estén disponibles en HTML y que, por lo tanto, el diseño no aparezca en la forma que esperábamos, pero las pérdidas son mínimas.

Para guardar un documento *Word* como archivo HTML procedemos así:

◆ Verificamos que el documento está activo y en pantalla.
◆ En el menú **Archivo** elegimos **Guardar como Html**.
◆ Pulsamos **Aceptar**.

2.4. Utilizar una Página Existente como Modelo

Otro modo práctico y directo de crear y diseñar una página *Web* es abrir de Internet alguna página que tenga los elementos y el aspecto que necesitamos y modificarla adaptándola a nuestras necesidades específicas. Recordemos que para abrir una página *Web* desde *Word*, y que se vuelque todo el contenido, incluídos los gráficos, imágenes, tablas, dibujos, etc. hay que ingresar, en el Cuadro de Diálogo **Abrir** del menú **Archivo,** el tipo de servidor y la dirección adecuada de la página a abrir, por ejemplo ¨http://disney. com¨.

Cuando la página aparece en pantalla, cortamos la conexión con Internet y procedemos a modificar las direcciones de los Hipervínculos, el contenido del texto, la posición de las viñetas, etc. para adaptarla a nuestras necesidades.

Para obtener una vista previa de la página *Web* que estamos creando, es necesario tener instalado un explorador de *Web*. Cuando pulsamos el botón **Vis-**

ta previa de una página *Web*, que se muestra en la **Figura 19,** pasamos al Explorador y vemos nuestra página.

Figura 19. *Un clic en este botón y tenemos una idea de cómo está quedando nuestra página.*

Para regresar a *Word* pulsamos el ícono de *Word* en la barra de tareas, o cerramos el explorador.

2.5. ¿Qué elementos podemos agregar a las páginas Web?

Los siguientes elementos pueden agregarse a una página *Web*.

- Números y Viñetas.
- Líneas horizontales.
- Colores de fondo y texturas.
- Tablas.
- Imágenes, gráficos, dibujos, etc.
- Texto desplazable.
- Formularios.

La mayoría de estos elementos se agregan y modifican siguiendo el mismo procedimiento que en los documentos de *Word*. A continuación se sintetizan las principales diferencias entre unos y otros.

2.5.1. Números y Viñetas

Existen dos tipos de viñetas que podemos utilizar para crear una página *Web*.

- Viñetas de Texto.
- Viñetas Gráficas.

Las Viñetas de Texto son las que ya conocemos y que usamos en los documentos. Las Gráficas tienen las siguientes características:

- Son imágenes y por lo tanto se comportan como tales.
- No podemos eliminarlas pulsando el botón **Viñetas,** como lo haríamos normalmente. Para eliminarlas debemos seleccionarlas y pulsar SUPRIMIR.
- Las Viñetas Gráficas se guardan como archivos GIF (. gif) o JPEG [. jpg] en la

La Web 5

misma ubicación donde se encuentra la página *Web*.

◆ Para acceder a las Viñetas Gráficas elegimos **Formato** y luego **Numeraciones y Viñetas**. En pantalla tiene que estar activo un documento HTML, de lo contrario no accederemos a la ventana de las **Viñetas Gráficas** que se muestra en la **Figura 20**.

Figura 20. *Modelos de Viñetas Gráficas para páginas Web con que cuenta Word.*

En las páginas *Web*, la numeración es similar a la de los documentos de *Word*, exceptuando que no existen los Esquemas Multinivel. Para realizar un Esquema Multinivel debemos crearlo manualmente aplicando diferentes estilos de numeración y las correspondientes sangrías.

2.5.2. Líneas Horizontales

Las líneas Horizontales que utilizamos en las páginas *Web* son imágenes y no líneas comunes. En general, aplicamos una línea Horizontal para separar secciones con diferente contenido. El procedimiento es el siguiente.

◆ Ubicamos el cursor en el lugar en donde aparecerá la línea Horizontal.
◆ En el menú **Insertar** elegimos **Línea Horizontal**.
◆ En el Cuadro de Diálogo que aparece, y que se muestra en la **Figura 21** , seleccionamos la línea y pulsamos **Aceptar**.

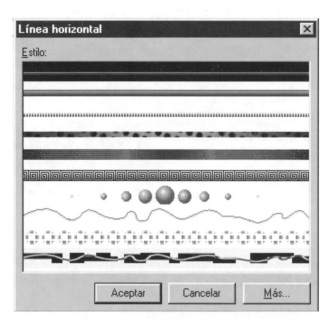

Figura 21. *Modelos de línea para páginas Web con que cuenta Word.*

Los archivos gráficos que contienen las líneas horizontales, por ejemplo, línea1. gif, línea2. gig, etc., deben guardarse en la misma ubicación que la página *Web*.

2.5.3. Fondo en las páginas Web

El principal elemento de una página *Web* es el fondo, ya que es lo que le da una apariencia atractiva. Para el fondo podemos utilizar texturas, colores lisos, imágenes, etc. La designación del fondo se hace seleccionando una del comando **Fondo del menú Formato,** como se muestra en la **Figura 22**.

La Web 5

Figura 22. *Modelos de fondo para páginas Web con que cuenta Word.*

2.5.4. Tablas en las Páginas Web

Las tablas se utilizan generalmente en segundo plano, para organizar el texto y los gráficos de una página *Web*. De forma predeterminada las tablas no incluyen bordes al insertarlas, para agregárselos hay que utilizar la barra de Herramientas TABLA y BORDE. Los bordes generalmente tienen un aspecto tridimensional en los exploradores de Web.

Para dar formato al fondo de una tabla ubicamos el cursor sobre ella y pulsamos el botón derecho del *Mouse*. En el menú contextual **Tabla** que aparece, seleccionamos la opción **Propiedades** y una vez allí, encontraremos todos los comandos para variar la apariencia del fondo de la tabla.

2.6. ¿Qué características tienen las imágenes de las páginas Web?

Las imágenes de una página *Web* tienen las siguientes características:

♦ Se insertan, modifican y eliminan del mismo modo que en los documentos *Word*.

♦ Los dos formatos admitidos en la *Web* son: GIF y JPEG.

♦ La primera vez que guardemos una página *Web* en formato HTML todos los archivos de imágenes se convertirán a formato GIF o JPEG. Si la imagen estaba en formato JPG, cuando la insertemos *Word* la guardará en ese mismo formato. Si las imágenes eran un archivo TIF, *Word* lo convertirá a formato GIF.

♦ Los archivos con las imágenes que insertemos en una página *Web* serán copia-dos en la misma carpeta en la que guardamos la página *Web*.

♦ Si incluimos objetos, una vez cerrada la página *Web* no podremos volver a abrirlos, dado que éstos se convertirán en imágenes GIF estáticas. Esto significa que si vamos a modificar los objetos conviene guardar la página como documento *Word* hasta que logremos la versión definitiva.

♦ Las imágenes de gran tamaño incrementan el tiempo de descarga de una página cuando los usuarios las abren. Las páginas muy cargadas de imágenes son lentas de descargar y corren el riesgo de ser menos visitadas.

♦ Dado que algunos usuarios desactivan la presentación de imágenes, no conviene incluir en ellas información importante que pueda ser pasada por alto.

2.7. ¿Qué se entiende por Texto Desplazable?

El Texto Desplazable es un efecto especial de texto en movimiento creado en esta versión de *Word* para otorgarle dinámica a las presentaciones o páginas *Web*. Este tipo de texto también se conoce como marquesina, y es compatible con todas las versiones del Explorador de Internet de *Microsoft*, excepto con la versión 1. 0. Existen exploradores de *Web* que no admiten el desplazamiento de texto por lo que en estos exploradores el texto aparece pero no se desplaza.

Para agregar una marquesina a una página *Web* hay que proceder del siguiente modo:

♦ En el menú **Insertar** elegir **Desplazamiento de Texto**.
♦ Escribir el texto que queremos desplazar.
♦ Seleccionar la configuración adecuada.
♦ Pulsar **Aceptar.**

Para eliminar una marquesina hay que seleccionarla y cortarla.

2.8. ¿Qué diferencias existen entre el formato DOC y HTML?

Las siguientes son algunas de las diferencias que existen entre estos dos tipos de formatos.

♦ En HTML hay una restricción en la variedad de tamaños disponibles para las fuentes, por lo que no disponemos de los miles de tamaños que existen cuando trabajamos con documentos *Word*.

♦ Los tipos de viñetas se ven diferentes y también se comportan de modo distinto. En el formato HTML, las viñetas son imágenes y para quitarlas tenemos que seleccionarlas y pulsar *DEL*.

♦ El formato de las páginas *Web* no admite columnas de estilo periódico, por lo

La Web 5

que para conseguir este efecto es necesario utilizar tablas.

♦ Los párrafos en formato HTLM llevan siempre un espacio antes y después. Para eliminar este espacio presionamos CTRL+ENTRAR.

♦ En HTML no están disponibles los formatos Relieve, Sombra y Grabado.

♦ En HTML no podemos modificar
   el interlineado,
   los márgenes,
   el espacio entre caracteres,
   el ajuste de espacio y
   los valores del flujo de texto.

♦ En HTML no podemos tabular, ya que en la mayoría de los exploradores las tabulaciones no se muestran como espacios. Para desplazar la primera línea de texto a la derecha debemos aplicar una sangría.

2.9. ¿Cómo subimos una página Web a la World Wide Web?

Subir una página *Web* a la *World Wide Web* significa ponerla a disposición de los usuarios que quieran consultarla. Este procedimiento se lleva a cabo teniendo en cuenta lo siguiente:

♦ Nuestro proveedor debe asignarnos un espacio en un servidor *Web*, y proporcionarnos las instrucciones adecuadas para subir la página.

♦ La primera página la llamamos Index.html y las otras con sus respectivos nombres. Deben estar vinculadas entre sí y con la primera página. Por ejemplo el sitio puede estar formado por la página principal Index.html, página 1.html, página2.html, etc.

♦ Nuestro proveedor nos da un código de acceso al servidor al cual accedemos con cualquier programa de manejo de servidores FTP. accedemos allí y copiamos las páginas a nuestro sitio como cualquier archivo.

♦ Una vez subida la página a un servidor *Web* debemos cargarla en los buscadores para que aparezca en las bases de datos. Cada buscador tiene su propia rutina de carga de información, que debemos seguir leyendo las instrucciones correspondientes.

Existe un asistente para subir páginas *Web* denominado *WebPost*, que viene con el *Office*. Para poder utilizarlo debemos primero instalarlo. Se encuentra en la carpeta *VALUPACK* subcarpeta *WEBPOST*.

PROBLEMAS

1. Gaspar creó un Hipervínculo, ahora quiere cambiar la dirección URL contenida en él, pero cuando pulsa el botón derecho del *Mouse* sobre el texto del Hipervínculo no aparecen los comandos correspondientes del menú contextual.

2. Marta hace un clic para saltar a la dirección contenida en un Hipervínculo pero, para su sorpresa, recibe un mensaje de error.

3. Ana está decidida a crear su propia página *Web* pero cuando se pone a trabajar no encuentran las herramientas *Web*.

4. A Tomás le entregan un disquete con una página *Web* para que agregue información adicional. Cuando lo abre aparecen corchetes y códigos HTML en lugar del contenido de la página *Web*.

5. María está diseñando su primera página *Web*. Todo va bien, sin embargo no encuentra algunos colores que pensó incluir en los títulos principales.

6. Rosa quiere utilizar una página *Web* que vio en Internet como modelo para crear su página personal, pero no sabe cómo abrirla sin perder las imágenes.

7. Juan abre un archivo de un sitio FTP, pero en la pantalla sólo aparece basura.

8. Daniel quiere seleccionar un Hipervínculo para modificarlo, pero cuando barre con el *Mouse* arriba de él, la pantalla pasa automáticamente a la dirección contenida en el Hipervínculo.

La Web 5

SOLUCIONES

1. El menú contextual Hipervínculo no aparece si el texto del Hipervínculo contiene un error gramatical u ortográfico. Si éste es el caso, Gaspar tiene que corregir el error antes de intentar hacer nada con ese Hipervínculo.

2. La causa de este problema puede ser alguna de las siguientes:

   ◆ Se cambió el nombre del destino del Hipervínculo. Por ejemplo, la dirección nos manda al documento ¨Antartida. doc¨ pero éste ahora se llama ¨Antartida2. doc¨.
   ◆ Se eliminó el archivo destino del Hipervínculo. Por ejemplo, el Hipervínculo nos manda a ¨c:\informes\trabajos. doc¨, pero este documento no existe.
   ◆ Se cambió de lugar el archivo de destino del Hipervínculo. Por ejemplo, la dirección nos manda a ¨c:\trabajos ¨cuando el documento está guardado en ¨c:\sueldos¨. Para evitar este tipo de errores es necesario desactivar el casillero **Utilizar ubicación de archivo fija** al momento de ingresar la dirección del Hipervínculo.
   ◆ Si la dirección de destino está en Internet, el problema puede estar en el acceso a Internet o también puede ser que el sitio esté ocupado. En este último caso debemos intentar abrirlo más tarde.

3. Las herramientas para creación de páginas *Web* se encuentran en el Cuadro de Diálogo **Nuevo** del menú **Archivo**. Si cuando elegimos **Archivo** elegimos **Nuevo** no aparece la ficha **Páginas** *Web* seguramente no están instalados los componentes adecuados. En este caso, Ana tendrá que ejecutar el programa instalador del *Office* y seleccionar los componentes relacionados con la creación de páginas *Web*. Esto se hace siguiendo las siguientes instrucciones.

   ◆ Cerrar todos los programas en uso.
   ◆ Hacer clic en el botón **Inicio de** *Windows*.
   ◆ Seleccionar el comando **Configuración** y luego **Panel de control**.
   ◆ Seleccionar el ícono **Agregar o quitar programas.**
   ◆ Seleccionar el programa de instalación del *Office*.
   ◆ Pulsar el botón **Agregar o Quitar**.
   ◆ Seguir las instrucciones que se indican en pantalla hasta habilitar los componentes para páginas *Web*.

   Recordemos que al abrir un documento de una página *Web* o al crear un nuevo documento basado en una plantilla o Asistente para páginas *Web* algunos de los menúes y barras de herramientas cambiarán para adaptarse al formato HTML.

4. Si aparecen corchetes y códigos, como <HTML>,<HEAD> o <P> en lugar del contenido de la página *Web*, puede ser debido a alguna de las siguientes razones:

   ♦ Se seleccionó la opción **Código HTML** en el menú **Ver**. Para regresar a la presentación visual de la página *Web* debemos seleccionar la opción **Salir de Código HTML** también en el menú **Ver**.
   ♦ El archivo es una página *Web*, pero no tiene ninguna de las siguientes extensiones: html, htm, htx, asp u otm. Para corregir este problema, tenemos que elegir **Herramientas** y luego **Opciones**, y en la ficha **General** activar el casillero **Confirmar conversiones al abrir**. Una vez hecho esto abrir nuevamente el archivo y en el cuadro de diálogo **Convertir archivo**, seleccionar la opción **Documento HTML**.

5. Al crear páginas *Web*, sólo podemos escoger entre 16 colores diferentes para las fuentes y el fondo de las tablas. Sin embargo, para el fondo de la página disponemos de una gama tan amplia que hasta podríamos crear nuestros propios colores. Los colores aplicables a las fuentes se encuentran en el Cuadro de Diálogo **Colores del texto** del menú **Formato**. Los colores para el fondo de las tablas están disponibles en el Cuadro de Diálogo **Propiedades de celda** y **Propiedades de Tabla** del menú **Tabla**.

6. Rosa tiene que elegir **Archivo** y luego **Abrir** y escribir, en el casillero **Nombre de Archivo**, el tipo de servidor y la dirección de la página. Puede escribir, por ejemplo, "http://www. duitres. edu". Cuando pulse **Aceptar** comenzará la transferencia de la página con todos sus elementos.

7. Existe un problema de incompatibilidad de formato. El archivo tiene un formato determinado y estamos intentando abrirlo en otro. Para evitar que esto ocurra conviene, antes de iniciar la transferencia, elegir **Herramientas** y luego **Opciones.** En la ficha **General** activar el casillero **Confirmar conversiones al abrir**. Una vez hecho esto Juan puede intentar abrir nuevamente el archivo, pero esta vez seleccionar el formato adecuado cuando aparezca el Cuadro de Diálogo **Convertir archivo**. Algunos formatos posibles son ASCII y Binario.

8. Daniel tiene que seleccionar el Hipervínculo utilizando el teclado o el botón derecho del *Mouse*.

La Web 5

APÉNDICE
LO NUEVO
EN WORD 2000

Tiempo de lectura y práctica:
1 hora y 25 minutos

Lo nuevo en Word 2000

1. INTRODUCCIÓN

La velocidad con la que van mejorando las aplicaciones de *Microsoft* en estos diez últimos años produce por lo general dos tipos de reacciones en los usuarios. Por un lado una sensación positiva al pensar que las nuevas herramientas agregadas a los "viejos" programas van a ayudarnos a producir mejores presentaciones con menor esfuerzo (hacer las maravillas que teníamos en mente con un solo clic). Pero, por otro lado, la pereza de saber que hay que adaptarse a una nueva interfase.

Todos deseamos que las mejoras que tenemos en mente aparezcan en una nueva versión de *Word.* Creo que una mejora positiva sería la incorporación de búsquedas inteligentes que pudieran automatizarse para facilitar reemplazos globales, como por ejemplo información en serie, palabras con cierta lógica, etc. Otra mejora podría ser la posibilidad de ver tablas e imágenes agrupadas en una sola pantalla para compararlas fácilmente, intercambiarlas de lugar, etc.

Pero no perdamos de vista el objetivo de este apéndice y pasemos de la expectativa a la realidad. La versión de prueba de *Word 2000* está lista. Este apéndice es un sumario de las principales diferencias respecto del *Word* 97, ordenadas con el mismo criterio que en el manual.

Ahora sólo queda que Ud., el futuro usuario, evalúe los pro y los contra y comience a familiarizarse con la nueva interfase. De este modo no se sentirá tan sólo cuando en el 2000 encienda la máquina para reemplazar a su viejo y querido procesador de texto por este nuevo, embellecido y mejorado *Word* 2000.

2. TECLADO Y *MOUSE*

2.1. Escritura

Lo más novedoso en este tema es sin duda la posibilidad de llevar el cursor a cualquier parte de la hoja con sólo hacer un doble clic. ¡No más desconcierto al querer escribir al final de una hoja en blanco y ver que no podemos llevar el cursor hasta allí! ¡No más ¨*ENTERS*¨ hasta llegar a la línea deseada! A partir del 2000 un doble clic en donde mejor se nos ocurra y empieza la carta. Recordemos que hasta ahora sólo se podía llevar el cursor al final de la hoja si ésta estaba escrita en su totalidad o si ingresábamos líneas en blanco.

Word 2000 pensó en todo, hasta en lo más simple. Los principiantes... ¡Agradecidos!

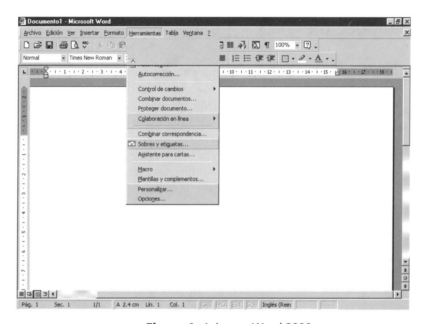

Figura 1. *Así se ve Word 2000.*

2.2. Mejoras para usuarios asiáticos

Hay muchas herramientas que fueron mejoradas y otras que fueron agregadas en relación con este tema. *Word 2000* incluye tipografía japonesa, personalización de caracteres y un sistema de traducción Chino simplificado/Chino tradicional que permite mejorar e integrar otro tipos de escrituras al procesador de texto ya desarrollado.

2.3. Nuevo Editor Global de ingresos (IME)

Esta es sin duda la novedad en materia de globalización, ya que permite que usuarios asiáticos escriban en japonés, coreano y chino (tanto tradicional como simplificado), aún teniendo un sistema occidental.

3. ENTORNO

3.1. Menúes Expandibles e Inteligentes

Tal vez lo más vistoso del nuevo *Word 2000*. El menú se expande automáticamente cuando el usuario ubica el puntero arriba y, en lugar de aparecer todos los comandos de ese menú (como ocurría hasta ahora), sólo aparecen los comandos más usados por ese usuario en particular. Haciendo un clic al final del menú mostramos todo lo que existe allí y que está oculto.

El siguiente ejemplo ilustra lo anterior. Supongamos que un usuario suele utilizar el menú **Formato** para realizar alguna de las siguientes acciones:

◆ Variar el tipo de letra de sus documentos.
◆ Modificar la alineación de los párrafos.
◆ Elegir el aspecto de números y viñetas.
◆ Cambiar la forma de los bordes de sus marcos.

Cuando este usuario ubique el puntero arriba del menú **Formato,** el mismo mostrará como únicas opciones los siguientes comandos:

◆ **Fuente.**
◆ **Párrafo.**
◆ **Números y Viñetas.**
◆ **Bordes y Sombreados.**

En caso de que quiera hacer algo completamente diferente a lo habitual, deberá hacer un clic al final del menú para mostrar las demás opciones ocultas allí.

De acuerdo al modo como trabajan los menúes podríamos decir que se trata de una interfase inteligente, ya que *Word* detecta los comandos más solicitados y los ubica al comienzo del menú, mientras que los que se usan poco o casi nada los quita y deja latentes para ser mostrados sólo si el usuario así lo desea.

La personalización de la interfase es una manera de no sobrecargar al usuario de comandos que no necesita. La dirección que tomó *Microsoft* en este sentido fue clara: no apabullar al usuario de opciones, ofrecerle las cosas de a poco y darle más a medida que pida, respetando sus propios tiempos.

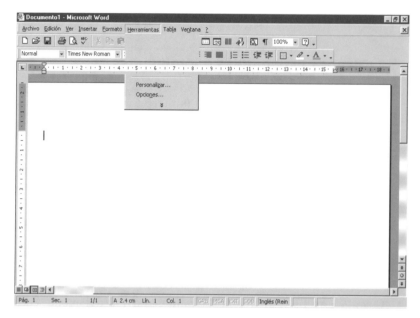

***Figura 2.** Menúes inteligentes. Una clave de Word 2000.*

3.2. Compatibilidad

Pensando en aquellos usuarios rezagados, *Microsoft* incorporó la posibilidad de poner sobre aviso al usuario de *Word 2000* sobre aquellos formatos que no podrán ser leídos por versiones anteriores de *Word*. El usuario *2000* tendrá entonces la posibilidad de deshabilitar estas funciones o atributos para evitar que se pierda información relevante cuando el documento sea abierto en un sistema con una versión de *Word* anterior a la que generó el documento. Es por eso que antes de guardar, *Word 2000* le advierte sobre la incompatibilidad, para que el usuario pueda tomar la mejor decisión en este sentido.

3.3. Ayuda poliglota

Con miras al año 2000, *Microsoft* tomó conciencia de que el 60% de los usuarios de *Word* no son angloparlantes. Es por eso que creó esta facilidad. Ahora el menú ayuda viene en varios idiomas y aún teniendo *Word* en inglés, podemos configurar la ayuda para que aparezca en español. Los archivos de ayuda fueron mejorados, hay mayor variedad de temas, se puede encontrar más fácilmente la información, etc.

4. EDICIÓN

4.1. Portapapeles Acumulativo

Tal vez, la novedad más esperada en el tema edición llega con *Word 2000*. Se trata de la posibilidad de cortar o copiar varios ítems y acumularlos en el Portapapeles, para luego pegarlos todos juntos donde corresponda. Algo que parecía evidente y sumamente necesario para los usuarios de todo nivel, llega recién ahora, después de muchas esperas. A decir verdad, las versiones de *Word* existentes en el mercado tienen esta facilidad, pero no como una herramienta más del entorno, sino como una macro especial que hay que instalar en la plantilla Normal.dot (algo poco frecuente de realizar, sobre todo para el que recién empieza). La característica acumulativa del portapapeles hace muy sencillo juntar información de diferentes fuentes y volcarla de una sola vez en el lugar adecuado.

Figura 3. Portapapeles con capacidad acumulativa.

5. MANEJO DE ARCHIVOS

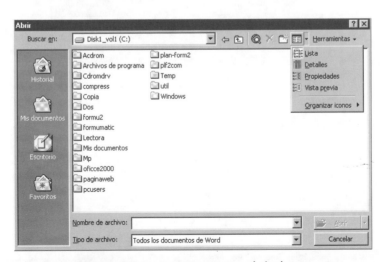

Figura 4. Nueva ventana para abrir documentos.

5.1. Impresión

La gran novedad en este tema es el nuevo comando de impresión que permite que el usuario redimensione el documento al momento de imprimirlo. Esto es realmente práctico, porque podemos adaptar una presentación que ya fue hecha, por ejemplo, para formato Oficio, a un formato Carta, recién al momento de imprimirla.

En *Word*, sin embargo, la gran utilidad de esta nueva herramienta parecería pasar más por el lado del *"preview"* (el equivalente en castellano de pantallazo, vistazo) que por el lado de la papelería.

Cuando hablamos de *preview* nos referimos a la posibilidad de disminuir el tamaño de las páginas del documento, de modo que varias de ellas entren en una sola carilla (por ejemplo en una carilla de hoja oficio). En otras palabras, volcar en papel la imagen de las pequeñas hojas que vemos cuando entramos a Presentación Preliminar.

La posibilidad de imprimir un "preview" es evidentemente una ayuda enorme para revisar gran cantidad de texto que antes estaba anclado en la pantalla y que a partir de *Word 2000* podremos llevar adonde se nos ocurra en un formato pequeño.

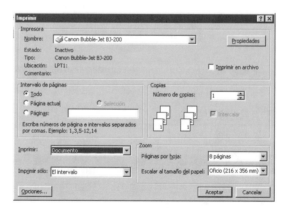

Figura 5. *Cuadro de diálogo Impresión.*

6. PRESENTACIONES

6.1. Presentación para páginas Web

Word 2000 incorpora una nueva presentación, que en inglés se denomina *Web Layout View*. Esta nueva presentación está pensada para mejorar la apreciación en pantalla de las páginas *Web*. A partir de esta versión de *Word*, pasar al Explorador para ver cómo está quedando nuestra página *Web* será algo anecdótico.

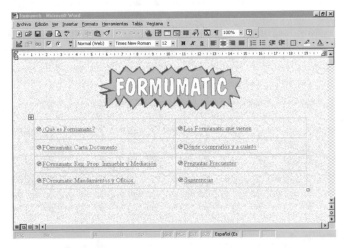

Figura 6. *Así se ven las páginas Web en Word con la nueva presentación.*

6.2. Menú Ver mejorado

Las consultas que se realizaron desde *Microsoft* sobre el uso de los distintos tipos de Presentación puso de manifiesto que la mayoría de los usuarios de *Word* presentan dificultades para mostrar en pantalla el mismo documento de diferentes modos. Esto hizo que se tomara la decisión de mejorar el menú **Ver**, que es el que contiene 7 de las 8 presentaciones que existen en Word.

A partir de *Word 2000* dicho menú está orientado, ya no al tipo de presentación a la que queremos llegar, sino a la tarea que vamos a desarrollar. Esto significa que, por ejemplo, si el usuario quiere imprimir, en vez de elegir en el menú **Ver** la opción **Presentación Preliminar**, elige en **Ver** la tarea que va a desarrollar (en este caso imprimir). *Word 2000* pasa automáticamente a la Presentación adecuada sin solicitar mayor información.

En síntesis, a la hora de presentar documentos en pantalla, *Word 2000* ¨se puso las pilas¨. Ahora el usuario sólo se limita a ¨explicar¨ lo que quiere hacer. Word salta inmediatamente a la presentación adecuada sin mostrar el viejo y resistido menú **Ver** con sus numerosas opciones.

7. TABLAS

7.1. Tablas Anidadas

La novedad en materia de tablas son sin duda las tablas anidadas. Las tablas anidadas son aquellas que se encuentran una adentro de otra. La idea de una tabla adentro de otra no parece demasiado relevante en apariencia, pero si pensamos un poco más nos damos cuenta de las ventajas. Las tablas anidadas nos permiten incluir todo un esquema que ya fue hecho en una tabla, en el interior de otra que tiene una configuración distinta. Esto tiene la ventaja de que no hay necesidad de desarmar la información para adaptarla a otras celdas, columnas, filas, etc. sino que con sólo arrastrarla con el Mouse y tirarla en la celda de la tabla destino, armamos un esquema de información que inmediatamente se adapta al formato que queremos.¡No más esfuerzo en adaptar las tablas existentes a un nuevo formato!. Ahora, una celda puede albergar a otra y a otra, y así sucesivamente.

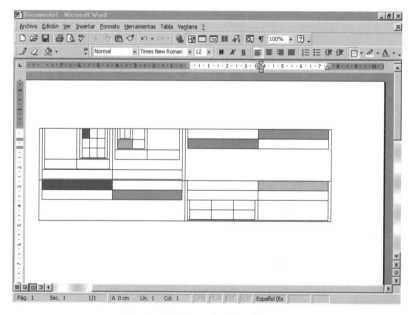

Figura 7. Ejemplo de tablas anidadas

7.2. Nuevo manejo de tablas

Word 2000 equipara el manejo de tablas al manejo de imágenes y objetos, y esto es sin duda... ¡una gran ventaja! A partir de ahora las tablas pueden arrastrarse con el *Mouse* a cualquier lugar del documento como si fueran verdaderos contenedores de información. Podemos moverlas al comienzo y al fin de la página, sacarlas fuera, al escritorio hasta decidir su ubicación final, poner una al lado de otra,etc. En las últimas versiones, no se las podía ubicar donde uno realmente quería, no se las podía sacar rápidamente de una página y llevarlas a otra, en fin, no existía el manejo flexible que se tiene a partir de esta nueva versión de *Word*.

7.3. Redimensión de tablas

A todas las ventajas que ya existían en *Word* 97 en materia de tablas ahora se suma la posibilidad de redimensionar tablas, utilizando los controladores de tamaño de las esquinas. Algo asombroso si pensamos que esto implica casi un doble comportamiento de la información. Decimos un doble comportamiento porque la tabla en sí, con sus disposiciones de columnas y filas, y sus marcadores de fin de fila y de fin de celda siempre fue casi una línea más de texto. Por lo tanto, pensar que ahora se puede redimensionar como un objeto nos lleva a imaginar un comportamiento dual que no deja de asombrar

Si pensamos en lo difícil que es manejar tamaños exactos de alto de fila y ancho de columna desde el menú tablas, la posibilidad de hacerlo manualmente tirando de una ¨oreja¨ es verdaderamente ventajosa. Seguramente cuando instalemos *Word 2000* vamos a jugar mucho con esto. Tirando del cuadradito de la esquina de una tabla y viendo cómo varía de tamaño toda la estructura nos vamos a reír de los viejos comandos del menú tablas, que nos pedían valores en puntos para definir el alto de una fila.

7.4. Ajuste de Tablas

Word 2000 permite ajustar texto alrededor de una tabla, (recordemos que esto antes estaba limitado sólo a las imágenes o a los Cuadros de texto). A partir del 2000, las tablas también podrán estar coronadas de letras y ubicadas en el medio de una hoja escrita. Y como si esto fuera poco, también podremos decidir el aspecto que tomará el texto alrededor de la misma: si estará a la misma distancia de todos los bordes, si aparecerá más cerca del borde izquierdo que del derecho, etc. Una innovación más en materia de tablas, que nos planta frente al desafío de toda nueva herramienta: aprender a utilizarla y que sus resultados se vean reflejados en nuestros documentos.

7.5. Nuevas Herramientas para manejo de tablas

Tal vez lo más novedoso en esta materia sean las herramientas que permiten dibujar casi intuitivamente tablas simples y complejas y borrarlas con sólo hacer un clic en ellas. A partir de esta versión de *Word*, las herramientas para dibujar una tabla ya no son más un proyecto de.... sino que pasan a ser verdaderos utensilios de trabajo. Un claro ejemplo de esto es la goma, que antes borraba bordes pero dejaba la estructura de la tabla intacta. Los usuarios poco experimentados se quedaban desconcertados frente a este comportamiento ilógico. Muchos creían que estaban usando mal la herramienta porque habían borrado y sin embargo la celda seguía estando. Con *Word 2000* esa duda desaparece. La goma borra tablas, celdas, bordes y todo lo que se le plante enfrente. La herramienta de dibujo crea celdas, filas, columnas, tablas simples, tablas complejas y todo lo que pueda imaginar el que la gobierne (hasta bordes diagonales). Nuevas herramientas de dibujo para tablas: sólo necesitamos paciencia para entenderlas, un poco de creatividad y el trabajo está listo.

Figura 8. *Nuevas Herramientas para tablas.*

7.6. Gráficos en tablas

Los usuarios de *Word 2000* podrán insertar imágenes dentro de una tabla y obtener el mismo manejo de gráficos tanto dentro como fuera de la tabla. No creo que valga la pena agregar mucho más. Una maravilla, como todo lo que nos está mostrando la Beta de *Word 2000* en materia de tablas.

8. OBJETOS

8.1. Más colores

Aumenta la variedad de colores tanto para texto como para bordes y sombreados. Ahora se puede sombrear en cualquier color o elegir colores de fuentes lilas, fucsias o el que se nos ocurra. Las versiones anteriores de *Word* estaban limitadas a la paleta de colores de una configuración VGA. Ahora podrán usarse colores de 24 bits, lo que significa... ¡Mucho más!

8.2. Objetos WordArt más flexibles

Word 2000 evolucionó mucho hacia la interfase Internet. El objetivo de los creadores de *Office* fue extender la funcionalidad de las herramientas de modo que pudieran servir a aquellos usuarios que no sólo necesitan un procesador de texto, sino que también quieren diseñar sus propias páginas *Web*, esquemas laborales, presentaciones gráficas, etc.

Dada la popularidad de las viñetas gráficas generada en los formatos de páginas *Web*, *Word 2000,* ahora, permite que podamos tomar cualquier gráfico y convertirlo en viñeta.

Es por todo lo anterior que a partir de esta versión de *Word*, las viñetas gráficas cobran importancia. Podemos definir objetos del *WordArt* como viñetas, cosa que implica una potencia enorme al momento de crear.

Preparémonos entonces para ver todo tipo de viñetas en aquellos carteles hechos en *Word*, que son tan comunes en las puertas de las oficinas, en la paredes de los negocios, etc. A partir de ahora las presentaciones convencionales serán sólo patrimonio de aquellos que no se animen a experimentar. ¡La carrera está casi por comenzar! ¿Quién se atreve a crear la primera viñeta gráfica e incluirla en sus escritos?

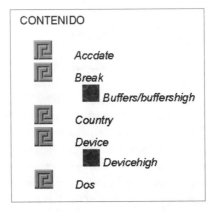

Figura 9. *Viñetas mejoradas.*

8.3. Librería de Imágenes

Esta librería tenía forzosamente que mejorar para ponerse a la altura de los requerimientos. Aumenta la variedad de imágenes y sobretodo se incorporan imágenes mucho más profesionales de lo que eran hasta ahora.

Figura 10. *Librería de Imágenes.*

9. HERRAMIENTAS

9.1. Autocorrección Inteligente

La evolución de *Word* en materia de Autocorrección no estuvo dirigida tanto hacia la cantidad como hacia la calidad. *Word 2000* ya no sólo basa la Autocorrección Ortográfica en una comparación ˝mecánica˝ frente a una lista de palabras incorporada en su diccionario, sino que detecta errores obvios que pueden ser de tipeo (y para los cuales evidentemente no existe sugerencia) y los corrige automáticamente sin preguntar al usuario si aprueba o no el cambio, y sin mostrar el famoso letrero ˝No existe sugerencia˝. En ese sentido, *Word 2000* quita la pesada carga que significaba responder una y otra vez a la interrogación del corrector frente a palabras mal escritas cuya corrección evidentemente no se encuentra en un diccionario.

9.2. Autocorrección Gramatical

No más subrayados verdes donde no corresponde. *Word 2000* finalmente tomó en serio la gramática e incorporó mejores sugerencias para los verdaderos errores (y no las obviedades que mostraba antes). Además ahora deja de detectar como faltas estructuras poco convencionales pero no por eso erróneas.

9.3. Detector inteligente de idiomas

Se trata de una función que permite identificar, tan pronto como se ingresan las primeras palabras, en qué idioma está la escritura, y cargar automáticamente el diccionario correspondiente a fin de que quede disponible en caso de que el usuario realice una Corrección Automática de Ortografía y Gramática. Esto antes se hacía seleccionando el texto y definiendo el idioma correspondiente, lo que traía aparejado el problema de que si no se definía bien el idioma antes de abrir el documento, o antes de empezar a escribir, *Word* desconocía todas las palabras y las subrayaba en rojo. Algo molesto como carta de presentación de un procesador de texto internacional, y en el que ya estaban automatizadas tareas no relacionadas directamente con la escritura, como por ejemplo el autoformato de Tablas, o las automatizaciones de todo tipo de tareas utilizando macros.

10. PÁGINAS *WEB*

10.1. Introducción

Sin duda el hincapié de *Word 2000* está puesto en integrar el ambiente de la oficina o el escritorio en el que se encuentra el usuario con el maravilloso entorno generado por Internet.

Si bien las herramientas de acceso a Internet ya se encontraban desarrolladas en *Word* 97, es recién en esta nueva versión de *Word* donde podríamos considerar que el escritorio de trabajo se amplía verdaderamente para integrar al individuo y su PC a las comunicaciones interactivas, los grupos de noticias, las páginas *Web*, etc.

Una necesidad concreta de los usuarios de *Word* y el paquete *Office* resutaba evidente: contar con herramientas *Web* para crear documentos-páginas *Web* que pudiesen ser publicados fácilmente en Internet, y a la vez que estas herramientas no fueran desconocidas, de modo de no tener más cosas que aprender.

Word 2000 consideró estas exigencias, y en esta versión de prueba ya se ve algo de los resultados: un entorno similar al de *Word* 97, las herramientas ya conocidas, otras herramientas nuevas pero de similares características a las ya existentes, y la posibilidad de que un documento ¨doc¨ pueda ser enviado vía E-mail a cualquier parte, o bien publicado en una Intranet o en la misma Internet sin contar con demasiados conocimientos adicionales a los necesarios para llevar ese documento al papel.

Las siguientes son algunas de las nuevas propuestas de *Microsoft* para *Word 2000* y su interacción con Internet.

10.2. Formato de archivos HTML absolutamente compatible

Lo que varía con respecto a la versión anterior es la flexibilidad con que se maneja el formato HTML. Todos los documentos HTML podrán ser leídos en *Word*, independientemente del programa en el que hayan sido creados. Esto significa que el usuario podrá incorporar a su documento páginas *Web* simplemente eligiéndolas y abriéndolas como si se tratara de cualquier documento ¨doc¨ . A su vez, el usuario podrá crear documentos *Word*, salvarlos como HTML, reabrirlos como ¨doc¨, etc. Es decir, no se perderá información en el pasaje de un tipo de formato a otro, aún cuando no tengan demasiado sentido, ni se usen los comentarios en el formato HTML. Esto fue pensado para que el usuario pueda hacer cambios a las páginas HTML fácilmente.

En caso de que exista algún tipo de incompatibilidad, el archivo se abrirá y se presentará lo que se pueda ver. *Word 2000* conservará aquellos códigos HTML que no pudieron ser interpretados en un archivo separado, para que el usuario maneje esta información a su conveniencia: los deje de lado, intente reconvertirlos, editarlos.

10.3. Automatización de Codificación HTML

La Codificación Automática de formatos HTML es una de las claves de la compatibilidad HTML que presenta *Word 2000*. Los archivos HTML pueden guardarse con diferentes tipos de codificación HTML. Una codificación HTML es un modo de representar texto en formato binario. Existen muchos formatos binarios a lo largo del mundo. La codificación HTML más común es la ISO-8859-1, sin embargo existen algunos idiomas que no son compatibles con este tipo de codificación, como por ejemplo el japonés. La gran ventaja de *Word 2000* es que detecta todo tipo de codificaciones HTML y aplica los filtros necesarios para que toda la información sea comprendida y pueda ser importada y exportada en forma adecuada y de modo que no se pierda el contenido.

Otra clave de la compatibilidad HTML es la asignación que hace *Word 2000* del tipo apropiado de fuente, basado en los estándares de cada codificación HTML. Esto es muy importante en Asia, en donde la asignación de un tipo de fuente equivocado provoca que se pierda la información contenida en esa página.

10.4. Creación de páginas Web

Las novedades en este tema son las siguientes:

Posibilidad de crear sitios Web utilizando un Asistente.

La mayoría de los usuarios de *Word* que necesitan confeccionar una página *Web* no conocen el lenguaje HTML ni tienen intención de conocerlo. Pensando en ellos, *Microsoft* desarrolló un Asistente para páginas *Web* que, incluido como una herramienta más de *Word 2000*, guía al usuario en la creación de varias páginas *Web*. Este Asistente contempla el caso de que dichas páginas necesiten estar vinculadas entre sí de modo de formar un ¨*Site*¨ que pueda ¨subirse¨ a la red para ser visitado como cualquier otro de los tantos sitios que ya existen en Internet.

Indudablemente, el plato fuerte de *Word 2000* es la posibilidad de acceso a Internet a través de aquellas herramientas con las cuales el usuario está familiarizado y se siente seguro. De hecho, *Word* cuenta con otros asistentes, como lo son el Asistente para envío de Fax o el Asistente para confección de etiquetas, que el usuario ya conoce y con los que se siente seguro.

Páginas Web compatibles con cualquier tipo de Navegador

Microsoft encontró que muchas empresas y la mayoría de los usuarios independientes son más reticentes a actualizar sus navegadores que a actualizar su procesador de texto. Esto trae aparejado el riesgo de que, al reemplazar el procesador de texto, las nuevas herramientas que se incorporan en él para el diseño de páginas *Web*, incluyan elementos en estas páginas no soportados por el viejo navegador aún instalado en el sistema. Por decirlo de otro modo, que la PC evolucione de forma despareja incorporando, por un lado formatos modernos para creación de páginas *Web*, y por el otro, quedándose afuera de estos adelantos al no contar con un navegador adecuado para la interpretación de los mismos. Afortunadamente, *Word 2000* se adelanta a este posible conflicto con una función que permite declarar en el procesador de texto el navegador instalado en el sistema, a fin de que se desactiven automáticamente aquellos elementos que no podrán ser interpretados por este último. La ventaja en este caso es que el usuario tiene la posibilidad de utilizar herramientas de última generación para crear sus páginas *Web*, y a la vez manejar esta información de modo que pueda ser interpretada por todos los sistemas, independientemente de que cuenten o no con esos adelantos. Esta característica surge a partir de la incorporación de herramientas de *Font Page*.

Nueva Vista Preliminar para Páginas Web

Si bien existe una compatibilidad absoluta entre el formato ¨doc¨ y el formato ¨html¨, las páginas *Web* no se ven exactamente igual en *Word* que lo que se verán en Internet cuando sean accedidas por un navegador. Es por eso que cuando diseñamos una página *Web* en *Word* necesitamos permanentemente evaluar su aspecto en el navegador instalado en el sistema. *Microsoft* pensó en esto al incorporar a *Word 2000* la nueva **Vista Preliminar para Páginas Web**. La misma se accede desde el botón **Vista Preliminar** de la barra **Estándar**, o bien haciendo un clic en **Archivo** y seleccionando la opción **Vista Preliminar**.

Plantillas para Páginas Web(Themes)

Las Plantillas para Páginas *Web* no son otra cosa que diferentes modelos entre los cuales elegimos uno al momento de crear una página. Cada uno de estos modelos cuenta con un diseño adecuado para el estilo que se pretende. Son ejemplo de elementos el fondo, las fuentes, los gráficos, las viñetas, las líneas, etc. Este tipo de plantillas no son nuevas en *Word 2000*, sin embargo las incluimos entre las novedades porque ahora existen por decenas y son absolutamente compatibles con otras aplicaciones de *Microsoft*, como por ejemplo *FontPage*.

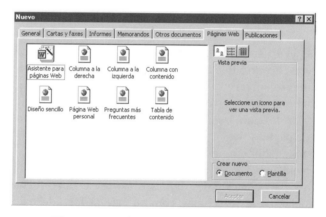

Figura 11. *Nuevas plantillas para páginas Web.*

Hipervínculos más fáciles de crear, configurar, etc.

Word 2000 propone una interfase absolutamente nueva en materia de Hipervínculos. Esta novedad apunta, no sólo a mejorar la dificultad que existía al tratar de configurar un Hipervínculo (ya que la pantalla saltaba automáticamente a la dirección de dicho Hipervínculo.), sino a permitir el ingreso no sólo de Hipervínculos que direccionen a otras páginas, sino también de aquellos que disparen el acceso a un correo electrónico para enviar un *E-mail*. Entre las novedades con que cuenta la intrefase para Hipervínculos está la nueva facilidad que controla las direcciones incluidas en ellos al momento de cerrar la página *Web*. En el caso de que hubiera novedades en los archivos a los que se hace referencia en cada uno de los Hipervínculos, se produce una actualización automática que evita futuros errores.

Figura 12. *Nueva Interfase para Hipervínculos.*

Nuevos Marcos y Tablas de Contenidos

En el tema Marcos aparece una nueva barra de Herramientas que muestra mayor variedad de diseños.

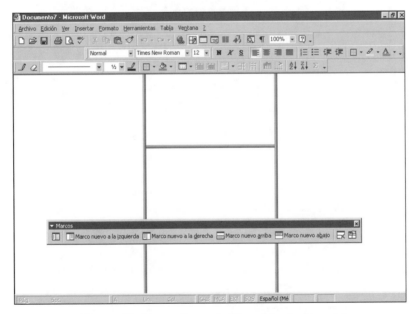

Figura 13. *Nueva Barra de Herramientas para Marcos.*

Las Tablas de Contenidos se comportan de modo distinto en las páginas *Web* que en los documentos comunes. En el lugar en donde normalmente aparece un número de página se disponen Hipervínculos. Haciendo un clic en ellos saltamos automáticamente a la dirección donde se encuentran esos temas. Esto es algo muy práctico, ya que la Tabla de Contenidos no sólo es un temario sino también la puerta de entrada a esos contenidos a través de los Hipervínculos existentes en ella.

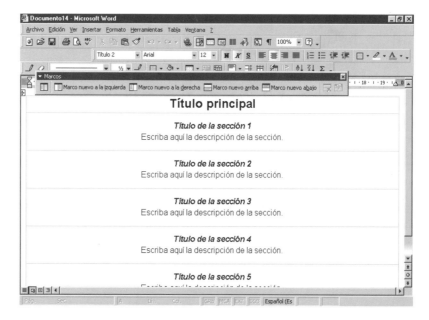

Figura 14. *Tabla de Contenidos para Páginas Web.*

11. INCORPORACIÓN DE *E-MAIL* A *WORD*

Estas nuevas herramientas surgen a partir de la realidad de que los trabajos grupales, los negocios, los contratos y todo otro tipo de transacciones tienden a realizarse vía *E-mail*. La idea de incorporar *E-mail* a *Word 2000* fue también consecuencia de otros dos hechos. El primero tiene que ver con la practicidad. Es evidentemente más práctico iniciar la comunicación directamente desde el mismo escenario en el que guardamos la información que vamos a enviar, que estar pasando de un programa a otro. El otro hecho tiene que ver con el desarrollo y las mejoras que se hicieron al lenguaje HTML. En *Word 97* existía la posibilidad de un intercambio vía *E-mail* utilizando *Word Mail*, sin embargo esos correos sólo podían ser leídos por otros usuarios de *Word Mail*. Esto implicaba dejar afuera a aquellos usuarios de muchos otros productos de correo electrónico muy populares como *Outlook, Eudora,* etc.

Las novedades de *Word 2000* respecto a *E-mail* son las siguientes.

♦ E-Mail mejorado

Word 2000 incorporó una versión revisada de *Word Mail*, que ahora se denomina *Microsoft Office E-mail*. Esta versión utiliza HTML como formato de intercambio, lo que implica que cualquier usuario que cuente con cualquier tipo de programa de correo electrónico pueda recibir el envío con absoluta fidelidad, sin perder información, sin perder formatos, etc.

Sin embargo, la mejora más importante no reside sólo en la compatibilidad, sino en el concepto en sí del componente *Word Mail*. Antes, *Word Mail* se cargaba como un componente OLE de *Outlook*. El usuario no veía nada especial, pero cuando intentaba abrir *Word Mail*, en realidad abría primero *Outlook, que* cargaba a *Word Mail* como un gran componente OLE. Esto provocaba una enorme demanda de memoria temporal con la consiguiente baja de *perfomance* en el sistema. El usuario tenía que esperar mucho tiempo hasta ver el programa abierto en pantalla, situación que muchas veces lo desalentaba a continuar la operación.

Esto afortunadamente cambió en *Word 2000*. El correo electrónico se carga como una aplicación independiente, de ejecución rápida, de fácil acceso y que demanda los recursos normales que puede demandar un programa de *E-Mail*, como puede ser *Eudora*.

♦ Papelería propia

Los usuarios de *Word 2000* pueden incluir papelería personal en el envío de sus *E-Mails*. Esto implica incluir sus datos personales, logos, tipos de fuente y fondo especiales, estilos que los indentifiquen, etc. A su vez, en los *E-mails* en los que se envíe una charla *on line*, cada uno de los participantes estará automáticamente identificado con un color y un tipo de sangría especial, de modo que el que reciba el *E- Mail* pueda seguir fácilmente la conversación, saber quién hizo tal o cual comentario, etc.

◆ Herramienta Autofirma

Gracias a la nueva herramienta *Autosignature*, las firmas ya no se limitan más al papel. *Word 2000* incorpora la firma en pantalla, de modo de poder enviar un *E-Mail* debidamente firmado. A su vez, haciendo un clic en el botón derecho del *Mouse* podemos modificar la firma, elegir entre varios modelos de firma, etc.

La incorporación de *E-mail* a *Word* abre una puerta de comunicaciones enorme. El usuario no sólo puede hablar *on line* con el personal de la oficina de al lado. Ahora también puede ingresar desde su escritorio a los grupos de noticias de todo el mundo, intercambiar ideas *on-line*, recibir la últimas noticias de boca de quien las está viviendo, y por ende tomar la decisión acertada en el momento preciso.

APÉNDICE
INSTALACIÓN DE
COMPONENTES

B

Tiempo de lectura y práctica:
45 minutos

Apéndice

B

Instalación de componentes

PASO A PASO

Para instalar o desinstalar componentes de Word es necesario contar con el CD o el disco fuente desde donde se instaló *Word* originalmente. Una vez insertado el disco o CD de instalación original puede proceder del siguiente modo:

Paso 1

En el menú **Inicio** de *Windows* elegir **Configurar** y luego **Panel de Control** como se muestra en la **Figura 1**.

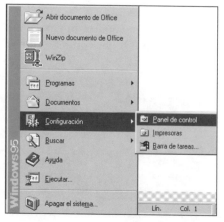

Figura 1. *Primer paso para instalar un componente de Word.*

Paso 2

En la ventana que aparece y que se muestra en la **Figura 2** elegir la opción **Agregar/Quitar Programas.**

Figura 2. *Elegir Agregar/Quitar Programas para agregar o quitar un componente.*

Paso 3

De la lista de programas que aparecen elegir *Microsoft Office* y luego hacer un clic en el botón **Agregar/Quitar** como se muestra en la **Figura 3**.

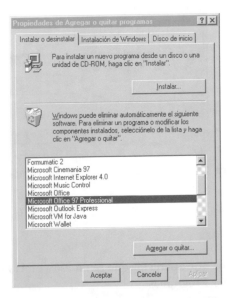

Figura 3. *En esta ventana elegir Microsoft Office para agregar un componente a Word.*

Paso 4

En la ventana de la **Figura 4** elegir la opción *Word* y luego hacer un clic en el botón **Modificar Opción**.

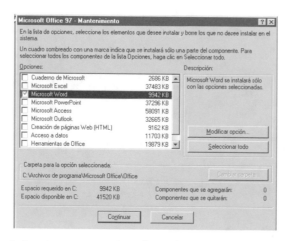

Figura 4. *Cuarto paso para instalar o desinstalar componentes de Word.*

Paso 5

En la ventana que aparece habilitar los componentes que se quieren instalar o deshabilitar aquellos que se quieren desinstalar como lo muestra la **Figura 5** y salir aceptando.

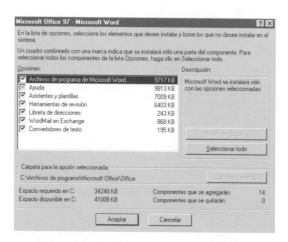

Figura 5. *Así termina la instalación o desinstalación de componentes.*

INFORMACIÓN ÚTIL

- Atajos de teclado

- Los mejores sitios Web

- Índice alfabético

Tiempo de lectura y práctica:
45 minutos

Información útil

■ Atajos de teclado

EL TECLADO Y SUS ATAJOS

TECLAS	FUNCIÓN	SHIFT	CTRL	CTRL+SHIFT	ALT	ALT+SHIFT	CTRL+ALT
F1	Llama a la ayuda	Llama a la ayuda contextual			Salta al campo siguiente	Salta al Campo anterior	Muestra Información sobre Microsoft
F2	Mueve texto o gráficos	Copia texto	Pasa a Presentación Preliminar			Guarda un documento	Abre un documento
F3	INSERT a un Autotexto	Cambia de Mayúscula a Minúscula.	Ejecuta Cortado Especial	INSERTa el contenido de Especial	Crea un elemento de Autotexto		
F4	Repite la última acción	Repite una acción de Buscar o de Ir a	Cierra la ventana		Sale de Word	Sale de Word	
F5	Ejecuta Edición/ Ir a	Salta a la revisión anterior	Restablece el tamaño de la ventana del documento	Modifica un marcador	Vuelve al tamaño original de la ventana		
F6	Salta al siguiente panel	Salta al panel anterior	Salta a la siguiente ventana	Salta a la ventana anterior			
F7	Ejecuta Herramientas/ Ortografía	Ejecuta Herramientas/ Sinónimos/ Idioma.	Ejecuta el comando Mover del menú Control	Actualiza la información vinculada en un documento origen de Word	Busca el error ortográfico siguiente. (Revisar ortografía mientras escribe activada)		
F8	Extiende una selección	Reduce una selección	Ejecuta el comando Tamaño del menú Control de documentos	Extiende una selección	Ejecuta una macro		
F9	Actualiza los campos seleccionados	Pasa de un código de campo a su resultado	INSERTa un campo vacío	Desvincula un campo	Pasa todos los códigos de campo a sus resultados	Ejecuta BOTóN IR A o BOTóN MACRO desde el campo que muestra los resultados de campo	
F10	Activa la barra de menús	Muestra un menú contextual	Maximiza la ventana del documento	Activa la Regla	Maximiza la ventana del programa		
F11	Salta al campo siguiente	Salta al campo anterior	Bloquea un campo	Desbloquea un campo	Muestra el código de Visual Basic		
F12	Ejecuta Archivo/ Guardar Como	Ejecuta Archivo/ Guardar	Ejecuta Archivo/ Abrir	Ejecuta Archivos/ Imprimir			

ATAJOS DE TECLADO PARA COPIAR Y PEGAR TEXTO Y ELEMENTOS GRÁFICOS

PARA	PRESIONE
Copia texto o elementos gráficos	CTRL+C
Copia formatos	CTRL+MAYúS+C
Mueve texto o elementos gráficos	F2
Pega texto o elementos gráficos	CTRL+V
Pega formatos	CTRL+MAYúS+V

ATAJOS DE TECLADO PARA EDITAR TEXTO Y ELEMENTOS GRÁFICOS

PARA	PULSAR
Elimina un carácter a la izquierda del punto de inserción	RETROCESO (Backspace)
Elimina una palabra a la izquierda del punto de inserción	CTRL+RETROCESO (Backspace)
Elimina un carácter a la derecha del punto de inserción	SUPR(Del)
Elimina una palabra a la derecha del punto de inserción	CTRL+SUPR(Del)
Corta texto seleccionado y lo copia al Portapapeles	CTRL+X
Deshace la última acción	CTRL+Z
Corta al Especial	CTRL+F3
Cancela una acción	ESC
Deshace una acción	CTRL+Z
Rehace o repetir una acción	CTRL+Y

ATAJOS DE TECLADO PARA INSERTAR CARACTERES ESPECIALES

PARA	PULSAR
Campo	CTRL+F9
Elemento de Autotexto	Escriba el nombre del elemento de Autotexto y, a continuación, presione CTRL+ALT+G
Salto de línea	MAYúS+ENTER
Salto de página	CTRL+ENTER
Salto de columna	CTRL+MAYúS+ENTER
Guión opcional	CTRL+GUIóN
Guión común	CTRL+MAYúS+GUIóN
Espacio común	CTRL+MAYúS+BARRA ESPACIADORA
Símbolo de Copyright	CTRL+ALT+C
Símbolo de registrado	CTRL+ALT+ R
Símbolo de marca registrada	CTRL+ALT+ T
Puntos suspensivos	CTRL+ALT+ PUNTO
Comillas de apertura	CTRL+`"`
Comillas de cierre	CTRL+`"`

ATAJOS DE TECLADO PARA SELECCIONAR TEXTO

PARA	PULSAR
Un carácter a la derecha	MAYúS+FLECHA DERECHA
Un carácter a la izquierda	MAYúS+FLECHA IZQUIERDA
Hasta el final de una palabra	CTRL+MAYúS+FLECHA DERECHA
Hasta el principio de una palabra	CTRL+MAYúS+FLECHA IZQUIERDA
Hasta el final de una línea	MAYúS+FIN (END)
Hasta el principio de una línea	MAYúS+INICIO(HOME)
Una línea abajo	MAYúS+FLECHA ABAJO
Una línea arriba	MAYúS+FLECHA ARRIBA
Hasta el final de un párrafo	CTRL+MAYúS+FLECHA ABAJO
Hasta el principio de un párrafo	CTRL+MAYúS+FLECHA ARRIBA
Una pantalla abajo	MAYúS+AV PáG
Una pantalla arriba	MAYúS+RE PáG
Hasta el final de un documento	CTRL+MAYúS+ FIN
Hasta el principio de un documento	CTRL+MAYúS+ INICIO
Para incluir el documento entero	CTRL+E

ATAJOS DE TECLADO PARA CAMBIAR EL FORMATO DE CARÁCTER.

PARA	PULSAR
Cambia la fuente	CTRL+MAYúS+F
Cambia el tamaño de la fuente	CTRL+MAYúS+M
Aumenta el tamaño de la fuente	CTRL+MAYúS+>
Disminuye el tamaño de la fuente	CTRL +<
Aumenta 1 punto el tamaño de la fuente	ALT+CTRL+<
Disminuye 1 punto el tamaño de la fuente	ALT+CTRL+>
Ejecuta los comandos Formato/Fuente	CTRL+M
Cambia mayúsculas o minúsculas	MAYúS+F3
Aplica formato a las letras como todas mayúsculas	CTRL+MAYúS+U
Aplica el formato de negrita	CTRL+N
Aplica un subrayado	CTRL+S
Subraya palabras pero no espacios	CTRL+MAYúS+P
Aplica doble subrayado	CTRL+MAYúS+D
Aplica formato de texto oculto	CTRL+MAYúS+O
Aplica el formato de cursiva	CTRL+K
Aplica el formato de versales	CTRL+MAYúS+L
Aplica el formato de subíndice (espaciado automático)	CTRL+SIGNO IGUAL
Aplica el formato de superíndice (espaciado automático)	CTRL+SIGNO MáS
Elimina manualmente el formato de caracteres	CTRL+BARRA ESPACIADORA
Cambia la selección a fuente Symbol	CTRL+MAYúS+Q
Muestra caracteres no imprimibles	CTRL+"("
Revisa el formato del texto	MAYúS+F1 (después, haga clic en el texto cuyo formato desee revisar)
Copia formatos	CTRL+MAYúS+C
Pega formatos	CTRL+MAYúS+V

ATAJOS DE TECLADO PARA CAMBIAR EL FORMATO DE PÁRRAFOS.

PARA	PULSAR
Define un interlineado simple	CTRL+1
Define un interlineado doble	CTRL+2
Define un interlineado de 1,5 líneas	CTRL+5
Agrega o suprime un espacio de una línea antes de un párrafo	CTRL+0 (cero)
Centra un párrafo	CTRL+T
Justifica un párrafo	CTRL+J
Alinea un párrafo a la izquierda	CTRL+Q
Alinea un párrafo a la derecha	CTRL+D
Sangra un párrafo a la izquierda	CTRL+H
Quita la sangría a la izquierda de un párrafo	CTRL+MAYúS+R
Crea una sangría francesa	CTRL+F
Reduce una sangría francesa	CTRL+MAYúS+G
Elimina el formato de párrafo	CTRL+W

ATAJOS DE TECLADO PARA TRABAJAR CON ESTILOS.

PARA	PULSAR
Aplica un estilo	CTRL+MAYúS+E
Inicia rutina de Autoformato	CTRL+O
Aplica el estilo Normal	CTRL+MAYúS+A
Aplica el estilo de Título 1	CTRL+!
Aplica el estilo de Título 2	CTRL+"
Aplica el estilo de Título 3	CTRL+MAYúS+3
Aplica el estilo de Lista con viñetas	CTRL+MAYúS+I

ATAJOS DE TECLADO PARA TRABAJAR
CON DISTINTAS PRESENTACIONES.

PARA	PULSAR
Pasa a presentación Diseño de Página	ALT+CTRL+D
Pasa a presentación Esquema	ALT+CTRL+E
Pasa a presentación Normal	ALT+CTRL+N
Permite desplazarse por un documento maestro y sus subdocumentos	ALT+CTRL+MAYúS+°

LOS MEJORES SITIOS WEB

MICROSOFT

www.microsoft.com/office/word/default.htm

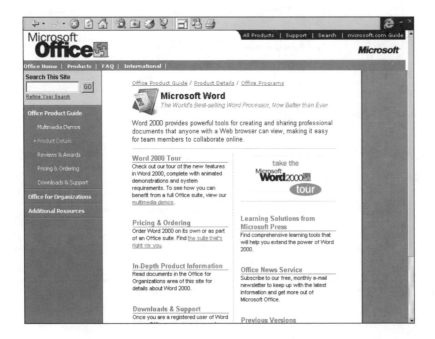

Este es el sitio oficial de Word 2000, mantenido por Microsoft. Su contenido se renueva periódicamente. Tiene trucos, una lista de las preguntas más frecuentes (FAQs), archivos para bajar a nuestro disco (*download*) y otros servicios. La estructura del sitio también se renueva cada tanto, por lo que las distintas páginas que lo forman pueden cambiar de dirección con el tiempo.

MICROSOFT ESPAÑA

www.microsoft.com/spain/office/word.htm

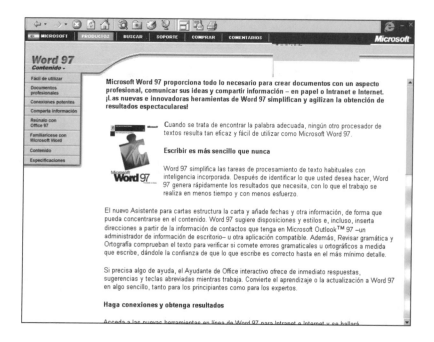

Toda la información oficial en idioma español.

ETHEK & FRIENDS

www.ethek.com/office2000/novedades/word2000novedades.html

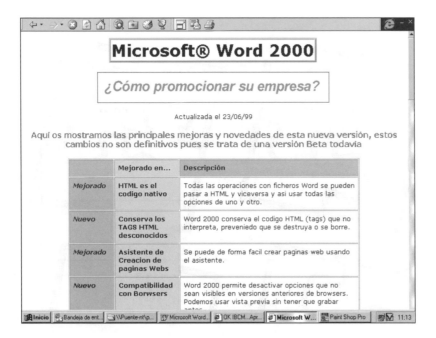

Este sitio no sólo está totalmente en castellano, sino que, además, es publicado en Barcelona. Con el formato de una revista, tiene para todos los gustos, desde trucos y técnicas básicas hasta páginas activas, y creación de macros. Además de un canal de chat y una lista de correo. Para descansar de tanto inglés.

BAARNS OFFICE 97

www.baarns.com

Baarns Publishing es una consultora especializada en computación personal en general y en Microsoft Office en particular. Su sitio en Internet contiene muchísima información acerca de los productos de la línea Office. Hay desde preguntas y consejos básicos para usuarios principiantes hasta documentación especialmente dirigida a desarrolladores. Hay también una página de humor.

ALKI SOFTWARE WORDINFO

www.wordinfo.com

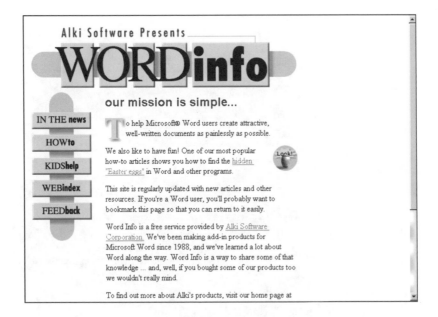

Esta página no está dedicada a Excel, sino a Word. Alki Software es una empresa que desde su fundación (en 1988) está especialmente dedicada al desarrollo de software para Microsoft Word y, por extensión, para los demás productos Office. En esta página nos enteramos de trucos y comandos pocos conocidos así como de consejos para el mejor uso del programa. También se incluyen los huevos ocultos en Word 2.0, 6 y 95, además de otros productos. También hay un curso rápido on line. Se supone que está dirigido a chicos pero, claro, está en inglés.

OK INTERNATIONAL BUSINESS CORPORATION MEXICO

www.okibcm.com/word97.html

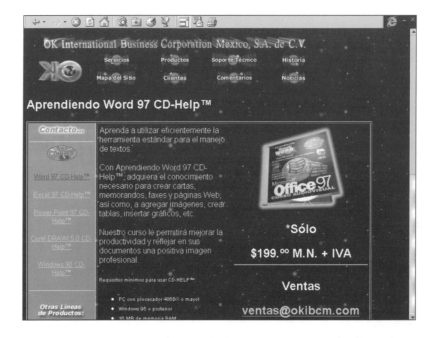

Una serie de cursos para mejorar la productividad y reflejar una positiva imagen profesional.

ÍNDICE ALFABÉTICO

Visitá nuestro sitio en la Web
www.mp.com.ar/libros

Curso práctico de computación
$19,90

Un completísimo curso diseñado para aprender paso a paso y en tiempo récord todo lo que hay que saber para ser un experto usuario de la PC. Toda la información para los que recién empiezan y para quienes quieren perfeccionar sus conocimientos.

COLECCIÓN: APRENDIENDO PC

Guía de funciones de Excel (volumen 1)
$13,90

Claudio Sánchez, el especialista en Excel, explica una por una las 327 funciones de Excel, en sólo 2 volúmenes. En esta primera entrega, las funciones financieras, de fecha y hora, matemáticas y para bases de datos.

COLECCIÓN: PC USERS EXPRESS

Guía de funciones de Excel (volumen 2)
$13,90

El segundo volumen de esta valiosa obra, que todo usuario del programa estaba esperando, incluye todas las novedades de la nueva versión Excel 2000. Además, el desarrollo de las funciones de información, de ingeniería, lógicas, estadísticas y de manejo de textos.

COLECCIÓN: PC USERS EXPRESS

111 preguntas sobre Correo Electrónico
$15,90

No nos quedamos atrás y seguimos indagando sobre lo que la gente quiere saber acerca del uso del correo electrónico. Gracias a los lectores de PC Users, todas las respuestas a las preguntas más frecuentes están en este libro.

COLECCIÓN: PC USERS RESPONDE

Estudiar con la PC
$13,90

Con los adelantos de la PC, las posibilidades de investigación, elaboración y presentación de textos se abren infinitamente. Por medio de este libro, usted dominará todas las herramientas necesarias para hacer los mejores trabajos.

COLECCIÓN: PC USERS EXPRESS

LINUX, Manual de referencia
$19,90

Sumáte al "proyecto Linux", el sistema operativo de distribución libre y gratuita. Lo que empezó como un simple hobby hoy hace temblar a Microsoft.
CD-ROM: versión completa de RED HAT LINUX.

COLECCIÓN: COMPUMAGAZINE

Proyectos con macros en Excel

$13,90

La mejor manera de dar respuesta a un tema difícil de abordar. Esta propuesta de nuestro especialista brinda las soluciones para el manejo de las técnicas de programación en Office y Excel, con ejemplos claros.

COLECCIÓN: PC USERS EXPRESS

Access para PyMEs

$16,90

El manejo a fondo de Access permite integrar datos, generar métodos de búsqueda y elaborar informes completos de una base de datos, de modo que la información de una empresa se optimice.

COLECCIÓN: PC USERS PYMES

Visual FoxPro 6.0

$19,90

Introduce al lector en la programación por eventos y orientada a objetos, a través del lenguaje más poderoso para aplicaciones de gestión. Dirigido también a quienes vienen de una plataforma xBase, como Fox, Clipper o Dbase.

COLECCIÓN: COMPUMAGAZINE

Macros en Office

$13,90

Asomáte al universo de las macros y comenzá a descubrir el poder del editor de Visual Basic, accesible desde Word, Excel o PowerPoint. Opciones avanzadas, técnicas, recursos y soluciones integradas con bases de datos.

COLECCIÓN: CM SOLUCIONES

La Biblia de Internet

$19,90

Contesta las preguntas más frecuentes: ¿Cómo elegir un buen proveedor? ¿Cómo hacer una compra en la Web?...

CD-ROM: con 10 horas gratis de Internet y todos los programas necesarios.

COLECCIÓN: PC USERS

Creación de aplicaciones multimedia con Visual Basic

$19,90

Todos los secretos para crear aplicaciones multimedia. Desde cero hasta un proyecto completo con imágenes, sonido, video y animación.

CD-ROM: soft de diseño, sonido, utilitarios, etc.

COLECCIÓN: PC USERS

Los mejores libros de computación
Entregá este cupón a tu canillita

✂ -

APELLIDO Y NOMBRE

DIRECCIÓN **LOCALIDAD**

CP **PROVINCIA** **PAÍS**

TELÉFONO **FAX**

TÍTULOS SOLICITADOS:

ADJUNTO CHEQUE/GIRO N° **C/BANCO** **A FAVOR DE MP EDICIONES S.A.**

DEBÍTESE DE MI TARJETA DE CRÉDITO EL IMPORTE $ **A FAVOR DE MP EDICIONES S.A.**

MASTERCARD ☐ **AMERICAN EXPRESS** ☐ **VISA** ☐ **VTO.** / /

NÚMERO DE TARJETA **CÓDIGO DE SEGURIDAD**

FIRMA DEL TITULAR **FIRMA DEL SOLICITANTE**

NOMBRE DEL VENDEDOR

PAQUETE N°: ☐☐ ☐☐☐ ☐☐☐
           D   L   V

Completá este cupón y envíalo por fax al (011) 4954-1791 o por correo a:
MP Ediciones S.A. Moreno 2062 (1094) Capital Federal o llamando al (011) 4954-1884.